Language and Culture in Learning

DEDICATION

We dedicate this volume to our children, Cristina, Juliana, Diana, Laura and Phillip, and to all other members of the next generation of Spanish speakers in the United States. May their language and culture be nurtured and valued.

Dedicamos este volumen a nuestros hijos, Cristina, Juliana, Diana, Laura y Phillip, y a todos los miembros de la próxima generación de hispanohablantes en los Estados Unidos. Ojalá que su lengua y su cultura sean fomentadas y respetadas.

Language and Culture in Learning:
Teaching Spanish to Native Speakers of Spanish

Edited by

Barbara J. Merino
Henry T. Trueba
Fabián A. Samaniego

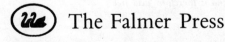

The Falmer Press

(A member of the Taylor & Francis group)
Washington, DC • London

USA   The Falmer Press, Taylor & Francis Inc., 1900 Frost Road, Suite 101,
         Bristol, PA 19007
UK   The Falmer Press, 4 John Street, London WC1N 2ET

First published in 1993

A catalogue record for this book is available from the British Library

Library of Congress Cataloging-in-Publication Data are available on request

ISBN 0 75070 230 3 cased
ISBN 0 75070 231 1 paper

Jacket design by Caroline Archer

Typeset in 9.5/11pt Bembo by
Graphicraft Typesetters Ltd., Hong Kong.

Printed in Great Britain by Burgess Science Press, Basingstoke on paper which has a specified pH value on final paper manufacture of not less than 7.5 and is therefore 'acid free'.

Contents

Part I: Theoretical Advances

Part II: Practical Advances: Redefining the Content and
Process of the Curriculum

Contents

List of Tables, Figures and Activities

List of Tables, Figures and Activities

Acknowledgments

Obviously it would be impossible to list all the scholars who have inspired us throughout our careers and stimulated our interest in language and culture. Their names are often mentioned in these pages. This volume began as a summer institute for teachers of native Spanish speakers with funds from an Eisenhower Grant sponsored by the California Post-Secondary Education Commission and the California State Department of Education. The Division of Education at the University of California, Davis, and the Butte County Office of Education implemented the program under the leadership of Fabián Samaniego and Barbara Merino with Evelyn Vargas Castaneda as Director. We are grateful to Jerry Allred of the Butte County Office of Education and Keith Prior of the Division of Education for their assistance in the planning process. We owe a special debt to Jon Wagner, Acting Director of the Division of Education, for supporting our Curriculum Development Project for Teachers of Spanish for Native Spanish Speakers. This support allowed several of the Fellows to continue their collaboration once the institute was completed. We are especially grateful to Carol Saumarez for her valuable inputs, suggestions and editorial corrections. We want to thank the many helpers that at one time or another gave us generously of their time, such as Carolyn Hackler, Brenda Spychalla and Yali Zou; but we have a significant debt of gratitude to Jackie M. Captain for her prompt, comprehensive and detailed analysis of the queries, for calling our attention to numerous inconsistencies, finding out references and helping us complete the information required in various parts of the volume. Finally, we are grateful to the participants of the institute and the other teachers of Spanish who have continued to collaborate with us in meeting the needs of native Spanish speakers at the secondary level.

Foreword

Now, when a volume on the interaction between anthropology, linguistics, and pedagogy in the teaching of Spanish to native speakers has been prepared at long last, it is time to face and admit the shame that we should feel over the fact that there has been no such volume until now. The lack of such a volume is a classic example of how political and ideological biases are immediately reflected in intellectual blinders and applied handicaps.

Because we have looked down upon foreign languages ('foreign' even if they were 'here', in what is now the territory of the United States, before English arrived), we did not hesitate to perpetrate conceptual and pedagogic approaches which we would not dream of inflicting upon the field of English instruction. In connection with English we not only differentiate between pedagogical and curricular issues pertaining to English as a native language and English as a non-native language, but in the latter we carefully distinguish between English as a second language and English as a foreign language. In connection with Spanish, spoken by millions natively and studied by other millions post-natively, no such distinctions have been recognized until very recently.

Because we have looked down upon native speakers of Spanish, stemming as they mostly do from 'south of the border' and from the Caribbean, we have disparaged their native varieties of spoken Spanish. Indeed, we considered them doubly expendable (expendable both because they were not Iberian and expendable because they were foreign) and required no particular native-speaker expertise from the Spanish teachers to whom they were entrusted. As a result, a two-directional antipathy was permitted (even encouraged) to develop. The teachers deprecated their native Spanish-speaking students, because the latter would not/could not accept the teachers' dubious non-native expertise in Spanish, and the students deprecated their teachers' expertise precisely because it was non-native. Mixed classes of native and non-native students were even greater travesties upon language teaching and language learning than our foreign language classes usually are.

As a native speaker of Yiddish who worked his way through college and graduate school by being a teacher of Yiddish to non-native speakers (and as the husband and father of native-Yiddish speaking teachers of Yiddish to non-native speakers of that language) it has long been apparent to me that a *difference* between a teacher's nativeness-status with respect to the language being taught and the learners' nativeness-status with respect to that language requires special pedagogical knowledge and skill and patience, on the one hand, and special curricular content, both cultural and linguistic, on the other hand. In addition, similarity between these two statuses also requires special handling. Even as a child attending Yiddish supplementary schools in Philadelphia in the mid-30s, my native-Yiddish-speaking teachers gave me special things to read and write, because I alone, among all the students in class, was really a fluent native speaker. My teachers quite conscientiously helped me cultivate my mother tongue and treated it and me as matters of great value.

My teachers were firm language maintenance advocates, proud cultural pluralism protagonists, conscientious multilingualism promoters. Pedagogy is never ideologically neutral, primarily because education itself is never neutral. All of education is society-building as well as individual potential-developing. Every teacher must answer the question: 'What kind of society am I trying to foster?', if only not to fall under the sway of unconscious mainstream biases which provide ready-made answers to that question. Foreign language teachers must be doubly conscious of asking and answering that question, precisely because they are suspect as subversive in a good bit of the mainstream. Finally, the teacher of Spanish to native speakers of Spanish, within the usually inhospitable context of the American school system, must be triply sensitive to this respect. Like my own clearly superior teachers of some sixty years ago, today's teachers of Spanish to native speakers of Spanish must have the view that the students and the language skills being developed are matters of great value.

These students and skills are matters of great value, not only to the students being taught, not only to their families and communities, but to a richer, more accepting, more creative American society.

The book now before the reader, whether that reader be a teacher or teacher of teachers, is a book that recognizes that it is dealing with skills, ideas and values whose time has finally come. The fostering of these skills, ideas and values is long overdue and so is this book. I greet both them and it wholeheartedly, as harbingers of better times to come for America's foreign language teachers, students, speakers, and cultivators of whatever nativeness-status. They are the most American of all, in the very best sense and in the very fullest promise of the term American!

Joshua A. Fishman, *Professor Emeritus
(Social Sciences) and Visiting Professor
(Linguistics) Yeshiva University, New
York and Stanford University,
California*

Part I

Theoretical Advances

Introduction

Henry T. Trueba

This is a very unusual volume. It is a volume produced almost in its entirety by Latino scholars with different social experiences in the Spanish-speaking world of their immigrant families, various degrees of proficiency in Spanish, and with plenty of common experience in the English-speaking world of academia and public life. It is also unusual because it deals with a rather controversial theoretical topic, the relationship of language and culture to learning, and it attempts to go beyond traditional theory to the real life issues of practical methods of teaching and qualitative evaluation of pedagogical effectiveness. Furthermore, it is a volume that deals with these topics in an unusual manner; it uses multiple analytical levels and multiple approaches from specialized and even esoteric discourses on linguistic theory to actual demonstrations of teaching strategies and samples of lessons.

The content of the book is divided into three parts: theory, pedagogical approaches, and actual case studies of successful curriculum development and teaching effectiveness. The linkages between these three parts are obvious. The first and second parts are mirror images of effective instruction; the first part is intended to lay the foundations for the second, that is, the theory behind a new pedagogy advocating the use of culturally and linguistically relevant and appropriate approaches to teaching Spanish to persons exposed to some variety of the Spanish language. The third part examines and illustrates the more practical aspects of problems in the application of this pedagogy.

Part I on Theoretical Advances presents seven important chapters assessing the state of the art in second-language teaching and learning, with special reference to Spanish. Chapter 1, by Merino, Trueba and Samaniego, provides a broad theoretical panorama for the study of first language (L1) maintenance. Given the demographics of the Spanish-speaking population in the United States and the international context of L1 maintenance, questions are raised about the role of schools and ethnic communities in the maintenance of home languages, especially in the case of the Spanish language. Chapter 2 by Trueba examines the relationship between language and culture, from the perspective of anthropological research, in the context of learning. He points out their intimate and permanent unity or inseparability of language and culture from the early stages of children's socialization to their full participation in social and political institutions.

1

Chapter 3 by Politzer explores the distinction between dialects and standardized languages in the context of the relationship of the acquisition of a second language (L2). Is Chicano or Black English a dialect of English? The author presents a review of current research from the perspectives of psycholinguistics, sociolinguistics and neurolinguistics. His discussion of the application of theory to classroom practice touches on the development and use of several languages for instruction, the problems of how to teach languages for instruction, and what variety of languages (standard or nonstandard) to teach.

Chapter 4 by Hernández-Chávez, Chapter 5 by Sánchez, and Chapter 6 by Hidalgo focus on issues related to Chicano Spanish, language loss and issues of inequality in the classroom. These issues are intimately related because they all point to the fundamental problem of status inequality of the Spanish-speaking persons who have to face structurally created barriers that prevent them from fully acquiring a second language (L2), while maintaining oral and written proficiency in their home language. Hernández-Chávez provides an excellent description of the social and political contexts leading to language loss among Chicanos. He deals with the issue of high and low prestige languages and the establishment of social mechanisms to maintain literacy in the home language. Sánchez provides a strong rationale to examine scientifically the issue of language status with her historical analysis of language change (the impact of Nahuatl on Spanish, for example). The dynamic nature of languages leads to borrowing and change; therefore standardization may be a social mechanism to maintain status inequalities in a society and ultimately to discourage bilingualism or multilingualism. Hidalgo pursues the issue of politics as it perpetuates status inequality among Latinos and the lack of support for the teaching of foreign languages in the United States. She points out that at times English-speaking secondary and university students receive an excellent education in Spanish while their Spanish-speaking counterparts do not have access to it.

Chapter 7 by Timm deals with the difficult issue of bilingual code-switching with examples that allow the reader to understand the complexity of the theoretical issues involved and the patterns in code-switching. The study, presented from a solid sociolinguistic perspective, makes an important contribution to our understanding of the role of the speech community in determining the function of specific types of code-switching. With this chapter Part I ends.

Part II moves to practical issues of classroom instructional approaches and the challenge of attempting to redefine the content and process of the curriculum. Chapter 8 by Merino and Samaniego offers a historical overview of norms in teaching rural non-standard speakers of Spanish, namely contrasting non-standard dialect forms with standard forms through oral or written exercises. They discuss teaching techniques based on principles of sociolinguistic variation focusing on composition, vocabulary, and reading. Chapter 9 by Chabram Dernersesian shows how Chicano literature can be used to teach Spanish to native speakers thus using their 'linguistic capital', rather than humiliating them by undermining the legitimacy of their dialects. She provides a broad conception of Spanish literature in which Chicano literature has a distinguished place. Chabram also discusses the problems faced by teachers in using Chicano literature. The richness and specificity of the chapter will be of great help to teachers of Spanish. The message that Chicano literature is linked to other prestigious forms of literature underlies the entire chapter. Chapters 10 and 11 are other examples of attempts at using culturally congruent pedagogical approaches to teach Spanish more effectively. Chapter 10 by Gorman deals with cooperative learning models and specific activities, and Chapter 11 by Carrillo Hocker offers examples of folk art use in the classroom.

Chapters 12 and 13 discuss the important theme of informational technology's use in classroom instruction. Chapter 12 by Faltis and DeVillar reviews methods and materials associated with different approaches: 1) the limited normative approach that attempts to extirpate non-standard forms of Spanish; 2) the teaching of standard forms of the language through sentence and sound patterns; and 3) the socio-academic approach which downplays skill development and advocates the use of language for effective communication in specific sociocultural and pedagogical contexts. The authors suggest that the socio-academic approach maximizes L1 maintenance and learning of content at the same time, and that it is best suited to the use of computers in the classroom. They discuss the use of specific software for drill and practice, simulations, games, and for editing written compositions. The key to this approach is to provide a real-life context in which communication through language takes place. Computer programs offer a rich social and cultural context for communicative exchanges. Chapter 13 by González-Edfelt offers a broad historical overview of computer-assisted instruction, research on computers for L2 teaching and acquisition, and the specific contributions of computer-assisted instruction. The author also presents a typology of the potential uses of software programs: tutorial, drill and practice, problem solving, instructional games, text manipulation, text generation, conversational simulations, situational simulations, and adventure games. An important contribution of this chapter is the clarification of the purpose and method of programming language software and the use of audio devices, digitized speech, synthesized speech, speech processing and other devices to enrich instructional effectiveness. At the end the author shows how interactive videodisc technology, now being pioneered for language instruction, can be extremely useful and can indeed revolutionize Spanish language teaching and learning.

Part III offers very brief case studies of successful innovation in the use of curriculum. Chapter 14 by D'Ambruoso presents the case of East Side Union High School District in San Jose, California, characterized by clearly defined mastery objectives in English and Spanish for writing, reading, listening and speaking; the emphasis is on bilingual communicative competence. Chapter 15 by Quintanar-Sarellana, Huebner and Jensen presents a case in Campbell Union High School District, also in San Jose. It is based on Cummins' theoretical premise that L1 is needed for the development of L2, and that before one can acquire difficult concepts in L2 one must have communicative competence in L2. Chapter 16 by Samaniego and Merino (with the assistance of teachers) describes the summer institute for expert teachers at the University of California, Davis. The summer institute and follow-up activities combine lectures by nationally- and internationally-recognized experts with hands-on individualized construction of lessons under the supervision of mentors. Chapter 17 by Trueba articulates the theoretical and pedagogical implications of the previous chapters around the central theme of the relationship of language and culture to the process of learning and cognitive development. It argues that this relationship of language and culture is central to the organization of curriculum and instruction as well as to their effectiveness.

The overall contributions of this volume are important because they address pedagogical issues ignored in the literature and pursue sociolinguistic issues that, having started in the 1960s, were never carried to their logical pedagogical consequences in the following decades. It is truly an interdisciplinary attempt at linking theory and practice under the joint umbrella of anthropology, sociolinguistics, second language acquisition, foreign language teaching and teacher education research.

Chapter 1

Towards a Framework for the Study of the Maintenance of the Home Language in Language Minority Students

Barbara J. Merino, Henry T. Trueba and Fabián A. Samaniego

Introduction

The education of language minority students is one of the most critical issues facing educators in the United States and many other countries where language minorities constitute large segments of the population. In the United States, the Spanish-speaking are by far the largest language minority. The 1990 Census data indicate that there are 23.4 million Hispanics in the United States (US Bureau of the Census, 1990). This represents an increase of approximately 60 per cent from 1980, when there were 14.6 million Hispanics in the United States. Based on 1980 US Census figures (Waggoner, 1988), there were 11,116,000 people five years or older who spoke Spanish at home. Table 1.1 indicates the number of Spanish speakers by state, based on 1980 census figures. There are no statistics yet on the number of people who speak Spanish from the 1990 data. In the school population the proportion of Hispanic students is even more dramatic, particularly in some states. California, with the largest number of Hispanics, counted 1.5 million Hispanics in its K-12 population in 1990. Moreover, the projections by the Department of Finance of the State of California are that by the year 2005 there will be 3.1 million Hispanics in California schools. (See Table 1.2). In 1989–90, there were 655,000 limited English proficient (LEP) students who were Hispanic in California. Thus, approximately one-third of Hispanics were limited in their proficiency in English and it must be assumed fluent in Spanish. The number of functional bilinguals among the rest of the Hispanic population can only be guessed at since most US Census surveys rely on self-report of proficiency and language use (See Table 1.1). However, Veltman (1988) found that, in the sample he studied, by the third generation Hispanic immigrant families have almost totally lost their Spanish, with seven out of ten children of immigrant Hispanic parents using English predominantly.

Table 1.1: *Percentage of Spanish-Origin population and language spoken at home by selected states*

State	Spanish Language	English Language
Arizona 386,088	296,909 (77 per cent)	89,179 (23 per cent)
California 3,431,245	2,734,008 (80 per cent)	697,237 (20 per cent)
Colorado 246,574	153,624 (62 per cent)	92,950 (38 per cent)
Florida 814,782	689,475 (85 per cent)	125,307 (15 per cent)
New Mexico 400,174	316,582 (79 per cent)	83,592 (21 per cent)
New York 1,411,235	1,201,668 (85 per cent)	209,567 (15 per cent)
Texas 2,630,302	2,278,381 (87 per cent)	351,921 (13 per cent)

Source: US Bureau of the Census (1983) *General Social and Economic Characteristics* (by state), December, Washington, DC: Department of Commerce.

Table 1.2: *California schools K-12 enrollment by ethnicity*

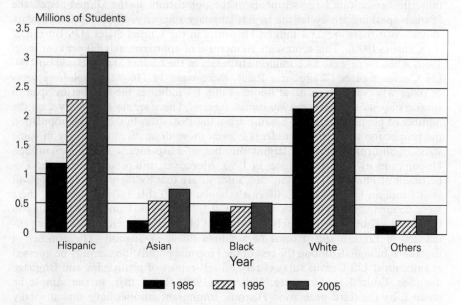

Source: California Department of Finance (1991) *Actual 1985, and Estimates for K-12 Enrollment by Ethnicity*, Sacramento, CA: Department of Finance.

This book is directed to researchers and practitioners interested in understanding how theory and empirical research can inform the practice of teaching Spanish to native Spanish speakers in the United States. The focus of this volume is on the secondary and university student of Spanish. The scope of the book is interdisciplinary. Theoretical and empirical research and its implications for practice are viewed from the perspective of a variety of disciplines: anthropology (Trueba), psycholinguistics (Politzer, Merino and Samaniego), sociolinguistics (Sánchez, Hidalgo, Timm, Hernández-Chávez) and literature (Chabram Dernersesian). Pedagogical innovations in instruction are analyzed from two perspectives. One focuses on the description and analysis of specific tools, techniques and curriculum content: the computer (González-Edfelt; Faltis and DeVillar), cooperative grouping strategies (Gorman), Chicano literature (Chabram Dernersesian) and folk art (Carrillo Hocker). The other integrates theory and pedagogy illustrating innovation through case studies at the secondary level (D'Ambruoso; Quintanar-Sarellana, Huebner and Jensen; Samaniego, Merino and collaborators).

In this introductory chapter, we propose a model for the study of the maintenance and development of the first language and culture in language minority groups. Our model is influenced by other models of second language (L2) acquisition but redirects the focus on the home language. The model we propose seeks to answer four broad questions:

1 How are language and culture acquired and maintained in bilingual communities in general and in the Hispanic community in the United States in particular?
2 What role have the schools had in the maintenance of the Spanish language in the United States?
3 What role do characteristics of the community play in maintenance and shift of Spanish in the United States?
4 Why do maintenance, loss and arrested language development occur in bilinguals?

We begin this discussion by briefly describing language minority groups in an international context. We turn then to an overview of previous models of language acquisition in bilinguals and propose an integrated model of instruction for the maintenance of Spanish in Hispanic bilinguals. The model posits that three basic clusters of variables can affect the maintenance of language and culture in bilinguals: the community, the school and individual differences in the learner. At the community level, the model posits both macro-variables (the role of literacy in the languages in contact, for example) as well as micro-variables, (proximity to a monolingual community). At the school level, the model posits macro-variables such as the program model articulated for instruction in the schools as well as micro-variables such as techniques used to develop awareness of linguistic variation or curricular approaches. At the individual level, the model explores macro-variables such as the role of access to monolingual individuals in the family cluster as well as micro-variables such as language use patterns in the home. We conclude with a discussion of how community and school variables interact with individual differences in the learner, modifying input into intake and yielding a unique profile of linguistic and cultural competencies as output.

Barbara J. Merino, Henry T. Trueba and Fabián A. Samaniego

Language Minority Groups in an International Context

One of the most prevalent myths of nationhood is that nations are largely limited to speakers of the same language group. In the African continent, for example, thirty-five of its fifty-nine countries (59 per cent) have language minority populations that account for at least a third of the total population (McConnell and Roberge, 1987). This level of linguistic diversity is less pronounced in the other continents of the world, but no area of the world goes unaffected. In some countries, Uganda, is one such example, the majority mother tongue or most claimed language (MCL) is spoken by as few as 16 per cent of its population.

In studying linguistic heterogeneity (LH) in a global context, Joshua Fishman and his associates (Fishman, Solanto and McConnell, 1991) use the most claimed language (MCL) as an index of LH. When LH in a country is great, the MCL is smaller. When the International Center for Bilingualism analyzed the percent for the most widely claimed mother tongue (MWCMT) across countries and continents around the world (1987), it found that even Europe, a continent often regarded as very homogeneous, showed considerable heterogeneity. Only three countries: Portugal, Norway and Iceland showed a 99 per cent of MWCMT. In the United States the percentage of MWCMT is 89 per cent for English.

Claims are frequently made that linguistic heterogeneity is irrevocably linked to civil strife. Yet two of the world's countries most torn by civil strife, Lebanon and Ireland, have one unified language. Moreover, Banks and Turner (cited in Fishman *et al.*, 1991) two political scientists, have devised a global index to measure predictors of civil strife. They identify three variables that predict or are related to civil strife: 1) long term and short term deprivation 2) absence of a central authoritative power and 3) the presence of organized lawless groups. When these variables are held constant, linguistic heterogeneity does not correlate with civil strife. However, when each variable is viewed on its own, linguistic heterogeneity does have a modest effect. Thus, Fishman argues (1991), linguistic heterogeneity should be viewed as an asset and resource, not a liability.

Linguistic Diversity Among Major Immigrant Groups in the US

Many of the countries that have contributed immigrants to the United States in large numbers are very linguistically diverse. In China, for example, 70 per cent of the population speaks Mandarin, but six other major dialect groups constitute significant numbers of the population: Wu, spoken by 8.4 per cent; Xiang, 5 per cent; Gan, 2.4 per cent, Hakka, 4 per cent; Min, 1.5 per cent; and Yue, 5 per cent (Li and Thompson, 1981). Many of these so-called dialects are actually mutually unintelligible and linked only by the writing system.

Spanish is one of the most widely spoken languages in the world. McConnell and Roberge (1987) calculate that approximately 259 million people in seventeen different countries in North and South America speak Spanish as a mother tongue. Others estimate that this number is even larger, with some estimates reaching as high as 297 million (Wallechinsky, Wallace, and Wallace, 1983). This wide geopolitical distribution contributes in large part to the heterogeneity of the Spanish language. Although all of its varieties are mutually intelligible, variation in the

Spanish language can be found not only in the sound system, but also in the syntax and most especially in the lexicon (Galván and Teschner, 1975; Cotton and Sharp, 1988; Sánchez, this volume). Spanish in the Americas has been influenced by indigenous as well as other European languages. In several countries where Spanish is spoken, it is the mother tongue for less than half of its population. In Bolivia, for example, Spanish is spoken as a mother tongue by only 35 per cent of its population. In Paraguay, a stable bilingual community of Guaraní and Spanish speakers, Guaraní is the majority mother tongue for most of its people.

Countries with widespread linguistic variation face complex decisions in language planning, particularly in determining appropriate educational programs that further the development of language minority children in their mother tongue as well as the majority language. Canada, a country where only 61 per cent of its people speak English as a mother tongue, has become a model for many other countries in creating educational programs that successfully promote bilingualism in its population (Swain, 1985). Another educational innovator is the Philippines. There, the largest mother tongue group is Cebuano, spoken by 24 per cent of its people. However, there are twenty-four other indigenous languages (Llamzon, 1978). But in spite of the earlier influence of Spanish, English has become the language of education and appears to be in a stable relationship with other mother tongues (González, 1980). Influenced by Canada, the Philippines have also become a fertile laboratory of educational experimentation (Galang, 1988). The Philippines provided one of the first systematic evaluations of the use of the vernacular or home language for initial reading instruction. These early experiments have resulted in a policy by which most Filipinos will receive instruction in both their mother tongue and English. Thus, immigrants from the Philippines face very different experiences from other immigrant groups arriving in the United States, since they generally arrive with higher levels of proficiency in English than many other immigrant groups (Beebe and Beebe, 1981).

Towards an Integrated Model of Instruction for the Development and Maintenance of Spanish in Hispanic Bilinguals

Through the years a variety of models has been proposed to account for the disparity in academic achievement often seen among language minorities compared with language majority students. These models have varied in their approach and attribution of the root causes for this disparity, and include attributing academic deficits to a linguistic mismatch, showing differences in the nature of the linguistic code used for social and academic contexts (Cummins, 1979), relating the threshold level of proficiency reached in the L1 to the degree of context and cognitive demand in which language is used in the schools (Cummins, 1981), relating differences in the sociolinguistic characteristics of the communities in which instruction takes place (Gumperz, 1981; Hernández, 1984) and pointing out complex interactions between immigrant groups and the status assigned them by the receiving culture (Ogbu, 1978). These models have been generated from the perspective of a variety of disciplines. Notable among linguists' proposals are Krashen, (1981) and Schumann (1978); among psychologists, beside Cummins, McLaughlin (1987) and Padilla and Sung (1991); among anthropologists beside

Ogbu (1974), Trueba (1987), Spindler and Spindler, (1987), DeVos and Suárez-Orozco, 1990). Often these scholars bring to bear the orientation of the base discipline in which they were schooled. Indeed, Lightbown (1984) has asserted that any theoretical framework for L2 acquisition must be interdisciplinary and incorporate at least five disciplines: linguistics, sociolinguistics, social psychology, neurolinguistics and cognitive psychology. To this list, we should add cultural anthropology.

In addressing the learning and instructional processes of the native speaker maintaining or re-triggering the development of the first language (L1), these models suffer from one basic flaw. Their focus is on the acquisition of the second language (L2). Here we will propose an interdisciplinary model that seeks to address the context of the bilingual's development of the primary language in a bilingual society and its role in the development of the L2. The model seeks to account for the role of the educational context as well as the community context in interaction with individual learner differences that contribute to both individual and collective outcomes.

As more and more industrialized countries experience the influx of immigrants in their midst, there is an emerging consensus that the view of immigrants has been too limited, focusing principally on their 'success' as defined by the mainstream culture in terms of the immigrants' ability to participate in the social, cultural, linguistic and economic life of the host country (Suárez-Orozco, 1991). From the immigrants' perspective, 'success' can be defined more broadly as the ability to return home, to purchase land and other benefits that ensure upward mobility at home or at a minimum to continue to support family members left behind and gain status in relationship to other immigrants in the host country. This immigrant view of success has been documented by studies of Central American communities in the US (Suárez-Orozco, 1989) and Turkish immigrants in Germany (Wolbert, 1991).

However, these perspectives of success are most prevalent in the voluntary immigrant generation and less frequent in their off-spring, sometimes termed involuntary immigrants. In Ogbu's model, involuntary entry into the dominant society is seen as one of the key qualities of caste-like or disparaged minorities. While this term has typically been used in connection with African Americans and American Indians, European researchers also use the term for second and third generation children of immigrants who do not 'choose' to immigrate (Roosens, 1989). The social and psychological orientation of second and third generation immigrants is significantly different from that of their parents. Some may be cushioned by a strong family structure that helps children cope with the effects of social and economic discrimination (DeVos and Suárez-Orozco, 1990). The Japanese coming to the United States at the turn of the century (DeVos, 1973) and in current times, the Sikh Punjabis (Gibson, 1988) are examples of immigrant communities that have successfully withstood adverse discrimination. Other immigrants however, do not fare as well. Many Turkish and Moroccan second and third generation immigrants in Belgium experience low achievement in school and a high incidence of drug use and criminal involvement (Roosens, 1989).

What then is the destiny of the Hispanic community in the United States? Will the strong family structure typical of the Hispanic community help to maintain Hispanic cultural and linguistic traditions? To build a greater understanding of the currents which play a part in the Hispanic, Spanish-speaking community we turn first to a discussion of the educational contexts in which the teaching of Spanish occurs.

What Role have the Schools Played in the Maintenance of Spanish in the United States?

Spanish is taught in a variety of educational contexts in the United States. It is taught as a second language or a foreign language, largely at the secondary and university level, but increasingly at the elementary level as well. Spanish is also taught as a mother tongue, as a transition language to Spanish speakers entering the US school system for the purpose of developing academic skills while these are not yet accessible in English. This approach is largely used at the elementary level. Another context for the teaching of Spanish as a mother tongue is when it is taught as a maintenance language with the goal of maintaining and developing the language as a written language. While maintenance of the primary language was a principal goal in many of the early, bilingual programs in the United States, it was not generally applied in practice. In recent years, maintenance of the primary language has become a primary goal of double immersion programs.

At the macro level, depending on the program model chosen in any one of these contexts, the learning of Spanish can be seen as additive or subtractive bilingualism. As conceptualized by W. Lambert (1978), in additive bilingualism, both languages and cultures are seen as complementary, positive elements in the child's development. Both languages and cultures are given equal importance and valued in both home and school. In subtractive bilingualism, the acquisition of the second language, usually the majority language is given greater prestige, seen as more important, and the first language is perceived as having little value. It should be remembered that in the context of the complex sociolinguistic Spanish-speaking community of the United States, bilingualism is further complicated by the influences of both standard and non-standard varieties. As Figure 1.1 illustrates, when bilingualism is viewed as a continuum that may or may not include bidialectalism, the native Spanish-speaking population in the schools may consist of a wide variety of students. (See Sánchez; Hidalgo; Hernández-Chávez; and Timm, this volume). American institutions, such as the schools, have reacted within an additive framework when Spanish speakers are speakers of a standard variety and come from an educated class, as in the case of Cuban Americans in Florida. When the Spanish speakers are from a rural background, speak a non-standard variety and or come from non-literate backgrounds, the reactions of the schools have been subtractive. The context and program model in which the instruction of Spanish is delivered have great influence on the goals of instruction and the degree to which Spanish will be taught in the schools. See Figure 1.3, for a listing of other sample macro- and micro-variables.

The Foreign Language Context

In the L2 or foreign language context, particularly at the secondary and university level, Spanish is perceived as adding to the educational baggage necessary for the survival of an educational elite. When instruction is provided to a limited degree, with little contact with native speakers of the language, the prognosis for success is very limited. Thus, for example, Carroll (1967), in his landmark study of

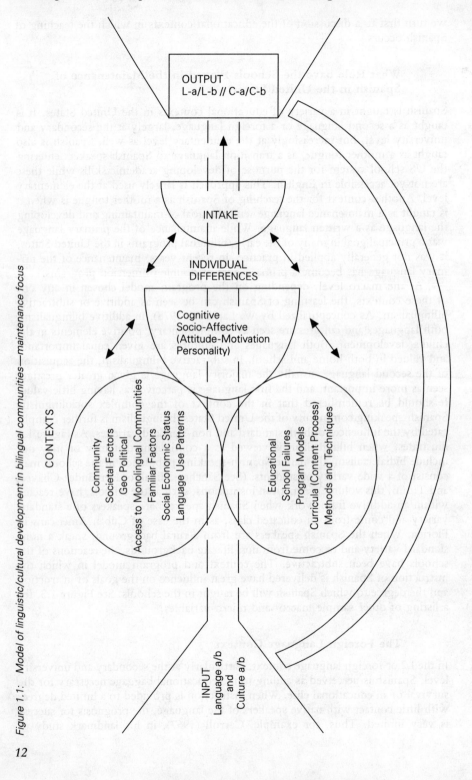

Figure 1.1: *Model of linguistic/cultural development in bilingual communities—maintenance focus*

OUTPUT
L-a/L-b // C-a/C-b

INTAKE

INDIVIDUAL
DIFFERENCES

Cognitive
Socio-Affective
(Attitude-Motivation
Personality)

CONTEXTS

Community
Societal Factors
Geo Political
Access to Monolingual Communities
Familiar Factors
Social Economic Status
Language Use Patterns

Educational
School Failures
Program Models
Curricula (Content Process)
Methods and Techniques

INPUT
Language a/b
and
Culture a/b

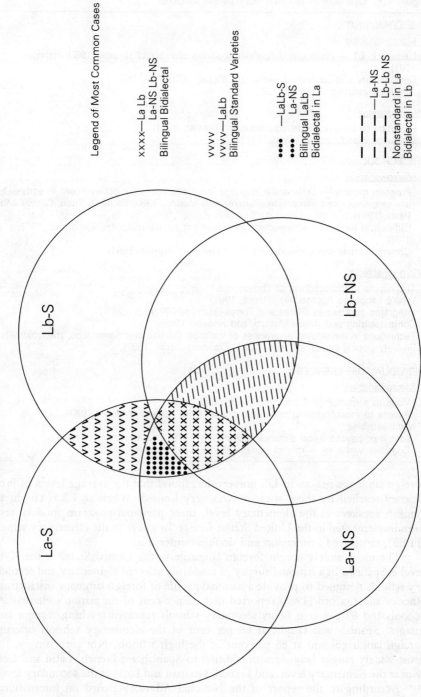

Figure 1.2: A bilingual/bidialectical model of language proficiency

Figure 1.3: Overview of contexts with sample variables

THE COMMUNITY

Macro-variables —

Literacy in L1 — Hmong and Spanish speaking community (Trueba, 1989; Fishman, 1991).
Discontinuity and contextual interaction (Ogbu, 1978).
Linguistic variation (Sánchez, 1983).

Micro-variables

Proximity to a monolingual coummunity (Gaarder, 1971).
Language island context (Kloss, 1977).

THE SCHOOL

Macro-variables

Program models — Differential language input and academic achievement in early-exit; late-exit, structured immersion (Ramirez and Merino, 1990; Ramirez, Yuen, Ramey and Pasta, 1991)
Differential input and achievement in concurrent vs. alternate day (Legarreta, 1977; 1979).
Commitment to the development of L1 literacy (Fishman, 1991).

Micro-variables

Techniques in the teaching of literacy in L1
Whole Language Approaches (Flores, 1981)
Integrated approaches (Perez and Torres-Guzman, 1992).
Contextualizing text (Mace-Matluck and Hoover, 1985).
Techniques in developing awareness of variation (Merino and Samaniego, this volume)
Problem posing curricula (Freire, 1981; Crawford-Lange, 1987).

INDIVIDUAL DIFFERENCES

Macro-variables

Visits to a monolingual community (Leopold, 1949).
Access to monolingual interlocutors in the family nucleus (Merino, 1983)
Micro-variables
Attitudes, psychological distance (Schumann, 1978; Silva-Corvalán, 1991).
Cognitive variables — role of transfer (Faltis, 1982; Edelsky, 1982)

---

foreign language majors in US universities, found that the average levels of proficiency reached by these students was very limited. When an L2 is taught to English speakers at the elementary level, three principal program models have been implemented in the United States: foreign language in the elementary school (FLES), structured immersion and double immersion.

The most widely taught foreign language in the United States at the K-12 level is Spanish. In a national survey of randomly selected elementary and secondary schools designed to provide a national profile of foreign language instruction, Rhodes and Oxford (1988) reported that 22 per cent of the nation's elementary schools and 87 per cent of its secondary schools reported teaching foreign languages. Spanish was taught at 68 per cent of the elementary schools offering foreign languages and at 86 per cent of the high schools. Not surprisingly, the most widely taught languages in addition to Spanish are French, Latin and German at the elementary level, and French, German and Latin at the secondary level.

According to the report of the National Advisory Board on International Education Program to the US Secretary of Education (1983), the number of students enrolled in foreign language in United States high schools had declined steadily from a previous peak of 36 per cent in 1915 to only 15 per cent in 1980. Moreover, many students, especially those students enrolled in schools with large numbers of minority students were not offered the opportunity to learn a foreign language at all. According to the Rhodes and Oxford survey (1988), only 23 per cent of the secondary schools that offered foreign language programs reported that at least half of their students were enrolled in foreign language study. This trend is beginning to reverse itself as universities and business have rekindled an interest in foreign language study (Dandonoli, 1987). For many students in the United States, access to development of languages other than English is severely limited.

The Mother Tongue Context

There are three principal types of programs that can provide opportunities for continued development of the mother tongue in US schools: transitional bilingual education, two-way bilingual immersion and courses for native speakers.

Transitional bilingual education (TBE) is an option that exists primarily at the elementary level. In this type of program, both English and the mother tongue are used as languages of instruction. Programs however, may vary in the degree to which they offer instruction in reading in two languages. Programs in Spanish usually do, but programs in Chinese often do not. The sequence in which reading in the second language is offered may also vary. In some programs, initial reading begins in the first language; in others, initial reading instruction is offered in both languages at the same time. Programs also vary by the number of years instruction is offered in the mother tongue. Early-exit programs, exit students at third grade; late-exit, do so at sixth grade. These programs were originally intended to provide second language learning opportunities for both language minority and majority children. Thus, original legislation required that at least one-third of the students in bilingual classrooms be monolingual English speakers. In practice, however, these children were perceived as models and sources of peer input, but little emphasis was given to the instruction of English speakers in the second language. Finally, transitional bilingual programs vary widely by the amount of instruction actually offered in the mother tongue and the way the languages are delivered. In one study of a bilingual Chinese-English and a Spanish-English program in upper elementary school, it was reported that based on live observation, classroom teachers ranged in use of the L1 from a low of zero to a high of 22 per cent (Wong-Fillmore, Ammon, McLaughlin and Ammon, 1985). Studies of bilingual classrooms at lower grade levels and in well articulated programs tend to report higher percentages of mother tongue use (Legarreta, 1977; Ramírez and Merino, 1990).

In the United States, approximately one third of the Hispanic population eligible for bilingual services is being provided these services in a self-contained classroom through bilingual education. In a national random survey of instructional services provided language minority students, Development Associates (1984) found that only 28 per cent of academic teachers of language minority-limited English proficient students had bilingual credentials. Fifty per cent of academic teachers of LM-LEP students reported speaking a language other than English and in most cases (88 per cent), that language was Spanish. Not surprisingly, teachers with bilingual credentials and teachers who spoke another language were more likely to emphasize the importance and utility of the use of the mother tongue in their teaching philosophy, in contrast to other teachers. Based on a sample of 1516 students, Spanish-speaking students received on average 3.1 hours per week of oral development in the native language and 3.9 in reading at the first grade. At the third grade, the hours/week quotient was lower. This survey confirmed that, in fact, in most cases, children may receive limited mother tongue instruction in transitional bilingual education programs. California, one of the states with the highest number of certified bilingual teachers, has only enough teachers to meet about 54 per cent of the demand (California Department of Education, 1991).

Two way bilingual education is a program, 'which employs two languages, one of which is English, for the purposes of instruction, and involves students who are native speakers of each of those languages'. Both groups of students — limited English proficient (LEP) and English proficient (EP) are expected to become bilingual. (New York State Education Department, 1986, cited in Campbell and Lindholm, 1987; p. 7). As in transitional bilingual education, there are roughly one-third native English speakers and two-thirds other mother tongue speakers. The mother tongue is used primarily from kindergarten to second grade, with thirty minutes a day in English at kindergarten and sixty minutes at first grade. The amount of English increases to 20 per cent at grades two and three and to 50 per cent at grades four through six. Languages are separated during instruction. Most of the programs using this model are Spanish/English although some are offered in other languages (Arabic, for example in Hamtramck, Michigan). See Lindholm, (1987) for a directory of two-way bilingual programs. Very little evaluation data are currently available on this type of program. Most of these programs are being implemented in New York and California and are typically at the lower elementary level, although a few are offered at the secondary level.

Native Speaker Programs

These are programs designed to provide instruction in the mother tongue to mother tongue speakers only. The Carpinteria Project in the Santa Barbara area in California is probably one of the more famous examples at the elementary level. In this kind of program, the intent is to develop the first language of the child as an academic language and to subsequently introduce L2. At the high school level, these programs are in place for part of the instructional day and offer courses in oral and written language. They also offer courses in at least one other content area of the required curriculum, anthropology, government or multicultural education. The goal of these programs is to build up skills in the mother tongue with the assumption that these skills will transfer to L2, or will facilitate the acquisition of those same skills in the L2. At the university level, model programs for native speakers of Spanish (NSS) are beginning to surface, at, for example, the University of California, Santa Cruz and in Miami, Florida, at Dade County City College (Roca, 1990).

According to the random survey of the nation's schools offering instruction in a foreign language, 1 per cent of the elementary schools offered Spanish for Spanish speakers (Rhodes and Oxford, 1988). Two per cent offered immersion, a program modeled on the Canadian French programs designed for English speakers. At the secondary level, only 4 per cent of schools sampled offered a language course for native speakers. Thus, it appears that, on the whole, native speaker programs are very scarce indeed. The lack of availability of programs is in part the result of the scarcity of native speaker teachers and the lack of training offered teachers in teaching NSS courses at the secondary level. According to the national survey, 67 per cent of the secondary schools sampled indicated that none of their foreign language teachers were native speakers.

In sum, the population of native speakers of languages other than English continues to be neglected in terms of their mother tongue development in US public schools. There are, however, several recent developments that offer some encouragement. First, the vitriolic attacks against bilingual education and its use of the mother tongue for instruction so characteristic of the early eighties have diminished, and there is a renewed recognition of the educational advantages of providing instruction in the first language. Thus, Willig's (1985) meta-analyses of bilingual education effectiveness research showing that bilingual education has a positive effect in promoting achievement among bilingual students did much to dispel the myth that bilingual education did not work. Recently, the final report of a study designed to compare the effectiveness of structured immersion, early- and late-exit bilingual programs has shown that the most sustained gains were made by students in the late-exit bilingual program model, where students had the highest proportion of Spanish language use (Ramírez, Yuen, Ramey and Pasta, 1991). Further, the increasing interest among researchers in the study of transfer and language loss (Merino and Samaniego; and Hernández-Chávez, this volume), is developing the educational community's awareness of the potential the mother tongue has for maximizing the academic achievement of the language minority population. Finally, the number of programs designed for native Spanish speakers in the United States continues to grow as older models are revitalized and newer models are proposed (D'Ambruoso; Merino and Samaniego; Quintanar-Sarellana, Huebner and Jensen, this volume).

In the educational context, other micro-variables such as curriculum approaches (Crawford-Lange, 1987; Freire, 1981) and specific teaching approaches for teaching literacy (Flores, 1981; Ada, 1988) contextualizing text (Mace-Matluck and Hoover, 1985) and developing awareness of language variation (Merino and Samaniego, this volume) may also affect the prospects of maintenance of the first language. Thus, if parents collaborate with teachers in defining the content of the curriculum to be learned as they did in the literacy project directed by Alma Flor Ada, (scholar and advocate of the continued development of the home language through literacy) parents, teachers and children are more likely to perceive the value the Spanish language and Hispanic culture have in the educational and emotional development of children. Expert teachers working with native Spanish-speaking secondary students have found that the use of themes that relate the development of a positive self concept to Chicano literature and art increase students' interest and participation in school (Samaniego, Merino and collaborators, this volume).

What Role have Community Contextual Variables had on the Maintenance of Spanish?

A question frequently asked of Spanish-speaking immigrants and proponents of the maintenance of Spanish in education and the community is, put simply, 'Why?'

Some argue that the continued use of Spanish in the schools has been a disabling influence for Hispanics in the United States (Pedalino-Porter, 1990). Often bilingual education is blamed for the continued low achievement of Hispanics. However, these assertions are frequently motivated by political ideology or simplistic analyses of educational achievement and drop out rates. First, bilingual education has been available for a very small portion of language-minority Hispanics and thus cannot be blamed for national statistics on achievement among this group. Second, studies comparing language-minority children who continue to use Spanish to those who do not, show an academic advantage for those who maintain Spanish (Dolson, 1985). Third, Hispanics underachievement is a highly complex and interactive process that cannot be explained by contextual variables alone but must also incorporate a theory of social identity (Bernal, Saenz and Knight, 1991). Finally, empirical research on the transfer of skills across languages among bilingual speakers argues for the continued viability of educational interventions that successfully transmit content and process from one language to the other (Kauffman, 1968; Faltis, 1982; Merino and Samaniego, this volume).

What Factors are Instrumental in Promoting Maintenance of the Home Language in Immigrant Communities?

Factors in the community that affect maintenance and shift have been studied by a variety of scholars. Fishman (1991), perhaps more than any other scholar, has done much to investigate those variables that affect maintenance and shift in a variety of immigrant communities in the US. Some of these variables can have either positive or negative effects. For example, the size of the group can lead to so much influence and power within mainstream society, as it did with the German immigrant group who settled in the Midwest in the late nineteenth century and advocated German as the national language of the US, that eventually the group's agenda becomes part of the mainstream. Initially, however, size may be a facilitator in gaining special services and programs (Kloss, 1977). Other variables generally help to maintain the immigrant language, cohesion and isolation in a language island situation, for example. Still others usually promote shift — for example, ease of entry into the educational system and access to its institutions and benefits. Following in this tradition, Gaarder (1971) found that Hispanics as a community in the United States had many variables in their favor helping them to maintain the viability of a Spanish community in the United States. These included what he termed 'access to the hinterlands', i.e., communities where the immigrant language is spoken as a native tongue and continuous immigration which supported the Spanish-speaking community by constantly bringing new speakers of Spanish. It is important to remember however, that the immigration patterns and the experiences encountered by immigrants in the US are not all the same for all subgroups of Hispanics.

Cubans, for example, have tended to be the most educated on arrival, particularly those in the early waves of immigration. This educational advantage has been maintained in the US (US Bureau of the Census, 1985). They also have the highest income levels, the highest number of workers per family, the highest rates of exogamy (out marriage) and the highest proportion of managerial and professional occupations of any Hispanic group.

In understanding the reasons some Hispanic minority groups have fared better than others in US society, the role of culture and its interaction with language must be considered. For some immigrants, many Central American Hispanics, for example, who were driven from their homelands by the strife of war and sent to the United States at substantial family sacrifice, scholastic achievement and economic success are an absolute necessity (Suárez-Orozco, 1987). Many of these students do achieve at very high levels, learning English quickly and gaining entry into university. Besides the press to achieve for the sake of other family members, some researchers have suggested that the lack of exposure to racism and discrimination in early childhood helps recent immigrants gain greater achievement (Ogbu and Matute-Bianchi, 1986). Others propose that a high level of linguistic development in the first language helps to promote achievement in the second (Cummins, 1981). Hernández-Chávez (this volume) believes that maintenance of the first language in the Hispanic community is a necessary ingredient for its structural integrity as a community. However, while first generation immigrants may have some advantages over second and third generation immigrants, subsequent generations can perform well particularly if they are provided with both effective programs and schools, as Tomlinson (1991) indicates with examples from England, and Merino (1991) demonstrates with Hispanics in the United States. Trueba (1987; this volume) argues that Chicanos have created a binational social structure supported by economic, social, political and cultural organizations. He proposes that the solution to the problem of differential achievement among linguistic and cultural minorities can only come from an understanding of the interplay of linguistic, cultural and cognitive abilities and how these are acquired at home and at school.

What is the Role of Individual Differences in the Maintenance or Loss of the Primary Language for the Individual?

While it is possible to speak of educational and community variables in general terms, every individual ultimately brings into play a unique array of characteristics and circumstances that affect the continued development of the primary language or its loss. Birth order (Ervin-Tripp, 1975), visits to a monolingual community (Leopold, 1949), language use patterns in the family and access to monolinguals (Merino, 1983), access to schooling and literacy in the primary language, all seem to contribute to continued development in the first language, but it is nonetheless difficult to establish a specific cluster of variables that can predict maintenance of the primary language consistently (Silva-Corvalán, 1990). Some of these variables seem to exert a more important influence than others, for example, a monolingual family member can exert a tremendous influence in the continued use of the primary language but certainly does not guarantee it. In some studies, gender appears to differentiate patterns of language proficiency, with Puerto Rican women in New York displaying greater proficiency than men (Zentella, 1988).

A variety of types of native speakers of Spanish may be seen in classes in which instruction in Spanish is offered. The range of linguistic profiles may be captured best as seen through two intersecting continua that can be represented graphically through Venn diagrams. On one continuum is the range of standard to non-standard proficiency. Thus a speaker may exhibit none or many of the dialect variants of a non-standard variety. (See Hidalgo, this volume for further discussion of the intricacies of defining this construct). On another continuum is the range of development possible in the L1 and L2. Full development would imply literacy at the highest levels as well as full mastery of the oral systems, while partial development may signal loss as a result of lack of exposure to the L1 over time or arrested development (See Hernández-Chávez, this volume for further discussion.)

There are several intersections possible in this configuration of proficiency. Here the notion of balance applies. Thus individuals may be balanced bidialectal or able to control both a standard and non-standard variety with equal ability. Liza Doolittle in 'My Fair Lady' is an example from the popular literature. Individuals may be balanced bilinguals in their two languages or have only partial development in one of their two languages (Hernández-Chávez, this volume). A typical example among immigrant communities may involve control of a standard dialect in the L2 majority language with control of a non-standard variety in the L1 (Sánchez, 1983; and this volume). All the possible combinations of this construct can be seen in Figure 1.2. (See p. 13)

How Does Bidialectalism Develop?

Many factors influence the conscious and unconscious choices speakers make in filtering input into intake. As Beebe (1985) has shown, these may be unmarked or marked choices, that is either in expected or unexpected directions. Thus speakers may choose the variety of their own social group over that of another, as is the case of black gangs choosing black English varieties (Labov, 1972). But at times, speakers may choose another social group over their own, the case of a white using black creole (Hewitt, 1982). A wide variety of factors have been shown to influence these choices. Feelings and motivations affect input preferences as well as social and situational factors (Beebe, 1985). Affect and input preferences may be viewed from a variety of theoretical perspectives: group identity theories, such as Gardner and Lambert's (1972) ethnocentrism theory and Fishman's (1966) loyalty theory. Other theoretical perspectives include speech accommodation theory (Giles and Byrne, 1982) as well as sociocultural and psychological distance (Schumann, 1978). Situational factors such as gender may also have an effect and play a role in determining intake (Zentella, 1987). A model that seeks to explain bilingual and bidialectal development must incorporate the construct of intake with input.

To sum up then, the framework for understanding maintenance in language minority students who are Hispanic encompasses two broad clusters of variables that influence the individual: educational and community clusters. These clusters interact and mediate the input that becomes intake for the individual in the acquisition of language and culture. (See Figure 1.1) The components of the framework are interwoven in the chapters of the book. Although there is substantial empirical research supporting many of the underlying assumptions and hypotheses of the framework, at this juncture the framework still includes heuristic elements that remain to be explored more systematically through further research.

This book seeks to expand the perspective of teachers of language minority students by highlighting the role of the home language and culture in the educational process. Hispanics in the United States represent a community of sub-stantial numbers and influence. Their access to the benefits that the United States offers immigrants is developing slowly but steadily. The stability of the US Hispanic community and its success in the American system are intertwined with the success of the United States as a society. The development and maintenance of a viable, bilingual Spanish/English community offers both a challenge and a resource. This book offers a framework for promoting a better understanding of this community and suggests innovative approaches to improve the education of Spanish-speaking students in the United States through a recognition of the value of the home lan-guage and culture. The destiny of the Spanish-speaking community in the United States is still in the process of evolution. Future generations of researchers must continue to describe and understand this evolutionary process. Teachers and policy makers must seek to develop a context of support for this community, allowing it thus to develop to its full potential.

References

ADA, A.F. (1988) 'The Pajaro Valley experience: Working with Spanish-speaking parents to develop children's reading and writing skills in the home through the use of children's literature', in SKUTNABB-KANGAS, T. and CUMMINS, J. (Eds), *Minority Education: From Shame to Struggle*, Philadelphia, PA, Multilingual Matters, pp. 223–8.

BEEBE, L. (1985) 'Input: Choosing the right stuff', in GASS, S. and MADDEN, C. (Eds) *Input in Second Language Acquisition*, NY, Newbury House Publishers, pp. 404–14.

BEEBE, J. and BEEBE, M. (1981) 'The Filipinos: A special case' in FERGUSON, C.A. and HEATH, S.B. (Eds) *Language in the United States*, Cambridge, Cambridge University Press, pp. 322–38.

BERNAL, M., SAENZ, D. and KNIGHT, G. (1991) 'Ethnic identity and adaptation of Mexican American youths in school settings', *Hispanic Journal of the Behavioral Sciences*, **13**, pp. 135–54.

CALIFORNIA DEPARTMENT OF EDUCATION (1991) *Remedying the Shortage of Teachers for Limited English-proficient Students*, Sacramento, CA, California Department of Education.

CAMPBELL, R.N. and LINDHOLM, K.J. (1987) *Conservation of Language Resources*, Los Angeles, CA, Center for Language Education and Research, University of California.

CARROLL, J. (1967) 'Foreign language proficiency levels attained by language majors near graduation from college', *Foreign Language Annals*, **1**, pp. 131–51.

COTTON, E.G. and SHARP, J.M. (1988) *Spanish in the Americas*, Washington, DC, Georgetown University Press.

CRAWFORD-LANGE, L.M. (1987) 'Curricular alternatives for second-language learning', in LONG, M. and RICHARDS, J.C. (Eds) *Methodology in TESOL*, New York, NY, Newbury House, pp. 120–44.

CUMMINS, J. (1979) 'Linguistic interdependence and the educational development of bilingual children', *Review of Educational Research*, **49**, pp. 222–51.

CUMMINS, J. (1981) 'The role of primary language development in promoting education success for language minority students', in *California State Department of Education* (Ed) *Schooling and Language Minority Students: A Theoretical Framework*, Los Angeles, CA, Evaluation, Dissemination and Assessment Center, California State University, pp. 3–50.

DANDONOLI, P. (1987) 'Report on foreign language enrollments in public secondary schools', Fall, 1985, *Foreign Language Annals*, **20**, pp. 457–70.

DEVELOPMENT ASSOCIATES (1984) *LEP Students Characteristics and School Services: The Descriptive Phase Report of the National Longitudinal Evaluation of the Effectiveness of Services for Language-minority Limited English Proficient Students*, Arlington, VA, Development Associates.

DEVOS, G. (1973) *Socialization for Achievement: Essays on the Cultural Psychology of the Japanese*, Berkeley, CA, University of California Press.

DEVOS, G. and SUÁREZ-OROZCO, M. (1990) *Status Inequality: The Self in Culture*, Newbury Park, CA, Sage Publications.

DOLSON, D.P. (1985) 'The effects of Spanish home language use on the scholastic performance of Hispanic pupils', *Journal of Multilingual and Multicultural Development*, **6**, pp. 135–55.

EDELSKY, C. (1982) 'Writing in a bilingual program: The relation of L1 and L2 texts', *TESOL Quarterly*, **16**, pp. 211–18.

ERVIN-TRIPP, S. (1975) Classroom lecture in 'Child Language and Bilingualism.' Dept. of Psychology, University of California, Berkeley, CA.

FALTIS, C. (1982) 'Transfer of beginning reading skills from Spanish to English among Spanish-speaking children in second grade bilingual classrooms', unpublished doctoral dissertation, Stanford, CA, Stanford University.

FISHMAN, J. (1966) *Language Loyalty in the United States*, The Hague, Netherlands, Mouton & Co.

FISHMAN, J. (1991) *Reversing Language Shift*, Clevedon, England, Multilingual Matters.

FISHMAN, J., SOLANTO, F. and MCCONNELL, G. (1991) 'A methodological check on three cross-polity studies of linguistic homogeneity/heterogeneity', in MCGROARTY, M. and FALTIS, C. (Eds) *Languages in School and Society: Policy and Pedagogy*, Berlin, Germany, Mouton de Gruyter, pp. 21–9.

FLORES, B. (1981) 'Bilingual reading instructional practices: The three views of the reading process as they relate to the concept of language interference', *Journal of Teacher Education*, **8**, pp. 45–52.

FREIRE, P. (1981) *Education for Critical Consciousness*, New York, NY, Continuum.

GAARDER, A.B. (1971) 'Language maintenance or language shift: The prospect for Spanish in the United States', (Mimeo) Washington, DC, Department of Commerce. Paper presented at the Conference on Child Language, Chicago, IL, November 22–24.

GALANG, R. (1988) 'The language situation of Filipino Americans', in MCKAY, S. and WONG, S.C. (Eds) *Language Diversity: Problem or Resource?* Cambridge, MA, Newbury House Publishers, pp. 229–51.

GALVÁN, R. and TESCHNER, R.V. (1975) *A Dictionary of Chicano Spanish*, Silver Spring, MD, Institute of Modern Languages.

GARDNER, R.C. and LAMBERT, W.E. (1972) *Attitudes and Motivation in Second Language Learning*, Rowley, MA, Newbury House.

GIBSON, M. (1988) *Accommodation Without Assimilation: Sikh Immigrants in an American High School*, Ithaca, NY, Cornell University Press.

GILES, H. and BYRNE, J.L. (1982) 'An intergroup approach to second language acquisition', *Journal of Multilingual and Multicultural Development*, **3**, pp. 17–40.

GONZÁLEZ, A.B. (1980) *Language Nationalism: The Philippines Experiences Thus Far*, Quezon City, Philippines, Ateneo de Manila University Press.

GUMPERZ, J. (1981) 'Conversational inferences and classroom learning', in GREEN, J.L. and WALLET, C. (Eds) *Ethnography and Language in Educational Settings*, Norwood, NJ, Ablex, pp. 3–23.

HERNÁNDEZ, E. (1984) 'The inadequacy of English immersion education as an educational approach for language minority students', in *Studies on Immersion Education:*

A Collection for United States Educators, Sacramento, CA, California State Department of Education, pp. 144–83.

HEWITT, R. (1982) 'White adolescent creole users and the politics of friendship', *Journal of Multilingual and Multicultural Development*, **3**, pp. 217–32.

KAUFFMAN, M. (1968) 'Will instruction in reading Spanish affect ability in reading English?', *Journal of Reading*, **11**, pp. 521–27.

KLOSS, H. (1977) *The American Bilingual Tradition*, Rowley, MA, Newbury House.

KRASHEN, S. (1981) *Second Language Acquisition and Second Language Learning*, Oxford, England, Pergamon Press.

LABOV, W. (1972) *Language in the Inner City: Studies in the Black English Vernacular*, Oxford, England, Blackwell.

LAMBERT, W. (1978) 'Cognitive and socio-cultural consequences of bilingualism', *Canadian Modern Language Review*, **35**, pp. 537–47.

LEGARRETA, D. (1977) 'Language choice in bilingual classrooms', *TESOL Quarterly*, **11**, pp. 9–16.

LEGARRETA, D. (1979) 'The effects of program models on language acquisition by Spanish-speaking children', *TESOL Quarterly*, **13**, pp. 521–34.

LEOPOLD, W. (1939–1949) *Speech Development of a Bilingual Child: A Linguist's Record*. 4 Vols. Evanston, IL, Northwestern University Press.

LI, C.N. and THOMPSON, S.A. (1981) *Mandarin Chinese: A Functional Reference Grammar*, Berkeley, CA, University of California Press.

LIGHTBOWN, P.M. (1984) 'The relationship between theory and method in second language acquisition', in DAVIS, A. CRIER, C. and HOWATT, A.P.R. (Eds) *Interlanguage*, Edinburgh, Scotland, Edinburgh University Press.

LINDHOLM, K.J. (1987) *Directory of bilingual immersion programs: Two-way bilingual education for language minority and majority students*, Los Angeles, CA, Center for Language Education and Research, University of California.

LLAMZON, T.A. (1978) *Handbook of Philippines Language Groups*, Quezon City, Philippines, Ateneo de Manila University Press.

McCONNELL, G.D. and ROBERGE, B. (1987) *Statistiques sur la Language Maternelle Majoritaire des Pays et Territoires du Monde*, Quebec, Canada, Centre International de Recherches sur le Bilinguisme.

MACE-MATLUCK, B. and HOOVER, W.A. (1985) 'Language, reading, and instruction in bilingual classrooms: Integrating the findings from a six-year longitudinal study', paper presented at the Meeting of the National Association of Bilingual Education, San Francisco, CA, March 11–16.

McLAUGHLIN, B. (1987) *Theories of Second-language Learning*, Baltimore, MD, Edward Arnold.

MERINO, B.J. (1983) 'Language loss in bilingual Chicano children', *Journal of Applied Developmental Psychology*, **10**, pp. 477–94.

MERINO, B.J. (1991) 'Promoting school success for Chicanos: The view from inside the bilingual classroom', in VALENCIA, R. (Ed) *Chicano School Failure and Success: Research and Policy Agendas for the 1990s*. London, England, Falmer Press, pp. 119–48.

NATIONAL ADVISORY BOARD ON INTERNATIONAL EDUCATION PROGRAMS (1983) *Critical Needs in International Education: Recommendation for Action*, (Report to the US Secretary of Education), Washington, DC, US Government Printing Office.

OGBU, J.U. (1974) *The Next Generation: An Ethnography of Education in an Urban Neighborhood*, New York, NY, Academic Press.

OGBU, J.U. (1978) *Minority Education and Caste: The American System in Cross-cultural Perspective*, New York, NY, Academic Press.

OGBU, J.U. and MATUTE-BIANCHI, E. (1986) 'Understanding sociocultural factors: Knowledge, identity, and school adjustment', in *Beyond Language: Social and*

Cultural Factors in Schooling Language Minority Students, Sacramento, CA, Bilingual Education Office, California State Department of Education, pp. 73–142.

PADILLA, A. and SUNG, H. (1991) 'A theoretical and pedagogical framework for bilingual education based on principles from cognitive psychology, in PADILLA, R.V. and BENAVIDES, A.H. (Eds) *Critical Perspectives on Bilingual Education Research*, Tempe, AZ, Bilingual Review Press, pp. 11–41.

PEDALINO-PORTER, R. (1990) 'The disabling power of ideology: Challenging the basic assumptions of bilingual education', in IMHOFF, G. (Ed) *Learning in Two Languages*, New Brunswick, NJ, Transaction Publishers, pp. 19–37.

PEREZ, B. and TORRES-GUZMAN, M.E. (1992) *Learning in Two Worlds: An Integrated Spanish/English Biliteracy Approach*, New York, NY, Longman.

RAMÍREZ, J.D. and MERINO, B.J. (1990) 'Classroom talk in English immersion, early-exit and late-exit transitional bilingual education programs', in JACOBSON, R. and FALTIS, C. (Eds) *Language Distribution Issues in Bilingual Schooling*, Clevedon, England, Multilingual Matters.

RAMÍREZ, J.D., YUEN, S.D., RAMEY, D.R. and PASTA, D.J. (1991) *Final Report: Longitudinal Study of Structured English Immersion Strategy, Early-exit and Late-exit Transitional Bilingual Education Programs for Language-minority Children*, San Mateo, CA, Aguirre International.

RHODES, N.C. and OXFORD, R.L. (1988) *A National Profile of Foreign Language Instruction at the Elementary and Secondary School Level*, Los Angeles, CA, Center for Language Education and Research.

ROCA, A. (1990) 'Teaching Spanish to the bilingual college student in Miami', in BERGEN, J.J. (Ed) *Spanish in the United States: Sociolinguistic Issues*, Georgetown, DC, Georgetown University Press, pp. 127–36.

ROOSENS, E. (1989) 'Cultural ecology and achievement motivation: Ethnic minority youngsters in the Belgian system', in ELDERING, L. and KLOPROGGE, J. (Eds) *Different Cultures, Same School Ethnic Minority Children in Europe*, Amsterdam, Netherlands, Swets & Zeitlinger, pp. 85–106.

SÁNCHEZ, R. (1983) *Chicano Discourse: Socio-historic Perspective*, Rowley, MA, Newbury House Publishers.

SCHUMANN, J. (1978) 'The acculturation model for second-language acquisition', in GINGRAS, R.C. (Ed) *Second Language Acquisition and Foreign Language Teaching*, Arlington, VA, Center for Applied Linguistics, pp. 27–50.

SILVA-CORVALÁN, C. (1990) 'Current issues in studies of language contact', *Hispania*, **73**, pp. 162–176.

SILVA-CORVALÁN, C. (1991) 'Spanish language attrition in a contact situation with English', in SELIGER, H.W. and VAGO, R. (Eds) *First Language Attrition: Structural and Theoretical Perspectives*, New York, NY, Cambridge University Press, pp. 151–71.

SPINDLER, G. and SPINDLER, L. (1987) *Interpretive Ethnography of Education at Home and Abroad*, Hillsdale, NJ: Lawrence Erlbaum Associates, Inc.

SUÁREZ-OROZCO, M. (1987) 'Towards a psychosocial understanding of Hispanic adaptation to American schooling', in TRUEBA, H. (Ed) *Success or Failure: Learning and the Language Minority Student*, Cambridge, MA, Newbury House Publishers.

SUÁREZ-OROZCO, M. (1991) 'Migration, minority status, and education: European dilemmas and responses in the 1990s', *Anthropology and Education Quarterly*, **22**, pp. 99–120.

SUÁREZ-OROZCO, M. (1989) *Central American Refugees and US High Schools: A Psychosocial Study of Motivation and Achievement*, Stanford, CA, Stanford University Press.

SWAIN, M. (1985) 'Communicative competence: Some roles of comprehensible input and comprehensible output in its development', in GASS, S.M. and MADDEN, C.G. (Eds) *Input and Second Language Acquisition*, Rowley, MA, Newbury House, pp. 235–53.

TOMLINSON, S. (1991) 'Ethnicity and educational attainment in England — An overview', *Anthropology and Education Quarterly*, **22**, pp. 121–39.

TRUEBA, H.T. (1987) (Ed) *Success or Failure? Learning and the Language Minority Student*, Cambridge, MA, Newbury House Publishers.

TRUEBA, H.T. (1989) *Raising Silent Voices: Educating the Linguistic Minorities for the 21st Century*, New York, NY, Newbury House Publishers.

US BUREAU OF THE CENSUS (1983) *General Social and Economic Characteristics* (by state), December, Washington, DC, Department of Commerce.

US BUREAU OF THE CENSUS (1985) 'Persons of Spanish origin in the United States: March 1985 (Advance report), Washington, DC, US Government Printing Office.

US BUREAU OF THE CENSUS (1990) 'Statistical Abstract of the US: 1990', Washington, DC, US Government Printing Office.

VELTMAN, C.J. (1988) *The Future of the Spanish Language in the United States*, Washington, DC, Hispanic Policy Development Project.

WAGGONER, D. (1988) 'Language minorities in the United States in the 1980s: The evidence fom the 1980 census', in MCKAY, S. and WONG, S.C. (Eds) *Language Diversity: Problem or Resource?*, Cambridge, MA, Newbury House Publishers, pp. 69–108.

WALLENCHINSKY, D., WALLACE, I. and WALLACE, A. (1983) *The Book of Lists*, New York, Morrow.

WILLIG, A. (1985) 'A meta-analysis of selective studies on the effectiveness of bilingual education', *Review of Educational Research*, **55**, pp. 269–317.

WOLBERT, B. (1991) 'More than a golden bangle. . . The significance of success in school for returning Turkish migrant families', *Anthropology and Education Quarterly*, **22**, pp. 181–99.

WONG-FILLMORE, L., AMMON, P., MCLAUGHLIN, B. and AMMON, M. (1985) 'Learning English through bilingual instruction', final report submitted to the National Institute of Education, Berkeley, CA, University of California.

ZENTELLA, A.C. (1987) 'Language and female identity in the Puerto Rican community', in PENFIELD, J. (Ed) *Women and Language in Transition*, Albany, NY, SUNY Press.

ZENTELLA, A.C. (1988) 'The language situation of Puerto Ricans', in MCKAY, S. and WONG, S.C. (Eds) *Language Diversity: Problem or Resource?*, Cambridge, MA, Newbury House Publishers, pp. 140–65.

Chapter 2

Culture and Language:
The Ethnographic Approach to
the Study of Learning Environments

Henry T. Trueba

The learning of languages, be it the mother tongue, or a second, third or fourth language, as well as the loss of languages, are presumed to be related to the differential status of languages and their various functions. Likewise, the acquisition of biliteracy is influenced by the value attached to the functional use of written languages (in contrast with the use of oral language). These are all phenomena reflecting human ecology, that is, social and cultural environmental forces surrounding individuals, families and social groups, and leading them to make important decisions related to migration and acculturation. Those forces can be drastic religious, political and economic movements, war, ethnic and social class conflicts, social class, and other similar events. Migration waves are often the last resort in efforts to survive or escape unbearable oppression. Immigrants in the host country must communicate with new peoples in a language often unknown and through a culture that is perceived as hostile, conflicting, and even destructive of one's own personal and collective values. The acquisition of the new language and culture, however, is the *sine qua non* of full participation in the social, political, economic, and educational institutions of the host country. Here is the dilemma faced by immigrants: to accept or not to accept the language and culture of the host country. To commit to the acquisition of the new language associated with the new culture is viewed as equivalent to giving up one's own cultural identity; not to commit is equivalent to remaining in isolation and being deprived of opportunities to improve and fulfill one's own dreams.

Part of the problem is, first, that language and culture are inseparable and one cannot be acquired without the other. Second, besides being merged as an instrument of communication, language and culture are key to the acquisition of new knowledge, the knowledge needed to participate and succeed in the host country. In the minds of recent immigrants, participation in the host country's institutions is limited by the lack of linguistic and social skills. In turn, the very acquisition of these skills depends on the brokerage of persons who know both the immigrants' language and culture and the language and culture of the host country.

Whatever knowledge we acquire, it is always acquired through language and culture, two interlocked symbolic systems considered essential for human interaction and survival. Culture and language are so intricately intertwined that even trained scholars find it impossible to decide where language ends and culture begins, or which one of the two impacts the other the most. They agree, however, that culture is a broader umbrella concept, and that, during the years of early socialization, both linguistic and cultural symbolic systems are highly instrumental in preparing children to become full members of a human group and active participants in its institutions.

In situations of rapid change and mobility, as is the case with the increasing number of immigrant families in America and Europe, children are uprooted from the home countries by their parents, who are in search of a better life. How do these children deal with the psychological trauma of being uprooted? How do they adapt to new settings with new symbolic systems and socialization patterns? How does socialization in the host country affect the home language and culture? We know that the loss of the mother tongue, often accelerated under social pressure from school teachers and peers, alienates children from their own family and community. What are the long-term effects of language loss and its consequences for the loss of cultural values and cognitive modes of learning? How do immigrant children cope with cultural conflicts embedded in most adaptive strategies they may choose? These and many other questions continue to worry educational researchers and social scientists. The issues alluded to in these questions go to the heart of the achievement problems faced by many Hispanics and other ethnic groups in the United States. Indeed, these issues are relevant worldwide because migration waves are an international phenomenon, and consequently, many ethnic immigrant children and their families are facing rapid changes in language and culture. These changes can have deleterious effects for school achievement. This is the case for Turks, Moroccans, Italians and Spaniards in Germany, Belgium and France. Similar problems are faced by South Americans and Lapps in Sweden; by Koreans in Japan, by Vietnamese, Cambodian and other Indochinese in Australia, Europe, Canada and the United States; by Chinese in Hawaii and in the Americas, as well as many other minority groups.

Thousands of political refugee families from Russia, China, Africa, the Middle East and Central America will soon face and continue to face painful cultural dilemmas and crises in ethnic identity. Linguistic changes (such the loss of the home language) occurring in the lives of immigrant and refugee families are always accompanied by changes in the home culture. The Spanish spoken by Mexicans and Mexican-Americans (Chicanos) in the United States becomes as unique as their English, and their life style evolves to a point that it is typical neither of the white mainstream population nor of the Mexicans living in Mexico.

This cultural and linguistic differentiation has led to cultural and even political conflicts within and between ethnic groups and the white mainstream segment of society. Hostility attributed to ethnic group boundaries is another worldwide phenomenon, unfortunately frequent and violent, as in Northern Ireland, Chad, and Lebanon. Conflicts over ethnic group boundaries have sometimes resulted in open warfare in Burma, Bangladesh, the Sudan, Nigeria, Iraq, and the Philippines. Similarly, cultural and linguistic diversity has exacerbated violent confrontations resulting in the Somali invasion of Ethiopia, the Turkish invasion of Cypress, the killings in Uganda, Syria, India-Pakistan, Burundi, and Indonesia; the terrorist activities of Sikh, Basque, Corsican, and Palestinian groups; the expulsion of Chinese from Vietnam, and of Asians from Uganda (Horowitz, 1985:3).

More recently, following the collapse of the former Soviet Union, the practice of ethnic cleansing in Yugoslavia, now broken up into Serbia, Croatia, Bosnia and Herzegovina, has led to atrocities (by Christians and Muslims against each other) comparable to those committed against the Jews in Germany during the late 1930s and early 1940s: concentration camps, systematic rape of women, assassination of children, women and elderly persons, physical torment, denial of all human and civil rights to prisoners and genocide. *New York Times* reporters David Binder and Barbara Crossette state:

> Policy makers say that the current ethnic conflicts are actually the third wave of this century, with the first two having taken place after World War I and the explosion of anticolonial movements in Africa and Asia after World War II. But the newest wave is seen as even more complex, potentially more threatening to international peace and almost certain to grow in the years ahead (Binder and Crossette, *New York Times*, February 7, 1993:1).

The same authors document ethnic struggles in forty-eight countries in Europe (Bosnia and Herzegovina, Croatia, Spain, Great Britain, Germany, Romania, Russia, Maldova and Georgia), in the Middle East and North Africa (Azerbaijan, Turkey, Iraq, Israel, Algeria, Egypt and the Sudan), in Africa south of the Sahara (Mauritania, Mali, Chad, Somalia, Senegal, Liberia, Togo, Nigeria, Uganda, Rwanda, Burundi, Kenya, Zaire, Angola, and South Africa), in Asia (Tajikistan, Afghanistan, Pakistan, India, Bhutan, Sri Lanka, Bangladesh, Myanmar, China, Cambodia, Indonesia, Papua New Guinea, and Fiji) and in Latin America (Guatemala, Colombia, Peru and Brazil) (*Ibid.*, p. 12).

Ethnic identity and ethnic boundaries are truly important in international conflicts. But what are ethnic groups, and who are the members of such groups? In a broad world context, ethnic groups can be defined as autochthonous or indigenous groups living in the social and territorial fringes of powerful societies. These groups become marginalized and disempowered and do not participate fully in mainstream societal institutions. While some conservative figures suggest that there are some 5000 such groups (Bacal, 1990:15), it is important to remember that the lowest socio-economic strata of industrialized and non-industrialized countries is extremely large. China alone has a total population of 1,103,900,000; from them, in 1982 about 93.3 per cent (some 937 million) belong to the Han (Chinese who speak Mandarin as *lingua franca*; at least ten other major languages are spoken by the Han peoples who have considerable cultural diversity among themselves). The Han people settled in the north where the lower Yellow and Wei Rivers spread the cradle of Chinese civilization. The rest of the population (167 million) belong to a number of ethnic groups or nations. It is estimated that there are at least fifty-five formally recognized national minority groups totalling over 100 million — of them fifteen groups have populations of over 1 million each: the Zhuang 13.4 million, the Hui 7.2 million, the Uygurs 6 million, the Yi 5.5 million, the Miao, ancestors of the Hmong, 5 million, the Manchus 4.3, the Tibetans 3.9 million, the Mongols 3.4 million, the Tujia with 2.8 million closely related to the Tong with 1.4, the Buyi 2.1 million, Koreans, 1.8 million, Yao 1.4 million, Bai 1.1 million, and Hani 1.1 million (Yuan Tien, 1989:501–503). Many other countries, especially the United States and Europe attract tens of thousands of *de facto* 'underclass' immigrants looking for an opportunity to live a good life.

Immigrants' Home Languages and Learning Environments

Anthropologists and linguists doing research on learning have focused on the relationship of language and culture. This relationship is inherently dependent on the social context and on the characteristics of the learning environment. Both language and culture seem to become not only the object of adaptive strategies for groups undergoing social change, but also the instruments of such change. Schools and other social institutions can adopt policies supporting home languages and cultures as important resources to produce learning environments for children of immigrant families that are qualitatively superior in comparison with other schools and social institutions that discard such resources. The cultural context of communication through the mother tongue and the development of adaptive stra-tegies that permit immigrants to retain their cultural values and traditions are shaped by national goals, traditions, and philosophies. These in turn, determine the treatment of immigrants and whether a climate of national tolerance of pluralism develops.

For the reasons given above, the status of native languages spoken by immigrant families is often a reflection of prejudice or cultural bias against such families. The Spanish spoken by a Chicano is quickly identified as a dialect primarily characterized by key phonological, syntactic and lexical features, and is often seen by academicians as 'bad' or 'deficient.' Consequently, the tendency is to place as a norm the standard forms of Spanish spoken by Spaniards (preferentially Castilian Spanish) or by upper-class Mexican or South American persons who retain a close association with peninsular forms of the language.

Social scientists (especially anthropologists) have developed various concepts and theoretical models based on ethnographic approaches intended to handle issues of cultural conflict, cultural congruence, cultural continuities and discontinuities, communication or miscommunication, incompatibility, interference, deficit, differential achievement, and many others. A careful reading of the ethnographic research literature suggests that there are intimate relationships between method and theory with important consequences for an in-depth understanding of the role of language and culture in learning contexts. In contrast with other research approaches to the study of culture, language and ethnicity, ethnographic research requires that theory and method be complementary and inseparable. Yet the nature of the relationships between method and theory varies in different disciplines using ethnography.

Two of the best examples of ethnographic researchers are George and Louise Spindler. Consistently for the last forty years, the work of the Spindlers has focused on the study of culture and cultural transmission and its implications for the choice of adaptive strategies during culture change (Spindler, 1955, 1963; and Spindler and Spindler, 1990 — see references in Note[1]). The work of George and Louise Spindler is today considered seminal in the study of culture and the process of cultural transmission, as well as in the use of ethnographic approaches to study this process. One of their major concerns, in the context of studying cultural transmission, has been the development of appropriate ethnographic methods and techniques to establish the supportive evidence behind inferences from observed behavioral patterns towards the construction of theories of behavior. In other words, the Spindlers have been particularly helpful in the development of theoretical models relevant to cultural patterns adopted by immigrants, refugees and minorities in their attempt to cope with culture change and culture conflict. They have focused on the learning environments of minority students, and have produced powerful accounts that invite reflection on serious theoretical issues by virtue of their insights obtained through systematic, close range field-based experiences.

The politics of language use and language teaching, especially in the context of a continuous flow of immigrants from lower socioeconomic levels, is an expression of cultural and social class values (or biases) that requires close examination. In turn, the study of the context of second language and culture acquisition requires a better understanding of the concept of culture.

Culture and Ethnography

Debates on the use of the concept of 'culture' and 'ethnography' must be contextualized by a number of methodological, theoretical and ideological currents that make the discussion difficult and seemingly politically loaded. The interest in naturalistic, field-based research methods has increased substantially, and a wide range of studies using approaches other than quantitative are indiscriminately dumped into the single category of 'qualitative'.

Ethnographers welcome with mixed feelings the popularity of qualitative research and the technological advances used in gathering and analyzing data (via computers, video-tape and other electronic means). Ethnographers often express feelings of anxiety over the possible misunderstanding of the concept of culture and its consequences for ethnographic research. The discussion of qualitative research methods in the absence of specific research designs within recognized disciplinary and theoretical frameworks has become rather popular in professional meetings, in spite of the fact that such practices may look dysfunctional to the professional ethnographer. The proliferation of workshops, oral presentations, articles, and books on qualitative research discussed generically, without pointing at any specific characteristics or a common denominator for all studies, is viewed with alarm by ethnographers.

In the face of such a proliferation, it is reasonable to distinguish between *methodological techniques*, (that is, tools utilized in many different types of qualitative studies, such as interviews, video-taping, audio-taping, photography, life histories, case studies, vignettes, journals, participant observations, unobtrusive observations, note-taking, sociolinguistic approaches, ethnohistorical approaches) and *methodological approaches*, (cohesive research designs using selected tools for specific research purposes, leading to different types of qualitative studies). It is also reasonable to describe a few examples of the types of qualitative studies that share certain common features, but also clearly exhibit distinct and unique characteristics separating them from each other:

1 Ethnohistorical studies. These studies focus on the 'emic' reconstruction of history, emic meaning from the perspective of the members of the culture under study. Frequently, these studies are based primarily on oral histories, of particular group members via interviews, as well as on archival research and research on existing monuments, cemeteries, and archaeological monuments;

2 Ethnolinguistic studies. These are studies on language use by members of the various social groups, and focus on the changes affecting language

during intensive culture conflicts. Linguistic analysis is used and enriched with ethnographic descriptions of the cultural context of language use;

3 Interactional studies. These are studies conducted by ethnomethodologists (in sociology) who look at oral and written language in order to make inferences about individual and collective behavior in the face of organizational and structural changes. These studies can be complemented by larger macrosociological research of institutional change, for example, in the case of changes in health service Federal policies — which may drastically change the relationship of doctor and patient, as well as patient treatment;

4 Ethnographic studies. These studies are characterized by their emphasis on the role of culture on behavior, and are amenable to theoretical frameworks from a number of disciplines (sociology, anthropology, psychology, and linguistics). They share, however, important theoretical and methodological characteristics which are discussed below.

All ethnographic studies are, at least ideally, long-term, grounded in empirical evidence collected through any of the methodological techniques alluded to above, and most of all they are interpretive. The main purpose of ethnographic research is to interpret the meaning of behavior by providing its appropriate social and cultural context. However, the social and cultural context is often found in a cross-cultural context. This is a particularly stringent requirement for ethnographic studies designed by anthropologists, but it has proven useful to psychologists, socio- and psycholinguists, ethnographers of communication, sociologists, and other social scientists.

Not every aspect of behavior is equally important across disciplines. Psychological frameworks often focus on cognitive processes, motivation, or developmental issues. Vygotskian researchers conducting ethnographic studies belong here (Diaz, Moll and Mehan, 1986; Moll and Diaz, 1987; Moll, 1990). Sociolinguists, ethnomethodologists and ethnographers of communication, in turn, may focus on the use of language to make inferences about institutional structures in society, about group boundaries, interactional patterns reflective of social status, or about the use of opportunity structures and closure structures via the use of class privileges (Gumperz and Hymes, 1964, 1972; Hymes, 1974; Cook-Gumperz, 1986).

It is precisely these enormous numbers of possibilities and varieties of potential theoretical frameworks that have attracted large numbers of educational researchers. The study of issues of equity, cultural diversity, multicultural settings, class and caste structures, ethnicity, academic achievement and performance in schools and society can have many and complex dimensions accessible only from a variety of qualitative approaches, and not necessarily through ethnographic approaches alone.

Indeed, ethnographic approaches are avenues of inquiry to build theoretical models, or mental constructs, or explanatory artifacts, in order to make sense of behavior from the perspective of a shared value system. Ethnographic research is compatible with a number of theoretically cohesive approaches that focus on different disciplinary areas of interest, yet *all ethnographic studies share a single methodological thrust; that is, a genuine long-term, interpretive, historically grounded, systematic, ethnographic approach guided by coordinated bodies of literature and subordinated foci via the use of the same data corpus.*

There is another important common characteristic of ethnographic studies across disciplines that is not shared by other qualitative approaches. Ethnographic studies, precisely because they attempt to provide a broad (holistic) context for the interpretation of behavior, and to portray the emic (or inside) view of the individuals' culture (an explanation based on their cultural assumptions that make sense of observed behavior), must be inherently long-term and reflective of the dynamics of change as ethnographers make progress in their understanding. This means that the actual data gathered impact the research goals and the nature of the inquiry itself continuously. Thus, the goals of the research are restructured with every new piece of information obtained. New questions are asked to get to the bottom of data, and new inquiry goals are constructed if they prove to be 'emically significant' or functionally relevant to the overall research objectives, in other words, useful to the ethnographer's understanding of the culture and behavior of the people under study, from their own standpoint.

At the university, there is an increasing pressure to prepare students coming from a variety of disciplinary backgrounds and interests in ethnographic methods. Some students clearly seek expertise in applied social science fields whose research has implications for policy and practice. We must examine the functional relevance of the data to the theoretical framework, the choice of a central topic, and the choice of particular methodological techniques. The choice of life histories, case studies, vignettes, audio-taping, interviews, or any other technique must be made with reference to the theoretical framework inspiring the research inquiry, the overall research design, and the constraints of time, resources and abilities of the researcher. Choices of techniques prior to identification of a theoretical thrust and/or focus of the research inquiry may be premature and counterproductive. The specific conditions for sound ethnographic research will be better understood after a discussion of the concept of culture. In general, however, these conditions have to do with the quintessential nature of ethnographic research as interpretive, depending on the contextual knowledge that allows the judicious ethnographer to make legitimate inferences. The ethnographer is indeed the weakest link between exhibited behavior and its interpretation through ethnographic research. The context of behavior may well be accessible, rich in clues, and clearly pointing in some interpretive direction, yet, ethnographers may be blinded by biases or unwillingness to consider certain contextual factors as functionally relevant or significant to their interpretive task. To counteract possible biases and to prevent blind spots in interpretation, the experienced ethnographer uses cross-cultural comparisons, faithful description of observed behavior and a rich contextualization of events described. It is expected that presenting the actual empirical evidence gathered and the perspectives of the researchers will help the reader to generate alternative interpretations.

Concept of Culture

Post-modernistic social science research trends, with an emphasis on construction and deconstruction of behavioral phenomena, have persuaded ethnographers to pursue empirical evidence backing inferences in the form of ethnohistorical documentation and comparative studies across cultures. The methodological challenges faced by researchers in the collection and interpretation of ethnographic data have rekindled enthusiasm for linguistic approaches that emphasized the analysis of text. Ethnographic research designs continue to lead to richer descriptions and ultimately to better understanding of behavior. Good ethnographic descriptions are the result of systematic inquiry executed with wisdom and methodological rigor, resulting in reasonable interpretations, in spite of the ethnographer's biases.

The 'discovery' of ethnographic research and the unrestricted use of 'culture' in non-technical contexts has resulted in pseudo-scientific explanations of behavior via popular 'ethnographic studies' which range from casual observations to serious research designs. Many of these studies have nothing to do with ethnography as understood here, but they may represent other legitimate qualitative approaches to investigation. Is it worth attempting to restrict the use of such terms? Is it possible? It may not be, but at the very least we suggest the advantages of using appropriately terms such as 'culture', and 'ethnography', 'acculturation', 'cultural conflict', 'cultural continuities or discontinuities', 'cultural involution', and others. It would be reasonable to:

1 Try to clarify our basic understanding of how these concepts are used in theoretical and methodological contexts deemed appropriate by trained ethnographers;
2 Point to the functional value of these concepts when used appropriately.

The latitude used by educational researchers and contributors to education journals suggests to the casual reader that culture is some sort of amorphous, reified, static entity that causes people to behave in certain ways, to express and exhibit certain values, beliefs and practices. Furthermore, the popular belief is often held that culture is an entity that can be packaged and transferred from one generation to the next with relatively few changes. In other cases, culture is seen by researchers as an interactional style shared with other members of the same working unit or social institution or ethnic group. Examples given by these researchers are the similarity of behavior in members of the same church, military unit, bureaucratic organization, public health office, etc. These individuals seem to share etiquette and patterns of behavior related to their roles played in those interactional settings. A superficial analysis of a given ethnic group behavior may persuade casual observers that most group members frequent parks, or raise their voices when they talk with each other, or litter, or eat peculiar foods, or laugh and play in ways not shared with other members of society.

Culture for other persons is simply an attachment, an appendix affecting our affiliation to a social group, to a social class, or to an organization. This culture is identified by group members within certain domains only. We talk, for example, about the culture of academia, the culture of schools, the culture of poverty, the culture of violence, the drug culture, and the military culture, the culture of academia, the 'superculture' of the rich and famous.

In contrast, the use of culture in well defined institutional contexts (schools, ethnic enclaves, cultural ecological niches) as noticed by local people when they speak of 'the culture of the Bronx' versus 'the culture of Tijuana', may help us characterize segments of society which share common behavioral features, enjoy a certain amount of internal self-sufficiency, and are a strong force determining individual behaviors, at least within certain contexts (see the study of poverty and ethnicity in the ghettos between 1840 and 1925 by David Ward, 1989). In a more restricted and technical sense, we refer to the culture of a single type of institution, or to specific institutions sharing high levels of control over the life of the individuals associated with it, as, for example, when we talk about total institutions — prisons, mental hospitals, religious seminaries, military training units, and others defined by Irving Goffman (1959). These institutions re-socialize individuals into a new self-concept, redefine the ranges of acceptable behavior and develop new reward systems in terms of institutional needs for control.

Through manipulation of incentives and sanctions, total institutions create new goals, norms of behavior, cognitive codes and new identities that facilitate the control of individuals, and thus enhance a more uniform behavior, at least in public. Goffman notes that often these institutions must keep a dual standard of conduct, one for the public and another internally. In a mental hospital, for example:

> . . . if attendants in a mental ward are to maintain order and at the same time not hit patients, and if this combination of standards is difficult to maintain, then the unruly patient may be 'necked' with a wet towel and choked into submission in a way that leaves no visible evidence of mistreatment (Goffman, 1959:45).

In some institutions jobs cannot be obtained through competition, or they require the candidates to suffer abuse or to make secret deals. This unwritten policy is adopted in order to:

> . . . foster the impression that they [the candidates] have ideal qualifications for the role, and that it was not necessary for them to suffer any indignities, insults, and humiliations, or make any tacitly understood 'deals'. . . . Reinforcing these ideal impressions there is a kind of 'rhetoric of training', whereby labor unions, universities, trade associations, and other licensing bodies require practitioners to absorb a mystical range and period of training, in part to maintain a monopoly, but in part to foster the impression that the licensed practitioner is someone who has been reconstituted by his learning experience and is now set apart from other men (Goffman, 1959:46).

In brief, the culture of total institutions is characterized by changing individual behavior in ways deemed appropriate by those who govern the institutions. How does the culture of a military institution differ from that of a hospital or a religious order? There are important differences in policies, demands and philosophy which result in preferential use of certain types of control (internal, based on supernatural beliefs, or external, such as coercive measures to obtain compliance).

While the previous usages of culture are widespread, to the trained social scientist and traditional anthropologist, culture is still *composed* of socially shared elements, socially shared norms, codes of behavior, values, and assumptions about the world that clearly distinguish one sociocultural group from another. Goodenough stated that culture 'is made up of the concepts, beliefs, and principles of action and organization' (Goodenough, 1976:5). Anthropologists have agreed that sharing a group's culture means being able to function effectively in that

group. Contemporary societies, however, are complex and in continuous movement, because there is a great deal of social mobility and migration from one
country to another caused by economic crises in the home country and the opening
of economic opportunities in another. Individuals take their families in search of
a better life and find themselves in places with languages and cultures that are
unfamiliar to them or even entirely unknown. As suggested earlier, the result of
immigration waves and cultural change is often ethnic pluralism and cultural
diversity (two sides of the same phenomenon); but not just as a beautiful mosaic
of ethnic and linguistic groups in harmony, but as a complex series of interactional
conflicts and problems related to the unemployment, violence, poverty, low educational levels, and isolation of disenfranchised individuals. At times these conflicts
seem to become crises of international dimensions affecting a number of technologically and industrially developed Western countries.

Ethnic Pluralism in the Americas

The frequent use of ethnographic approaches to study ethnic pluralism, multilingual and multicultural settings has brought to light the complex relationships
between culture, race, class and ethnicity. In the United States alone, continuous
questions arise as to how the Chicano, African American, American Indian, Asian,
Indochinese and other members of ethnic groups who spread over the various
social classes, can together form in conjunction with white mainstream persons a
single *American culture*? In the construction of these 'ethnic' cultures what is the
role of the class and race dimensions? Some of the ethnic groups remain cohesive
in their ethnic identity as long as they stay within a single social class (often in
the low income brackets), but lose their cohesiveness as they become members of
the middle or upper classes. Upward social mobility and the loss of ethnic identity
are important phenomena since they entail drastic changes in life-style and level
of participation in the American political, economic and social institutions. Some
individuals (and this is a truly remarkable accomplishment in adaptive behavior)
within the same ethnic group seem to move freely from one social stratum to
another, and communicate effectively with members of different social strata.
Scholars, on one extreme, and common immigrants and refugees on the other,
continue to ask themselves questions such as the following: What is American
culture? What is the essence of American democracy? Who determines cultural
values? What is the role of schools in determining cultural values? Do the schools
have a culture of their own? Do age groups have a culture of their own? Do the
homeless, drug addicts, and minorities have a culture of their own? How do you
define culture in these diverse contexts? These questions transcend any one culture
in particular. Cultural contrasts and culture change underline the unique nature of
Western cultures in industrial societies, especially those like the US facing the flow
of large numbers of immigrants and refugees.

We know that at different times in American history *culture* has had various
definitions applied to a variety of contexts and settings. In the specific context of
educational research some of the concepts of culture have enjoyed significant
continuity and consistency. Culture is here viewed as instrumental in the study
of dynamic and complex educational institutions. A cultural system cannot be
described adequately unless it is compared and contrasted with other systems.

It is only in the light of other cultural norms, codes of behavior and cognitive approaches that we realize what our own culture is all about. Cross-cultural comparisons have been most helpful in anthropological research. Cross-cultural research is not an easy task. The problem is not 'to state what someone did but to specify the conditions under which it is culturally appropriate to anticipate that he, or persons occupying his role, will render an equivalent performance' (Frake, 1964:112). Knowing another culture is being able to anticipate peoples' observed behaviors; this requires cultural knowledge and an understanding of their cultural values. Yet, the understanding of ongoing cultural changes, processes of adaptation in cultural contact and adaptive strategies (see Trueba, Cheng and Ima, 1993) require a better understanding of the process of culture acquisition and transmission.

Culture, as the Spindlers have consistently argued, is a transactional process, intrinsically dynamic, because it is precisely during cultural transmission from one generation to another that culture is recreated, restructured and redirected by the people involved in that process. The Spindlers' discussion of the nature of culture in a cross-cultural perspective represents the best of their anthropological research (see Note 1 for references). During the last decade, a number of other scholars have embraced both the notion of culture as a transactional process and the need to describe cultures in a cross-cultural perspective (Alvarez, 1988; Boos-Nunning and Hohmann, 1989; Boggs, 1972, 1985; Cazden and Mehan, 1989, and many others — see Note 2 for additional references). Cultural contrasts in the context of school performance have been mentioned often in the literature (Gibson, 1987a, 1987b, 1988; Goldman and Trueba, 1987; Hornberger, 1988; Jordan, Tharp and Vogt, 1985; Macias, 1987; for additional references see Note[2]).

For the above scholars, culture has become a powerful instrument in the conceptual organization and implementation of research projects. As such, culture has become an integral part of the educational research kit. It is definitely not just an abstract construct of complex relationships between observed behavior and cognitive codes presumed to generate such behavior, nor a cumbersome and amorphous sum total of cultural values and traditions presumed to characterize a society. George and Louise Spindlers' contribution is to present culture as a vital force encompassing values, perceptions and goals *shared* and *transmitted* in a given social group, motivating individuals to pursue specific actions enhancing goals related to the values (Spindler, 1959, 1977, 1982; Trueba, Spindler and Spindler, 1989; Spindler and Spindler, 1990). In turn, education is a collective transaction that perpetuates the community's attachment to cultural values. If culture is recreated in the process of being transmitted, education is the mechanism that facilitates the two key components of cultural transmission: learning and motivation.

One of the most controversial and penetrating contributions by the Spindlers is their most recent book *The American Cultural Dialogue and its Transmission* (1990). Their candid discussion of the America they have lived in with its ethnic and social classes, its diversity, cultural conflicts, contradictory demands and future orientation may surprise the readers. The Spindlers confront issues about ethnic identity and minority status, culture maintenance, cultural values and the dialectical nature of American democratic institutions. They summarize the views of Crevecoeur, Jefferson, Martineau, Toqueville, von Hubner, Turner and other important historical figures. They refer to binary polar forces driving cultural movements and the cultural dialogue in opposite directions: cultural continuity and discontinuity, change and resistance to change, conformity and individualism, and minority success and failure. In their discussion of continuities and discontinuities of cultural groups, the Spindlers have discovered the cycles of recurring similarities, for example, in their study of German schools and their study of the American cultural dialogue. They see a remarkable consistency in cultural values and themes. The myth that American society has overcome its racist biases is often brutally shattered with examples of racially motivated violence. Racism is not just a simple attitudinal problem on the part of the white mainstream population; it is an integral part of a structural arrangement, created through centuries of European control that have shaped up Western cultural values resulting in an American 'quasi-apartheid' life-style. Attempts at integration show the far-reaching structural changes needed in our institutions and the values behind determining their organization.

Concepts such as those of mainstream culture and cultural pluralism, (with the shock, dissonance and incongruence experienced by the various ethnic groups) and cultural adjustment (congruence, harmony, balance) have moved the Spindlers to recognize the complexity and depth of the conflicts faced by individual Americans and the entire society. The individual *enduring self* (the consistent self-perception as being culturally attached to a given cultural setting) and the *situated self* (the part of ourselves adapting continuously to new settings) are an attempt to resolve the conflict of rapid cultural change we face (Spindler and Spindler, 1989). The world moves too fast and does not permit us to anchor ourselves and families in any value system. As an effort to help resolve the dissonance resulting from conflict, the Spindlers have offered *cultural therapy* (Spindler and Spindler, 1989), a process which has also most recently occupied their attention and that seems to gain momentum as a theoretical framework for both individual and collective healing processes. Cultural therapy has two basic components, cultural knowledge to understand one's own culture (one's own enduring self and changing self) and the motivation to embrace a new culture.

American Cultural and Linguistic Diversity

Ethnic diversification and pluralism are a phenomenon that characterizes most modern Western societies. What is peculiar to the United States and in what ways are these diversification currents unique?

> Within the USA the diversification is particularly impressive. All of the skills and insights gained by anthropologists in cultures away from home can be used to good advantage at home. Anthropologists attend to symbols, ceremonies, rituals, communities, language and thought, beliefs, dialects, sex roles and sexuality, subsistence and ecology, kinship, and a multitude of other topics in ways that historians, sociologists, political scientists, and psychologists will not, because of the heritage of experience with 'other' cultures from primitive to peasant to urban away from home (Spindler and Spindler, 1983:73).

There is no simple way of categorizing all Americans. Can we divide Americans into 'ethnic' and 'non-ethnic', or into mainstream and marginal? If America was divided into the first two major categories, 'ethnic' and 'non-ethnic', would there be a consensus as to who qualifies as 'ethnic' and who does not? Along the spectrum of possible 'ethnics' in current folk taxonomies we could find people who have been in this country for generations, who may have lost their parents' language and culture, and who may have moved away from their ethnic community, but despite all, who still insist on calling themselves Italian, German, Scottish, or Hispanic. . . . The 'non-ethnic' category also has problems. It seems to be a category frequently chosen and applied by other individuals and imposed on Americans on the basis of physical appearance, speech patterns and behavioral characteristics. It is quite possible, however, that many people looking 'non-ethnic' see themselves as mainstream Americans from an 'ethnic extraction', but not totally uprooted from their parents' ethnic culture.

Inter-ethnic marriages and informal unions essentially did away with the classificatory system brought to the new world by the European colonizers and resulted in a broad range of physical types. When economic differences were combined with physical differences, inter-ethnic and interracial marriages did away with prejudice, at least to some extent. Latin American society is still viewed by some scholars as profoundly racist and class-conscious. Cultural diversity and cultural conflict are at the center of European concern because of the unexpected arrival of unwanted immigrants who are perceived as a threat to European cultural unity and as a drain to scarce public resources, jobs and opportunities created with European tax monies. In order to become competitive in the world economy, European nations supported for many years a policy of hiring (at low wages) guest workers from their African colonies and other poor countries. Guest workers and their families have now become a permanent population in Germany, Belgium, France, Holland and other countries.

The case of Belgium is particularly enlightening. Belgium is a country of 10 million people with a very large population of immigrants (20 per cent) who were recruited to work in the mines and in other jobs not wanted by the Belgians (Roosens, 1989a, and 1989b). The latest available figures (Roosens, 1989b:127–128) indicate that there are 270,521 Italians, 119,083 Moroccans, 70,033 Turks, and 55,952 Spaniards. In a relatively small territory, where the historical division between the Walloons and the Flemish has been reflected in the legislated use of French in some areas and of Dutch in others, the use of other languages either for public instruction or for services can create serious political problems.

The clue to an understanding of the nature of ethnic pluralism and cultural diversity created in Europe lies in an analysis of the region's economic needs coupled with European cohesiveness that led to the use of temporary immigrants. In contrast, pluralism and diversity of the United States or of Latin America requires understanding of the role of native languages and cultures in the adaptation of immigrants who want to stay permanently in the Americas as 'insiders' or full participants. In Europe immigrants face nationalist norms that permanently exclude them as outsiders. Why do European industrial entrepreneurs consistently invite those outsiders to come and work for lesser wages, knowing well that they will want to stay and that their children will see themselves as Europeans? The left hand of European economic development is only concerned with the use (in some instances, exploitation) of cheap immigrant labor, and it does not want to know about what the right hand is doing to improve the life of immigrants, or about the social consequences of immigration. What the right hand is doing with those children of immigrants who are born in the host country is essential to prepare them to participate fully in European social institutions.

One could argue that the White European cultural values, the life style, the amenities of industrial affluent societies, the Culture with a capital 'C', are intimately related to their colonial philosophy and the use of cheap labor. Are cultural values and patterns of behavior wedded to class values? Are some of these values and patterns inherently racist and prejudicial in that they require services from guest workers in conditions unacceptable to white Europeans? Does this mean that there is no racism in the Americas?

Of course, there is a great deal of racial prejudice in the United States, Mexico and Latin America, but it is of a different nature. First, it is condemned by the law and, in many cases, also by social practice as well. African Americans can move up the social ladder, enter the ranks of executives in businesses and industry, become professors in major universities, and marry white persons. These benefits, upward mobility, intermarriage, high ranks in industry, the military and business, are possible in the United States and Latin America, precisely because class and culture concepts were forged differently, and have changed drastically in these countries without destroying their national unity and core values. Cultural diversity is part of the definition of these countries and is recognized as an asset. These societies, being deeply diversified, pluralistic, and ethnically rich, allow persons of color and of different ethnic groups to create social institutions that cross-cut class and racial strata. Everybody recognizes that the pluralistic nature of American society is based in its fundamental democratic philosophy of equal rights for all. The payoff is a rich culture where jazz is not just black music, but as American as apple pie. At the very foundations of the United States' economic and political development is a respect for civil rights, for ethnic differences and for individual belief systems.

Notes

1 The discussion of cultural transmission pioneered by George Spindler since the mid-1950s was pursued during his entire academic career; he has written about it in 1968, 1970a, 1970b, 1971; 1974a, 1974b, 1974c, 1977, 1978, 1982; both George Spindler and Louise Spindler discussed the topic in 1982, 1983, 1987a, 1987b, 1987c, and 1989.

2 The literature on cross-cultural research that explores concepts of cultural conflict, cultural socialization and learning is abundant. Much of this literature was influenced by the Spindlers. See, for example, McDermott, 1977, 1987a, 1987b; Moll and Diaz, 1987; Ogbu, 1982, 1987; Philips, 1982; Roosens, 1989a, 1989b; Suárez-Orozco, 1987, 1989, 1990; Trueba, 1987a, 1987b; 1988a, 1988b, 1988c, 1988d; 1989a, 1989b; 1990a, 1990b, 1991; Trueba and Delgado-Gaitan, 1988; Trueba, Spindler and Spindler, 1989; Trueba, Jacobs and Kirton, 1990; Warren, 1982. There are also other ethnographers and sociolinguistics who explore a number of theoretical frameworks combining anthropological and linguistic concepts. Among others, Cazden, and Hymes, 1972; Cheng, 1987; Chilcott, 1987; D'Andrade, 1984; Delgado-Gaitan, 1986a, 1986b; 1987a, 1987b, 1990; Deyhle, 1987; LeCompte and Goetz, 1984. Finally, others have used the sociohistorical approaches of Vygotsky and some anthropological concepts, such as Diaz, Moll and Mehan, 1986; Erickson, 1986, 1987; Fujita and Sano, 1988; Delgado-Gaitan and Trueba, 1991).

References

ALVAREZ, R. (1988) 'National politics and local responses: The nation's first successful school desegregation court case', in TRUEBA, H. and DELGADO-GAITAN, C. (Eds) *School and Society: Learning Content Through Culture*, New York, Praeger Publishers, pp. 37–52.

BACAL, A. (1990) 'The emergence of ethno-development in the social sciences', in ALVARSSON, J. and HORNA, H. (Eds) *Ethnicity in Latin America*, Uppsala, Sweden Centre for Latin American Studies, Uppsala Universitet, pp. 15–27.

BINDER, D. and CROSSETTE, B. (1993) 'As ethnic wars multiply, US strives for a policy', *New York Times*, February 7, **CXLII**, No. 49, 235, pp. 1 and 12.

BOGGS, S.T. (1972) 'The meaning of questions and narratives to Hawaiian children', in CAZDEN, C.B., JOHN, V.P. and HYMES, D. (Eds) *Functions of Language in the Classroom*, New York, NY, Teachers College Press, pp. 1–28.

BOGGS, S.T. (1985) *Speaking, Relating, and Learning: A Study of Hawaiian Children at Home and at School*, Norwood, NJ, Ablex Publishing Corp.

BOOS-NUNNING, U. and HOHMANN, M. (1989) 'The educational situation of migrant workers' children', in ELDERING, L. and KLOPROGGE, J. (Eds) *Different Cultures Same School: Ethnic Minority Children in Europe*, Berwyn, PA, Swets North America, pp. 39–59.

CAZDEN, C. and MEHAN, H. (1989) 'Principles from sociology and anthropology: Context, code, classroom, and culture', in REYNOLDS, M.C. (Ed) *Knowledge Base for the Beginning Teacher*, Oxford, England, Pergamon Press.

CAZDEN, C., JOHN, V. and HYMES, D. (Eds) (1972) *Functions of Language in the Classroom*, New York, NY, Teachers College Press.

CHENG, L. (1987) 'English communicative competence of language minority children: Assessment and treatment of language "impaired" preschoolers', in TRUEBA, H. (Ed) *Success or Failure? Learning and the Language Minority Student*, New York, NY, Newbury/Harper & Row, pp. 49–68.

CHILCOTT, J.H. (1987) 'Where are you coming from and where are you going? The reporting of ethnographic research', *American Educational Research Journal*, **24**, 2, pp. 199–218.

COOK-GUMPERZ, J. (Ed) (1986) *The Social Construction of Literacy*, Cambridge, England, Cambridge University Press.

D'ANDRADE, R. (1984) 'Cultural meaning systems', in SHWEDER, R.A. and LEVINE, R.A. (Eds) *Culture Theory*, New York, NY, Cambridge University Press, pp. 88–119.

DELGADO-GAITAN, C. (1986a) 'Mexican adult literacy: New directions for immigrants', in GOLDMAN, S. and TRUEBA, H.T. (Eds) *Becoming Literate in English as a Second Language*, Norwood, NJ, Ablex, pp. 9–32.

DELGADO-GAITAN, C. (1986b) 'Teacher attitudes on diversity affecting student socio-academic responses: An ethnographic view', *Journal of Adolescent Research*, **1**, pp. 103–114.

DELGADO-GAITAN, C. (1987a) 'Traditions and transitions in the learning process of Mexican children: An ethnographic view', in SPINDLER, G. and SPINDLER, L. (Eds) *Interpretive Ethnography of Education: At Home and Abroad*, Hillsdale, NJ, Lawrence Erlbaum Associates, Publisher, pp. 333–59.

DELGADO-GAITAN, C. (1987b) 'Parent perceptions of school: Supportive environments for children', in TRUEBA, H. (Ed) *Success or Failure?: Learning and the Language Minority Student*, Cambridge, MA, Newbury/Harper & Row, pp. 131–55.

DELGADO-GAITAN, C. (1990) *Literacy for Empowerment: The Role of Parents in Children's Education*, London, England, Falmer Press.

DELGADO-GAITAN, C. and TRUEBA, H. (1991) *Crossing Cultural Borders: Education for Immigrant Families in America*, London, England, Falmer Press.

DEYHLE, D. (1987) 'Learning failure: Tests as gatekeepers and the culturally different child', in TRUEBA, H. (Ed) *Success or Failure?: Learning and the Language Minority Student*, New York, NY, Newbury Publishers, a division of Harper and Row, pp. 85–108.

DIAZ, S., MOLL, L. and MEHAN, H. (1986) 'Sociocultural resources in instruction: A context-specific approach', in *Beyond Language: Social and Cultural Factors in Schooling Language Minority Students*, Sacramento, CA, Bilingual Education Office, California State Department of Education, pp. 187–230.

ERICKSON, F. (1986) 'Qualitative methods in research on teaching', in WITTROCK, M.C. (Ed) *Handbook of Research on Teaching*, New York, NY, Macmillan Publishing Co, pp. 119–58.

ERICKSON, F. (1987) 'Transformation and school success: The politics and culture of educational achievement', *Anthropology and Education Quarterly*, **18**, 4, pp. 335–56.

FRAKE, C. (1964) 'Notes on queries in ethnography', *American Anthropologist*, **66**, 3, pp. 132–45.

FUJITA, M. and SANO, T. (1988) 'Children in American and Japanese day-care centers: Ethnography and reflective cross-cultural interviewing', in TRUEBA, H. and DELGADO-GAITAN, C. (Eds) *School and Society: Teaching Content Through Culture*, NY, Praeger, pp. 73–97.

GIBSON, M. (1987a) 'Playing by the rules', in SPINDLER, G. (Ed) *Education and Cultural Process: Anthropological Approaches* (Second Edition) Prospect Heights, IL, Waveland Press, Inc., pp. 274–83.

GIBSON, M. (1987b) 'The school performance of immigrant minorities: A comparative view', *Anthropology and Education Quarterly*, **18**, 4, pp. 262–75.

GIBSON, M. (1988) *Accommodation Without Assimilation: Sikh Immigrants in an American High School*, Ithaca, NY, Cornell University Press.

GOFFMAN, I. (1959) *The Presentation of Self in Everyday Life*, Garden City, NY, Doubleday Anchor Books.

GOLDMAN, S. and TRUEBA, H.T. (Eds) (1987) *Becoming Literate in English as a Second Language*, Norwood, NJ, Ablex Corporation.

GOODENOUGH, W. (1976) 'Multiculturalism as the normal human experience', *Anthropology and Education Quarterly*, **7**, 4, pp. 4–7.

GUMPERZ, J. and HYMES, D. (Eds) (1964) 'The ethnography of communication', *American Anthropologists*, **66**, 6.

GUMPERZ, J. and HYMES, D. (1972) *Directions in Sociolinguistics: The Ethnography of Communication*, New York, NY, Holt, Rinehart & Winston.

HORNBERGER, N. (1988) 'Iman Chay?: Quechua Children in Peru's Schools', in TRUEBA, H. and DELGADO-GAITAN, C. (Eds) *School and Society: Teaching Content Through Culture*, New York, NY, Praeger, pp. 99–117.

HOROWITZ, D.L. (1985) *Ethnic Groups in Conflict*, Berkeley, CA, University of California Press.

HYMES, D. (1974) *Foundations in Sociolinguistics*, Philadelphia, PA, University of Pennsylvania Press.

JORDAN, C., THARP, R.G. and VOGT, L. (1985) *Compatibility of Classroom and Culture: General Principles, with Navajo and Hawaiian Instances*, (working paper), Honolulu, HA, Kamehameha Schools/Bishop Estate, Center for Development of Early Education.

LECOMPTE, M. and GOETZ, J. (1984) 'Ethnographic data collection in evaluation research', in FETTERMAN, D. (Ed) *Ethnography in Educational Evaluation*, Beverly Hills, CA, Sage Publications, pp. 37–59.

MACIAS, J. (1987) 'The hidden curriculum of Papago Teachers: American Indian strategies for mitigating cultural discontinuity in early schooling', in SPINDLER, G. and SPINDLER, L. (Eds) *Interpretive Ethnography of Education: At Home and Abroad*, Hillsdale, NJ, Lawrence Erlbaum Associates, Publishers, pp. 363–80.

MCDERMOTT, R. (1977) 'Social relations as contexts for learning in school', *Harvard Educational Review*, **47**, 2, pp. 198–213.

MCDERMOTT, R. (1987a) 'Achieving school failure: An anthropological approach to illiteracy and social stratification', in SPINDLER, G. (Ed) *Education and Cultural Process: Anthropological Approaches* (Second Edition), Prospects Heights, IL, Waveland Press, Inc, pp. 173–209.

MCDERMOTT, R. (1987b) 'The explanation of minority school failure, again', *Anthropology and Education Quarterly*, **18**, 4, pp. 361–64.

MOLL, L. (1990) *Vygotsky and Education: Instructional Implications and Applications of Sociohistorical Psychology*, Cambridge, Cambridge University Press.

MOLL, L. and DIAZ, E. (1987) 'Change as the goal of educational research', *Anthropology and Education Quarterly*, **18**, 4, pp. 300–11.

OGBU, J. (1982) 'Cultural discontinuities and schooling', *Anthropology and Education Quarterly*, **13**, 4, pp. 290–307.

OGBU, J. (1987) 'Variability in minority school performance: A problem in search of an explanation', *Anthropology and Education Quarterly*, **18**, 4, pp. 312–34.

PHILIPS, S. (1982) *The Invisible Culture: Communication in Classroom and Community on the Warm Springs Indian Reservation*, New York, NY, Longman.

ROOSENS, E. (1989a) 'Cultural ecology and achievement motivation: Ethnic minority youngsters in the Belgian system', in ELDERING, L. and KLOPROGGE, J. (Eds) *Different Cultures Same School: Ethnic Minority Children in Europe*, Amsterdam, The Netherlands, Swets & Zeitlinger, pp. 85–106.

ROOSENS, E. (1989b) *Creating Ethnicity: The Process of Ethnogenesis*, in BERNARD, H.B. (Series Editor) *Frontiers of Anthropology, Volume 5*, Newbury Park, CA, Sage Publications.

SPINDLER, G. (Ed) (1955) *Education and Anthropology*, Stanford, CA, Stanford University Press.

SPINDLER, G. (1959) *Transmission of American Culture*, The Third Burton Lecture, Cambridge, MA, Harvard University Press.

SPINDLER, G. (1963) *Education and Culture: Anthropological Approaches*, New York, NY, Holt, Rinehart & Winston.

SPINDLER, G. (1968) *Culture in Process: An Inductive Approach to Cultural Anthropology* (with A. BEALS and L. SPINDLER), Revised 1973, New York, NY, Holt, Rinehart and Winston.

SPINDLER, G. (Ed) (1970a) *Being an Anthropologist: Fieldwork in Eleven Cultures* (with L. SPINDLER) republished by Waveland Press in 1987.

SPINDLER, G. (1970b) 'The education of adolescents: An anthropological perspective', in EVANS, E. (Ed) *Adolescents: Readings in Behavior and Development*, Hindsdale, IL, Dryden Press.

SPINDLER, G. (1971) *Dreamers Without Power: The Menomini Indians* (with L. SPINDLER), New York, NY, Holt, Rinehart and Winston, republished by Waveland Press in 1984.

SPINDLER, G. (1974a) 'Schooling in Schoenhausen: A study of cultural transmission and instrumental adaptation in an urbanizing German village', in SPINDLER, G. (Ed) *Education and Cultural Process: Toward an Anthropology of Education*, New York, NY, Holt, Rinehart & Winston, Inc., pp. 230–71.

SPINDLER, G. (1974b) 'The transmission of American culture', in SPINDLER, G. (Ed) *Education and Culture: Anthropological Approaches*, New York, NY, Holt, Rinehart & Winston, pp. 279–310.

SPINDLER, G. (1974c) 'From omnibus to linkages: Models for the study of cultural transmission', *Council on Anthropology and Education*, **1**, pp. 2–6.

SPINDLER, G. (1977) 'Change and continuity in American core cultural values: An anthropological perspective', in DERENZO, G.D. (Ed) *We the People: American Character and Social Change*, Westport, CT, Greenwood, pp. 20–40.

SPINDLER, G. (Ed) (1978) *The Making of Psychological Anthropology*, Berkeley, CA, University of California Press.

SPINDLER, G. (1982) *Doing the Ethnography of Schooling: Educational Anthropology in Action*, New York, NY, Holt, Rinehart & Winston.

SPINDLER, G. and SPINDLER, L. (1982) 'Roger Harker and Schoenhausen: From the familiar to the strange and back again', in SPINDLER, G. (Ed) *Doing the Ethnography of Schooling*, New York, NY, Holt, Rinehart & Winston, pp. 20–47.

SPINDLER, G. and SPINDLER, L. (1983) 'Anthropologists' view of American culture', *Annual Review of Anthropology*, **12**, pp. 49–78.

SPINDLER, G. and SPINDLER, L. (1987a) 'Cultural dialogue and schooling in Schoenhausen and Roseville: A comparative analysis', *Anthropology and Education Quarterly*, **18**, 1, pp. 3–16.

SPINDLER, G. and SPINDLER, L. (Eds) (1987b) *The Interpretive Ethnography of Education: At Home and Abroad*, Hillsdale, NJ, Lawrence Erlbaum Associates.

SPINDLER, G. and SPINDLER, L. (1987c) 'Teaching and learning how to do the ethnography of education', in SPINDLER, G. and SPINDLER, L. (Eds) *Interpretive Ethnography of Education at Home and Abroad*, Hillsdale, NJ, Lawrence Erlbaum Associates, Inc., pp. 17–33.

SPINDLER, G. and SPINDLER, L. (1987d) 'In prospect for a controlled cross-cultural comparison of schooling Schoenhausen and Roseville', in *Education and Cultural Process: Anthropological Approaches*, (Second Edition), Prospect Heights, IL, Waveland Press, Inc., pp. 389–400.

SPINDLER, G. and SPINDLER, L. (1989) 'Instrumental competence, self-efficacy, linguistic minorities, and cultural therapy: A preliminary attempt at integration', *Anthropology and Education Quarterly* **10**, 1, pp. 36–50.

SPINDLER, G. and SPINDLER, L. (1990) *The American Cultural Dialogue and its Transmission*, (with chapters by TRUEBA, H.T. and WILLIAMS, M.D.), London, England, Falmer Press.

SUÁREZ-OROZCO, M.M. (1987) 'Towards a psychosocial understanding of Hispanic adaptation to American schooling', in TRUEBA, H. (Ed), *Success or Failure: Linguistic Minority Children at Home and in School*, New York, NY, Harper & Row, pp. 156–68.

SUÁREZ-OROZCO, M.M. (1989) *Central American Refugees and US High Schools: A Psychosocial Study of Motivation and Achievement*, Stanford, CA, Stanford University Press.

SUÁREZ-OROZCO, M.M. (1990) 'Speaking of the unspeakable: Toward a psychosocial understanding of responses to terror', *Ethos*, **18**, 3, pp. 353–83.

TRUEBA, H.T. (Ed) (1987a) *Success or Failure: Linguistic Minority Children at Home and in School*, New York, NY, Harper & Row.

TRUEBA, H.T. (1987b) 'Organizing classroom instruction in specific sociocultural contexts: Teaching Mexican youth to write in English', in GOLDMAN, S. and TRUEBA, H.T. *Becoming Literate in English as a Second Language*, Norwood, NJ, Ablex Corporation, pp. 235–52.

TRUEBA, H.T. (1988a) Comments on L.M. Dunn's *Bilingual Hispanic Children on the US Mainland: A Review of Research on their Cognitive, Linguistic and Scholastic Development*, in a special issue of the *Hispanic Journal of Behavioral Sciences*, **10**, 3, pp. 253–62.

TRUEBA, H.T. (1988b) 'Culturally-based explanations of minority students' academic achievement', *Anthropology and Education Quarterly*, **19**, 3, pp. 270–87.

TRUEBA, H.T. (1988c) 'English literacy acquisition: From cultural trauma to learning disabilities in minority students', *Journal of Linguistics and Education*, **1**, pp. 125–52.

TRUEBA, H.T. (1988d) 'Instructional effectiveness: English only for speaker of other languages?', *Excellence and Equity in Education: Models for Success*, **20**, 4, pp. 341–62.

TRUEBA, H.T. (1989a) *Raising Silent Voices: Educating Linguistic Minorities for the 21st Century*, New York, NY, Harper & Row.

TRUEBA, H.T. (1989b) 'Compassion and equity: Culture and English literacy for linguistic minority children', in BAPTISTE, JR., H.P. ANDERSON, J.E. WALKER DE FELIZ, J. and WAXMAN, H.C. (Eds) *Leadership, Equity and School Effectiveness*, Newbury Park, CA, Sage Publications, Inc., pp. 97–108.

TRUEBA, H.T. (1990a) 'The role of culture in literacy acquisition', *International Journal of Qualitative Studies in Education*, **3**, 1, pp. 1–13.

TRUEBA, H.T. (1990b) 'The role of culture in the acquisition of English literacy for minority school children', in IMHOFF, G. (Ed) *The Social and Cultural Context of Instruction in Two Languages: From Conflict and Controversy to Cooperative Reorganization of Schools*, New Brunswick, NJ, Transaction Publishing Co., pp. 123–37.

TRUEBA, H.T. (1991) Comments on Foley's 'Reconsidering anthropological explanation . . .', *Anthropology and Education Quarterly*, **22**, 1, pp. 87–94.

TRUEBA, H.T. and DELGADO-GAITAN, C. (Eds) (1988) *School and Society: Learning Content Through Culture*, New York, NY, Praeger Publishers.

TRUEBA, H., CHENG, L. and IMA, K. (1993) *Myth or Reality: Adaptive Strategies of Asian Americans in California*, London, England, Falmer Press.

TRUEBA, H.T., JACOBS, L. and KIRTON, E. (1990) *Cultural Conflict and Adaptation: The Case of the Hmong Children in American Society*, London, England, Falmer Press.

TRUEBA, H., SPINDLER, G. and SPINDLER, L. (Eds) (1989) *What do Anthropologists Have to say about Dropouts?*, London, England, Falmer Press.

WARD, D. (1989) *Poverty, Ethnicity, and the American City, 1840–1925: Changing Conceptions of the Slum and the Ghetto*, New York, NY, Cambridge University Press.

WARREN, R. (1982) 'Schooling, biculturalism, and ethnic identity: A case study', in SPINDLER, G. (Ed) *Doing the Ethnography of Schooling: Educational Anthropology for Action*, New York, NY, Holt, Rinehart & Winston, pp. 382–409.

YUAN TIEN, H. (1989) 'China: Population', in *The Encyclopedia Americana: International Edition*, **6**, Danbury, CT, Grolier Incorporated, pp. 501–3.

Chapter 3

A Researcher's Reflections on Bridging Dialect and Second Language Learning: Discussion of Problems and Solutions

Robert L. Politzer

Introduction

First a brief clarification of the title and the scope of this chapter. From the purely technical, linguistic point of view there isn't really a clear-cut difference between languages and dialects. According to some points of view a language is merely the total of all the dialects subsumed or classified as being part of the language. According to other definitions languages are the dialects that, so to speak, 'got the breaks' and which for political or other (for example, literary) reasons became recognized and standardized, while dialects — usually, at least — lack official recognition. Mutual intelligibility, by the way, is not a factor which can be used to clarify the general use of the terms dialect and language: e.g. Spanish (based on the Castilian dialect) and Portuguese (strongly related to the Spanish Gallego dialect) probably share higher mutual intelligibility than Spanish (Castilian) and the Spanish dialect of, let us say, the Alto Aragon. The exact nature of the similarities and differences between second language learning and second dialect learning will depend partly on the magnitude of the differences between the dialects involved, just as in second language learning it is at least partly a function of the difference between the first (L1) and second (L2) languages involved in the process. For the purpose of the presentation and discussion of this chapter I shall assume that First and Second Language differences are greater than differences between first and second dialects, and that First and Second languages (L1, L2) share little mutual intelligibility (as, for instance, English and Spanish) but that dialect differences are no greater than those between standard Spanish and so-called Chicano Spanish or standard English and Chicano English or black English vernacular. In introducing these terms I fully realize that Chicano English or Chicano Spanish or even black English are not well defined, clearly delineated speech varieties — but a detailed discussion of their characteristics and the problems of their exact definition and delineation might take us far afield (see Wolfram and Christian, 1988, Sánchez, 1988, González, 1988). At any rate this discussion will assume that intelligibility

between L1 and L2 is relatively small or absent, while mutual intelligibility between dialects or language and dialect is relatively large. The languages I have in
mind in this presentation are English and Spanish, and the non-standard dialects
are vernacular (Mexican-American) Spanish and African-American or black vernacular English. The discussion itself will focus on the problem of the similarities
and possible differences between second language (L2) learning and teaching and
the learning of Standard Languages (SL) by speakers of Non-Standard Dialects
(NSD).

The ideas expressed in this paper occurred to me when — after a few years
of being relatively out of touch with research in Second Language Acquisition
(SLA) and Second Dialect Acquisition (SDA) — I tried to catch up on recent
developments in the field by reading two anthology type publications (Leslie
M. Beebe, editor, *Issues in Second Language Acquisition*, 1988, and Dennis Bixler-
Márquez and Jacob Ornstein-Galicia, editors, *Chicano Speech in the Bilingual
Classroom,* 1988). The anthology on Chicano speech contains thirteen articles
divided in three sections ('Language, Society and Education', 'Description of the
Dialects', and 'Educational Issues and Practices'). The anthology on *Issues in
Second Language Acquisition* contains six presentations, namely 1. 'Psycholinguistic
Perspective' (Herbert Seliger), 2. 'Sociolinguistic Perspective' (Leslie M. Beebe), 3.
'Neurolinguistic Perspective' (Fred Genesee), 4. 'Classroom Research Perspective'
(Michael H. Long), 5. 'Bilingual Education Perspective' (Jim Cummins), 6.
'Implications of SLA Research' (a summary of highlights relevant for teachers, by
Thomas Scovel). In this chapter I will comment in turn on each section of the
SLA anthology (Beebe, 1988), though my discussion is not meant to be a review
of the anthology. As a matter of fact, I personally have little quarrel with most
of its findings. The scholars who wrote the six sections of the book are highly
competent individuals, and I am in personal agreement with most of what they
have to say. I will simply outline very briefly what each has to say, comment on
it, and present my own views on how SDA is or may be different from SLA as
discussed in the book.

1. Psycholinguistic Perspective: Psycholinguistic Issues in
Second Language Acquisition

Dr. Seliger's article starts with a brief historical sketch of psycholinguistic views
of language acquisition during the last twenty or twenty-five years. This period
started with the 'Chomskyan' revolution against behavioristic views and Skinner's
psychology, which emphasized learning through reinforcement of stimulus>response
patterning. Language was viewed by Chomsky as a complex system of rules
acquired thanks to an innate language acquisition device and linguistic universals.
The system of language (competence) was distinguished from instances of actual
use of the system (performance).

In developmental psycholinguistics the concern with describing competence
led to a great deal of research showing general (and perhaps universal) stages of
LA and eventually also SLA. SLA began to be pictured as going through successive stages of competences in which the learner advanced from L1 to L2. Each
stage ('interlanguage', 'approximative system') could be studied primarily by
showing the systematic *mistakes* made by the learner and distinguishing them from

the occasional non-systematic (not competence but performance connected) *errors.* Error analysis thus became one of the most popular research topics of the day. Errors were classified in various ways, dealing mainly with efforts to distinguish overgeneralizations on the part of the learner, the influence of L1, and inappropriate teaching as the probable causes.

The other main psycholinguistic theory mentioned by Seliger — perhaps less directly traceable to the Chomsky revolution — is the so-called Krashen theory, which has caused a great deal of discussion in recent years and given rise to some methodological approaches, especially the so-called Natural Way of teaching languages. S.D. Krashen's theory is really a series of hypotheses: 1. In order to reach the second language acquisition device input has to become intake and penetrate the affective filter. 2. Acquisition has to be distinguished from Learning; the former is a subconscious process, the only one which results in the ability to actually produce language for any kind of natural communicative purpose. 3. Learning — conscious awareness of rules — can only activate the monitor — which can correct language output but not produce it. 4. Acquisition takes place because meaningful input is provided. Meaningful input must of course be comprehensible and be at a level slightly beyond what the student already knows (input must be i+1).

The historical discussion introduced by Dr. Seliger gives me the opportunity for a slight historical digression. Some twenty years ago most of us would probably have assumed that the similarity between SLA and SDA was quite great — all types of learning seem to resemble each other in a strongly behavioristic paradigm. Second language teaching was still greatly influenced by three assumptions: (1) Most of the real problems offered by L2 could be isolated or perhaps even predicted by the contrastive analysis of L1 and L2. (2) A good way of teaching L2 was to present phonological, morphological and above all syntactic patterns in procedures ultimately derived from the so-called 'discovery procedure' of structural linguistics. (3) The core of at least initial language teaching consisted of so-called pattern drills. Following advice that came from various methodologists (for example, especially Christina Bratt Paulston, (see C.B. Paulston and M.N. Bruder, 1976) the drills proceeded from 'mechanical' to 'meaningful' to 'communicative'.

At any rate, when in 1969 my research associates and I prepared some teacher training materials for teachers of Standard English as a Second Dialect (D.E. Bartley and R.L. Politzer, 1972) we took for granted that drills should emphasize differences between Standard English and the dialects — specifically black English and 'Hispanized English'. In the process we realized that at that time very little was known about the realities of the dialects — especially Chicano English or Puerto Rican English, but we assumed that Chicano English was mainly due to interference coming from Spanish. Thus we advised to proceed with drills which would most likely follow the progression from 'automatic' to 'communicative'.

To conclude the digression with a brief example: The dropping of the third person singular *-s* is a well-known feature of NSD — especially black Vernacular. An automatic drill (which can, theoretically at least, be performed without knowing or paying attention to the meaning) dealing with this problem consists of responding to questions of the type, 'Does your father work in an office?' with 'Yes, he works in an office'. The next step — the 'meaningful drill' — could be introduced by a little story dealing with the habitual daily routines of Mr. Smith: 'He gets up at six o'clock, he brushes his teeth, he eats breakfast,' etc. This story is followed by questions: 'Does he get up at eight o'clock?' 'No, he gets up at six o'clock'. 'What does he do before breakfast?' 'He brushes his teeth,' etc.

The 'communicative drill' of 1970 did not really deal with the complex issues of 'communicative competence' referred to in the next section (3) of this chapter. 'Communicative' was any drill in which the student could provide unpredictable answers and thus communicate new information. The teacher may now ask questions like: 'Do you have a sister?' (Yes). 'When does she get up?' ('She gets up at seven o'clock' — Let's hope the student doesn't get too communicative and say 'I don't know', or 'What's the diff?'). 'Where does she go to school?' ('She goes to the same school I do' — Hopefully not 'Right here', or 'She doesn't go to school', or 'She don't go to no school').

Most of the discussion in this paper really deals with the underlying question of the extent to which this contrastive analysis based pattern drill methodology has become totally inapplicable and to what extent and under what circumstances it should be totally abandoned, especially in the process of learning and teaching standard language to speakers of NSD.

Let us turn to the question of what implications the psycholinguistics of SLA have for SDA. Differences of error and mistake and exact stages in the acquisition of second languages are difficult to demonstrate in SLA. In SDA the tasks may be even more formidable. As we shall point out presently multiple causes of variation such as switching of register, style, etc. are built into the use of dialects even more than in the acquisition of a second language. When does the use of a non-standard as opposed to standard form constitute an error, a mistake, or even an intentional or subconscious device to make a statement of political or ethnic identity? The research problems are challenging and indeed a bit overwhelming.

Diachronic ('time related') stages or levels in SLA may well exist. The documented levels or stages relevant to problems in SDA seem to be intricately interwoven with levels of formality of speech and speech style and different levels of sociolinguistic communication (see section 2) available to speakers within the same community that typically range from a highly educated prestigious speech variety ('Acrolect') to a low level, uneducated, low prestige variety ('Basilect'). Again research opportunities are still abundant. Teachers of SL to speakers of NSD should undoubtedly be aware of the existence of the complex and often intentionally employed options of style and social dialect at least potentially available to speakers of any language.

The 'Krashen' theory of language acquisition provides an important framework for the discussion and solution of many problems of SLA and SDA as well. Like Seliger and many other researchers I have some reservations concerning the usefulness of the hypotheses on which the theory rests. Let us say that I like them better as a teacher than as a researcher and that I think of them primarily as common-sense principles to be considered by the teacher and as a challenge for the researcher to be turned into provable, perhaps quantifiable propositions. To elucidate this point very briefly: In order for input to become intake and to be utilized, the input must pass through an 'affective filter'. In other words, if the students do not like the language or dialect to be learned, dislike the people speaking and/or teaching it, they probably won't 'acquire' (or even 'learn') very much — an extremely important point to keep in mind, but hardly a new or surprising truth or insight. In order for input to lead to acquisition it can't be so 'far out' that the student doesn't understand it, nor can it consist of material already known to the student; in either case the student won't acquire or learn — we are just wasting time. A very important fact to be kept in mind, in SD teaching perhaps even more than in SL teaching, but again not a very new truth. If a student is not concerned with grammatical rules at all and pays no attention to them whatsoever, he is probably an 'underuser of the monitor'. If he becomes so involved with grammar that concern with rules interferes with communication, he is an overuser. If he communicates easily and without any or very many mistakes, he is undoubtedly a good user of the monitor, and so on.

Many problems facing us in teaching SD to speakers of NSD are, as stated above, similar to problems of teaching of SL. The dangers of 'turning off' the student, of confusing enthusiasm for the tasks of teaching standard with a communicable dislike for the non-standard, overdrilling to the point of producing tongue-tied 'overusers of the monitor' are very real. Obviously we must keep them in mind.

A very real problem in applying the 'i+1' part of the Krashen theory to teaching of NSD is the difficulty of defining 'comprehensible input'. At least in the situations envisaged in this chapter, NSD and SD are largely mutually comprehensible. As a matter of fact I (and others) have often measured the degree of dominance of standard over non-standard in tests in which students were asked to repeat standard sentences. Many students — especially when not paying attention to the grammatical problem — process the input in such a way that the repetition of the standard takes place in non-standard! Comprehension is likely to break down in the area of vocabulary rather than grammar and/or phonology. Perhaps the conclusion to be drawn is that unlike in the teaching of L2, teaching of SD may require a great deal of attention to the teaching of vocabulary and — at least beyond the elementary school level — a certain amount of attention to rules and the utilization of the monitor.

2. Sociolinguistic Perspective: Five Sociolinguistic Approaches to Second Language Acquisition

For our topic the sociolinguistic perspective presents a kind of reverse shift in orientation. Most sociolinguistic research that has influenced second language acquisition theory comes from situations involving the various levels of standardness and the vernacular — we do not have to speculate as to how SLA theory may influence it. Most of the flow of theoretical thinking goes from Sociolinguistic to SLA theory, not in the reverse direction.

Dr. Beebe divides his presentation into five topics: (1) the so-called 'Labov' paradigm (named after the famous researcher in black English), (2) the dynamic paradigm, (3) the description of communicative competence, (4) the accommodation type of research, and finally (5) the motivation-attitude research, largely initiated and originally associated with the Canadian research of Gardner and Lambert.

To comment only briefly on some of the above (and skipping the dynamic principle paradigm about which relatively little is said in the book): Labov's research showed, among other things, just how various factors, especially attention paid to the language, the place in which language is used, the interlocutors, and the purpose of its use, result in at least quantifiably predictable variation. People asked to read minimal pairs (such as *main/men*) will produce sounds and sound differences they are unlikely to use in any other kind of speech. The degree of non-standardness, for example, the use of *he be* in vernacular black English, will vary according to who speaks to whom and where.

The description of certain speech acts and their appropriateness according to certain circumstances and occasions represents a long tradition of ethnographic research. During the past ten or fifteen years it has had tremendous impact in creating the awareness of communicative in addition to linguistic competence. In other words, we keep in mind that our students must not only speak in grammatically correct sentences, they must also learn when to speak and when to keep silent, how to perform speech acts (such as apologizing or expressing regrets or congratulations, etc.) in the culturally appropriate form.

Accommodation theory deals with ways in which individuals change their speech in order to adapt it (convergent accommodation) or differentiate it (divergent accommodation) from the speech of other individuals. In second language acquisition certain factors may either favor acquisition (convergent accommodation) or refusal to learn. Among these factors are the intensity of intra-group identity felt by individuals, perceived vitality of the group, perceived openness of group boundaries, and the degree to which individuals feel themselves to be a member of various groups rather than just a single one.

Motivation and attitude research can be regarded as a way of making quantifiable and concrete the affective filters of the Krashen theory. Various approaches such as the matched guise technique are utilized in attitude research. In the latter the subjects listen to various voices using either L1 and L2 or D1 and D2. Without the subjects' knowledge, the voices belong to bilingual or bidialectal speakers who are asked to use first the one and then the other guise of their voices. The differential ways in which subjects react to the voices (making estimates about their intelligence, educational level, size, other personal characteristics) reveal the subjects' attitudes and their stereotypes related to languages and or dialects. Motivational research usually takes the form of subjects ranking various reasons for learning languages, reasons which have traditionally been grouped into instrumental (learning for material advantage) and integrative (liking and/or wanting to become or be like people speaking the L2 or D2 to be learned).

Since sociolinguistic research and socially conditioned (SC) research have always been heavily involved in NSD learning and teaching, we can be brief in our comments. Knowledge of socially conditioned language variation will obviously make the task of a teacher of SD to speakers of NSD easier. Knowledge of pupils' motivation and attitudes will also make the task easier — at least it will explain the problems and difficulties involved in it, and perhaps will keep the teacher from inadvertently getting the students to lower their affective filters.

For many students learning Standard English and/or Standard Spanish in school, the NSD is the speech of the ethnic community, of the home, of the parents, of part of the historical heritage. In the usual circumstances of teaching L2 to speakers of L1, the extinction of L1, its replacement by L2, is, or at least should, never be an issue. In the teaching of D1 (SD) to speakers of D2 (NSD) this point is often not quite so clear-cut. Often we are in danger of getting on slippery ground. If we approach the teaching of standard language in such a way that we 'attack' the non-standard, imply its inferiority, and suggest that it be abandoned, we may very well cause the students to 'filter out' input from the outside. If we teach the standard form of a language by stereotyping non-standard forms, we will screen out natural influences from the social environment that keep changing language in order to function and serve us effectively in new situations. Language is a dynamic symbolic system that changes with culture change and new experiences. Further, let me here make a very simple point: I believe that it is the business of schools to teach languages and speech variations and not extinguish or make people forget anything — and this involves first dialects and non-standard dialects as well as languages.

3. Neurolinguistic Perspective: Neuropsychology and Second Language Acquisition

Fred Genesee's article deals with three aspects of language related neurophysiology: (1) localization of certain functions in the brain; (2) the way languages with very · different characteristics, such as Chinese with an ideographic writing system or English with an alphabet-based orthography, may be represented in the brain; (3) the possible existence of a critical period for second language acquisition. Dr. Genesee stresses that some aspects of linguistic neurophysiology (like location of most language functions for most people in the left hemisphere or the existence of a critical period for the acquisition of L1) are fairly well established by research. Others are debated, highly speculative, and not to be taken literally in a physiological sense (like *plasticity* of the brain in early childhood, right brain learning which may be less formal and more like *acquisition*, and left brain learning which may be more like *learning*: — in the sense used by Krashen, see section 2 above).

To comment extensively on applications of neurophysiologically oriented research to problems of NSD acquisition and teaching would mean adding more speculation to speculation. A few comments will suffice. The debate of whether there is a critical period (perhaps before onset of puberty) after which certain second language acquisition abilities are lost or at least diminished, has been going on, relatively inconclusively, for some time. As Dr. Genesee points out, the problem with research conducted in the area is that in any experimental design the age of the learner is very difficult to isolate as a unique independent variable. In other words, differences in outcome of SLA or SDA can not be attributed to differences in age alone. The tests to be used to measure outcome — time of exposure, general nature of input, method of instruction, interest, motivation, etc. — can not be meaningfully equated on adult and child levels. Various experiments comparing adult and childhood second language learning have been inconclusive. In general they tend to show that acquisition may be easier for the child, that formal learning (relying on the monitor) may be better suited and even accelerate acquisition of proficiency in older learners. This conclusion can be reached just on the basis of insights from purely psychological ideas about motivation and cognitive development. It is a conclusion which seems fully applicable to SD learning and teaching also.

Another well known fact, related to the critical period but not necessarily to neurophysiological changes or lateralization of brain functions, is that with the advent of puberty it becomes increasingly unlikely (but not impossible) that an individual will acquire a perfect native-like pronunciation in L2. The same, or at least a similar phenomenon exists also in the acquisition of the pronunciation of another dialect. For instance, linguistic geographers have known for some time that an individual who has moved from one dialect area to another after puberty is likely to acquire the pronunciation habits of the post-puberty residence. In Great Britain it has been known for a long time that pupils learn the upper-class Standard English pronunciation (Received Pronunciations or RP) by going to the 'right' private schools before the onset of puberty. At any rate, I am not sure that pronunciation habits of an individual — especially if they do not really interfere with intelligibility — should or ought to be that great a concern by themselves in SD teaching.

4. Classroom Research Perspective: Instructed Interlanguage Development

Michael Long's discussion of the classroom research perspective in SLA centers on the question of whether there is any evidence at all that language instruction of any kind — in other words, intervention dealing with language *per se* — serves any purpose. This is a question which would probably not be asked twenty years ago when the research problems dealt with *how* to teach languages, not *whether* to teach. The question of whether it is at all necessary to teach language (in the sense that the organization of material and the instruction process pays attention to linguistic categories) has of course been asked for a long time. Languages are often acquired more successfully in the real world, outside rather than inside classrooms and through informal contact rather than through instruction. The evident success of bilingual immersion types of programs in which language is acquired by subject matter being taught in the language rather than through formal language teaching makes it even more reasonable to ask the question: Why instruction at all? If we believe with Krashen that the main prerequisite for language acquisition to take place is the provision of comprehensible input at the i+1 level, the role of organized instruction is of course rather limited.

Dr. Long reviews various studies dealing with a comparison of the effects of organized instruction and the lack of it — and finds that it is very difficult to come to any conclusion, primarily for the obvious reason that instruction may be carried out by various methods, may be of varying quality and intensity, and that as a result any conclusion about instruction as a whole is impossible. He suggests that some research shows that sequence of acquisition may be pretty much the same under planned instruction and in natural acquisition. He himself seems to believe that instruction does have a positive effect, though he admonishes the reader to keep in mind that instruction does not necessarily mean sequential planning of discrete grammar points. The minimum attention paid to language which distinguishes instruction from untutored naturalistic acquisition, according to Long, consists of (1) manipulation of input and (2) determination of required production tasks. In other words, potentially successful instruction as envisaged by Long could be organized not according to any grammatical categories, but by functional categories, vocabulary input, speech acts to be performed by the student, etc.

The question of applicability of Long's presentation and tentative conclusions concerning the efficiency or necessity of formal instruction to the SD teaching situation deals again with the problem of whether or to what extent grammar and 'monitor focused' learning may be necessary for acquisition of a relatively easily comprehensible variety. As I have already intimated, I feel that, at least with older learners, some focus on grammar may be difficult to avoid. The acquisition of a second dialect (or standard dialect) does not seem to occur like second language acquisition in demonstrable successive stages following specific rules characterized and marked by commission and finally abandonment of systematic errors. For the speaker of a non-standard dialect the rules of D1 may become or be responsible for errors in D2 (the standard language). Those features of the non-standard that intrude in the standard resemble rather the so-called 'fossilized' mistakes or errors of SLA, errors which, perhaps because they do not interfere with communication — do not 'cry out' to be removed — have become part of the speaker's permanent repertory. We all know that these are the errors which are most difficult to combat and which are not likely to disappear without specific instructional effort and without being called to the learner's attention.

The other second dialect or standard language teaching problem which may necessitate overt instructional intervention rather than or at least in addition to untutored naturalistic exposure occurs quite frequently in the context of Bilingual Education, especially in the USA. There the classroom exposure in the school language (e.g. Spanish and English) occurs in the standard language. We hope, of course, that both standard languages will be acquired primarily through subject matter and literary skills being taught in those languages, but in both languages a far more massive and decisive exposure to non-standard dialects may occur at home, by and with the peer group. Under those circumstances we may not be able to put our trust only in natural methods and natural acquisition. If we do, we may produce students who are fluent speakers of only two non-standard dialects (e.g. Chicano Spanish, Chicano English). Tutored, planned instruction which pays some attention to standard grammar may be the only way out — provided we observe some of the cautions already mentioned earlier in this presentation.

5. Bilingual Education Perspective: Second Language Acquisition within Bilingual Education Programs

Cummins reviews the main research studies contributing to and occasioned by the educational policy debate in the United States. Why is it that bilingual education in Canada, which started as a replacement of middle-class second language teaching, was, or at least seemed to be, greatly successful? Why was bilingual education in the USA, thought of primarily as a way of helping the poor and disadvantaged, not an immediate resounding success? Why did immersion in the second language work in Canada? Why doesn't it do the job in the USA where it becomes *sub*mersion rather than *im*mersion? These questions and the research studies relating to them are very neatly reviewed by Cummins, and to review his review goes beyond our scope and space limits. The interesting aspect of Cummins' presentation is that he does not go beyond language and does not belabor the obvious political and social class differences between the USA and the Canadian programs and all the factors that can be connected with them. He finds that successful programs in Canada and the USA share certain language related aspects, specifically:

1 L1 of the pupil is considered a very important part of the curriculum. This is also true in Canada where in the French immersion programs most or

all subject matter is taught in French, but literacy skills in English are taught in early grades;

2 Input is modified so as to make it comprehensible and enable the student to learn L2;

3 This modification of the input and the solution of other cultural/linguistic problems is made possible by bilingual/bicultural teachers. In other words, the importance of the bilingual/bicultural teachers in the process of L2 acquisition in the bilingual program is not that they teach bilingually by going from one language to the other, but that they adapt and modify the L2 input so that the pupils can understand it.

Thus Dr. Cummins' main message for language acquisition is simply this: optimal input is the best, if not the only, prerequisite for successful acquisition of L2. Optimal input is interesting, relevant, comprehensible, probably not grammatically sequenced, emphasizes function rather than form. Bilingual Education is better than Second Language Instruction only insofar as it provides that kind of input. In bilingual education we must always keep in mind that the main goal of any educational endeavor, especially in the early grades, is not only creation of a specific communication skill but an underlying Cognitive Academic Learning Proficiency (dubbed CALP by Dr. Cummins in some of his earlier publications) which can be transferred across languages.

All, or at least most, of Dr. Cummins' findings concerning L2 learning and teaching in the bilingual education context seem quite valid. The real issue at this point is the extent to which they are applicable to the problem of standard language teaching. Granted that L2 acquisition takes place primarily or even exclusively through providing unstructured, interesting input, will the same happen if we simply use standard L1 rather than NSD in all our presentations? What about the L2 input which occurs in the form of a NSD? In a way, Cummins' findings pose a kind of dilemma. On the one hand we must utilize the students' L1 to create literacy skills to bring about the all-important Cognitive Academic Learning Proficiency, on the other hand we also have an obligation to teach the student the use of standard language. A good solution has been suggested in a recent article by R. Milk (1988): (1) When the two goals — teaching standard and creating cognitive proficiency — seem in conflict, remember that the latter is really the more important goal, especially in the elementary grades. Do not produce tongue-tied, language and form rather than content-conscious students, for the sake of drilling some grammatical standard forms and/or pronunciation. (2) Develop acquaintance with and use of the standard by utilizing and discussing written materials rather than through oral drill *per se*. Connect teaching standard with the creation of literacy. And here I may add, do not make the mistake illustrated by Cummins' example of the inappropriate reading lesson: utilize literacy and reading for modeling and for illustrating the use of standard, but do not let the goals of teaching standard drown out the more important one of teaching cognitive skills. The mistake made by the teacher of English reading in Cummins' example of the bad input lesson was not that he corrected the students' pronunciation and asked them to imitate the correct one, but that he spent an hour doing something boring and incidental to the main goal of instruction.

Our insistence that the students' L1 should be considered in the creation of literacy skills which can then be transferred to L2 leads us to the brief discussion of yet another problem and possible analogy between L1/L2 and DS1/D2 teaching situations. If the L1 is really a non-standard dialect, are we really following the principle of teaching initial literacy in the first language if we approach it through D2 (the standard dialect)? This problem has been discussed quite a bit with specific reference to initial teaching of reading to children dominant in black Vernacular English or Chicano English (see Bixler-Márquez, 1988). There are, first of all, some purely technical problems with producing reading materials in a vernacular dialect. The very nature of the vernacular implies that it is neither codified nor standardized, that some people may feel uneasy about seeing it in print at all, that there may be disagreement as to what forms are really part of the vernacular, what constitutes extremely local variation, etc. My own feeling is that in the case of black English vernacular and Chicano Spanish the distance between vernacular and standard is probably not large enough to justify the large scale creation of vernacular reading materials. True enough, at times the pupil who speaks vernacular who is faced with a standard text will be at a disadvantage compared to a pupil whose speech is totally or virtually identical with the standard, but I think that a teacher who understands the pupil's problem and the problem created by the difference between standard and vernacular can compensate for the disadvantage. If pupils in their reading lesson produce forms like *muncho* or *ámonos* or experience some difficulty because they can't find them on the page, the teacher's intervention can be brief and be utilized to introduce some of the features of the standard. Obviously it would be a good idea to avoid combining the teaching of initial reading skills and introduction of a great deal of unfamiliar vocabulary of the standard language. I think that the real reason or excuse for the advocacy of the creation of special initial reading materials in the vernacular is the desire to take the consideration of vernacular interference in initial reading instruction out of the hands of teachers. It is probably very true that a lesson dealing with reading skills using standard text for speakers of vernacular could easily change — deteriorate, if you wish — into a lesson dealing with correct pronunciation and grammar, and thus become an example of the type of inappropriate input lesson described by Cummins. I think that teachers who either know or are at least aware of some of the features of the students' L1 (or rather D1) and who do not lose track of the goals of reading instruction in the process of teaching reading, can handle the situation without having to fall back on vernacular reading texts. To conclude this point: at least in the situation of teaching reading in English or Spanish to vernacular black English or Chicano Spanish dominant students, I believe that initial reading texts can be in D2 — the standard language to be learned — provided teachers are sensitive to D1/D2 differences and massive introduction of new standard vocabulary is avoided.

6. Summary

In the summary of this discussion I shall of course highlight the points which relate to Second dialect teaching rather than the SLA related points chosen by Dr. Scovel in his excellent summary of the five articles.

Second dialect acquisition (SDA) and teaching share many features of second language acquisition (SLA). Among them I would like to stress the following:

1 Motivation and attitude on the part of the pupil are undoubtedly among the most important factors influencing any outcome.
2 The creation of linguistic competence must be accompanied by communicative competence. Grammaticality is not the only goal of teaching.

Some of the important areas of concern in which SLA and SDA differ, at least in degree of emphasis:

1 It may be difficult to determine natural stages of acquisition in SDA. Some of the speech forms of NSD resemble fossilized forms of arrested SLA and may be difficult to deal with, especially without specific drill and high motivation on the part of the student.
2 The use of NSD on the part of a speaker is related to the choice of specific register and style and should not be interpreted as necessarily constituting lack of knowledge or ability on the part of the speaker.
3 Comprehensible input as prerequisite for acquisition of SD by speakers of NSD is probably difficult to define, and unlike in the case of SLA, is in some situations not even a meaningful and useful concept.
4 Especially with students above the elementary school level, SDA in a school context is likely to require some grammar-oriented teaching, in other words 'learning' and activation of the 'monitor'.
5 Even more than the teacher of SL, the teacher of SD has to walk a narrow path between a concern with grammar and correctness and the stimulation of communicative competence and the avoidance of tongue-tied 'overusers of the monitor' who pay attention to form rather than to function. In the long run, in any use of language, *what* is still more important than *how*.
6 Students who learn a standard language as a second dialect should not be given the same training as students who learn it as a second language. Meaningful input for acquisition or useful rules for the monitor for L2 learners may be boring, useless or even insulting for speakers of D1 learning D2.

A final reminder of an already mentioned similarity between Second Language and Second (Standard) Dialect teaching: in neither case can or should it be the goal of instruction to replace the home language variety which represents the student's ethnic heritage. The goal of instruction is to teach, not to extinguish. The second language and the standard variety of the first must and can become an addition to the students' repertory.

References

BEEBE, L.M. (Ed) (1988) *Issues in Second Language Acquisition, Multiple Perspectives*, New York, NY, Newbury House Publishers.
BIXLER-MÁRQUEZ, D.J. and ORNSTEIN-GALICIA J. (Eds) (1988) *Chicano Speech in the Bilingual Classroom*, American University Studies, Series VI, New York, NY, Peter Lang Publishing, Inc.

Other References:

BARTLEY, D.E. and POLITZER, L. (1972) *Practice-Centered Teacher Training: Standard English for Speakers of Non-standard Dialects*, Philadelphia, PA, The Center for Curriculum Development, Inc.

BIXLER-MÁRQUEZ, D.J. (1988) 'Dialects and Initial Reading Options in Bilingual Education' in BIXLER-MÁRQUEZ, D.J. and ORNSTEIN-GALICIA, J. *Chicano Speech in the Bilingual Classroom*, American University Studies, Series VI, New York, NY, Peter Lang Publishing, Inc.

GONZÁLEZ, G. (1988) 'Chicano English' in BIXLER-MÁRQUEZ, D.J. and ORNSTEIN-GALICIA, J. *Chicano Speech in the Bilingual Classroom*, American University Studies, Series VI, New York, NY, Peter Lang Publishing, Inc.

MILK, R. (1988) 'The Role of Chicano Spanish in the Early Grades: Clarification of Issues' in BIXLER-MÁRQUEZ, D.J. and ORNSTEIN-GALICIA, J. *Chicano Speech in the Bilingual Classroom*, American University Studies, Series VI, New York, NY, Peter Lang Publishing, Inc.

PAULSTON, C.B. and BRUDER, M.N. (1976) *Teaching English as a Second Language: Techniques and Procedures*, Cambridge, MA, Winthrop Publishers, Inc.

SÁNCHEZ, R. (1988) 'Chicano Spanish: Style varieties and functions' in BIXLER-MÁRQUEZ, D. and ORNSTEIN-GALICIA, J. (Eds) *Chicano Speech in the Bilingual Classroom*, American University Studies, Series VI, New York, NY, Peter Lang, pp. 55–68.

WOLFRAM, W. and CHRISTIAN, D. (1988) 'Dialect, Society and Education' in BIXLER-MÁRQUEZ, D.J. and ORNSTEIN-GALICIA, J. *Chicano Speech in the Bilingual Classroom*, American University Studies, Series VI, New York, NY, Peter Lang Publishing, Inc.

Chapter 4

Native Language Loss and Its Implications for Revitalization of Spanish in Chicano Communities

Eduardo Hernández-Chávez

The loss of first language skills by native speakers of Spanish is a problem that, until recently, has received scant attention either in the linguistics literature or among educators of language minority students. Large numbers of Chicano children and young people from Spanish-speaking families either no longer learn the language or acquire but a limited facility in it. As a result, patterns of communication are disrupted, cultural and social structures break down, and youth become alienated from their communities. The institutional processes that lead to native language loss are well established, and the shift to English is very far along in many Chicano communities. Responsible for these conditions are the truly rapid changes in American society in recent decades involving urbanization, technological growth, and the spread of mass culture. Additionally, many educational and governmental policies are driven directly by social and political philosophies whose ultimate aims are the linguistic and cultural assimilation of ethnic minorities.

In this chapter, I will first provide an overview of language loss processes and will then discuss the linguistic manifestations of loss among Chicanos, the relationship of loss to language acquisition and use, the sociocultural mechanisms that give it shape, and its effects on individuals and society. In the final section I will discuss some of the implications of these concepts for educators, especially bilingual educators and teachers of Spanish for native speakers.

The Loss of Language

Much existing research on language loss has been concerned with the attrition of language skills by learners of a foreign or second language after varying periods away from formal study. Considerable work has also been done among aphasics, persons who have undergone partial or complete loss of linguistic functioning due to some physical trauma. (Studies on second language loss in Spanish include Pratella, 1970, and Cohen, 1974. For a sampling of relevant research on bilingual aphasia, see Paradis, 1977; Albert and Obler, 1978; and Galloway, 1978.) Among normal populations, loss of first or native language has, until fairly recently, been studied largely in sociolinguistic contexts in which the language varieties themselves are dying. This research on 'language death' includes studies on Irish (Breatnach, 1964), Biloxi (Haas, 1968), Scots Gaelic (Dorian, 1978, 1981), Tlaxcalan Náhuatl (Hill and Hill, 1977), and Aravanitka Albanian (Trudgill, 1976–77), among others. Recently, a number of researchers have investigated native language loss in different ethnic group contexts in the United States, such as Saltrelli, 1975a; and Henzl, 1977. A few studies have begun to focus on the progressive decrease in Spanish proficiency by Chicano speakers (Saltarelli, 1975b; Ostyn, 1972; Merino, 1983; Silva-Corvalán, 1983a, 1983b, 1986, 1988; Gutiérrez, 1990; Ocampo, 1990; and Hernández-Chávez, 1990a, 1990b, 1990c). For a compendium of studies on language loss see Williamson (1982).

The loss processes described by these investigators have been observed in mostly cross-generational studies. In general, they find that the first, or immigrant generation, is monolingual or highly dominant in Spanish and evinces a proficiency fully comparable to that of native speakers in any other Spanish-speaking region. As subsequent generations become increasingly proficient in English, they tend also to become progressively less proficient in Spanish, a situation described by Silva-Corvalán (1988) as the 'bilingual continuum.'

It should be noted that it is not generation of residence in the US *per se* that is the key variable in explaining language loss. Silva-Corvalán, for example, has conducted a number of studies investigating the effects of bilingualism among three different generations of Mexican Americans in Los Angeles. In a recent report on this project (Silva-Corvalán, 1988), she notes that some of her Generation III speakers, who have been in the US the longest, retained more Spanish than some Generation II speakers. Also, there exist numerous communities, especially in New Mexico but also throughout the Southwest, where Chicanos have lived for many generations, not just three or four. Until fairly recent times, most of these communities have maintained a stable bilingualism, and loss has been minimal. We need to look for other factors — rapid social change comes to mind — that, together with patterns of inter-generational transmission of language, account for language loss.

In the decline of native language proficiency from one generation to the next, the more complex linguistic structures, which are learned late in normal acquisition, *fail to be learned* and are thus lost. It is also entirely possible that, at lower levels of proficiency, previously acquired structures might *actually be forgotten* by particular individuals. However, in cross-generational studies, the forgetting of structures, once they are learned, would be extremely difficult to ascertain.

The direct investigation of language forgetting requires the study of loss in the same individuals over time. One of the studies reviewed for this paper, Merino (1983), was conducted in this way with a group of kindergarten to fourth grade children in a bilingual education program. In a longitudinal portion of the study, Merino retested the children after a two-year lapse. She found that not only did most of the children fail to progress, but some 50 per cent actually *forgot* some of the structures they had learned previously.

As with the cross-generational studies, the lost structures are those, such as the subjunctive and relative clauses, that are normally acquired late. This gives some support to the notion that forgetting involves processes that are a 'mirror image' of those of acquisition (Bailey, 1973; cited in Merino, 1983; Silva-Corvalán, 1990). However, in Merino's data, not all of the structures lost, such as the past tense, are late-acquired forms, so at least some other processes are operating as well. Preliminary results from one of my own studies among Spanish speakers in New Mexico (Hernández-Chávez, 1990a) are suggestive in this regard. Such strategies may be involved as the elimination of redundancy (for example, the indirect object marker *a* in *Mi abuela le daba un ataque de corazón*) or the restructuring of certain semantic contrasts like the use of *estar* instead of *ser* with predicate nouns to indicate change of status (for example, *Cuando ya yo nací, yo creo que [él] ya estaba panadero*). Additionally, this study shows that the borrowing of structures from English may also violate the mirror image hypothesis. Thus, *Yo fui nacida en Las Vegas, Nuevo México* seems clearly to be a calque on the English passive of 'I was born in Las Vegas, New Mexico.' And *Muy limpiecita viejita* uses the English word order of 'A very clean little old lady.' In all these cases, the changed structures demonstrate a pattern of loss, yet they involve less advanced structures than some which are retained. Thus, the linguistic processes of loss, though clearly related to acquisition processes, are seen to be fairly complex.

Language loss exhibits important differences between speaking and comprehension proficiencies, also observed by Merino (1983). Speaking performance in Spanish dropped sharply, especially by grade four, but comprehension showed no change across the grades. She suggests that comprehension may be more resistant to loss. This is consistent with language acquisition research which has shown that comprehension normally precedes and is superior to speaking performance (see Fraser, Bellugi, and Brown, 1963). Merino's findings also receive confirmation from the experience and common knowledge within Chicano communities that, even where speaking skills are almost entirely lost, comprehension may be quite active.

Although the studies reviewed focus mainly on the grammatical system, loss may occur differentially in any of the various linguistic skills. Beside the differences just noted in comprehension and production, loss may occur in discourse skills, the lexicon, and presumably phonology as well. Silva-Corvalán (1988), observes that preferential use of particular grammatical structures correlates with certain parts of narratives. Thus, only the most proficient speakers used direct quotations or the historical present as evaluative devices (that is, certain constructions or types of expressions that create or maintain a high level of interest as, for example '*Ven a la casa*', *me dice*. 'Come over to the house', she tells me.) Speakers in the second and third generations will also tend to produce narratives that are much less fluent in their delivery than first generation speakers.

Silva-Corvalán (1983a and b) also observes, along with Koike (1987), that where fully developed evaluative devices are not available in narratives because of loss, speakers will often code-switch to English when using Spanish. On the other hand, in a recently completed study of the role of New Mexican Spanish (Hernández-Chávez, 1990c), I found that, while gaps in vocabulary do trigger some switches among English-dominant speakers, a more common occasion for lexical and phrasal switching was cultural content. Words and phrases referring to activities or events most generally experienced in English and in the dominant culture (for example, school, work, commerical transactions) would tend to trigger switches to English — even though the relevant vocabulary is familiar to the speaker. The more a speaker had contact with Anglo-American activities, the greater the reliance on code-switching in speaking of those contexts. Nevertheless, lexical skills are most certainly an important aspect of language loss, either through failure to acquire certain vocabulary or through forgetting.

We have little evidence of loss in phonological systems, though much of what has been called interference may, in fact, be loss in relation to monolingual community norms. Indeed, experience by members of the Chicano community indicates that certain distinctions such as *r:rr* tend to accompany other forms of loss and are interpreted by community members as indicating diminished proficiency.[1]

As suggested above, any of these forms of loss implies a fully developed norm. This norm cannot be some idealized standard described in handbooks nor even a widely accepted spoken standard. Were this the case, monolingual speakers of regional or social class varieties of the language might be deemed to have undergone language loss if, in their variety, certain distinctions were no longer made. Thus, it cannot be considered loss if a Spanish speaker fails to use the future subjunctive (e.g., *viniere* 'will perhaps come') or the preterite perfect, (e.g., *hubo llegado* 'had once arrived') found only in certain frozen expressions and as archaic literary forms. Similarly, speakers of non-standard varieties are not necessarily losing Spanish if they use periphrastic constructions in the place of the tense functions of the inflected future or conditional, (*voy a volver* 'I am going to return' instead of *volveré* 'I will return') or if they use the imperfect for the past subjunctive in certain constructions (e.g., *Le ofreciera trabajo si podía* [*<si pudiera.*].

Such differences from other forms of Spanish may represent autonomous changes or changes due to cultural or social factors rather than to loss (Sánchez, 1983). At the same time, for Chicanos, it is striking that such forms are found mainly in native-born speakers who demonstrate other characteristics of loss, so it is not a straightforward matter to distinguish loss from dialectal variation or from change across generations. The principal criterion must be the language proficiency of monolingual or Spanish dominant speakers within the community in question. The assumption is that such speakers are fully proficient in the language and that differences from other varieties are dialectal in nature. Changes among English-dominant speakers not shared by the Spanish-dominant speakers in the same community would then be considered strong indications of language loss.

Linguistic Processes in Loss

The research on language loss uniformly demonstrates that loss of native language skills, far from being random or idiosyncratic, is a highly regular process. Indeed, it can be seen as obeying certain general principles found in other dynamic systems of language such as language acquisition, sociolinguistic variation, and historical change. Thus, for example, Henzl (1977, cited in Merino, 1983), in her study of four generations of Czech-Americans undergoing loss will *regularize* certain case endings where alternate forms are normally used with different classes of nouns. In language acquistion, children use similar processes of regularization, not only with case systems but also with irregular tense or number markings. For example, at certain stages in the acquisition of English, children will use forms like *goed* for *went* and *mans* for *men*. At other stages they will simplify redundant marking, as where gender is marked on both articles and nouns. Henzl notes a similar elimination of redundancies in the Czech case system as does Hernández-Chávez (1990a) for Spanish indirect objects.

Another common acquisition process is what is often referred to as *overmarking*, as when child learners of English say 'Nobody don't like me', or 'I didn't broke it', doubly marking the negative and the past tense. Merino (1983) provides a clear example of this process in loss. In her longitudinal study, subjects who earlier used the conditional conjunction *a menos* 'unless' as well as *si* 'if', later used the overmarked form *a menos si* to express the notion 'unless.'

Both Merino and Henzl observe the *'overextension'* or generalization to forms of one class from those of other, minor, classes as in the use of the *-ar* conjugation endings in Spanish for verbs from the *-er* and *-ir* conjugations. This is most certainly related to general word formation processes in Spanish by which new words and borrowings are overwhelmingly assigned to the *-ar* conjugation.

Other language change patterns are seen to be recapitulated in language loss through the *simplification* and *neutralization* of grammatical structures reported by several investigators. Henzl (1977) shows that, in the later stages of loss, the case system in Czech is replaced by word order. Similarly, loss of a variety of verbal inflections is noted for Chicano Spanish by Merino (1983) and Silva-Corvalán (1988). Among these are the future, conditional, past and present subjunctives, and the perfect tenses which tend to be substituted by less complex forms. Thus, the inflected future is replaced by the *ir a* construction; the conditional and the past subjunctive by the imperfect; the present subjunctive by the indicative; and the perfect tenses by the simple past. In certain narrative contexts, the imperfect and preterite verb forms become neutralized. That is, there is a tendency for only the imperfect to be used with stative verbs such as *ser*, *tener*, and *haber* and for the preterite to be used with event verbs. Similarly, the distinction between *ser* and *estar* becomes blurred in certain pragmatic contexts (Silva-Corvalán, 1988, 1990; Hernández-Chávez, 1990a).

An important characteristic of loss processes observed by most of these investigators is that until loss is quite well advanced, the substitutions, simplifications, neutralizations, etc. are variable rather than categorial. Loss first appears as a decrease in frequency of use, in appropriate contexts, of the more complex forms. For example, Pousada and Poplack (1979), in a study of Spanish- and English-dominant Puerto Ricans in New York, found a decrease among English-dominant speakers in the use of the future, conditional, and plusperfect tenses. They also showed a reduction in occurrence of the subjunctive as did Ocampo (1990). As noted above, Silva-Corvalán (1988) reports a diminished preference for certain constructions like the historical present and rhetorical questions within evaluative structures of narratives where those constructions are normally prevalent. Gutiérrez (1990) shows similar patterns in the decreasing use of various subordination structures.

Language Acquisition, Language Use, and Language Loss

Child language acquisition studies demonstrate that the basic structures of the native language are normally learned by the age of five or six. Yet, we also know that language learning continues well into adulthood. Several studies have shown, for example, that the mastery of complex syntax and semantics continues throughout the elementary school years. (General introductions to child language acquisition are found in Clark and Clark, 1977, and in Moskowitz, 1978; for more comprehensive, cross-cultural studies, see Ferguson, 1973. For work on older children, refer to Chomsky, 1968, and Kessel, 1970). Research on sociolinguistic variation among pre-teens and teens reveals that there is considerable development of phonological, lexical, and grammatical variables related to style and social groupings (Fischer, 1958; Labov, 1964; Wolfram, 1969). Moreover, in literate, technological societies, many individuals strive throughout their careers to elaborate their vocabulary and grammatical structure and to fine tune their writing and speaking styles.

All of this amounts to normal language development, and the normal range of proficiencies attained is delimited by such factors as social and cultural interactions, formal schooling and individual aptitude. For all but perhaps the most standardized and specialized forms of speech and writing, which depend on explicit tuition, full natural language learning depends principally on what Krashen (1981), writing about second language acquisition, has called 'comprehensible input'. In a first language context, we interpret this to mean interactions through language in ways that are cognitively, socially, and culturally significant for the learner. They must include sufficient and continual linguistic communication with family members, peers, and other members of the community over the crucial periods of natural language learning. Anything short of this kind and amount of sufficient meaningful interaction will result in a curtailed or otherwise incomplete development of language, i.e. language loss.

In a monolingual community or in a bilingual community with a clear separation of functions for each language by societal domain ('bilingualism with diglossia', Fishman, 1972), the most likely learning conditions will include availability of the full range of interactions necessary for completely normal language acquisition. However, in bilingual communities where the language of a dominant society encroaches on domains that are critical for the acquisition of a subordinate, ethnic language, conditions strongly disfavor the full development of the latter.

Diminished language use, then, goes hand in glove with language loss. As the social functions of an ethnic language become more restricted, so do the opportunities for the broad variety of meaningful interactions that are necessary for successful transmission of the language to the next generation. Imperfect learning is the result. The mainstream language then becomes dominant, and a steep downward spiral in the use and acquisition of the ethnic language is set in motion. A shift in language use, in this analysis, is seen as the social-functional precursor of loss, which reflects incomplete learning by individuals. Similarly, the maintenance of language use patterns is the social-functional concomitant of natural language acquisition.

Sociocultural Mechanisms of Loss

Fifteen years ago Spanish speakers in the United States numbered 10.6 million and today are estimated at 19.4 million persons (US Bureau of the Census, 1990). A large percentage of these are recent immigrants, and with the proximity of Mexico and other areas of Latin America, their numbers will undoubtedly continue to grow for the forseeable future. And, although Spanish speakers are found in all of the states, they are concentrated in just a few. Most are poor.

Given these demographic facts — numbers, recency of arrival, continued immigration, concentration of population, low socio-economic status — all favoring the native language, the prospects for the maintenance of Spanish would seem extremely bright: large size and geographic concentration provide the ethnic community the resources to develop cultural maintenance institutions, and in their daily lives, members of the community have greater opportunities for interaction with each other; new immigration is generally drawn to areas of ethnic concentration, increasing the size of the group and regenerating the pool of dominant speakers of the language; and the relative lack of social mobility reinforces the geographic concentration at the same time that it enhances a sense of group solidarity.

These plus other factors such as relationship to the homeland, attitudes toward language and ethnicity, discrimination, etc., are generally considered to favor maintenance (Grosjean, 1982). Indeed, many earlier studies concluded, mostly on the basis of language use patterns, that Spanish in the US was being maintained. (See, for example, Patella and Kuvlesky, 1963; Fishman and Hofman, 1966; Hayden, 1966; and Skrabanek, 1970). Yet, it is becoming increasingly clear that such factors are not sufficient to staunch the linguistic hemorrhage. A review of several of these studies by Hernández-Chávez (1978) reveals that the presumed maintenance was largely an artifact of the growth of population through immigration. In recent years, study after study shows a progressive shift to English in the second and third generations and even in younger first generation immigrants, mirroring the language loss studies cited above. (See Gaarder, n.d.; Thompson, 1970; Laosa, 1975; Ortiz, 1975; Faltis, 1976; López, 1978; Gutiérrez, 1980; Hudson-Edwards and Bills, 1982; and Floyd, 1982. Floyd, 1985, reviews several of these works).

An important sociolinguistic question, then, especially for educators and other language planners dedicated to linguistic and cultural pluralism, is what processes — powerful enough to override the maintenance factors noted above — operate within and outside the Chicano community that lead so forcefully and, perhaps, inexorably toward shift and loss.

Although English is not the official language of the United States, there are strong Anglo-Saxon traditions and a multitude of federal and state laws that make English the *de facto* national language. Since at least the middle of the nineteenth century, conflicts between Mexicans and Anglos in the Southwest and anti-foreigner bias generated by Southern European immigration in the East led to a series of repressive laws mandating schooling, official publications, and court proceedings to be in English. In the latter half of the 1800s, English was mandated in the Territories for government business. During that same time, several of the states passed legislation with similar provisions as well as laws requiring English literacy for voting. By the end of the century, no fewer than thirty-nine states had enacted statutes restricting non-English schools. (See Liebowitz, 1969; Kloss, 1977; Hernández-Chávez, 1990b; and Piatt, 1990, for extended historical treatments of language policies).

In this century the Mexican Revolution, two World Wars, the Great Depression, the Cold War, and the Oil Crisis have all fed xenophobic attitudes which have been reflected in further discriminatory legislation and practices that have generally been upheld by the courts. For example, the Nationality Act of 1940 required English for the first time for naturalization of citizenship; the Internal Security Act of 1950 added reading and writing to those requirements. Lassiter v. Northhampton Election Board (360 US 45, 1959), upheld those provisions in a

North Carolina case. Later, Castro v. California (2 Cal. 3d 223, 1970) ruled that the state interest in a common language was such that election materials in Spanish could not be required. There have been similar decisions in various areas of language law.

Such statutory and judicial mandates follow from and comprise an integral part of Anglo-American principles of cultural hegemony. Non-English speaking peoples are to be subjected to the 'great melting pot', not so much to create a new and hardened alloy, but to be recast, as English-speaking replicas conforming to Anglo cultural molds. Non-Europeans have generally been considered inferior, and according to the influential educator Elwood Cubberly early this century, society must instill in them, 'so far as can be done, the Anglo-Saxon conception of righteousness, law and order, and our popular government. . . .' (Cubberly, 1909, pp. 15–16). Also in the same period, Theodore Roosevelt insisted that we 'have room for but one language here and that is the English language, for we intend to see that the crucible turns our people out as Americans, of American nationality. . . .' (US English, 1987).

These notions continue to modern times. Heller (1966) decries the kind of socialization by Mexican-American families that promotes 'family ties, honor, and masculinity', neglecting the values conducive to a dynamic, industrialized society — 'achievement, independence, and deferred gratification'. More recently, the official English movement has launched an all-out campaign against linguistic pluralism. It is expressly opposed to multilingual ballots and bilingual education, though its underlying impetus seems to be fear of Hispanic political power and the desire to control Mexican immigration. Giving voice to these feelings in a statement under an *English First* letterhead, Representative Jim Horn of Texas warns that if bilingual balloting is allowed to continue, 'the next American President could well be elected by people who can't read or speak English!' (Californians United, 1987, p. 80). In a similar vein, reporter Harold Gilliam, who covers the environment for *This World*, states 'The time has come to risk being politically incorrect. . . . There are too many people in California. Immigration must stop'. (Gilliam, 1993). Columnist George Wills expresses clearly the underlying philosophy:

[The government] should not be bashful about affirming the virtues of 'Anglo culture' — including the political arrangements bequeathed by the men of July 4, 1776, a distinctly Anglo group. The promise of America is bound up with the virtues and achievements of 'Anglo culture', which is bound up with English. (*Newsweek*, July 8, 1985).

It is this political context in which local and state governments have passed English-only legislation, educators have imposed Spanish sanctions and sought English immersion curriculums, and employers have dismissed employees for using Spanish in the workplace.

The effect on Spanish speakers is chilling. Not only does English come to be seen by Chicanos as the highly valued language of education and commerce, Spanish is viewed as a hindrance, a language that blocks advancement and acceptance by the broader society. Many schoolchildren, experiencing embarrassment and shame in their desire to be accepted, reject the use of their native language and even deny their ethnicity. Parents attribute their own socioeconomic conditions, not to a history of poverty, lack of education, and political powerlessness, but to a lack of English skills. Understandably, they fear for their children's future without English. They easily accede to the insistence of teachers and other authority figures that they discourage the use of Spanish in the home while they encourage the use of English. There is little awareness that, under such conditions, their children's knowledge of Spanish will inevitably deteriorate or what the social and cultural consequences might be.

We must add to these attitudinal factors the ubiquitousness of English: at school both in and out of the classroom, in the popular entertainment media, in the workplace, in commerce, in social services and government, etc. Under these circumstances, the acquisition and use of English is inevitable. The fears of parents and the English-only advocates alike in this regard are quite unfounded.

What is not inevitable is the retention of Spanish. English becomes the usual and preferred mode of communication, not only in ethnically mixed domains, but soon for intra-ethnic communication in Chicano barrios themselves. From there it is a short leap into the home, the final refuge of the ethnic language. Older children begin to use it with younger siblings. Parents, most of whom have no explicit ideology concerning language and culture, begin to accept English from their children, even if they barely comprehend it themselves. Reasons for the young people to use Spanish are reduced to communication with monolingual family members and to stylistic codeswitching for re-affirming group identity (Gumperz and Hernández-Chávez, 1970). There are no longer 'sufficient meaningful interactions', and the native language begins to slip away.

Revitalization Strategies in Education and Society

A shared language embodies peoplehood — and in this we can agree with the proponents of official English. It encodes the customs and traditions of ethnicity; it is the means of social interaction in the family and community; it carries with it the emotional attachments of upbringing and the values that give meaning to a shared existence; in short, it is crucial to the notion of culture.

Language loss threatens to destroy these relationships. Communication between different-language community members is weakened; the sense of a shared destiny is lost; intra-ethnic conflicts arise; historical knowledge fails to be passed on; and individuals suffer feelings of alienation from their historical ethnicity. These are some of the consequences, at least in part, of language loss. There are possibly others. Cultural alienation can have as its products poor educational performance, socioeconomic marginalization, and a host of other ills. (See Hernández-Chávez, 1978, 1985, 1990b for further discussion of these points).

It would seem to follow, then, that contrary to the wisdom of the advocates of forced assimilation, a healthy society demands an enlightened cultural pluralism. Such a society is one in which the cultures of ethnic groups, far from being prohibited or even merely tolerated, are actively encouraged by the majority institutions. It is a society in which ethnic communities, and thereby their individual members, are strengthened in their own institutions and ways of life and in which powerful ways are found for interethnic collaboration and cooperation. Forced assimilation weakens the assimilated and, thus, the whole; pluralism provides variety, liberates the ethnic group, and strengthens the entire society.

It is not the intent of this chapter to explore in depth all the ramifications of this model except to provide a number of comments about education as it relates to the development of Spanish for Chicanos. We cannot, however, limit our discussion to methodological questions since the revitalization of Spanish in communities where the language is being lost is not just a technical issue. Rather, it is a fundamentally philosophical one and one of setting goals and defining principles from which flow the educational approaches to be taken. We will briefly discuss these issues and their sociopolitical setting as a context for our discussion of education.

The goals for Spanish revitalization cannot be separated from those for cultural pluralism in the sense discussed above. While language is seen as a critical aspect of pluralism, it is not the only component (and perhaps not even the central one). The important goal is the development of the community — educationally, economically, socially, politically — through Spanish, through English, or bilingually. For the individual, we must add a strong sense of self, grounded in the native culture, and the full development of cognitive capabilities. The native language is a critical ingredient in all of this precisely because it can contribute to these goals, and without it, individuals are uprooted, and the community tends to fragment. (See Hernández-Chávez, 1978 and 1985).

We have emphasized the importance of language to the development, participation in, and transmission of culture and we have seen that both the language and the ethnic culture in many Chicano communities is stigmatized. Few people will regularly choose to use a stigmatized language without a strong ideological commitment. These realities give rise to a first principle in language revitalization efforts, namely that *ways must be found to infuse the ethnic language and culture with a positive image and value*, both within and outside the ethnic community. In many Chicano communities, there exist a variety of cultural activities and organizations which serve to promote ethnic solidarity and pride. Such communities must be encouraged to develop these kinds of activities as a way to bolster community pride and ethnic identity.

In addition to such efforts within the community itself, a crucial requisite of social value for a minority language is official standing. Although Spanish enjoys some legal status through such measures as bilingual ballots under the Voting Rights Act, federal and state bilingual education statutes, the Court Interpreters Act, and a few favorable court rulings, it must be pointed out that most of this is grudging and limited support, at best, or else it is for the benefit of the state (see Hernández-Chávez, 1989). Legal recognition that the language minority has the right to use and to maintain its own language for a wide variety of public and private purposes would best serve revitalization efforts. Such recognition would have far-ranging implications for public policy and for the use and prestige of the ethnic language.

Weinreich (1953) defines prestige as 'the value of a language in social advance' (p. 79). An obvious measure of this value is the usefulness of the language for employment. Currently, there exist positions for interpreters, bilingual educators, secretaries, clerks, etc. Most of these, however, have a sort of negative prestige in that they generally involve more responsibilities, yet they pay no more than their monolingual counterparts. Moreover, they are generally created for the convenience and purposes of the employer, not to enhance linguistic pluralism. There exist other positions, as in the foreign service or in international commerce, but Chicanos have either not entered these in great numbers or their native language skills are not sufficiently developed to be a source of personal or professional pride. Similarly, the linguistic preparation of persons in the service professions is entirely left to chance. Revitalization movements, therefore, need to ally themselves with efforts to achieve language rights both in the public and private sectors. Researchers, educators, and other persons interested in language revitalization must, at the very least, become informed about the needs in these areas.

A critical source of prestige is the incorporation of the ethnic language and culture into public school curricula. It is believed by many that cultural values have no place in the curriculum, yet this belief is wholly contrary to long-established educational practice. Though they are often considered to be neutral, the history, arts, social studies, and literature taught in American schools are patently English and Anglo-American. This is certainly legitimate and necessary, but for minority children the failure to teach through their own culture is alienating and is a major contributor to language and cultural loss.

Many people call for the establishment of private after-school ethnic classes to maintain the language and culture. This position is taken not only by official-English advocates, but by ethnic group spokepersons as well, such as Armas (1990). There is no question that ethnic communities can and should engage in a variety of this kind of activity on their own behalf. But we can accept them as strategies for language retention only with reservations. First, that kind of effort is often too late and it is certainly too little, especially given the resources available to most Chicano communities. Retention and/or revitalization of language requires a much more massive effort. The public schools and other majority group institutions are to be held largely responsible for the negative attitudes of students toward the native language and culture and for the failure to develop skills and knowledge in them. Therefore, they have an obligation to attempt to undo that damage. Moreover, ethnic groups themselves, as taxpayers and as citizens or residents, have the right to expect the schools to meet their children's needs in such a vital area.

Nor is the undertaking to teach the minority culture to be taken lightly. Periodically focusing on Mexican national holidays and heroes, for example, only reinforces the idea that culture is an academic exercise and incidental to real life. The culture to be taught needs to be integral to the curriculum, a regular and systematic part of the everyday subjects. Equally as important, cultural instruction must be relevant to students' lives and those of members of their community. Its goal must be to establish a strong sense of cultural identity (as it does for Anglo students), a goal that implies the development of an awareness of the social, economic and political conditions that define the community.

Thus the language of the community must also permeate the curriculum. This follows both from the first principle, enunciated above, and from a second principle of language revitalization: *steps must be taken to insure sufficient native language interactions for full acquisition to take place*. Bilingual education programs, as currently structured, are totally inadequate for this purpose. The principal (and irremediable) difficulty with these programs is that they follow an openly assimilationist philosophy that is codified into law by all the relevant federal and state statutes (see Hernández-Chávez, 1978, 1979, 1985, for discussion). Daily classes in Spanish language arts can certainly be of help, but unless these are supported by important use of the language as a medium of instruction, the criterion of sufficient meaningful interactions cannot be met.

Compare English instruction for Anglo students. Were all their subjects except English given in a foreign language, there would likely develop important gaps in their English knowledge of terms in mathematics, social studies, science, etc. — not just technical terms, but terms in these fields that are necessary for any educated discourse — even though the rest of their world is surrounded by English. For most language minority students, the rest of their world *is* surrounded by English, which they will learn fluently in due course. Development and maintenance of their native language skills demands the use of that language in significant and useful ways as part of their normal scholastic activities, not just in structured language lessons, which are necessarily restricted in their linguistic input to the student. Full language acquisition must have available to it the total range of communicative possibilities by which the learner may selectively recreate the language in a natural order (Chomsky, 1965).

It follows that other opportunities need to be sought outside the curriculum for students to use the language. Many suggestions come to mind. In schools, the active use of Spanish by students, teachers and other staff can be encouraged outside the classroom. Library and other reading materials in Spanish can be given high visibility and use, and increasing use can be made of Spanish-language films, videos, audiotapes and other educational materials. Students and staff can be encouraged to use Spanish in extracurricular and enrichment activities.

Depending upon the commitment of students, faculty, administrators, and the community at large, more intense and creative efforts can be made to raise the prestige of the language and to provide ample meaningful interactions in it. An example might be a native language immersion program on the model of one in Woodland, California. Essential features of this program are that it includes among its students dominant speakers of both Spanish and English, but the language use and curriculum are geared to meet the characteristics and needs of the Spanish-dominant children. (For the English speakers, the methodology applied is similar to that in immersion programs that have many demonstrated successes). Parents are closely involved in all aspects of the program (See Trueba, *et al.*, 1993).

Another example is a proposal for a high school program in Española, New Mexico. This program will use Spanish as a medium of instruction for several hours a day using the local variety[2] as a basis while expanding students' comprehension and use of other varieties for academic purposes. Central to this model is the involvement of students in summer camps, where Spanish will be the medium of interaction and exchange programs for teachers and students with counterparts in Mexico and other Spanish-speaking countries (Davis, 1990).

These two programs have in common *the active involvement of parents and other segments of the community*, a third principle of a revitalization program. The schools are clearly a central institution in this effort because of their tremendous influence on children. But, ultimately, the language and culture must have enough vitality within families and communities to continue to develop across generations. For this, the participation of many different parts of the community is essential. Members of the community must become aware of all aspects of language and cultural loss and must become active partners with their children and with a variety of societal institutions in their revitalization.

The principles of native language revitalization efforts and the modes of implementation suggested above impose heavy burdens on parents, students, educators and language planners concerned with language and culture loss. There are surely other principles and other ways of putting them into effect. But we are convinced that they are no less difficult. Language loss is very far advanced in many Chicano communities, to the point that it may involve heroic efforts to make Spanish viable again. We need to ask whether such efforts are possible and, if so, whether they are feasible or even desirable. The position taken here is that much harm has accrued due to the breakneck pace of change and that it is imperative that communities work, at the very least, to slow it down and make it more manageable and less destructive.

Notes

1 'r:rr' means that some persons tend to substitute the rr (double r sound, as in *perro* = dog) for the r (single r sound, as in *pero* = but). The reason is that the rr is a difficult sound that must be mastered.
2 'Variety' is used in order to rank-order different dialects or to distinguish them from the 'standard' form which some people believe does not exist in real life (i.e., all forms are varieties). 'Dialect' often conveys the meaning of localized varieties in contrast with wider communication varieties. Often 'dialect' and 'variety' are used interchangeably.

References

ALBERT, M.L. and OBLER, L.K. (1978) *The Bilingual Brain*, New York, NY, Academic Press.
ARMAS, J. (1990) 'Preserving culture: If we want the job done right, do it ourselves', *Alburquerque Journal*, July 1, p. B3.
BAILEY, C.J. (1973) 'The patterns of language variation', in BAILEY, R.W. and ROBINSON, J.L. (Eds) *Varieties of Present Day English*, New York, NY, MacMillan.
BREATNACH, R.B. (1964) 'Characteristics of Irish dialects in process of extinction', *Communications et Rapports du Premier Congres de Dialectologie Generale*, Louvain, France, Centre International de Dialectologie Generale.
CALIFORNIANS UNITED (1987) 'Californians United Against Proposition 63: English-Only Opposition Campaign Kit', San Francisco, CA, Californians United.
CHOMSKY, C. (1968) 'The acquisition of syntax in children from 5 to 10', *Research Monograph*, **57**, Cambridge, MA, The MIT Press.
CHOMSKY, N. (1965) *Aspects of the Theory of Syntax*, Cambridge, MA, The MIT Press.
CLARK, H.H. and CLARK, E.V. (1977) *Psychology and Language*, New York, NY, Harcourt Brace Jovanovich.
COHEN, A. (1974) 'The Culver City Spanish immersion program: How does summer recess affect Spanish speaking ability?', *Language Learning*, **24**, pp. 55–68.
CUBBERLY, E.P. (1909) *Changing Conceptions of Education*, Boston, MA, Houghton Mifflin Co.
DAVIS, P. (1990) *An internationalist focus for the revitalization of Spanish in northern New Mexico*, unpublished manuscript, Albuquerque, NM, University of New Mexico, Department of Linguistics.
DORIAN, N. (1978) 'The fate of morphological complexity in language death', *Language*, **54**, pp. 590–609.

DORIAN, N. (1981) *Language Death*, Philadelphia, PA, University of Pennsylvania Press.

FALTIS, C. (1976) *A Study of Spanish and English Usage Among Bilingual Mexican Americans Living in the Las Calles Barrio of San Jose, California*, MA Thesis, San Jose, CA, San Jose State University.

FERGUSON, C.A. (1973) *Studies of Childhood Development*, New York, NY, Holt, Rinehart and Winston.

FISCHER, J.L. (1958) 'Social influences on the choice of a linguistic variant', *Word*, **14**, pp. 47–56.

FISHMAN, J.A. (1972) 'Societal bilingualism: Stable and transitional', in FISHMAN, J.A. *The Sociology of Language*, Rowley, MA, Newbury House.

FISHMAN, J.A. and HOFMAN, J.E. (1966) 'Mother tongue and nativity in the American population', in FISHMAN, J. *et al.* (Eds) *Language Loyalty in the United States*, The Hague, Netherlands, Mouton.

FLOYD, M.B. (1982) 'Spanish language maintenance in Colorado', in BARKIN, F., BRANDT, E.A. and ORNSTEIN-GALICIA, J. (Eds) *Bilingualism and Language Contact: Spanish, English, and Native American Languages*, New York, NY, Teachers' College Press.

FLOYD, M.B. (1985) 'Spanish in the Southwest: Language maintanence or shift?' in ELIAS-OLIVARES, L., LEONE, E.A., CISNEROS, R. and GUTIERREZ, J. (Eds) 'Spanish Language use and public life in the USA', in FISHMAN, J.A. (Ed) *Contributions to the Sociology of Language*, **35**, The Hague, Netherlands, Mouton.

FRASER, C., BELLUGI, U. and BROWN, R. (1963) 'Control of grammar in imitation, comprehension, and production', *Journal of Verbal Learning and Verbal Behavior*, **2**, pp. 121–35.

GAARDER, A.B. (n.d.) *Language Maintenance or Language Shift: The Prospect for Spanish in the United States*, Mimeo.

GALLOWAY, L. (1978) 'Impairment and recovery in polyglot aphasia', in PARADIS, M. (Ed) *Aspects of Bilingualism*, Columbia, SC, Hornbeam Press.

GILLIAM, H. (1993) 'Bursting at the seams', *This World, San Francisco Chronicle*, February 21, p. 12.

GROSJEAN, F. (1982) *Life With Two Languages: An Introduction to Bilingualism*, Cambridge, MA, Harvard University Press.

GUMPERZ, J. and HERNÁNDEZ-CHÁVEZ, E. (1970) 'Cognitive aspects of bilingual communication', in WHITELY, H. (Ed) *Language Use and Social Change*, London, England, Oxford University Press.

GUTIÉRREZ, J.R. (1980) 'Language use in Martineztown', in BARKIN, F. and BRANDT, E. (Eds) *Speaking, Singing, and Teaching: A Multidisciplinary Approach to Language Variation*, Proceedings of the Eighth Annual Southwestern Area Language and Linguistics Workshop, *Anthropological Research Papers*, **20**, pp. 454–459. Tempe, AZ: Arizona State University.

GUTIÉRREZ, M. (1990) 'Sobre el mantenimiento de las cláusulas subordinadas en el español de Los Angeles', in BERGEN, J. (Ed) *Spanish in the United States: Sociolinguistic issues*, Washington, DC, Georgetown University Press.

HAAS, M.R. (1968) 'The last words of Biloxi', *International Journal of Applied Linguistics*, **34**, pp. 77–84.

HAYDEN, R.G. (1966) 'Some community dynamics of language maintenance', in FISHMAN, J. *et al.* (Eds) *Language Loyalty in the United States*, The Hague, Netherlands, Mouton.

HELLER, C. (1966) *Mexican-American Youth: Forgotten Youth at the Crossroads*, New York, NY, Random House.

HENZL, V. (1977) 'On similarity between language acquisition and language loss', paper presented at the Second Annual Boston University Conference on Language Development, Boston, MA.

HERNÁNDEZ-CHÁVEZ, E. (1978) 'Language maintenance, bilingual education, and philosophies of bilingualism in the United States', in ALATIS, J. (Ed) *International Dimensions of Bilingual Education*, Georgetown University Round Table Monograph, Washington, DC, Georgetown University Press.

HERNÁNDEZ-CHÁVEZ, E. (1979) 'Meaningful bilingual bicultural education: A fairytale', in ORTIZ, R. (Ed) *Language Development in a Bilingual Setting*, Pomona, CA, National Multilingual Multicultural Materials Development Center.

HERNÁNDEZ-CHÁVEZ, E. (1985) 'The inadequancy of English immersion education as an educational approach for language minority students', in *Studies on Immersion Education: A Collection for United States Educators*, Sacramento, CA, California State Department of Education.

HERNÁNDEZ-CHÁVEZ, E. (1989) 'Language policy and language rights in the United States: Issues in bilingualism', in SKUTNABB-KANGAS, T. and CUMMINS, J. (Eds) *Minority Education: From Shame to Struggle*, Clevedon, Multilingual Matters Ltd.

HERNÁNDEZ-CHÁVEZ, E. (1990a) *'Gracias por viniendo'* — *Language Loss in the Spanish of New Mexico*, Paper presented at the Linguistic Association of the Southwest Annual Conference, El Paso, Texas, October 19–21.

HERNÁNDEZ-CHÁVEZ, E. (1990b) 'The role of suppressive language policies in language shift and language loss', Estudios Fronterizos, *Revista del Instituto de Investigaciones Sociales*, **7**, 8, pp. 18–19, 123–35.

HERNÁNDEZ-CHÁVEZ, E. (1990c) 'Sociocultural sources of Spanish-English codeswitching in language loss', paper presented at the Rocky Mountain Modern Language Association, 44th Annual Meeting, Salt Lake City, Utah, October 11–13.

HILL, J. and HILL, K.C. (1977) 'Language death and relexification in Tlaxcalan Náhuatl', *International Journal of the Sociology of Language*, **12**, pp. 55–70.

HUDSON-EDWARDS, A. and BILLS, G. (1982) 'Intergenerational language shift in an Albuquerque barrio', in AMASTAE, J. and ELIAS-OLIVARES, L. (Eds) *Spanish in the United States: Sociolinguistic Aspects*, Cambridge, England, Cambridge University Press.

KESSEL, F.S. (1970) 'The role of syntax in children's comprehension from ages six to twelve', *Monograph of Social Research and Child Development*, **35**, 6.

KLOSS, H. (1977) *The American Bilingual Tradition*, Rowley, MA, Newbury House.

KOIKE, D. (1987) 'Code switching in the bilingual Chicano narrative', *Hispania*, **70**, pp. 148–54.

KRASHEN, S.D. (1981) 'Bilingual education and second language acquisition theory', in California State Department of Education, *Schooling and Language Minority Students: A Theoretical Framework*, Los Angeles, CA, Evaluation, Dissimentation and Assessment Center, California State University, L.A.

LABOV, W. (1964) 'Stages in the acqusition of standard English', in SHUY, R.W. (Ed) *Social Dialects and Language Learning*, Champaign, IL, National Council of Teachers of English.

LAOSA, L. (1975) 'Bilingualism in three United States Hispanic groups: Contextual use of language by children and adults in their families', *Journal of Educational Psychology*, **67**, 5, pp. 617–27.

LIEBOWITZ, A. (1969) 'English literacy: Legal sanction for discrimination', *Notre Dame Lawyer*, **45**, 7, pp. 7–67.

LOPEZ, D.E. (1978) 'Chicano language loyalty in an urban setting', *Sociology and Social Research*, **62**, pp. 267–78.

MERINO, B.J. (1983) 'Language loss in bilingual Chicano children', *Journal of Applied Developmental Psychology*, **10**, pp. 477–94.

MOSKOWITZ, B.A. (1978) 'The acquisition of language', *Scientific American*, **239**, pp. 92–108.

OCAMPO, F. (1990) 'El subjuntivo en tres generaciones de hablantes bilingues', in

BERGEN, J. (Ed) *Spanish in the United States: Sociolinguistic Issues*, Washington, DC, Georgetown University Press.

ORTIZ, L.I. (1975) *A Sociolinguistic Study of Language Maintenance in the Northern New Mexico Community of Arroyo Seco*, Ph.D. dissertation, Albuquerque, NM, University of New Mexico.

OSTYN, P. (1972) *American Flemish: A Study in Language Loss and Linguistic Interference*, Ph.D. dissertation, Rochester, NY, University of Rochester.

PARADIS, M. (1977) 'Bilingualism and aphasia', in WHITAKER, H. and H. (Eds), *Studies in Neurolinguistics*, **3**, New York, NY, Academic Press.

PATELLA, V. and KUVLESKY, W.P. (1963) 'Situational variation in language patterns of Mexican American boys and girls', *Social Science Quarterly*, **53**, 4, pp. 855–64.

PIATT, B. (1990) *Only English? Law and Language Policy in the United States*, Albuquerque NM, University of New Mexico Press.

POUSADA, A. and POPLACK, S. (1979) 'No case for convergence: The Puerto Rican Spanish verb system in a language contact situation', New York, NY, Centro de Estudios Puertorriqueños, Working Papers No. 5.

PRATELLA, W.C. (1970) 'The retention of first and second year Spanish over the period of the summer vacation', *Dissertation Abstracts*, 31.235–A.

SALTRELLI, M. (1975a) 'Emigrant languages in America: Acquisition, development, and death', *Studies in Language Learning*, **1**, pp. 186–87.

SALTRELLI, M. (1975b) 'Leveling of paradigms in Chicano Spanish', in MILAN, W., STACZEK, J.J. and ZAMORA, J.C. (Eds) *Colloquium on Spanish and Portuguese Linguistics*, University of Massachusetts. Washington, DC, Georgetown University Press.

SÁNCHEZ, R. (1983) *Chicano Discourse: A Socio-historical Perspective*, Rowley, MA, Newbury House.

SILVA-CORVALÁN, C. (1983a) 'Tense and aspect in oral Spanish narrative: Context and meaning', *Language*, **59**, pp. 60–80.

SILVA-CORVALÁN, C. (1983b) 'Code-shifting patterns in Chicano Spanish', in ELIAS-OLIVARES, L. (Ed) *Spanish in the US Setting: Beyond the Southwest*, Rosslyn, VA, NCBE.

SILVA-CORVALÁN, C. (1986) 'Bilingualism and language change: The extension of *estar* in Los Angeles Spanish', *Language*, **62**, pp. 587–608.

SILVA-CORVALÁN, C. (1988) 'Oral narrative along the Spanish-English bilingual continuum', in STACZEK, J. (Ed) *Colloquium on Spanish, Portuguese, and Catalan Linguistics*, Washington, DC, Georgetown University Press.

SILVA-CORVALÁN, C. (1990) 'Current issues in studies of language contact', *Hispania*, **73**, pp. 162–76.

SKRABANEK, R.L. (1970) 'Language maintenance among Mexican-Americans', *International Journal of Comparative Sociology*, **11**, pp. 272–82.

THOMPSON, R. (1970) 'Mexican American language loyalty and the validity of the 1970 census', in BILLS, G. (Ed) *Southwest Areal Linguistics*, San Diego, CA, Institute for Cultural Pluralism.

TRUDGILL, P. (1976–77) 'Creolization in reverse: Reduction and simplification in the Albanian dialects of Greece', *Transactions of the Philosophical Society*, pp. 32–50.

TRUEBA, H., RODRIGUEZ, C., ZOU, Y. and CINTRÓN, J. (1993) *Healing Multicultural America*, London, England, Falmer Press.

US BUREAU OF THE CENSUS (1990) 'Statistical Abstract of the US, 1990, Washington, DC, US Government Printing Office.

US ENGLISH (1987) 'In defense of our common language', in *Californians United. English-Only Campaign Kit*, San Francisco CA.

WEINREICH, U. (1953) 'Languages in contact: Findings and problems', Publications of the *Linguistic Circle of New York*, **1**.

Eduardo Hernández-Chávez

WILL, G.F. (1985) 'In defense of the mother tongue', *Newsweek*, July 8, Vol. **VI**, p. 78.
WILLIAMSON, S. (1982) 'Summary chart of findings from previous research on language loss', in LAMBERT, R. and FREED, B. (Eds) *The Loss of Language Skills*, Rowley, MA, Newbury House.
WOLFRAM, W. (1969) *A Sociolinguistic Description of Detroit Negro speech*, Washington, DC, Center for Applied Linguistics.

Chapter 5

Language Variation in the Spanish of the Southwest

Rosaura Sánchez

The events of recent weeks here at UC Davis[1] have struck a nerve throughout the state and helped to focus attention on what is more a social than a linguistic problem, more a problem of class and ethnic discrimination than one of language variation. But let me first address the linguistic situation, as a sociolinguist and as a Chicana.

All languages are characterized by linguistic variation. There is no language in the world that has only one variety unless it is a computer language or an artificial language of some sort, like Esperanto. No living language, moreover, is safe from change, as it is always evolving; as history changes, as social structures evolve, as technology develops, new interactional situations are created; new roles and functions arise; new networks of communication are established with new codes. Languages thus change to meet new needs. As new forms appear they compete with older forms so that eventually there is an overlapping of forms. Languages for the most part, however, favor simplification; they tend to favor regularization and avoid redundancy. For that reason certain forms are invariably lost; in popular varieties, for example, irregular forms tend to become regularized and they may eventually become the norm. For example, *roto* becomes *rompido*. Thus as societies change, languages change. These changes become evident at various levels of the grammar of every language.

Sound changes are one type of frequent linguistic change; changes may be widespread or localized, giving rise to regional or national variants. We know, for example, that we do not pronounce the word for *chicken* like the Argentinians of the Buenos Aires area. They say *pozo* and we say *poyo*. In central and northern Spain they say *polo*, with a palatal 'l.' Now when you realize that all three came from the Latin word *pullum* you know that the double 'l' went through several changes, becoming palatalized first and then a palatal fricative and finally in Argentina, Uruguay and Ecuador, a strident alveo-palatal fricative. Is only one of these pronunciations correct? That's a silly question in linguistics. All three pronunciations are native Spanish products, equally historical, equally acceptable in linguistics, equally explainable within the rules of a Spanish historical grammar. In fact what has happened to the palatal 'l' in *pollo* is a repetition of something that happened previously in the history of the language when another palatalized 'l' became a strident fricative. Thus the word for woman in Latin was *mulierem*, then

75

muliérem and for many centuries it was pronounced *muλerem* before it became *mu žer*, then *musér*, and finally, around the seventeenth century, our present *muxer* (*mujer*). Changes that occur once can thus happen more than once, as if there were certain tendencies within the language, or maybe we should say, within all languages, since similar things, like palatalization, occur in many languages including English; thus, to give an example, a 't' + 'i' as in the word *nation* is no longer anything like *nati-on* but rather *neyšan*.

Phonetic differences such as these are only one aspect of language variation. Differences can also occur at the level of vocabulary. Thus some Spanish-speaking regions prefer the term *maní* for peanuts and others, like most of us, use the word *cacahuates*. In Spain they prefer *cacahuetes*. However, since it is a word borrowed from the Náhuatl[2] *cacawatl* are we to say that they are wrong in preferring *hue* to *hua* and that we in Meso-America have the correct form of the word? No, all of these forms are equally appropriate; each is used in a particular area of the world by millions of Spanish speakers.

Changes may occur as well in grammar. You might be surprised to know that some forms that we continue to use today in popular Spanish, like *haiga* or *truje* or *ansí* or *ansina* were once written forms used by the so-called *cultos* — the lettered men of the fifteenth and sixteenth-century Spanish court. We know then that morphological forms also change; some are discarded and new ones created. We know, for example, that our future tense did not exist in Classical Latin. Oh, they had a future tense but it was not the form we inherited. No, it seems that people wrote one form and used another one orally. In spoken Latin, they preferred a future made up with the verb *habere*. Thus, their use of the infinitive + a conjugated form of *habere* is what gave us our modern future tense form. *Comeré* thus comes from *comer* + *he* — which when pronounced together rapidly gave *comeré*.

Many changes come simply from contact with other languages. Migration is a historical process as are invasions and conquests. Thus when the Romans invaded the Spanish peninsula they found a number of natives there of Celtic, Greek, Phoenician, Iberian, and Basque origin. The Romans were the powerful and culturally and technologically more advanced society, and their language became the dominant one of the entire peninsula. It appears that the population assumed the language of the dominant group for cultural and political reasons since the Romans allowed the colonized to become citizens of the Roman empire. Unwillingness to be dominated and to assimilate, on the other hand, kept the Basques isolated in the northern area and thus allowed them to retain their language for many centuries, although subsequent contact with Castilian and acculturation have led to a significant reduction of speakers of Euskera, the Basque language. Thus social contact as well as distance or segregation can also have an impact on language choice and language variation.

Subsequent contact with other groups, whether through invasion or commerce, but especially through conquest, brought the Iberian Romans into contact with a number of Germanic tribes and later with the Arabs who brought many changes to the peninsula, especially at the economic and social level. Intimate contact with the Arabs led to the incorporation into Spanish of thousands of loanwords that are now part of the Spanish language. Do we perhaps today reject the use of words like *almohada* [pillow] or *acequia* [irrigation ditch] or *azafrán* [saffron] because they are of Arabic origin? Does anyone question that the word *guerra*, our word for war, is Spanish even though it is of Germanic origin? No, those terms were absorbed into the language and adapted phonologically and morphologically to fit in with the rest of the grammar and today are considered a legitimate part of the language.

The same process of borrowing is evident in English. Is the word *rodeo* today rejected as a Spanish word? What about *barbeque*? Does anyone question the use of the loan-translation *cowboy* because it is a quasi-translation of the word in Spanish, *vaquero*? Yet today if we say *troque* or *troca* [from truck] for *camión* or *plogue* or *ploga* [from plug] for *enchufe* we are dismissed as ignorant Spanish-speaking peasants. Why is this the case if the process is historical and occurs whenever two linguistic groups come into contact? Perhaps, my friends, it is because the problem is not linguistic in nature. Let me explain.

All forms, let me repeat, are linguistically valid, but they do not all have the same social acceptance. In a society characterized by stratification, language varieties are also stratified. Some are dominant, some subordinated. The status of varieties is not, of course, linguistically determined, for they are all equally valid, equally the product of a rule-determined grammar. Their status is socially determined. All languages undergo or have undergone the process of standardization. In these cases, commissions, schools or academies are established by those in power to establish language policy, to determine the linguistic norms. The process involves selection and rejection of forms and rules of usage. Once these learned men and women, but mostly men, make their choices, their selections are published and disseminated throughout a given area and advocated by state apparatuses, especially by educational institutions. Subscribing to these norms is encouraged and benefits accrue to those that do. Consensus is thus generally the strategy used to enforce particular norms and particular segments of the population readily consent to their implementation. Coercion, however, can also be used, as in the case of language policy under Hitler or under the Chilean dictator Pinochet, in which particular terms or forms were prohibited from public use.

Standardization of a particular norm does not, however, automatically lead to the elimination of other norms or, as we say in linguistics, of other grammars. For that reason in some societies there is often a large gap between the written form of a language and the oral or spoken varieties. The acquisition of certain norms or of a particular variety of language may in fact imply or require instruction or long-term contact with individuals who use that particular norm as well as the opportunity to practice it.

Those of us of Mexican and Latino origin who are born in the United States do not, for the most part, receive instruction in the Spanish language. Even bilingual education has served primarily to facilitate the rapid transition from Spanish instruction to English instruction. For many of us, however, such bilingual instruction, limited as it may be, was not available when and where we grew up. We have thus acquired only the Spanish varieties spoken at home, varieties with particular functions and used for informal interpersonal interaction with family and community members. In many cases, our parents or grandparents immigrated from a rural area of Mexico, and they speak a rural variety of Spanish which shares many of the same features of all the other rural varieties used throughout Latin America and even Spain. Perhaps our ancestors came from urban barrios in Mexico, Texas, New Mexico or California. There too, the popular varieties reflect the particular regional origin of the population and the social standing of that group. In all of this we must recall that social barriers in society inevitably mean linguistic barriers as well, not at the level of competence, because all speakers are competent to learn additional varieties of their language, but at the level of performance.

Nonetheless, whatever the variety, the Spanish that is spoken in our homes is Spanish, let there be no doubt about that, but it is not necessarily academic Spanish; it may retain forms which are no longer considered part of the standard variety, regardless of the fact that they were once the 'king's castellano' and regardless of the fact that millions may continue to use them today. But our popular variety of Spanish shares practically all of the rules of grammar with a standard variety of Spanish. The question, however, is not really one of the standard vs. popular as if there were only two varieties of language throughout the Spanish-speaking world. No, in fact there are several standard and popular varieties which vary from one region to another, and from nation to nation, with, for example, the *voseo* of Argentina not being part of Mexican Spanish; all speakers of Spanish or of any language, moreover, are characterized by being heteroglossic, that is multidialectal, and able to participate in multiple interactional situations with different varieties of language, with different codes, with different discourses. Language varieties differ in terms of function and thus the use of one or another conveys different meanings, different connotations. It is thus not the same to say, *Están platicando* as it is to say, *Están periqueando* or *Están charlando*. Each one is appropriate in a different context with a different speaker.

Having a wide repertoire with a number of language registers does not imply that we have all the varieties that we need or would like to have. What it does mean is that the acquisition of additional varieties is easier for us than it is for someone to learn a second language. Once one is made aware of rule differences between given varieties, (learning, for example, that in the preterite, the standard form does not place an -s at the end, so that it is *estuviste* instead of *estuvistes* or *estuvites*, as in the popular varieties of Spanish), it is easy to make the shift; one simply applies a different rule when one needs to make use of a different variety of language. Learning to shift does not however, imply losing the varieties that one already speaks. One may need to use a standard form in writing or in class but prefer a popular form with one's friends or parents. In fact, the defining trait of an educated person should be the ability to shift from one variety to another according to the circumstances, at will and at one's pleasure.

For a linguist, the issue is one of distinguishing between different grammars since varieties within one language differ in terms of grammar rules, but the issue in an educational context is not strictly linguistic but rather social and economic. We need to recall that our ancestors quickly passed from being colonizers of the Southwest to being conquered back in 1848;[3] they subsequently became a source of cheap labor and a subordinated minority in this country. Latinos have been geographically deterritorialized, disempowered, linguistically oppressed and economically exploited in this country for over 140 years. That's really what it's about. Because of our social situation, the Spanish varieties that we speak are looked down upon, and we are said to speak 'Spanglish.' Make no mistake about it. Such descriptions are racist and classist and meant to demean not only our language but us as well. The putdown is not only uttered by English-speaking journalists, but by speakers of our own language from middle or upper classes of Spain and Latin America who resent having to deal with those of us who are primarily from the working class. Our class is of course revealed when we use particular varieties of Spanish, for we, like the British and indeed all people, 'are born branded on the tongue', since language use is a social marker. Moreover, they seemingly resent in us what is a historical process, that is, the incorporation of loanwords into our language and they look down upon popular varieties which are also spoken by millions in their own countries. Is it that only Chicanos and Latinos in this country incorporate English terms as loanwords into Spanish? No, a quick review of newspapers like *El País* from Spain would show the degree to which English vocabulary and phraseology have 'contaminated' Spanish journalism. Even the President of Mexico, Salinas de Gortari, says things like *removeré obstáculos*. Why then do they reject the process in us? The degree of borrowing may be greater here where contact between the two language groups is constant and a response to new information, new technologies and an ever-growing number of consumer goods and services that are not introduced in Spanish but rather in English. Unfortunately, the academic terms that we learn, whether to discuss government, politics, technology, literature, scientific topics or even cultural subjects, are generally in English. We are bombarded by language constantly and continually from the media, the university, our friends, society in general, and only a small part of that bombardment is in Spanish. Imagine a world in which all references to every conceivable subject were in Spanish; that unfortunately, is not our world in this country, at this time. For this reason we do not always develop the vocabulary in Spanish that we need to discuss any number of academic topics. As long as our discourses stay within certain domains within which we use the language daily, we do well, but as soon as we have to speak of the current situation in Eastern Europe or in Nicaragua we often feel an urge to shift to English because academic and political functions are monopolized by English. We can consciously determine to expand our repertoire and make it our business to acquire the terminology to deal with political, economic, technological and cultural issues in Spanish, if we so choose. University and high school classes to provide such strategies and vocabulary can, of course, be devised and should.

However, not all Latino or Chicano students are interested or so inclined. Many are happy with the few varieties that they already speak or with not knowing any Spanish at all. In a society where English is the dominant language and Spanish the subordinated language, it often occurs that some wish to assimilate and enter the mainstream, erasing all traces of ethnicity and linguistic background, a la Richard Rodríguez (see Rodríguez, 1982). Others, on the other hand, may perhaps wish to express their resentment and dissatisfaction with social conditions by stressing those very features and practices that identify one with certain minority groups, especially through the public use of the minority language. Yet, even when we speak Spanish to our friends to stress our group membership, we soon find ourselves dealing with topics which are marked 'English-dominant' in our mental linguistic files. We begin to code-switch. Of course, shifting from English to Spanish may also occur if the topic falls within the domain of that language for us. In fact, constant shifting from one language to another is common among bilingual Chicanos. I myself am a constant code-switcher with my friends; but here again the practice is not unique to us, as most bilingual people who interact with other bilingual individuals in an intimate or familiar setting do in fact code-switch to some extent. There is nothing wrong with code-switching as it indicates that one is competent in two grammars. But it cannot be our excuse for not developing our Spanish for a multiplicity of functions. It must be done intentionally, not by default, not because of a lack of options. The important thing is to be able to sustain a conversation in one language if one has to because the other person is not a friend or is not bilingual. It is, I think, politically important to be fully functional in both languages, and that is something that Latino and Chicano university students can attain, but it will undoubtedly take time and effort and most of all, the desire and willingness to do so.

Our Spanish is a skill that we need to develop and hone like any other skill. It is important that we see ourselves as part of an enormous Spanish-speaking world out there, a world with which we need to communicate. Language is a tool, an instrument of defense and attack, a way of being critical and making our voices heard. Socially and politically it is important that we have a great many linguistic resources to call upon, including a standard variety of Spanish. It may come in handy, especially if you have to do battle with those who only listen to other speakers of standard varieties of language. As long we are not the dominant group, others can put us down and dismiss us for social, racial, ethnic and even linguistic reasons. Let us not give anyone that pleasure. We must be ready, willing, and able to defend ourselves at a number of discursive levels. Knowing the rules of the linguistic game might prove to be to our advantage. For the time being, we can lick them at their own game. Tomorrow, the game, as well as the rules, may well be our own.

Notes

1 This talk was presented at the University of California, Davis, during a period of protest by several minority students who went on a hunger strike to protest, among several issues, the State Department's policy and attitude towards Chicano/Latino students. [Note by R. Sánchez]
2 Náhuatl is a Uto-Aztecan language, the most important language in pre-colonial Mexico which is still spoken by millions of people. Many of the Náhuatl words were taken by the Spanish language after 1521 (*tomate, zarape, chile*, etc.). The question is, are these words viewed as Spanish words or as Náhuatl words? Most probably they are viewed as Spanish words today.
3 The Guadalupe Hidalgo Treaty resulted in the acquisition of the Southwest by the United States. This treaty was signed in Veracruz, Mexico, on August 2, 1848, and represents the end of the Mexican War that had lasted for two years. Over one-third of the US territory was added: Texas, New Mexico, California and other significant parts of the Southwest.

Reference

RODRÍGUEZ, R. (1982) *Hunger of Memory: The Education of Richard Rodríguez, An Autobiography*, Boston, MA, David R. Godine.

Further Readings

AMASTAE, J. and ELÍAS-OLIVARES, L. (1982) *Spanish in the United States: Sociolinguistic Aspects*, Cambridge, Cambridge University Press.

COTTON, E.G. and SHARP, J.M. (1988) *Spanish in the Americas,* Washington, DC, Georgetown University Press.

GARCÍA, O. and OTHEGUY, R. (1988) 'The language situation of Cuban Americans', in MCKAY, S.L. and WONG, S.C. (Eds) *Language Diversity, Problem or Resource?,* NY, Newbury House Publishers, pp. 162–92.

HERNÁNDEZ-CHAVEZ, E., COHEN, A. and BELTRAMO, A. (1975) *El Lenguage de los Chicanos,* Arlington, VA, Center for Applied Linguistics.

PEÑALOSA, F. (1980) *Chicano Sociolinguistics: A Brief Introduction,* Rowley, MA, Newbury.

SÁNCHEZ, R. (1983) *Chicano Discourse: Socio-Historic Perspectives,* Rowley, MA, Newbury House Publishers.

VALDÉS, G. (1988) 'The language situation of Mexican Americans', in MCKAY, S.L. and WONG, S.C. (Eds) *Language Diversity: Problem or Resource?,* New York, Newbury House Publishers, pp. 111–39.

ZENTELLA, A.C. (1988) 'The language situation of Puerto Ricans', in MCKAY, S.L. and WONG, S.C. (Eds) *Language Diversity: Problem or Resource?,* NY, Newbury House Publishers, pp. 140–65.

Chapter 6

The Teaching of Spanish to Bilingual Spanish-Speakers: A 'Problem' of Inequality

Margarita Hidalgo[1]

Many shadows darken the teaching of the mother tongue to Spanish speakers living in the United States. Their traditional marginal position as minorities has caused the language of Hispanic Americans to become the object of suspicion, derision, and social discrimination, and on occasion, has even caused discrimination in the workplace. Paradoxically, the teaching of Spanish as a foreign language holds a more promising future, as evidenced by massive enrollments in a large number of major public universities and by the great quantity and quality of texts written for English speakers learning Spanish. Legitimate efforts to address the needs of bilingual students on the part of linguists and professors who are dedicated to the teaching of Spanish for native speakers (SNS) in the United States, have been cogently outlined in Valdés, Lozano and García-Moya (1981) and rearticulated some years later by the author of this work (Hidalgo, 1986). However, the texts prepared for Spanish-speakers at the university level are neither abundant nor varied, but rather reveal the philosophical worries and the pedagogical strategies of their authors (see Burunat and Starcevic, 1983; Marqués, 1986; Mejias and Garza-Swan, 1981; Valdés-Fallis and Teschner, 1985). This article touches on some of the many problems that plague the teaching of SNS. These problems can be identified as political, bureaucratic, pragmatic, and affective.

Problems of a Political Nature

The current political mood in the United States may be characterized as extremely conservative, due, in part, to the crisis that confronts the North American economic system and the fierce competition with economies that are perceived as being healthier and more prosperous than ours. Despite such an unfortunate crisis, the socioeconomic conditions of some Hispanics (in particular Cuban Americans in Florida and in the Northeast of the country) have improved in the last few years, giving way to a visible middle class that seems to stand out in the business world, in commercial arts, and in the most prestigious professions (García and Otheguy,

1988). This powerful and influential middle class is on its way, however, in continuous competition with the English-speaking majority at comparable levels, a majority who seems to resent the steady progress of some minority groups.

Other less fortunate Hispanic groups still combat one another in the 'daily struggle for life' and seem to be ambivalent towards the dominant North American current. This ambivalence is seen in the attitudes of attraction and rejection towards all that is Hispanic and Spanish as well as towards all that is North American and English (García *et al.*, 1988). Even more uncertain is the future of those United States Hispanics from Mexico and Central America who have welcomed amnesty, and the future of illegal immigrants from the same region whose numbers increase in large cities like New York, Houston, or Los Angeles, or who live with the imminent risk of being deported at any moment to their native countries. Whatever the conditions of United States Hispanics, they will all sooner or later realize that one of their most precious values is becoming irrevocably affected by their and their children's prolonged stay in the United States.

The millions of Hispanics who are residents of the United States are confronted, along with other ethnic minorities, with a system unwilling to educate them, even partially, in their native language. This is occurring on the threshold of the twenty-first century because the United States, upon becoming a nation, did not build a foundation for bilingual/bicultural education supported from the beginning by the guardian of the public well-being, that is, the State (Heath, 1981).

Spanish-speakers on both sides of the Atlantic are very conscious of the values (prestige and identity, for example) that their ancestors assigned to the Spanish language. It would not be surprising, therefore, that in the not very distant future, United States Hispanics begin to demand, on a massive basis, the right to bilingual/bicultural education for their children.

Up to the present time United States Hispanics have maintained their ancestral language — principally for sociodemographic and affective reasons — rather than due to the efforts of an organized and conscious movement. It is possible that in the near future, the elite among Hispanic Americans may protest against the intolerable pressures imposed from outside and from above by the dominant anglophone groups (Donahue, 1985).

Because of their conscious and unconscious desires to be accepted by the anglophone majority, United States Hispanics have forced themselves to conform to the general dictates of the North American ideology: the ability to speak English is one of the most effective routes in the process of acculturation, assimilation, and ultimately, in the acquisition of the North American dream: personal success. The Mexican-American workers from the 1940s as well as the elitist Cubans who were expelled by the Castro regime at the beginning of the Revolution have all been inclined to conform to the dominant ideology. They have become 'northamericanized' linguistically speaking, or rather, they have transformed their patterns of behavior and values, conforming them to those of the dominant group.

No period of North American history documents massive movements in favor of linguistic and cultural freedom for United States Hispanics; Hispanics have not participated in linguistic or national loyalty campaigns tied to their native language. The material compensation for first and second generation immigrants seems to be sufficient, so much so that the phenomena of language, culture or national identity have never turned up as part of a partisan political program.

Within the framework of an advanced capitalist system, such as exists in North America, the reclamation of linguistic rights is, without doubt, possible, but such a reclamation on the part of minority groups occurs at a certain time in history when these groups form select proto-groups that give intellectual or spiritual direction to the members of the masses with whom they feel a cultural identification (Fishman, 1985).

In the midst of the jingoistic environment that dominates the US and is exploited by reactionary groups such as those that direct the US Only English Movement, Hispanics are advancing slowly in the (re)conquest of their lost linguistic and cultural territory. A sign of this is the television programming in Spanish that has received favorable reviews by *Newsweek*, a weekly magazine that is the standard-bearer of the North American system. The (re)conquest of televised space is relevant to the masses of Hispanics because of the symbolic message that television carries — we are on the air and we have options at a personal level — we are able to choose programming in English or in Spanish. The massive existence of means of communication in Spanish obeys the economic motivations of United States Hispanic managers more than the conscious desire to maintain the minority language in question. In other spheres of more significant interaction, such as education and politics, United States Hispanics lack the comfortable options afforded by means of communication. The barriers that are erected in the field of education are, in the majority of the cases, insurmountable, due to promontory bureaucratic factors.

Bureaucracy and Education in Foreign Languages

The North American educational system, as that of any other country, involves general strategies and special tactics that are, in the majority of the cases, planned by the groups in power. Lacking a centralized educational system like those existing in some European and Latin American countries, the North American system is characterized by its elasticity and plasticity, in such a way that educational programs are regionally or locally formed in agreement with the specific needs of a school district, a county, or a state.

This very flexible educational framework allows for programs that are as strange as they are capricious. In the field of foreign languages, for example, material and human resources are invested at the secondary and post-secondary levels, while the primary and elementary levels become neglected and abandoned. This practice is extremely paradoxical if one takes into consideration linguistics applied to the teaching of foreign languages as well as popular wisdom; foreign languages are acquired and learned more easily when an individual has early contact with them. As a consequence, the great majority of North Americans are involuntarily educated in only one language and their educational system offers them few opportunities to become bilingual or multilingual at an early age. Those who by individual or economic motivation aspire to learn a foreign language with a certain level of acceptability, have to anxiously await their final years of high school to receive ineffective instruction, in the majority of cases, an instruction which is mediatized by the dictates of the school district of the corresponding jurisdiction. Those who are able to overcome the vicissitudes of the educational system are generally students with irrevocable motivation, English speakers who have had the opportunity to live and/or study in a Spanish-speaking country during their final years of high school or during their first years of university education. Some of them are able to become high school teachers as well as university professors.

Other individuals who have majored in Spanish are of Hispanic origin or United States Hispanics who have acquired Spanish at home and who have later relearned it in school, and who have overcome, as have the English speakers, the irrational bureaucracy that dominates public education.

At times English-speaking secondary and university students receive an excellent education in Spanish; their success as Spanish students is subject to purely individual factors as well as to factors outside their control — the school or university programs, the attitudes and dedication of their teachers, the accessibility of the courses in some Spanish-speaking country. If the students are lucky, they can receive several years of secondary or university instruction planned within the principles of a coherent curriculum, integrated with objectives that are both general and specific and with goals planned for short and long term. Within a reasonable period of time, the student can then master the language and fulfill the objectives of their program — master the spoken language on the various sociolinguistic levels, read works of literature and literary criticism, write papers that reflect their ability to understand literature and literary criticism. Given the vast production of literary works representative of the literature written in the Spanish language, one of the general objectives of the Spanish programs, secondary as well as university, is the knowledge, even superficial knowledge, of some Spanish and Latin American literary works. This objective, as praiseworthy as it is justifiable, is naturally disseminated in the great majority of the secondary and university programs and seems to reach, at least in theory, English as well as Spanish-speaking students.

United States Hispanics and Spanish Programs

Hispanic students who want to formally learn their native language are fortunate if they are able to attend a public secondary school or university that has a program which specializes in the teaching of Spanish as a native language. On the chance that such a program exists, it's probable that the student will receive instruction based on a philosophy promoted by Valdés-Fallis and Teschner (1985). This instruction attempts to create a linguistic awareness that helps the student distinguish the existing formal levels of the Spanish language while at the same time introduces lessons in reading, spelling, grammar, and writing, all designed for the specific needs of United States Hispanics.

The course, or series of courses, offered for United States Hispanics are generally known as SNS (Spanish for native speakers), and although the philosophy and methodology employed in SNS are the most pedagogically appropriate for the moment, only a handful of schools and universities can afford to offer them. A good number of public schools and universities lack this specialized teaching for United States Hispanics. This lack is due to many factors, such as: lack of specialized personnel; lack of orientation on the part of administrative personnel; negligence on the part of directors, parents and teachers; or simply ambivalence or openly negative attitudes on the part of the students who prefer to share learning with the English-speaking students because they consider it less demanding.

In the southern United States one can find structured programs that lead United States Hispanic students from a semi-literate level in their own language to a level of basic literary creation and criticism. For example, the programs at Florida International University, Arizona State University, The University of New Mexico, The University of Texas at El Paso, The University of Arizona, with large contingents of United States Hispanics, serve a large number of students who take advantage of this instruction and may continue to major in Spanish. However, the majority of the universities and secondary schools are faced with another problem that also affects the programs for English speakers: diagnostic tests and grade level exams. There are numerous inconsistencies in the diagnostic tests for English speakers, speakers who present relatively homogeneous characteristics if one compares them with groups of bilingual Spanish-speakers. The efforts to evaluate the oral and written production of United States Hispanics are lucidly exposed in Barkin (1981a and b), who not only presents a coherent four-level program, but also a series of strategies to test students at each level. A program so well-structured as Barkin's helps to minimize the problems of proficiency and to even out the levels of language mastery, as it is well known that United States Hispanics are bilingual to various degrees and have at their disposal a series of linguistic codes that are unfamiliar to English speakers.

United States Hispanics are active or passive bilinguals, and depending on the occasion, they master one language better than the other, they know how to read and write in one language better than in the other, and they have the ability to interact in sociocultural activities in one language with greater fluency and naturalness than in the other. In this heterogeneous group we find individuals who are totally bilingual, if it is understood that by bilingual we mean the perfect mastery of all oral and written linguistic levels of two or more languages. This type of bilingualism is very infrequent, and the educational system and the instructor are confronted with classifications that depend, at times, on their own criteria. Even in those countries that educate bilinguals with the greatest amount of efficiency, the educational system finds itself forced to classify in agreement with the school attended by the child, the personal criteria of the student, the grade obtained on an exam, or the linguistic antecedents (generally determined by the environment) of the individual in question (Baker, 1988). Balanced bilingualism that tends to produce functional individuals in both languages could be accomplished in circumstances identical to or similar to those experienced by Canadians in the Province of Quebec who have been fortunate enough to be educated in many academic subjects in two languages in an impeccable literary tradition. The bilingualism described by Lambert and Tucker (1972), based on the St. Lambert experiment, is bilingualism of the professional middle class, a product of efforts on the part of parents and educators belonging to a very advanced capitalist society.

United States Hispanics are, on the other hand, very far from acquiring the level of bilingualism attained by the Canadians. It would be more correct to affirm that United States Hispanics have been victims of an extremely erratic policy on bilingual education mediatized by the currents of the dominant majority. The education that United States Hispanics have received in their language is, in many respects, similar to that of the indigenous Mexicans, who have been denied global learning in their own language, a language which has been used as a mere transition in order to acquire the majority language: Spanish (Hamel, 1988).

The education of United States Hispanics in their own language has been erratic, insensitive, and very removed from the reality that daily bombards the speaker of a minority language or dialect. US Hispanics find themselves extremely limited in their interaction with speakers of the prestige language or variety. Although some United States Hispanics have preserved Spanish on a plane comparable to that of educated Hispanic Americans, a good proportion of them have not only lost the natural fluency of a native speaker, but what is perhaps even more unfortunate, they have lost confidence in their own linguistic competence. The home environment of United States Hispanics can encourage as well as frustrate the speakers if they compare themselves favorably or unfavorably with the members of their own family. The school environment, on the other hand, seems to cause more inhibitions than positive behavior oriented toward the maintenance of Spanish. The United States Hispanics then become the bearers of a bilingualism that is principally oral, a form of bilingualism in which only one variety tends to prevail: the colloquial variety of the family or the community. It should be noted, however, that a good number of United States Hispanics have constant contact with speakers from monolingual communities; this contact depends on a multitude of variables that the United States Hispanics cannot completely control: family visits, geographic proximity to the country of origin, access to means of communication in Spanish. These contacts with the country of origin give Hispanics the opportunity to at least listen to spoken Spanish by those who are monolingual, and at the same time it offers them opportunity to evaluate the speech of other Spanish speakers and to compare it with their own speech. United States Hispanics generally react positively toward the speech of Hispanic Americans and negatively toward their own. United States Hispanics then grow up with a devalued notion of their own speech, not because they have instruments to objectively consider it inferior, but because the majority society has imposed — at least at the psychological level — different norms that are 'better' or 'superior'.

Written Language, Standard Language and Curricular Problems

The objective of foreign language programs is to properly equip English-speakers with the ability to produce the language of educated speakers found in the large Spanish-speaking countries (Spain, Mexico, Columbia), because educated speech represents the norm of prestige, the correct style, the type of speech supposedly more like that of the written language. United States Hispanics, who have not received formal instruction in Spanish, can, on occasions, reorganize their oral structure and acquire or learn formal Spanish. Proof that this occurs is found in a handful of Mexican-American intellectuals who are dedicated to the teaching of Spanish.

However, not all of United States Hispanics have the time, the motivation, or the luck to (re)educate themselves in Spanish. The majority of them are confronted with a code that they have never written and that causes anxiety, fear, shame, or uncertainty, since they are aware that there is a correct form of saying things. United States Hispanics are convinced that their linguistic forms, whatever they might be, are not the correct ones. The task of Spanish for Native Speakers was, as was put forth in the articles and textbooks prepared for United States Hispanics, to gently lead the student to mastery of the written language. This form of education did not presuppose the *eradication* of United States Hispanics' dialect, but rather it presupposed that it would *complement* what educators considered that it lacked — the standard variety (Hidalgo, 1987a).

The teaching of the standard language is not an easy task; if this teaching is carried out, more years of instruction would be required in any educational program than in those that are currently dedicated to the teaching of Spanish for Native Speakers in the United States. This is so because the general objectives of the programs for Spanish as a second language (SSL) as well as the objectives of SNS are excessively ambitious and divorced from reality. Spanish programs in the United States have as their goal the preparation of students with the knowledge of the spoken and written language based on literary models. The patterns and structures of the oral language are not taught in their totality because they are not known. These objectives are very unrealistic, but they are also imposed, as we said, on United States Hispanic students who many times drop out of courses because they consider them to be intolerable.

Those professors, who by personal conviction or professional committment, want to teach SNS, are confronted not only with common bureaucratic barriers, but also with their own objectives and with the attitudes and uncertainties of their own students who seem to accentuate their ambivalence toward the written language: What use is it? Am I going to write well? How long will it take me to learn the correct vocabulary? How long will it take me to master the monstrous and at times contradictory Spanish grammar?

Around 1986–7 when I wrote the article that appeared in the *Hispanic Journal of Behavioral Sciences*, I was convinced that the teaching of the plural to speakers of Caribbean dialects and the teaching of gender and the subjunctive to all United States Hispanics was a necessary task, not only necessary, but beneficial for them. The restoration of such structures — based on the written language — could also restore United States Hispanics' confidence in themselves at the same time that it would put them in contact with a superior culture — the millenary Hispanic culture.

In this article I also proposed that we search for appropriate strategies and tactics in order to identify the more stigmatized morphosyntactic characteristics in the Spanish-speaking world, given that these characteristics seem to indicate with a certain precision the origin of an individual's class. The correction of these characteristics in United States Hispanics would, at least, help them to equate their way of speaking with that of educated individuals from Latin America. The morphosyntactic characteristics in question are the following: the addition of -s to the second person preterite form, i.e., *dijistes, trajistes, llegastes*, etc.; the accentuation of the antepenultimate syllable in the present subjunctive, i.e., *váyamos* instead of *vayamos, cómpremos* instead of *compremos*; and the use of -*nos* instead of -*mos* in the imperfect indicative as in *llegábanos* instead of *llegábamos*. In my opinion, these three morpho-syntactic characteristics are the most noticeable of the nonstandard structures heard from immigrants from the countryside to the city in the Republic of Mexico (Hidalgo, 1987b). These same characteristics also identify Mexican-American speakers of rural origin (Sánchez, 1983). My task in 1987 was to try to 'correct' such characteristics in Mexican-American students enrolled in Spanish classes at San Diego State University, a commuter university with an enrollment of about 3000 United States Hispanic students. Given that correction implies criticism of that which is perceived as erroneous or mistaken, the reaction of the Mexican-American students is confusion, shame, or contained anger, since this correction reminds the individual of the speech of their grand-parents, their parents, their older siblings, and all those people who they most love. The sporadic and asystematic correction of an adult implies, then, humili-ation by what is one's own, contempt for what is authentic, disdain for the le-gitimacy of the dialect or idiolect. Other reasons have prevented me from initiating the practice that I previously proposed; one of them is that I have frequently heard some of the characteristics previously described used by our graduate students who have come from Mexico City and Tijuana and in educated speakers from Chile and Argentina.

Better results are obtained when the standard forms are acquired over time (during childhood and adolescence), and they are unconsciously and naturally assimilated by means of daily contact with the standard variety that is taught, principally, at school. Mastery of the standard form, even in countries where Spanish is the majority language, requires a slow process which is subjected to a number of social and cultural variables that do not depend on the individual.

In Mexico, for example, where a good part of United States Hispanics come from, studies reveal the many problems of monolingual children enrolled in pro-grams designed for reading and writing Spanish. Achievement in spelling and academic subjects is superior among children from urban areas (versus children from rural areas), among middle-class children, and among female students (Avila, 1986). However, minimal discrepancies between oral and written language cause some problems in writing that can only be overcome with many hours of in-struction, even among students who speak the Castilian variety of Spanish, who need, according to a Spanish educator, at least 600 hours of study outside of the classroom in order to master Spanish spelling alone, as this spelling is based on the pronunciation of the Castilian variety (Avila, 1986).

Faced with this desolate panorama, professors of Spanish teaching United States Hispanics cannot and should not expect their students to attain a quasi-literate mastery of their mother tongue because the educational system has not offered them opportunities galore to educate themselves in their own language. We also cannot expect them to constantly utilize Spanish-speakers as a source, as a model, or as an instrument of aid. Along the same lines, we should desist in the anti-pedagogical practice of evaluating them unfavorably if they make orthographic and syntactic errors on their exams, compositions, or other written work, since writing in Spanish has been neither a general nor a specific objective in the public educational system nor in Spanish courses for English-speakers. The situation of those who want to major in Spanish within the universities seems to be more critical. United States Hispanics then find more obstacles, anti-professional atti-tudes on the part of the teachers, programs with extremely ambitious objectives which are out of reach for United States Hispanics as well as for English-speakers. We should ask ourselves if the objectives proposed up until now by those of us who teach Spanish — mastery of literary language — are realistic and can be attained within the framework of our academic programs. On the other hand, we should also question if the pseudo-programs for English-speakers, as well as for Spanish speakers, are completely congruent with the traditional humanistic edu-cation that those of us who belong to other generations received, or if we should transform them and readapt them to the needs of a pragmatic society that values competence in effective oral communication.

Oral Proficiency and United States Hispanics

According to Valdés (1989), the objectives of oral proficiency, initially proposed for speakers of Spanish as a second language (SSL), conflict with the sociolinguistic reality of United States Hispanics. One of the greatest problems stems from the criteria utilized in the evaluation and measurement of the linguistic proficiency of United States Hispanics, since the description of the features of the Foreign Service Institute (FSI) is based on criteria applicable to English speakers, although the model of such features is in itself a model that supposedly reflects the average linguistic behavior of an educated Spanish speaker. The features in question did not include United States Hispanics in their goals, something that could imply, as a consequence, that the objectives of the programs for United States Hispanics should be modified so that they abandon written practice and emphasize oral proficiency. This task would involve the tacit acceptance of the criteria of the FSI, that, according to Valdés (1989:397–401), are contradictory and elitist because they are based on the criteria that only the linguistic production of a limited number of inhabitants of the large Spanish-speaking capitals is inherently correct and acceptable.

We must remember, however, that the differences between Mexican and standard Chicano Spanish are minimal at the purely linguistic level. The discrepancies between one variety and the other operate at the functional level, and there are regions in the United States (the border between Mexico and the United States) where a Mexican is indistinguishable from a Chicano of urban origin. There are, on the other hand, United States Hispanics whose fluency is not totally native, but who have the motivation to (re)learn or acquire the standard variety. I do not believe, as Valdés affirms, that the criteria of the FSI are impossible to apply to United States Hispanics, because there is evidence that it has been done successfully (Barkin, 1981a and 1981b). Even if the criteria were totally arbitrary, I believe that SNS programs, instead of having as their ultimate objective the understanding of literary creation and literary creation itself, can be molded to help the students receive an acceptable score on the FSI exams, especially since this exam seems to have as much authority as the Dictionary of the Royal Spanish Academy itself.

The objectives of a SNS program are as utopian and inconsistent as the criteria of the FSI can be. Those of us who teach SNS are faced with, as I mentioned earlier, a conservative atmosphere that dominates the country, with a bureaucracy of intransigent educational policy concerning minorities, with the utopian objectives of an incoherent and inoperable curriculum in contemporary society and with attitudes that are overtly negative on the part of many Spanish professors. It is not surprising then that US Hispanics react with a painful ambivalence when confronted with a task that we have made nearly impossible.

Some Practical Suggestions

If the objectives of SNS are inoperable, at least for some Spanish speakers that have never had the opportunity to study the written language, and if the criteria of the FSI dismiss United States Hispanics who do not have mastery over an acceptable variety of Spanish, I propose to introduce introductory courses for oral proficiency that will serve as a transition as well as a common SNS program for a possible FSI exam. The activities of these introductory courses can also be used in the classroom where as many United States Hispanics as English-speakers are found. Some of the activities that I carry out in these introductory courses are:

1) *Comprehension exercises in standard dialects* (i.e., Castilian Spanish from Madrid, Mexican Spanish)

Frequently, United States Hispanic students indicate that they do not understand television and radio programs in Spanish because the language used in these programs is rapid, telegraphic and uses very sophisticated vocabulary. To raise the level of comprehension, I use commercial tapes from *La Puerta del Sol*, that utilize academic themes as well as popular ones. These commercial tapes were prepared for English speakers, but they are a magnificent resource for both groups. The more pedagogical component of this series is probably the varied vocabulary because it covers both the specialized lexicon from several disciplines (politics, psychology, etc.), and the daily expressions typical from Madrid. Students can listen to these tapes as many times as necessary and extract from them the main ideas, learned lexicon and colloquial vocabulary, etc.

In those areas of the United States where there is access to Spanish language television, we can use as resources soap operas, news programs, sports commentaries and documentaries that can be converted into academic assignments that raise the level of comprehension of the standard language. The language spoken on the radio and television can be used so that students learn to recognize the different levels of formality and the various dialects that exist in the Spanish-speaking world.

2) *Exercises for the production of the standard language*

Research in the area of foreign languages offers a series of strategies for communication that can be used in courses for United States Hispanics. Textbooks like *Pasajes: Actividades* (Bretz, *et al.*, 1987) are full of useful suggestions, for example, the formulation of questions, debate, argumentation, description, narration, creation of hypothetical situations, strategies for asking for help, advice, translation, interpretation, etc. Based on the themes of this very varied text, students can also prepare themselves to emulate real-life situations — helping monolinguals with translation and interpretation, looking for a job, asking professional advice, interviewing famous people or simply asking information in an imaginary Spanish-speaking country. The comprehension activities, as well as those for production, have as their objective improving the quality of the language, helping the United States Hispanics to recover confidence in themselves.

3) *The task of assigning grades*

The comprehension exercises can easily be graded if the students are asked to identify the principal ideas and the vocabulary selected by the professor. The exams should be based on the tapes that have become (almost) totally familiar from so much repetition. Grades can also be assigned for the formal vocabulary which was previously investigated, for grammatical precision, and for communication with an audience.

The correction of nonstandard grammatical structures should proceed with caution and the teacher should select those structures that are obviously rejected by the educated majority (i.e., *producí, conducí, pidía, muría*, etc.). However, there is no efficient formula that allows us to correct without hurting the feelings of the rest of the students. In my courses, I resort to a kind lie — the nonstandard forms approximate child language that is affective and spontaneous, but as adults we must mature and begin to recognize the linguistic forms found in books.

Conclusion

I hope that these suggestions help to alleviate the anxiety of a teacher who faces a group of Spanish speakers, or the anxiety of Spanish and English speakers. There is a great deal left for us to do concerning the education of minority groups. We could take a step forward in this titanic task if we Spanish professors accept the bilingual varieties that are being coined in the United States and if we bring them into the classroom in order to mold and sculpt them with firmness and compassion.

Note

1 Translation by Kathi Leonard, PhD., Department of Spanish, University of California, Davis.

References

AVILA, R. (1986) 'Sólo para tus oídos', in LARA, L.F. and GARRIDO, F. (Eds) *Escritura y Alfabetización*, México: Ediciones de Ermitaño, pp. 11–38.

BAKER, C. (1988) 'Normative testing and bilingual populations', *Journal of Multilingual and Multicultural Development*, 9, pp. 399–409.

BARKIN, F. (1981a) 'Establishing criteria for bilingual literacy: The case of bilingual university students', *The Bilingual Review/La Revista Bilingüe*, 8, pp. 1–13.

BARKIN, F. (1981b) 'Evaluating linguistic proficiency: The case of teachers in bilingual programs', in VALDÉS, G., LOZANO, A.G. and GARCIA-MOYA, R. (Eds) *Teaching Spanish to the Hispanic Bilingual: Issues, Aims, and Methods*, New York, NY, Teachers College Press, pp. 215–233.

BRETZ, M.L., DVORAK, T. and KIRSCHNER, C. (1987) *Pasajes Actividades*, New York, NY, Random House.

BURUNAT, S. and STARCEVIC, E. (1983) *El Español y su Estructura*, Ft. Worth, TX, Holt, Rinehart & Winston.

DONAHUE, T. (1985) 'US English: Its Life and Works', *International Journal of the Sociology of Language*, 56, pp. 99–112.

FISHMAN, J.A. (1985) *The Rise and Fall of the Ethnic Revival in the United States: Perspectives on Language and Ethnicity*, The Hague, Netherlands, Mouton Co.

GARCIA, O. and OTHEGUY, R. (1988) 'The language situation of Cuban-Americans', McKAY, S.L. and WONG, S.C. (Eds) *Language Diversity: Problem or Resource?* Cambridge, MA, Newbury.

García, O., Evangelista, I., Martinez, M., Disla, C. and Paulino, B. (1988) 'Spanish language use and attitudes: A Study of two New York City communities', *Language in Society*, **4**, 1, pp. 475–511.

Hamel, R.E. (1988) 'Determinantes sociolingüístícas de la educación indígena bilingüe', *Signos: Anuario de Humanidades*, México, Universidad Autónoma Metropolitana pp. 319–76.

Heath, S.B. (1981) 'English in our language heritage' in Ferguson, C.A. and Heath, S.B. (Eds) *Language in the USA*, Cambridge, MA, Newbury, pp. 6–20.

Hidalgo, M. (1986) 'Two recent contributions to the study of US Spanish', *Hispanic Journal of Behavioral Sciences*, **8**, 1, pp. 80–94.

Hidalgo, M. (1987a) 'On the question of "Standard" vs. "Dialect": Implications for teaching Hispanic college students', *Hispanic Journal Of Behavioral Sciences*, **9**, 4, pp. 375–95.

Hidalgo, M. (1987b) 'Español mexicano y español chicano: Problemas y propuestas fundamentales', *Language Problems and Language Planning*, **11**, 2, pp. 166–93.

Lambert, W.E. and Tucker, G.R. (1972) *Bilingual Education of Children: The St. Lambert Experiment*, Rowley, MA, Newbury House.

Marqués, S. (1986) *La Lengua que Heredamos*, New York, NY, John Wiley & Sons.

Mejías, H.A. and Garza-Swan, G. (1981) *Nuestro Español*, New York, NY: Macmillan.

Sánchez, R. (1983) *Chicano Discourse: A Socio-historic Perspective*, Rowley, MA: Newbury House.

Valdés, G., Lozano, A.G. and Garcia-Moya, R. (Eds) (1981) *Teaching Spanish to the Hispanic Bilingual: Issues, Aims and Methods*, New York, NY, Teachers College Press.

Valdés-Fallis, G. and Teschner, R. (1985) *Español Escrito*, New York, NY, Scribners and Sons.

Valdés, G. (1989) 'Teaching Spanish to Hispanic bilinguals: A look at oral proficiency testing and the proficiency movement', *Hispania*, **72**, 2, pp. 392–401.

Chapter 7

Bilingual Code-Switching:
An Overview of Research

Lenora A. Timm

Introduction

A prominent form of communication among Chicanos and other US Hispanics involves the alternating use of Spanish and English within and between sentences in ordinary conversation. This form of communication, usually called code-switching,[1] has received a great deal of attention in recent years, chiefly from linguists but also from educators, who are often concerned about the wisdom of encouraging this type of language behavior in the classroom. The purpose of this chapter is to provide an overview of the linguistic and sociolinguistic research on this widespread bilingual mode of talk, and then, later, to consider the question of code-switching in the classroom.

Code-switching may be defined as the alternating, or switching, of two different languages at the word, phrase, clause, or sentence level (Valdés, 1981:95). This alternation is not random or chaotic (as was once thought), but generally adheres to certain constraints or rules as to the types of switches that are acceptable.

The alternation of languages in code-switching must not be mistaken for interference, which refers to the importation of a linguistic structure from one language directly into another. Interference probably operates most clearly at the level of phonology — for example, when a native English speaker pronounces a Spanish tap or trill as an American English *r*, phonetically [r]: [*mira*] for [*mira*], etc. True alternation of languages, or code-switching, involves using integral swatches of one language followed by integral swatches of another, between or within sentences. Examples follow (the language which is switched to is indicated in capital letters; the Spanish portion is translated underneath):

1 '*Siga yendo, los dos*', *les digo*. THEY DON'T WANT TO. (Timm, 1975: 482). ('Keep going, the two of you', I tell them);

2 I went when I was twenty *A LA CAPITAL* (Jacobson, 1982:199). (to the Capitol);

3 . . . since he has been here fifty years *PERO MIS HERMANOS NO HABLAN EL ESPAÑOL TAMBIEN COMO YO* because . . . (*ibid.*:198). (but my brothers also don't speak Spanish, like me);

4 *Pero verdad que* IT WAS WORTH IT (Valdés, 1982:218). (But it's true that);

5 *No van a* BRING IT UP AT THE MEETING (Pfaff, 1979:271). (They're not going to);

Now, in hearing such bilingual talk, particularly as shown in 2–5, people customarily think that this is some confused mixture of two languages, evidence of insufficient competence in either one. Even bilinguals who engage in this kind of talk may characterize it as sloppy or improper — or deny that they even do it at all (because they regard it as a stigmatized way of communicating). However, the truth is that code-switching is a very frequent mode of discourse among bilingual (or multilingual) peoples whose languages have been in contact for a considerable period of time, where the majority of speakers in the speech community are, as a result, bilingual, and where the languages are not socially or functionally distinctly compartmentalized — by this I mean that there are not rather consciously drawn lines of demarcation between the languages with regard to which language is the only appropriate one for given situations or contexts. (Speech communities in which this happens are said to be diglossic, and in such cases code-switching is less likely to occur).

Many of the numerous Chicano speech communities in the Southwest US fulfill the requirements just mentioned, and accordingly they provide a setting conducive to code-switching. Although I will be focusing on Spanish-English code-switching within the Southwest context, it is important to point out that this type of bilingual communication has been documented in many other parts of the US and in other parts of the world, for that matter, in modern and historical times. For example, researchers have investigated the language alternation patterns of speakers of such other pairs of languages in this country as: English and Swedish, English and Greek, English and Italian; and, in other countries (and other times, in some cases), of switching between French and Russian, Latin and German, Italian and French, Hindi and English, Italian and German, Swahili and English, Swahili and Kikuyu, French and Bantu, and more. Examples of code-switching among a few of these pairs of languages are given in 6–9:

6 *Domine, MEIN ALLMECHTIGER GOTT, quam libenter fudissem sanguinem pro tuo verbo . . . tu es deus vitae et mortis. MEIN ALLERLIBSTER GOTT . . . DU HAST MICH IN DIE SACH GEFURTT, DU WEIST DAS ES DEIN WARHEIT UND WORT IST, ne glorific inimicos. . . .* (Stolt, 1969–70:433).
('Lord . . . you are the god of life and death./ My dearest God . . . you have led me to this circumstance., you know that it is your truth and your promise;/ do not praise enemies . . .') (German/Latin, Martin Luther, 16th c.);

7 *Je suis votre VERNY RAB, et à vous seule je puis l'avouer. MOI DETI-Ce sont les entraves de mon existence. ETO MOY KREST. YA TAK SEBYE OBYASNYAYU. Que voulez-vous?* (Tolstoy, 1960, vol. 1, p. 10). ('I am your/faithful servant,/and to you alone I can confess. / My children — they are the bane of my existence. / This is my cross, This is how I explain to it myself./ What can I do?') (French/Russian, 19th c. Russian aristocracy);

8 *Ik was achtenzestig jaar BEFORE ik kon GET mijn PENSION* ('I was 68
/ before / I could / get/ my / pension') (Dutch/English, 20th-c. Australia
[Clyne, 1987:754]);
9 *IL FAUT pe biso to-sala makasi*
(We must / make a serious effort') (Lingala Bantu/French, Republic of
Zaire [Bokamba, 1988:38]).

In encountering and documenting such forms of speech, linguists and sociolinguists have sought to answer a number of critical questions, including:

- Is code-switching linked in demonstrable ways with the level of profi-
  ciency of speakers as bilinguals?
- Is code-switching linguistically constrained (i.e., are their 'rules' about
  when to switch, or when not to switch)?
- What are the social-cultural dimensions of code-switching talk?
- What discourse functions does code-switching serve?
- What relationship does spoken code-switching bear to code-switching in
  literature?
- What is, and should be, the role of code-switching in the classroom?

In this chapter I shall try to provide an overview of the answers to these questions
that investigators have been pondering for nearly twenty years of researching this
phenomenon.

Inasmuch as code-switching has been a much maligned form of communication both within and outside of the speech communities in which it is practiced,
a first opinion formed by many who hear code-switched dialogue is that those
who do this must not have very good command of either or both of the languages
involved. This impression may be reinforced by personal experience in learning
a second language, in which learners find themselves trying to formulate a sentence in L2 (the 'target' language) and then resorting somewhere along the way
in the sentence to L1 (the native language) for lack of knowledge either about the
grammatical structures required to continue in L2 or to fill a lexical gap in L2
vocabulary. Language learners do this all the time, and although it does represent
a sort of code-switching — let's call it learners' code-switching — it results from
cognitive and linguistic processes quite unrelated to the code-switching under
discussion here, which is sometimes referred to in the literature as true code-
switching; one may also think of it as competent or proficient code-switching,
which serves various narrative and social purposes, unlike learners' code-switching,
which is chiefly a 'crutching' device.

True code-switching flourishes in bilingual environments (communities) of
more than one generation's depth in which both languages are used by most
speakers on a daily basis and each language corresponds to a distinct set of sociocultural institutions. While such conditions do not guarantee the presence of code-
switching, they are ones typically associated with it. Studies to date have also
indicated that the most proficient code-switchers are the most proficient bilinguals,
for while it is true that speakers obviously weaker in one language than the other
may also engage in some code-switching talk, the 'deepest' code-switchers need
to be highly competent in all linguistic aspects of both languages (Poplack, 1980).
'Deepest' here refers to speakers' ability to engage in complex code-switching
interpolations of the type shown in examples 10 to 12:

10   *Siempre está* PROMISING *cosas* (Poplack, 1980:243). (She is always promising things);

11   *Anda* FEELING *medio* NICE *y* START BLOWING AGAIN (Pfaff 1979: 276) (He starts feeling rather nice and starts blowing off again);

12   *LOS ÚNICOS* that we have to *WACHAR* for *SON* the county gringo cops (López, López and López, 1971) (The only ones that we have to look out for are the county gringo cops).

Intersentential vs. Intrasentential Switching

Sentences 10–12 above provide examples of what is called in the literature 'intrasentential' code-switching (that which occurs within a sentence or clause), which contrasts sharply with 'intersentential' switching in terms of the linguistic resources required to weave successfully this linguistic tapestry. Interestingly, it was only the latter type of switching that seemed to attract any notice in earlier days of research on bilingual speech; it is almost as if there were massive denial of the possibility of alternation within a single sentence. Yet, scholars who have focused their research attention primarily on code-switching in the past two decades have gleaned the most interesting results about the do's and don'ts of switching as a linguistic phenomenon and about what factors motivate code-switching in the first place.

Patterns Underlying Code-switching

There are two distinct types of patterns underlying code-switching that are important to discuss — the *linguistic* and the *extra-linguistic*. The linguistic patterning has been described chiefly in terms of constraints — limitations or rules — about what constituents are switchable in a sentence. Constraints have changed from being quite specific in formulation with regard to which stretches of constituents may not be switched to being more general, more abstract, more universalistic in nature. I was one of those investigators fifteen years ago working to develop the initial formulations about what cannot be code-switched, on the basis of data gathered in working with Southwestern Chicanos and Chicanas. In a work published in 1975, I proposed five constraints on code-switching; these are presented as 1–5 below:

1. No switching between a pronominal subject or object and adjacent verb. This prohibits sequences such as *I/fui, Yo* went (I went), *María traía*/it, Mary it *traía*, (María carried it) and many more.

2. No switching between a verb and a following preposition or particle that is in turn followed by an infinitive. This prohibits switches such as (They) want/*a venir, quieren*/to come (They want to come). In other words, the preposition or particle must be in the same code as the finite verb that precedes. Thus, it is permissible to have sequences such as They want to/*venir, quieren a*/come right away, *va a/ charter/un camion*, etc.

3. No switching between auxiliaries (including modals) and a following main verb. Thus, the following would be ungrammatical: I must/*esperar* (I must wait),

97

Debo/wait; She has/*visto*, *(Ella) ha*/seen (she has seen); They were/*caminando*, *Estaban*/walking (they were walking), etc. However, research subsequent to my own showed that sequences such as the last two — where there is a switch between an auxiliary and a present participle — are in fact allowable and not uncommon. For example, Rogelio Reyes (1982) documented (for Arizona Spanish) — sentences such as *Los están* BUSSING *pa 'otra escuela* (they were bussing them to the other school); and Carol Pfaff (1979) for California Spanish documented the following (among others): *Estaba* TRAINING *para pelear* (he was training to fight); *¿Dónde estás* TEACHING? (Where are you teaching?) *Yo creo que apenas se había* WASHED OUT (I think that it has just washed out).

Notice that the direction of the shift in these examples is always from a Spanish auxiliary to an English main verb. It seems likely to me that it is to a considerable extent the sociocultural semantic content of these English verbs that influences the switches: 'bussing', 'training', 'teaching' all refer to essentially Anglo activities. 'Wash out', on the other hand, has the force of an idiom, and researchers have documented repeatedly that idioms are not broken up by code-switching.

4. A constraint that I delineated in 1975 was: No switching in negative constructions between the negating element (or elements) and the verb. This is a powerful constraint that disallows such formulations as I don't/*quiero*, *(Yo)* no/want, I/no quiero, I/no/want, etc.

5. Adjectives in Noun Phrases are generally in the same language as the head noun and generally follow the rule for adjective placement that is operative in the language of the head noun. This last constraint is far more flexible than the others, but does suggest the following pattern: When the head noun of an NP is in English, the adjective is generally placed before it and when the head noun is in Spanish, the adjective generally follows it. Thus, we find NPs such as: *su*/favorite spot and not **su favorito* spot; his *lugar favorito* and not *his/lugar*/favorite, etc. Of course, if the two languages would place an adjective in the same slot in relation to the noun, the switching may occur — e.g., *el*/next day (Sp. *el próximo día*), *mi único*/pleasure (Sp. *mi único gusto* my sole pleasure), *el siguiente*/play (Sp. *el siguiente drama* the next play/drama).

There were so few data available in the early 1970s on linguistic aspects of code-switching among other pairs of languages that I was hesitant to do more than suggest that the constraints that seemed representative of my data might well turn up in other bilingual contact situations.[2] Subsequent research on Spanish and English code-switching as well as other language pairs gradually revealed that my constraints did not have the power of categorical rules, though they did still represent tendencies, even within the gradually massive amounts of data that were being collected on the phenomenon. It was becoming evident to all that, although difficult to characterize, there clearly were syntactic principles of some sort at work (in addition to semantic, pragmatic, stylistic ones) in the production of bilingual code-switching talk.

The More Generalizing Attempts

As a result of the counterexamples encountered using the constituent-specific sorts of rules that I, and others, had been proposing, several linguists in the late 1970s to early 80s began formulating constraints at a higher level of generalization. I shall not cover all of these here, but will explain a few that have been much cited in the literature. Lipski (1978:258), for example, proposed a constraint that he dubbed 'Hypothesis B', which may be informally stated as follows: 'Whereas the portion of a code-switched utterance that falls before the code switch may indeed contain syntactically divergent elements, those falling after the switch must be essentially identical'. What is meant by 'essentially identical' is not entirely clear, but an example he provided is shown in example 13:

13   There are many families on the block *QUE TIENEN CHAMAQUITOS* (who have kids)

According to Lipski's hypothesis, this code-switched sentence is acceptable because the English version of the switched-to portion, *who have kids*, is syntactically identical in its configuration with the Spanish *que tienen chamaquitos* (Lipski, 1985: 44). This hypothesis is attractive and does seem to account for many instances of code-switching within sentences, but nevertheless encounters some problems in light of sentences such as those illustrated in 10–12.

Shana Poplack (1981:175) formulated another, somewhat similar, hypothesis called the 'equivalence constraint' which states that 'codes will tend to be switched at points where juxtaposition of English and Spanish elements does not violate a syntactic rule of either language — i.e., at points where the surface structures of the languages map onto each other.' She illustrates the operation of this constraint with the following trio of related sentences (the first wholly in English, the second wholly in Spanish, and the third in code-switched format):

14   I. . . . told him. . . . that   so that. . . . he. . . . . would bring it. . . . fast
14a   (*Yo*). . . . . *le dije*. . . . . *eso*   *pa'que*. . . . (*el*). . . . . *la trajera*. . . . . . *ligero*
14b   I. . . . told him. . . . that   *pa'que*. . . . (*el*). . . . . *la trajera*. . . . . . *ligero* .

(Dotted lines represent the only points at which switching is possible according to this constraint).

Basically Poplack's claim is that switching cannot take place within a constituent generated by a rule from one language that is not shared by the other (this prohibits, for example, switching between the verb and the object pronoun, since the two languages have different rules for placement of a pronominal direct object). This constraint has been shown to have wide applicability to code-switching talk, and has been especially valid for the Spanish/English case. It has, however, been shown to be untenable for some cases of code-switching, which would take me too far afield to discuss here (see Bokamba, 1988).

Poplack (1980) also proposed a constraint called the 'Free Morpheme Constraint', which states that switching may not occur between a bound morpheme and a free morpheme — in other words, switches can only be at the boundaries of free morphemes. This prohibits the production of such items as *habling* or *talkiendo*. This constraint also has wide applicability.

In more recent years theoretical linguists working within the framework of 'government' and 'binding' have turned their attention to code-switching, and proposed a 'government constraint', to wit that 'switching is possible only between elements not related to government (for example V governs O and P governs the NP in a PP)' (DiSciullo, Muysken and Singh, 1986, cited in Clyne, 1987:748). However, it appears that although this constraint works for the Italian-French and Hindi-English data they present, it does not allow for very commonly heard switches between V and an object NP as in *Los hombres comieron*/the sandwiches (The men ate the sandwiches).

Thus, while the constraints have become loftier in compass, most have not become airtight. In two recent articles from non-Euro-American settings, Clyne (1987) for Australia and Bokamba (1988) for Africa (with a focus on Bantu languages in interaction with each other and with English and French), it is demonstrated that each of the above constraints admits exceptions. To date the most successful hypothesis about the syntactic limits on code-switching appears to be the 'Dual Structure Principle' formulated by S.N. Sridhar and K. Sridhar (1980), based on their work with English and a Dravidian language. This constraint is constructed around the concepts of a 'host' language (the base language) and a 'guest' language (the language of the switch). Their principle reads: 'The internal structure of the guest constituent need not conform to the constituent structure of the host language, so long as its placement in the host language obeys the rules of the host language' (1980:7). For example, consider 15 (the host language is Kannada):

15 *Avanu obba* MAN OF CONSIDERABLE COURAGE (he is)

Here we have a complex NP in English, *man of considerable courage*, which if it were translated word-for-word in Kannada would not be at all grammatical (since Kannada requires that nouns be modified pre-nominally, not post-nominally). Thus, the authors argue that the English portion of this sentence is not 'essentially identical' (*pace* Lipski) to the equivalent Kannada one, and yet the code-switch is quite acceptable.[3] This is accounted for by their Dual Structure Principle, which focuses on the *external relationship* that the switched-to constituents in the guest language bears to the constituents in the host language.

As helpful as the gradual refinements of the 'grammar' of switching have been in leading us to a greater understanding of the complexity of bilingual talk, it is arguable that no purely syntactic analysis will ever be wholly satisfactory for a full appreciation of the phenomenon. Rather, for each pair or triad of languages that enter into code-switching it will be necessary to consider the particulars not only of the relevant language structures but also of the semantics and discourse traditions of the particular speech communities in which switching is being documented. Future accounts of the possibilities and the limits of code-switching will also undoubtedly benefit from additional research by psycholinguists and others concerned with the mental (neurolinguistic) mechanisms of language processing.

Extra-linguistic Factors Involved in Code-switching

Although as a linguist I have been deeply interested in trying to track the syntactic limits of code-switching, I must admit finding equally fascinating the various functions code-switching plays in the discourse of bilinguals. In some ways, research into these aspects of switching has been more fruitful than the purely linguistic investigations, in the sense that we seem to have quite solid agreement among dozens of researchers as to at least some of the 'reasons'[4] bilinguals switch code. Over the years numerous classifications of 'reasons why' bilinguals code switch have been provided; they differ in detail, but, as noted, generally come up with similar inventories. Valdés-Fallis (1978), for example, offers a convenient tabular summary of 'Principal code-switching patterns' which suggests that switching occurs in response to two general categories of motivation — 'switching in response to external factors' [i.e., sociocultural and stylistic] and 'switching in response to internal [i.e., linguistic or conversational] factors.' This classification is indicative but not exhaustive; we may add, for example, under 'external factors' personal or affective motivations such as feelings of anger, frustration, affection, pride, etc. In my own data on Spanish-English switching, I found that

> a switch to S[panish] is a device for indicating such personal feelings as affection, loyalty, commitment, respect, pride, challenge, sympathy, or religious devotion . . . Conversely, a switch to E[nglish] often signals a speaker's feelings of detachment, objectivity, alienation, displeasure, dislike, conflict of interest, aggression, fear, or pain (Timm, 1975:475).

This Spanish-to-English shift is illustrated neatly in the following passage written by author Ricardo Sánchez (quoted in Pfaff, 1979:295):

16 Why, I questioned myself, did I have to daily portray myself as a gringo
    CUANDO MI REALIDAD TENÍA MAS SANGRE Y PASIÓN?
    ('when my reality encompassed more blood and passion')

Topic changes, of course, frequently trigger language shifts, and in Chicano speech communities it is natural enough for a switch to English to occur when there is a topic shift in the conversation to matters typically Anglo-American (such as national politics, the educational system, etc. — note Valdés-Fallis' example of shifting to English to discuss the details of a math exam). Another example may be seen in the following fragment of a conversation among family members in their home, reported in Huerta-Macías (1981:158). She uses it to illustrate specifically a switch to English, which she says takes place 'whenever a topic outside the home domain was discussed, particularly when the topic related to work or school.'

17 L: *Ví a Betsy con el DOCTOR*
        (I saw Betsy with the doctor)
    G: *¿Está trabajando?*
        (Is she working?)
    L: MR. PAGE GOT FIRED [*Mr. Page worked with Betsy*]
    G: MR. PAGE? WHY?
    L: I DON'T KNOW. SHE SAID HE WAS THERE ON A FRIDAY
        AND THEN ON MONDAY HE JUST DIDN'T COME BACK.
    G: *¡Hijo! ¡Qué monjas!*
        (Oh boy! What nuns!)

An earlier classification of motivations for code-switching proposes that switches activated by factors relating to topical and affective factors be termed 'metaphorical' switching; these are to be contrasted with 'situational' switching which is triggered by a change in the speakers' 'definition of each other's rights and obligations' (Blom and Gumperz, 1972) — in other words, a change in the nature of the social situation due to perceived changes in the roles of the interactants, in turn due to the entry into the scene of new speakers, or to the change of locale and/or domain of activity. The latter type of switching (situational) is indeed very common among bi- and multilingual peoples, especially when there are fairly clearly demarcated domains of appropriateness for one language or the other (as in diglossic societies). It is the same principle, in fact, which causes monolinguals to shift from one style of speech to another as they move from social domain to social domain — e.g., from a formal lecture to a dinner party conversation with friends. For many bilinguals there is the additional option, as legitimated by the norms of their speech community, of switching not just styles within one of their languages, but of switching languages entirely; additionally within each language, there is the option of selecting dialects, registers, or styles to suit the occasion. For example, in Chicano Spanish, many speakers have access to Caló[5] or other popular varieties of Spanish that may be drawn on as desired as the speech situation changes. To add one more technical term, we may say that bilinguals possess a more complex 'linguistic repertoire' (inventory of linguistic resources) than do monolinguals; for many there is the additional resource of code-switching. Schematically:

MONOLINGUAL LINGUISTIC REPERTOIRE

Language A

Styles/registers$_A$
Regional dialect(s)$_A$
Social dialect(s)$_A$
Standard$_A$

BILINGUAL LINGUISTIC REPERTOIRE

Languages A and B

Style/Registers$_A$ ←c/s→ Style/Registers$_B$
Regional Dialect(s)$_A$ ←c/s→ Regional Dialect(s)$_B$
Social Dialect(s)$_A$ ←c/s→ Social Dialect(s)$_B$
Standard Language$_A$ ←c/s→ (Standard Language$_B$)
(c/s and the arrows indicate the potential for bilingual code-switching)

I have placed Standard Language$_B$ in parentheses to indicate the possibility, frequently realized among bilinguals, that the standard or literary form of one of their languages — if it is a minority language — may not be part of their repertoire, given lack of exposure to it (since minority languages are not usually offered within the educational system).

A further perspective (in addition to the metaphorical and the situational) on why bilinguals switch code is found in the work of Sánchez (1983) on Chicano discourse. Sánchez argues that there is an 'ideological' dimension to

Spanish/English code-switching that may operate at the level of implicit oppositions in speakers' minds (deriving from their sociocultural background and interactions). She gives the example (p. 172) of

Chicano population — subordinate minority group
vs.   *vs.*
Anglo population — superordinate majority group

Such 'we/they' ideological oppositions may give rise to more specific psycho-social oppositions such as antagonism vs. solidarity, dominance vs. subordination, and acceptance vs. rejection (p. 175). Her discussion of this dimension is very useful, but I feel that, in the final analysis, this ideological dimension underlying code-switching is closely related to motivations for switching that were discussed above as 'metaphorical'.

To sum up this section, we can say that code-switching is a highly complex phenomenon that cannot be fully analyzed without recourse to many factors of both a linguistic and nonlinguistic nature. 'True' code-switchers are bilinguals competent in two languages, reflected in the richness of their linguistic repertoires. Linguistically it is never possible to predict when a person will switch code (any more than it is possible to predict when a monolingual will select a particular word or phrase over another one), though it is possible, on the contrary, to posit linguistic boundaries where switching is not likely to take place. None of the constraints on switching thus far proposed have proven exceptionless, but they are nevertheless indicative of powerful tendencies among bilingual speakers representing many sets of languages.

Motivations underlying code-switching discourse are diverse, but are strongly patterned, again, across many sets of languages. Both linguistic and extra-linguistic factors are clearly at work in producing code-switched discourse. As Sánchez concludes, what is involved is not only

... shifting from one language to another but shifting from one level of meaning to another. Shifted utterances are never mere translations; they carry additional connotations. . . . A study of code-switching entails knowledge of the speaker's cultural background and values as well as close contact with the dynamic bilingualism prevalent in the area, for this information is essential in analyzing the semiotic and ideological constraints determining code-switching (1983:176).

Code-switching in Literature

Although bilinguals have been code-switching for countless centuries, it is only in very recent times that this form of talk has been legitimized, so to speak, through its appearance in published literature. Spanish/English literature has flourished in the United States particularly in both the Chicano and Puerto-Rican communities. Poetry is the genre most frequently expressed in a code-switching mode, though short stories, children's stories, and novels have also made use of this resource. The code-switching that I have examined in literary works resembles

that heard in spoken discourse, but more frequently violates the syntactic constraints discussed above. This is not surprising, considering the visual effects that
a writer can achieve through code-switching that a spontaneous code-switching
speaker cannot. Nevertheless, my impression of literary code-switching texts that
I have examined is that they do not stray very far from the norms of the written
mode; they cannot if the writer wishes to be taken seriously. I have included for
consideration a selection of code-switched poems and samples of texts:

The first poem is by Alurista (Alberto Urista), a pioneer in bringing code-
switching into the literary arena, beginning in the late 1960s. Due in large measure
to his efforts and success, the bilingual approach to writing poetry has met with
wide acceptance and is exploited by many poets. Alurista's poems are meant to be
read (representing as they do the code-switching milieu in which he was raised
and first began composing poems). They are rich in layers of bicultural imagery
and allusions, which can be realized only through the use of both Spanish and
English (as well as dialect variants of these — especially of Spanish). Consider the
following fragment of a poem entitled 'Wheat Paper Cucarachas' (in Ybarra-
Frausto, 1979:122):

> wheat paper *cucarachas*
> *de papel trigo*
> *y la cosecha del sol*
> winged in autumn
> *de vuelo al sol*
> *y las alas de trigo*
> *a volar*
> *en la primavera*
> spring of youthful bronze
> melting in the lava of our blood
> *la cucaracha muere*
> *y muerde el polvo*
> powder wheat
> *de atole con el dedo*
> and they bleed
> crushed by florsheims

Translation of the Spanish portions: Line 1: 'cockroaches' (marijuana cigarettes);
lines 2–3: 'of wheat paper/and the harvest of the sun'; lines 5–8: 'flying to the sun/
and the wings of wheat/to fly/in the spring time'; lines 11–12: 'the cockroach dies/
and bites the dust'; line 14: 'of atole [cornmeal gruel] with the finger.'

One cannot fully understand the imagery of this poem without an understanding
of the bilingual/bicultural context which it represents; further, its very impact
depends on the use of this complex imagery. Thus, even the first line of the poem
is unfathomable unless one knows that *cucaracha* is the Spanish translation of English
(cock)roach, which is barrio slang for a marijuana cigarette (hand-rolled). Literary
critic Ybarra-Frausto (1979) provides a line-by-line interpretation of this fragment, concluding that 'the image is liberated by exploring the connotative and
denotative domains of the two languages. This is one of the major formal contributions of Alurista's bilingual poetry' (p. 123).

Another of Alurista's poems, widely admired, is entitled '*Nuestro Barrio*' ('Our Barrio') (in Castañeda Shular, Ybarra-Frausto and Sommers, 1972:157):

> *Nuestro barrio*
> *en las tardes de paredes grabadas*
> *los amores de Pedro con Virginia*
> *en las tardes*
>   *barriendo*
> Dust about
>   swept away in the wind of our breath
> *el suspiro de dios por nuestras calles*
>   gravel side streets of solitude
>   the mobs from the tracks are coming
> *en la tarde*
> *mientras Don José barre su acera*
> *mentras dios respira vientos secos*
>   *en el barrio sopla la vejez de Chon*
>   *y la juventud de Juan madura*
> *en la tarde de polvo*
> *el recuerdo de mi abuelo*
> *— de las flores en su tumba*
>   of dust
>   *polvorosas flores*
> blowing free to powdered *cruces*

Translation of the Spanish portions: Lines 1–5: 'Our barrio/in the evenings of walls etched/the loves of Pedro with Virginia/in the evenings / sweeping'; line 8: 'the breath of god through our streets'; lines 11–18: 'in the evening/while Don José sweeps his sidewalk/while god breathes dry winds/in the barrio the old age of Chon expires/and the youth of Juan ripens/in the evening of dust/the memory of my grand-father/of the flowers on his tomb'; line 19: 'dusty flowers'; line 20: 'crosses.'

'*Nuestro Barrio*' would undoubtedly be a fine poem in either Spanish or English, but, as with the preceding poem, the emotional impact and the power of its imagery would, arguably, be far less compelling in a unilingual format. (Note that, linguistically speaking, the poem does not violate any code-switching constraints *per se*; on the other hand, in the second to last line, in a Spanish NP, Alurista places the adjective before the noun (*polvorosas flores*), probably to create symmetry with the code-switched NP of the last line, powdered/ cruces.)

The next literary fragment is from a short story about barrio life as experienced by several male adolescents in the late 1960s. It is entitled simply '*Ese*' (López, López and López, 1971):

When I got to, '*El Ranchito*', *LOS BATOS RAUL* and Junior were already there talking to *El Grifo*, *UN BATO LOCO COMO CUATRO AÑOS* older. '*Quihubo esos, qué hay de nuevo, man?*'
'*Pos nada, ese*', *dijo Raúl*. 'I hear *qu'el viejo Carso t'echó de la'scuela*. 'YEAH,' *dijo Juan, un poco* SAD, *pero* THEY'LL SEND ME BACK TO SCHOOL *el martes*.

JUNIOR *dice que* HE WON'T GO BACK *mañana*. HE DON'T WANT
TO GO BACK AT ALL.
'YOU DON'T NEED IT', *dijo El Grifo*. 'I DIDN'T GO *y no necesito nada,*
AND BESIDES, *la lana en mi chamba es buena*'.

Translation of the Spanish portions: Line 1: The dudes Raul; Line 2: a crazy dude
about four years; Line 3: 'What's happenin' guys, what's new, man?'; Line 4:
'Well, nothing, dude', said Raul. 'I hear that old Carson threw you out of school';
Line 5: said Juan, a little sad, 'but . . . on Tuesday'; Line 6: says that . . . tomorrow;
Line 7: said El Grifo '. . . and I don't need anything'; Line 8: 'the bread (lit., wool
= pay) in my job is good'.

The story provides a rich illustration of the range of possibilities for code-switching
since switching is quite evident at both the language level (Spanish-English)
and the dialect level (with social dialects and slang of both English and Spanish
represented).

The final fragment to be offered here comes from a children's story 'Robin
El Chicano Bird', written by Trini Campbell (1977), deploying standard colloquial varieties of Spanish and English:

'Robin, get up', said Mrs. Bird.
The sun was coming up. *ERA UNA FRESCA MAÑANA EN
PRIMAVERA*.
'Robin, get up!' . . . repeated Mrs. Bird.
Robin could hardly open his eyes. He was so sleepy.
'Robin!' called Mrs. Bird, for the third time.
Robin *ESCUCHÓ EL CANTO DE UNOS PAJARILLOS QUE
CELEBRABAN* the arrival of spring.
'If only I could sing', said Robin. He got up and went to the window.
VIO lots of birds jumping from place to place, *MIENTRAS
CANTABAN* ALEGREMENTE.
'If only I could sing', Robin said again, with tears *EN SUS OJOS*. Then
he flew away *YENDO A PARAR* on top of a dried bush by a little pond.

Translation of the Spanish portions: Line 2: 'It was a fresh spring morning'; Line 6: '(he) listened to the song of some little birds who were
celebrating'; Line 8: '(he) saw'; Line 9: 'while they sang happily'; Line 10
'in his eyes'; Line 11 'going to land'.

To my knowledge, this type of reading material has been little exploited in elementary school reading classes; undoubtedly apprehension runs high among
educators that such visual reinforcement of code-switching will do more damage
than good to young minds tackling the hurdle of literacy. It would be very
interesting to do some research with pre-adolescent bilinguals to see whether or
not a code-switching approach to reading hindered or promoted their ability to
read and write, and also to investigate their attitudes about reading and writing
monolingually vs. bilingually. If they come from a code-switching background,
do they feel more comfortable with the bilingual text, and do they display more
eagerness to read?

Code-switching in the Classroom

In general, many linguists and sociolinguists, find nothing inherently objection-able about code-switching — quite the contrary, as this chapter has endeavored to show. Even within the classroom setting, I believe one can make a case for its being an acceptable form of communication in principle, and at times even a useful or beneficial one — for example, if children come to the classroom already accustomed to code-switching, the ready acceptance of this by the teacher will probably be conducive to a more relaxed classroom atmosphere which, in turn, can enhance learning. However, there are a number of important questions to ask and considerations to bear in mind before teachers decide whether or not to code-switch in their own classrooms.

First, it seems to me that teachers need to be exposed to the research on code-switching that has established this phenomenon as a legitimate and complex form of bilingual communication. Clearly, teachers would not initiate or encourage practices that they hold in low esteem and regard as basically wrong. Just as important, however, is ascertaining the attitudes of the parents and the commun-ity toward code-switching; even if parents do code-switch at home on a regular basis, they may very well think it's a bad thing to do and would be horrified to know that their children were also being exposed to it at school. Discussions between teachers and parents on this very issue need to be held, in which attitudes are explored and information presented.

Another consideration has to do with the position of Spanish *vis-à-vis* English in the community — i.e., how vigorously is Spanish being maintained? If a com-munity is showing clear signs of language shift (to English), the wiser pedagogical decision may be to reinforce Spanish in the classroom (i.e., use more Spanish than English and little or no code-switching).

If code-switching is already taking place in a bilingual classroom, one needs to pay attention to the balance in use between the two languages. Some studies have documented a higher incidence of shift to English over Spanish and the use primarily of English to exercise control over the class. Such language choice implicitly reinforces the image of English as the dominant and Spanish as the subordinate language.[6]

There have been very few ethnographic studies of code-switching in the classroom; this is an area that calls out for much more research. A few that I have seen document that classroom code-switching shares many of the same functions of conversational switching — e.g., to clarify, to emphasize, to attract attention or bid for a conversational turn; or a switch may be motivated by the need to refer to an item or concept specific to one culture, as in conversation (Olmedo-Williams, 1980).

A more pessimistic picture of classroom code-switching is painted by Alex-ander Sapiens (1982), who observed a bilingual high school civics class in which students' language skills ranged from Spanish only, to both Spanish and English, to English only — surely a fairly frequently encountered classroom situation. The teacher was a fully bilingual Chicano, versed in code-switching and clearly favorable to its practice in the classroom. This article is instructive because it showed, on the basis of detailed quantitative and qualitative measures, that in spite of the teacher's positive attitude towards both Spanish and code-switching, he neverthe-less used English to convey key concepts twice as often as Spanish, and English was overwhelmingly the language of classroom control. The author concludes that

> Although the strategy of code-switching helped motivate the students
> and maintain rapport with them, it did not serve as a good language
> model in either Spanish or English. The linguistic repertoires of the stu-
> dents were not developed equally in both languages because English was
> clearly favored in instruction, classroom control, and solidarity. From a
> quantitative and qualitative perspective, it was apparent that the students'
> language skills were shifting from Spanish to English and that Spanish
> was not being maintained in the classroom (1982:402).

One of the main lessons to be learned from this account is that the social distance between teacher and students can be a sufficient barrier to inhibit true code-switching, which, as we have seen in the review of the literature, is an intimate and spontaneous form of communication among people who feel comfortable with one another. The social hierarchy implicit in the classroom setting may therefore pose a formidable barrier to true code-switching; and it certainly challenges the bilingual teacher who would like to exploit the many resources that code-switching communication has to offer.

Notes

1 Terms on this phenomenon are abundant and include 'code-shifting', 'code-mixing', 'code-alternation'; some researchers prefer using 'language' as the first term in these compound words. 'Code-switching' is, however, probably the most widespread variant. A popular term that has been around for a while is 'Spanglish', which refers to the overall influence of English on Spanish, inevitably with negative and/or humorous connotations.

2 Curiousity, however, impelled me shortly thereafter to investigate code-switching between Russian and French in another historical and cultural milieu (Timm, 1978), the source of several of the examples cited above.

3 *Pace* is generally deployed with a trace of irony, since the researchers on Kannada-English switching found that a code-switch is indeed possible at a site within the clause that does not adhere to Lipski's concept of 'essentially identical' clause segments as the only potential sites for switching.

4 In quotation marks because these are not typically consciously expressed by bilinguals, but emerge, often indirectly, from discussions with code-switchers, who may be asked to listen to tapes of their own conversations and to consider why they switched when they did. This was, for example, a tactic I used early on with considerable success with bilingual Chicanos/as who were aware of their code-switching, *and who were also not embarrassed by it* (the latter is a critical attitude affecting the elicitation of explanations).

5 Referring to *la policía* (the police) as *la chota* or *la jura*, or to *zapatos* (shoes) as *calcos*. It has frequently been observed that Caló is chiefly a youthful male variety of Chicano Spanish; this remains to be corroborated by empirical studies, but it is clearly the impression of many. One researcher, for example, recorded this (code-switching) observation by a young Chicana: '*Conoci a una señora y usaba esas palabras, se oyían muy feas* (I knew a woman and she used these words, they sounded very ugly), that's not the kind of language . . . coming from *una mujer, no se oye bien* (coming from a woman, it doesn't sound good). It's all right for them [the men]

pero en una mujer se oye feo (but in a woman it sounds ugly)' (Elías-Olivares 1976: 11).

Sánchez (1983:174) attributes to Caló the connotations of 'virility, defiance of literary norm, artistic innovativeness'.

6   Another problem has to do with the variety of Spanish used by the teacher: If the latter is quite different from the children's vernacular, this mismatch and the attendant perception that the teacher's Spanish is 'better' help undermine the students attitude about Spanish and may thereby indirectly reinforce use of English.

References

BLOM, J.P. and GUMPERZ, J.J. (1972) 'Social meaning in linguistic structures: Code-switching in Norway', in GUMPERZ, J.J. and HYMES, D.H. (Eds) *Directions in Sociolinguistics: The Ethnography of Communication*, New York, NY, Holt, Rinehart & Winston, pp. 407–43.

BOKAMBA, E.G. (1988) 'Code-mixing, language variation, and linguistic theory: Evidence from Bantu languages', *Lingua*, **76**, pp. 21–62.

CASTAÑEDA SHULAR, A., YBARRA-FRAUSTO, T. and SOMMERS, J. (Eds) (1972) *Literatura Chicana: Texto Y Contexto*, Englewood Cliffs, NJ, Prentice-Hall.

CLYNE, M.G. (1987) 'Constraints on code-switching: How universal are they?', *Linguistics*, **25**, pp. 739–64.28.

DiSCIULLO, A., MUYSKEN, P. and SINGH, R. (1986) 'Government and code-mixing', *Journal of Linguistics*, **22**, pp. 1–24.

ELÍAS-OLIVARES, L. (1976) 'Language use in a Chicano community: Sociolinguistics approach', *Working Papers in Sociolinguistics*, Austin, TX, Southwest Educational Development Laboratory, No. 30, pp. 1–30.

HUERTA-MACÍAS, A. (1981) 'Code-switching: All in the family', in DURÁN, R.P. (Ed) *Latino Language and Communitive Behavior*, Norwood, NJ, ABLEX Publishing, pp. 153–68.

JACOBSON, R. (1982) 'The social implications of intra-sentential code-switching', in AMASTAE, J. and ELÍAS-OLIVARES, L. (Eds) *Spanish in The United States: Sociolinguistic Aspects*, New York, NY, Cambridge University Press, pp. 182–208.

LIPSKI, J. (1978) 'Code-switching and the problem of bilingual competence', in PARADIS, M. (Ed) *Aspects of Bilingualism*, Columbia, SC, Hornbeam Press, pp. 263–77.

LIPSKI, J.L. (1985) *Linguistic Aspects of Spanish-English Language Switching*, Tempe, AZ, Arizona State University (Center for Latin American Studies, Special Studies, #25).

LÓPEZ, D., LÓPEZ, E. and LÓPEZ, C. (1971) 'Ese', unpublished ms., Davis, CA, Dept. of Sociology, UC Davis.

OLMEDO-WILLIAMS, I. (1980) 'Functions of code-switching in a Spanish-English bilingual classroom', *Delaware Working Papers in Language Studies*, **13**, pp. 1–30.

PFAFF, C.W. (1979) 'Constraints on language mixing: Intrasentential code-switching and borrowing in Spanish/English', *Language*, **55**, 2, pp. 291–317.

POPLACK, S. (1980) ' "Sometimes I'll start a sentence in Spanish *y termino en español*": Toward a typology of code-switching', *Linguistics* **18**:581–618, reprinted in AMASTAE, J. and ELÍAS-OLIVARES, L. (Eds) *Spanish in The United States: Sociolinguistic Aspects*, New York, NY, Cambridge University. Press, 1982, pp. 230–63.

POPLACK, S. (1981) 'Syntactic structure and social function of code-switching', in DURAN, R.P. (Ed) *Latino Language and Communicative Behavior*, Norwood, NJ, ABLEX Publishing, pp. 169–84.

REYES, R. (1982) 'Language mixing in Chicano Spanish', in AMASTAE, J. and ELÍAS-OLIVARES, L. (Eds) *Spanish in The United States: Sociolinguistic Aspects*, New York, NY, Cambridge University, Press, pp. 154–65.

Lenora A. Timm

Sánchez, R. (1983) *Chicano Discourse: Socio-Historic Perspectives*, Rowley, MA, Newbury House.
Sapiens, A. (1982) 'The use of Spanish and English in a high school bilingual civics class', in Amastae, J. and Elías-Olivares, L. (Eds) *Spanish in The United States: Sociolinguistic Aspects*, New York, NY, Cambridge University Press, pp. 386–412.
Sridhar, S.N. and Sridhar, K.K. (1980) 'The syntax and psycholinguistics of bilingual code mixing', *Studies in the Linguistic Sciences*, 10, 1, pp. 203–15.
Stolt, B. (1969–70) 'Luther Sprach "*mixtim vernacula lingua*"', *Zeitschrift für Deutsche Philologie*, 88, pp. 432–35.
Timm, L.A. (1975) 'Spanish-English code-switching: *El porqué y* how-not-to', *Romance Philology*, 28, 4, pp. 473–82.
Timm, L.A. (1978) 'Code-switching in *War and Peace*', in Paradis, M. (Ed) *Aspects of Bilingualism*, Columbia, SC, Hornbeam Press, pp. 302–15.
Tolstoy, L.M. (1960) *Voyna I Mir* ['War and Peace'], 4 vols. Moscow, USSR: Gosudarstvennoe uchebno-pedagogicheskoe izadatel'stvo.
Valdés, G. (1982) 'Social interaction and code-switching patterns: A case study of Spanish-English alternation', in Amastae, J. and Elías-Olivares, L. (Eds) *Spanish in The United States: Sociolinguistic Aspects*, New York, NY, Cambridge University Press, pp. 209–29.
Valdés-Fallis, G. (1978) *Code-switching and the Classroom Teacher*, Arlington, VA, Center for Applied Linguistics.
Ybarra-Frausto, T. (1979) 'Alurista's poetics: The oral, the bilingual, the pre-Columbian', in Sommers, J. and Ybarra-Frausto, T. (Eds) *Modern Chicano Writers*, Englewood Cliffs, NJ, Prentice-Hall, pp. 117–32.

Further Readings

Berg-Seligson, S. (1986) 'Linguistic constraints on intrasentential code-switching: a study of Spanish/Hebrew bilingualism', *Language in Society*, 15, 3, pp. 313–48.
Breitborde, L.B. (1983) 'Levels of analysis in sociolinguistic explanation: Bilingual code-switching, social relations, and domain theory', *International Journal of the Sociology of Language*, 39, pp. 5–43.
Campbell, T. (1977) 'Robin el Chicano bird', *El Grito del Sol*, 2, 1, pp. 21ff.
Canfield, K. (1980) 'A note on Navajo-English code-mixing', *Anthropological Linguistics*, 22, 5, pp. 208–22.
Chana, U. and Romaine, S. (1984) 'Evaluative reactions to Punjabi/English code-switching', *Journal of Multilingual and Multicultural Development*, 5, 6, pp. 447–74.
Clyne, M.G. (1967) *Transference and Triggering*, The Hague, Netherlands, Mouton.
Clyne, M.G. (1978) 'Some (German-English) language contact phenomena at the discourse level', in Fishman, J.A. (Ed) *Advances in the Study of Societal Multilingualism*, The Hague, Netherlands Mouton, pp. 113–28.
Coupland, N. (1980) 'Style-shifting in a Cardiff work-setting', *Language in Society*, 9, 1, pp. 1–12.
Dearholt, D.W. and Valdés-Fallis, B. (1978) 'Toward a probabilistic automata model of some aspects of code-switching', *Language in Society*, 7, 3, pp. 411–19.
Denison, N. (1971) 'Some observations on language variety and plurilingualism', in Ardener, E. (Ed) *Social Anthropology and Language*, London, England, Tavistock, pp. 157–83.
Di Pietro, R. (1978) 'Code-switching as a verbal strategy among bilinguals', in Paradis, M. (Ed) *Aspects of Bilingualism*, Columbia, SC, Hornbeam Press, pp. 275–82.
Garcia, E. (1980) 'The functions of language switching during bilingual mother-child interactions', *Journal of Multilingual and Multicultural Development*, 1, 3, pp. 231–52.

GARDNER-CHLOROS, P. (1985) 'Language selection and switching among Strasbourg shoppers', *International Journal of the Sociology of Language*, **54**, pp. 115–36.

GENESEE, F. (1984) 'The socio-psychological significance of bilingual code-switching for children', *Applied Psycholinguistics*, **5**, 1, pp. 3–20.

GENESEE, F. and BOURHIS, R.Y. (1982) 'The social psychological significance of code-switching in cross-cultural communication', *Journal of Language and Social Psychology*, **1**, 1, pp. 1–26.

GIBBONS, J. (1979) 'Code-mixing and *koinés* in the speech of students at the University of Hong Kong', *Anthroplogical Linguistics*, **21**, 3, pp. 113–123.

GOKE-PARIOLA, A. (1983) 'Code-mixing among Yoruba-English bilinguals', *Anthropological Linguistics*, **25**, 1, pp. 39–46.

GUMPERZ, J.J. (1969) 'Communication in multilingual societies', in TYLER, S. (Ed) *Cognitive Anthropology*, New York, NY, Holt, Rinehart & Winston, pp. 435–49.

GUMPERZ, J.J. and HERNÁNDEZ-CHÁVEZ, E. (1971) 'Cognitive aspects of bilingual communication', in WHITELEY, W.R. (Ed) *Language and Social Change*, London, England, Oxford University Press, pp. 111–25.

HASSELMO, N. (1972) 'Code-switching as ordered selection', in FIRCHOW, E.S., GRIMSTAD, K., HASSELMO, N. and O'NEIL, W.A. (Eds) *Studies For Einar Haugen*, The Hague, Netherlands, Mouton, pp. 251–80.

KACHRU, B.B. (1976) 'Toward structuring code-mixing: An Indian perspective', *International Journal of the Sociology of Language*, **16**, pp. 24–46.

KACHRU, B.B. (1978) 'Code-mixing as a communicative strategy in India', in ALATIS, J.E. (Ed) *International Dimensions of Bilingual Education*, Washington, DC, Georgetown University Press, pp. 107–24.

LEDERBERG, A. and MORALES, C. (1985) 'Code-switching by bilinguals: Evidence against a third grammar', *Journal of Psycholinguistic Research*, **14**, 2, pp. 113–36.

LIN, J.S. and STANFORD, L.M. (1983) 'An experimental reappraisal of some syntactic constraints on code-switching', in MORREAL, J. (Ed) *The Ninth Lacus Forum*, Columbia, SC, Hornbeam Press, pp. 474–83.

LIPSKI, J.L. (1983) 'Spanish-English language switching in speech and literature: Theories and models', *The Bilingual Review*, **9**, 3, pp. 191–212.

McCLURE, E. (1981) 'Formal and functional aspects of the code-switched discourse of bilingual children', in DURAN, R.P. (Ed) *Latino Language Communitive Behavior*, Norwood, NJ, ABLEX Publishing Corp., pp. 69–94.

McDOWELL, J. (1982) 'Sociolinguistic contours in the verbal art of Chicano children', in AMASTAE, J. and ELÍAS-OLIVARES, L. (Eds) *Spanish in The United States: Sociolinguistic Aspects*, New York, NY, Cambridge University Press, pp. 333–53.

NARTEY, J.N.A. (1982) 'Code-switching, interference, or faddism? Language use among educated Ghanians', *Anthropological Linguistics*, **24**, 2, pp. 183–92.

PARKIN, D.J. (1974) 'Language switching in Nairobi', in WHITELEY, W.H. (Ed) *Language in Kenya*, Nairobi, Kenya, Oxford University Press, pp. 189–216.

SCOTTON, C.M. and URY, W. (1977) 'Bilingual strategies — Social functions of code-switching', *Linguistics*, **193**, pp. 5–20.

SHAFFER, D. (1978) 'The place of code-switching in linguistic contacts', in PARADIS, M. (Ed) *Aspects of Bilingualism*, Columbia, SC, Hornbeam Press, pp. 265–74.

SINGH, R. (1985) 'Grammatical constraints on code-mixing: Evidence from Hindi-English', *Canadian Journal of Linguistics*, **30**, 1, pp. 33–45.

SOBIN, N.J. (1984) 'On code switching inside NP', *Applied Psycholinguistics*, **5**, 4, pp. 293–304.

SRIDHAR, S.N. (1978) 'On the functions of code-mixing in Kannada', *International Journal of the Sociology of Language*, **16**, pp. 109–17.

ST. CLAIR, R. (1980) 'The sociology of code-switching', *Language Sciences*, **2**, 2, pp. 205–21.

THELANDER, M. (1976) 'Code-switching or code-mixing?', *Linguistics*, **183**, pp. 102–23.

Timm, L.A. (1983) 'Does code-switching take time? A comparison of results in experimental and natural settings, with some implications for bilingual language processing', *Hispanic Journal of Behavioral Sciences*, **5**, 4, pp. 401–16.

Valdés, G. (1981) 'Code-switching as deliberate verbal strategy: A microanalysis of direct and indirect requests among bilingual Chicano speakers', in Durán, R.P. (Ed) *Latino Language and Communitive Behavior*, Norwood, NJ, ABLEX Publishing Corp., pp. 95–107.

Verma, S.K. (1976) 'Code-switching: Hindi/English', *Lingua*, **38**, pp. 153–56.

Wu, Y.A. (1985) 'Code-mixing by English-Chinese bilingual teachers of the People's Republic of China', *World Englishes*, **4**, 3, pp. 303–17.

Zentella, A.C. (1982) 'Code-switching and interactions among Puerto Rican children', in Amastae, J. and Elías-Olivares, L. (Eds) *Spanish in The United States: Sociolinguistic Aspects*, New York, NY, Cambridge University Press, pp. 354–85.

Part II

Practical Advances: Redefining the Content and Process of the Curriculum

Chapter 8

Language Acquisition Theory and Classroom Practices in the Teaching of Spanish to the Native Spanish Speaker

Barbara J. Merino and Fabián A. Samaniego

The teaching of Spanish to native speakers (SNS) has seen a dramatic upheaval over the past ten years as increasing numbers of native Spanish speakers have enrolled in US schools. At the elementary school level in the backdrop of bilingual education, the teaching of SNS has focused on the acquisition of initial literacy, often as a vehicle for the acquisition of other academic skills in English (Cummins, 1981). At the secondary level SNS has been seen traditionally as an extension of the teaching of Spanish as a foreign language (Valdés-Fallis, 1974). With older learners at both the high school and the college level, two principal approaches have been identified: 'the limited normative approach' which focuses on the eradication of 'errors' or nonstandard dialect variants (Valdés-Fallis, 1978); and 'the comprehensive approach' which strives to expand the students' language skills principally through reading and writing (Valdés, Lozano and García-Moya, 1981).

It is important to acknowledge at the outset that the population of native Spanish speakers in the United States represents a very heterogeneous group. It numbered approximately 15 million people at the beginning of the last decade and was then principally composed of people of Mexican origin (60 per cent), but also included Puerto Ricans (14 per cent), Cubans (6 per cent) and increasingly Central Americans (US Bureau of the Census, 1980 and 1982). Although some Hispanics speak English fluently when they arrive in school, the unifying characteristic for most is the Spanish language. Eleven million of the close to 15 million Hispanics counted by the 1980 census reported speaking Spanish at home (Lopez, 1982). Almost (93 per cent) of Hispanic adults reported that Spanish was their primary language when they grew up (US Bureau of the Census, 1982) and only 14 per cent of all Hispanics in the United States report having an English language background (Brown, Rosen, Hill and Olivas, 1980). From this population, those of rural background are most likely to speak nonstandard rural varieties. Those who have lived in the United States for some time are most likely to be affected by the influence of English in the community (Peñalosa, 1982). Those of the second and third generation are most likely to exhibit loss of Spanish or arrested development in Spanish (Merino, 1983).

In this chapter, we will first provide a brief historical overview of trends in pedagogical approaches in the teaching of Spanish to native speakers. We will then analyze the relationship of first and second language acquisition theory to the teaching of SNS with a focus on current practices as they are reported in the literature.

Historical Overview

The limited normative approach described by Valdés-Fallis (1978) has been the tradition in teaching rural nonstandard speakers in the Spanish speaking world. It is characterized by selecting the most common features of non-standard dialect, contrasting them with the standard forms and providing oral or written exercises on their use. These exercises can be found typically in language arts texts used at the elementary level in Mexico even today. Dialect variants are identified as errors or *barbarismos* and not recognized as part of the systematic dialect variation process studied by sociolinguists. In the United States, this approach inspired *Español para el Bilingüe* (Barker, 1972) in one of the earliest attempts to address the needs of the native Spanish speaker (NSS). In addition to nonstandard dialect variants, variants developing in the Spanish-speaking community of the Southwest as a result of the influence of English were also included in the Barker text. This approach advocated direct error-correcting techniques, which highlighted dialect variants as features to be avoided in all circumstances. Necessarily, this approach tended to alienate students from their own Spanish-speaking community since it frequently devalued the language of their parents (Faltis, 1984).

Under the influence of sociolinguists such as Labov (1972) who studied black English varieties in the United States and Chicano linguists who were describing 'Chicano Spanish' (Sánchez, 1972), Valdés-Fallis (1974) challenged the normative approach with the comprehensive approach. As described by Faltis and DeVillar (this volume), this approach presents language as a tool for exchanging ideas about topics of interest to the students. Through a series of texts, Valdés-Fallis and her associates have sought to develop literacy skills in standard Spanish by providing varied and rich opportunities to talk, read and write about topics of interest to the students (Valdés-Fallis and Teschner, 1978, 2nd Edition 1984; Valdés, Hannum and Teschner, 1982).

The principal advantage of the comprehensive approach is that it seeks to extend the students' language skills in a natural way, launching into the functional uses of the standard variety through the media of print. Reading and writing thus become necessary skills to communicate with a broader community of standard Spanish speakers. Initially, correction is limited to that which is necessary for understanding. Conveying the message of the speaker is given primary status. To some extent, the comprehensive approach also reflects current second language theory which emphasizes the message being communicated rather than the grammatical forms being taught (Krashen, 1981).

For the past fifteen years scholarship on effective techniques for teaching SNS in the secondary school and beyond has largely been generated through the work of University-based departments of Spanish and high school foreign language teachers. This literature offers a rich array of strategies and techniques for the development of spoken and written language (Valdés, Lozano, García-Moya, 1981). Most of these instructional strategies represent the authors' own experience. The type of evidence presented to support their effectiveness is typically anecdotal accounts of courses taught to native Spanish speakers. Nonetheless, in this early stage of development in the field of teaching SNS, this literature can offer practitioners and researchers alike an array of treatments from which to begin to gather empirical data on the process of teaching Spanish to this population through more systematic inquiry.

Classroom Techniques

When to correct? Often the first question teachers have to address in teaching Spanish to NSS is what to do when dialect variants are produced in the classroom. Should these be corrected overtly, indirectly or not at all? First, it is important to understand that some dialect variants have been fairly well documented in descriptive studies of different communities and that some of these cannot be distinguished from the type of developmental error all learners of a language will make. Consider, for example, the form *fuistes* or *fuites* both nonstandard variants of *fuiste* (you went or you were). In the second person, this variant which affects all forms of the past, has been widely documented as a rural variant in the Spanish-speaking world (Peñalosa, 1982). It has sometimes been shown to occur among monolingual Spanish-speaking children learning Spanish in a standard community, although it appears to be rare in that context. Yet another form of the past, the past participle, in irregular verbs such as *rompido, roto* in standard, (broken) has been widely documented as occurring among both non-standard speakers of Spanish and L1 and L2 learners exposed to standard Spanish. The first problem then is to understand the nature of the error, if it can be labelled that. Does it reflect the speech of the student's community or family? Does it indicate an interim stage in the acquisition of Spanish?

In the pedagogical literature of Spanish, points of view on correction of forms have varied widely. Some propose that the teacher should repeat the form to be imitated and not the form be avoided (Aparicio, 1983). Thus, for example, students should be asked to provide alternatives for a word like *guachear* (to watch, or take care of). This technique should be used with the admonition that the appropriateness of *cuidar* or *guachear* depends on the community of speakers being addressed. From another point of view, Magaña (1972), a high school teacher, proposes giving stress to reading and writing and de-emphasizing grammatical analysis and pronunciation. Magaña based his suggestion on practical experience with high school students who were bored by grammatical analysis and pronunciation drills. Valdés echoes this strategy when reflecting on her own experiences teaching college students (Valdés *et al.*, 1981). She suggests focusing on reading and writing skills and avoiding correction of oral language. Politzer (this volume) reports that teaching standard English to black English speakers through traditional second language drills was not successful. Merino (1989) reporting on her experiences as a Berlitz teacher, teaching a Chicano speaker who wanted to eliminate the form-*istes* from his speech, found that while engaged in communicative games, this speaker was able to produce the standard form. However, once engaged in informal conversation outside of class, the nonstandard form often recurred. This speaker fits Krashen's description of a low monitor user (1981). It appears therefore that changing oral patterns, particularly when these are systemic, is a very difficult time consuming task. Can the acquisition of standard oral forms be addressed adequately in a traditional classroom? Important as the acquisition of the standard form may be for some speakers, this question has not been answered. Future research needs to address appropriate strategies to facilitate the process of acquisition of a standard form in oral discourse.

Study of Sociolinguistic Principles

Many have proposed the study of principles of sociolinguistic variation as a way of building awareness among students about the phenomena which they themselves are experiencing. Thus, Solé (1981) proposes the review of materials, such as print and visual media, as a means of giving students opportunities to observe various uses of standard and nonstandard varieties and thus learn to distinguish *español familar y español culto* (colloquial and formal Spanish). Lozano (1981) reports using a more elaborate approach to the study of sociolinguistic variation with his university students in Colorado. His approach included the study of transformational grammar analyses to understand formal differences between standard and nonstandard varieties combined with reading and discussion of the role of standard and dialect varieties in language communities. Lozano offers no data on the development of language skills using the approach but reports a generally positive student response, although some dropped out of the course.

Engaging students in learning the data collection methods of sociolinguists has been used by Gutiérrez-Marrone (1981) as a way of building students' awareness of standard regional variation. Her technique involved the comparison of lexical variation among standard varieties in the Spanish-speaking world in specific semantic domains — for example, office equipment. Students explored differences in standard lexical variants through interviews with informants or review of popular media, noting differences such as *sujetapapeles* (clip). This approach can be highly motivating to students and also results in the development of oral conversational skills. However, it assumes a great deal of student self-discipline and has been used principally with university level students. At the secondary level, a modified approach may be necessary, where informants come to the class, or interviews are homework assignments. Alternatively, students can monitor local Spanish print and other media. A strength of this approach is that students learn about local cultural resources as well as gain an understanding of sociolinguistic variation. (See Quintanar-Sarellana, Huebner and Jensen, this volume for further suggestions).

In a more focused approach to the study of sociolinguistic variation, based on experiences with black English speakers, Aparicio, (1983) proposes the use of contrastive analyses. Following a class presentation of audio tapes of major dialects of Hispanics in the US, students are given a listing of major dialect variants, combined with a non-technical description of the differences from standard variants. These differences are then discussed. Students may assist by generating their own tapes of informal conversations outside of class. This activity may also be used to analyze code-switching. (See Timm, this volume.)

Composition

Composition has been frequently viewed as the principal corpus of instruction in teaching SNS. Spanish-speaking students in the United States frequently reach secondary school with very limited opportunities for writing in Spanish. Thus, many of the texts reflecting a comprehensive skills philosophy, often focus principally on writing, including both composition and orthography. In this tradition, Valdés, Hannum and Teschner (1982), in a text for secondary students provide systematic activities to develop an understanding of the use of accents in Spanish. The approach they use is incremental, beginning with diphthongs and moving gradually to syllable division of formal rules of accentuation.

Aparicio (1983) advocates the use of written sources such as Chicano literature (poetry, short stories, etc.) which are representative of the student population. Chabram Dernersesian (this volume) provides many useful suggestions for sources that are representative of recent Chicano literature. One major advantage of the use of US-based Chicano literature is that students can begin to identify themselves as members of a community of Spanish speakers with their own special voice and place in world literature. Chicano literature also offers many written examples, used to dramatic effect, of the very language the students hear within their communities. Aparicio (1983) suggests using Chicano, Puerto Rican and Cuban American literature as part of controlled composition exercises in which students can change passages from informal to formal Spanish, from dialogue to narrative, form indirect speech to direct speech, from nonstandard to standard dialect. Students can then analyze the impact of these changes on the dramatic force of the text and thus gain greater understanding of the role of styles of discourse and language varieties.

Targeting another tradition, the teaching of writing to mainstream and nonstandard English speakers, Aparicio (1983), outlines a variety of activities that can be used to develop students' skills at composing while at the same time enhancing their awareness of dialect variation. Thus students can be engaged in self-editing exercises, writing of dialogues in standard and nonstandard varieties, acting these out in class as well as developing their own writing assignments. The process to be used includes, in the terms used by Rivers and Azevedo (cited in Aparicio, 1983) conceptualization/discussion, incubation-formulation and editing/revising, with appropriate activities targeted for each one of these steps. (See Samaniego, *et al.*, this volume, for further suggestions).

Vocabulary

Many have recognized that a particular need of the SNS is the development and expansion of vocabulary. Some have advocated traditional approaches of vocabulary development which focus on structural analysis that includes the functions of a word as well as its history (de las Casas, 1987). Others have pushed for the use of a wide variety of subject matter — science, art, music, math and social studies activities — as the best means to expand students' vocabulary while at the same time developing other academic skills (Merino and Faltis, 1986; Faltis, 1981, 1984 and 1986). Games, such as the 'dictionary game' have also been used as a way of developing the students' vocabulary and awareness of lexical variation (Merino, 1989). In this game, students are given dictionaries of lexical variation in Chicano

Spanish, for example, Galvan and Teschner's (1975) *Dictionary of Chicano Spanish*. In small groups, students must identify a word, invent two plausible definitions and then read out to the whole class the two false definitions as well as the real definition. The whole class takes an exam on the words and definitions generated by the class. As correct answers are presented, the relationship of the words to the standard variety are discussed. This activity has been used with high school and college level students and helps students realize how lexical variation functions in both standard and nonstandard varieties. It is a highly entertaining activity which also gives value to the knowledge that Chicano students in the class bring to the experience.

Reading

It has long been recognized that reading presents a unique set of problems and opportunities for the native Spanish-speaking student. Typically, the NSS students have already learned to read in English, although that is not always the case. When literacy has already been acquired, reading should proceed as part of a general transfer of skills. This phenomenon of transfer from Spanish to English has been largely explored with young children (Faltis, 1981, 1984, 1986). Hidalgo (1989) reporting on her experiences with college level students in New York and California, suggests approaching reading through systematic increments of isolated words, to sentences, to longer segments of text. Based on experiences with young bilingual children, we recommend the emphasis in beginning reading should be on words with those sounds that have a consistent pattern of fit with their graphemes and whose correspondence with English maximizes transfer. Thus, for example, reading words such as *cama* and avoiding initially words such as *viaje*. Guitart (1981) proposes another objective in using reading with nonstandard Spanish speakers. Based on his experiences with college level students, he finds that reading aloud in class gives students an opportunity to orally produce standard features that may not be part of their own oral repertoire. In addition, thematic courses that use authentic materials, such as job applications and advertisements, have been proposed as especially motivating for this population (Conway, 1986).

One very important and at times controversial reform movement which has had considerable influence at the elementary level in bilingual education, but which has had little impact at the secondary level with teachers of Spanish is the 'whole language approach' (Edelsky, 1986, 1990; McKenna, Robinson and Miller, 1990). This approach or philosophy links literacy, reading and writing to the functional use of the language by speakers in their communities. Reading and writing are drawn from the students' experience, and emphasis is given to communication. In many ways, the emphasis on the value of the learner's message and the tolerance of learner 'error' would suggest that this approach has much to offer the teacher of Spanish for native Spanish speakers at the secondary level.

Curricular Emphasis

Recently, school districts across the country, recognizing the needs of the native Spanish speakers, have begun to engage in curriculum development efforts designed to develop skills in Spanish beyond the traditional foreign language curriculum. In California, many districts are focusing on the Spanish high school class as a natural place to begin the academic development of recently arrived NSS, (See Part III of this volume). Activities in critical thinking, reading and writing are provided with the aim of developing skills which are necessary for survival in English (Cummins, 1981). In Dade County, Florida, a course of study for Spanish for Spanish speakers has been developed for the junior and senior high school, with the aim of integrating literature and business education with the teaching of Spanish (Dade County Public Schools, 1988). For example, Spanish courses in shorthand, dictation and transcription are offered as well as courses in Spanish literature and literary criticism. In Harlandale, Texas, Blanco (1987) has used the notional functional approach to develop communicative activities for a course for the native Spanish speaker at the high school level.

Future Directions

While many instructional strategies for teaching Spanish to the native speaker have been proposed and used, at this stage very little is known empirically about how these strategies work with students. Most of what is known about the effectiveness of these techniques is based on the reported experience of teachers. However, these experiences can now constitute the beginning steps for systematic inquiry, particularly through teacher research. An individual teacher, for example, could simply describe how students, who are literate in English, transfer their reading skills as they learn to read in Spanish.

It is also important to recognize that many instructional strategies have simply not been explored at all. Cooperative learning has been a very useful technique particularly in groups of heterogeneous ability levels and could enhance the experiences of both traditional and native Spanish-speaking students. (Gorman, this volume). Technological innovations such as the microcomputer also need to be explored, particularly as these can enhance the development of writing skills (See Faltis and deVillar, this volume).

The use of local cultural resources could similarly be the focus of a Spanish course for native speaking students. Here culture should be redefined to include the rules of social behavior. Ethnographic interviews, for example, could serve as the starting point for engaging students in structured activities with their own local culture (Trueba, Chapter 2 this volume). Even traditional definitions of culture which encompass art could be used productively in the classroom, particularly if folk art is used as a more accessible starting point (see Carrillo Hocker, this volume).

Finally, it is important to understand that we know very little about two psycholinguistic processes that frequently impact native Spanish-speaking students: standard dialect acquisition and language loss. The acquisition of a standard dialect such as standard Spanish that is closely allied to the nonstandard variety of Chicano Spanish presents unique problems. How do bidialectal speakers organize and activate two closely allied linguistic systems? For those who have experienced language loss, how can reacquisition be triggered once again? These and many other questions await further research.

References

APARICIO, F. (1983) 'Teaching Spanish to the native speaker at the college level', *Hispania*, **66**, pp. 232–39.

BARKER, M.E. (1972) *Español para el Bilingüe*, Skokie, IL, National Textbook Company.

BLANCO, G. (1987) *Español para el Hispanohablante: Función y Noción*, Harlandale, TX, Harlandale Unified School District, ED 294432.

BROWN, G., ROSEN, N., HILL, S.T. and OLIVAS, M. (1980) *The Condition of Education for Hispanic Americans*, Washington, DC, National Center for Education Statistics.

CONWAY, D. (1986) 'Theme courses for community colleges', *Hispania*, **69**, pp. 409–12.

CUMMINS, J. (1981) 'The role of primary language development in promoting educational success for language minority students', in CALIFORNIA STATE DEPARTMENT OF EDUCATION, (Ed) *Schooling and Language Minority Students: A Theoretical Framework*, Los Angeles, CA, California State University at Los Angeles, pp. 3–49.

DADE COUNTY PUBLIC SCHOOLS (1988) 'Spanish for Spanish speakers: Course of study for junior and senior high schools', Ed 254 068/069.

DE LAS CASAS, W. (1987) 'Curriculum guide for Spanish native language arts', *Hispania*, **70**, pp. 370–72.

EDELSKY, C. (1986) *Writing in a Bilingual Program: Había una Vez*, Norwood, NJ, Ablex.

EDELSKY, C. (1990) 'Whose agenda is this anyway? A response to McKenna, Robinson, and Miller', *Educational Researcher*, **21**, pp. 7–11.

FALTIS, C.J. (1981) 'Teaching Spanish writing to bilingual college students', *NABE Journal*, **6**, pp. 93–106.

FALTIS, C.J. (1984) 'Reading and writing in Spanish for bilingual college students: What's taught at school and what's used in the community', *The Bilingual Review/La Revista Bilingüe*, **11**, pp. 21–32.

FALTIS, C.J. (1986) 'Initial cross-lingual reading transfer in second grade bilingual classrooms', in GARCIA, E. and FLORES, B. (Eds) *Language and Literacy Research in Bilingual Education*, Tempe, AZ, Arizona State University, pp. 145–58.

GALVAN, R.A. and TESCHNER, R.V. (1975) *El Diccionario del Español Chicano/The dictionary of Chicano Spanish*, Silver Spring, MD, Institute of Modern Languages.

GUITART, J. (1981) 'The pronunciation of Puerto Rican Spanish in the Mainland: Theoretical and pedagogical considerations', in VALDÉS, G., LOZANO, A. and GARCÍA-MOYA, R. (Eds) *Teaching Spanish to the Hispanic Bilingual: Issues, Aims and Methods*, New York, NY, Columbia Teachers College. Press, pp. 46–58.

GUTIÉRREZ-MARRONE, N. (1981) 'Español para el Hispano: Un enfoque sociolingüisitico' in VALDÉS, G., LOZANO, A. and GARCÍA-MOYA, R. (Eds) *Teaching Spanish to the Hispanic Bilingual: Issues, Aims and Methods*, New York, NY, Columbia Teachers College. Press, pp. 69–80.

HIDALGO, M. (1989) *On the Question of Standard vs. Dialect: Hispanic Students*, Videocassette, Davis, CA, University of California Media Center, No. 927900, 60 min.

KRASHEN, S. (1981) *Second Language Acquisition and Second Language Learning*, London, England, Pergamon Press.

LABOV, W. (1972) *Language in the Inner City: Studies in Black English Vernacular*, Philadelphia, PA, University of Pennsylvania Press.

LOPEZ, D. (1982) *The Maintenance of Spanish over Three Generations in the United States*, Los Alamitos, CA, National Center for Bilingual Research.

LOZANO, A. (1981) 'A modern view of teaching grammar', in VALDÉS, G., LOZANO, A. and GARCÍA-MOYA, R. (Eds) *Teaching Spanish to the Hispanic Bilingual: Issues, Aims and Methods*, New York, NY, Columbia Teachers College Press, pp. 81–90.

MAGAÑA, C. (1972) 'The necessity of order in the teaching of Spanish to native speakers', *Hispania*, **53**, pp. 438–40.

MERINO, B.J. (1983) 'Language loss in bilingual Chicano children', *Journal of Applied Developmental Psychology*, **10**, pp. 477–94.

MERINO, B.J. (1989) Techniques for teaching Spanish to native Spanish speakers, Español para triunfar/Spanish for success: A summer institute for high school Spanish teachers of NSS students, Davis, CA, University of California.

MERINO, B.J. and FALTIS, C.J. (1986) 'Spanish for special purposes: Communication strategies for teachers in bilingual education', *Foreign Language Annals*, **19**, pp. 43–9.

PEÑALOSA, F. (1982) *Chicano Sociolinguistics*, Rowley, MA, Newbury House Publichers.

SÁNCHEZ, R. (1972) 'Nuestra Circumstancia Linguística', *El Grito*, **1**, pp. 45–74.

SOLÉ, Y. (1981) 'Consideraciones pedagogicas en la ensenanza del Espanol a estudiantes bilingües', in VALDÉS, G., LOZANO, A. and GARCÍA-MOYA, R. (Eds) *Teaching Spanish to the Hispanic Bilingual: Issues, Aims and Methods*, New York, NY, Teachers College Press, pp. 21–9.

US BUREAU OF THE CENSUS (1980) 'Age, sex, race, and Spanish origin of the population by regions, divisions, and states: 1980', *1980 Census of the Population, Supplementary Reports*, PC 80-S1-1, Washington, DC, US Government Printing Office.

US BUREAU OF THE CENSUS (1982) 'Ancestry and language in the US: November, 1979', *Current Population Reports*, Series P-23, No. 116, Washington, DC, US Government Printing Office.

VALDÉS-FALLIS, G. (1974) 'Spanish and the Mexican Americans', *The Colorado Quarterly*, **22**, pp. 483–93.

VALDÉS-FALLIS, G. (1978) 'A comprehensive approach to the teaching of Spanish to bilingual Spanish-speaking students', *The Modern Language Journal*, **3**, pp. 102–10.

VALDÉS-FALLIS, G. and TESCHNER, R.V. (1978; 2nd edition, 1984) *Español Escrito: Curso para Hispanohablantes*, New York, NY, Charles Scribner's Sons.

VALDÉS, G., HANNUM, T.P. and TESCHNER, R.V. (1982) *Cómo se Escribe: Curso de Secundaria para Estudiantes Bilingües*, New York, NY, Charles Scribner's Sons.

VALDÉS, G., LOZANO, A.G. and GARCIA-MOYA, R. (1981) *Teaching Spanish to the Hispanic Bilingual: Issues, Aims and Methods*, New York, NY, Teachers College Press.

Chapter 9

The Role of Chicano Literature in Teaching Spanish to Native Speakers[1]

Angie Chabram Dernersesian

To speak of the role of Chicano literature within the context of imparting know-ledge of Spanish to the native speaker in the milieu of Spanish departments or language programs across the United States is to engage in the dynamics of curriculum reform, language policy, cultural politics, and creative innovation. Traditionally language programs have focused on the pedagogical needs of the Anglo-American student who aspires to learn the Spanish language. Throughout the United States courses, textbooks and educational studies abound which exam-ine the processes involved in imparting the Spanish language to those speakers whose mother tongue is English. The proliferation of Spanish language text-books, which assume that the student is unfamiliar with the most basic of Spanish vocabulary and grammatical forms, and cultural readers which promise these students a symbolic partnership with 'foreign' cultures on the other side of the Atlantic, is an indication of this trend in pedagogical studies concerning language acquisition and development. To put it bluntly, Spanish has not been the terrain of native speakers, and this situation was substantially worse before than it is now.

In the not-so-distant past, (and unfortunately for us, in the vestiges of the historic present) native speakers were often scorned publicly for being so bold as to enter an elementary or intermediate Spanish class, even if the native speakers in question were authentically in need of learning accent placement, grammatical structures or expanding their vocabulary. Native speakers who entered these Spanish classes were immediately suspected of trying to engage in one-upmanship of the professor — trying to get away with an easy 'A'. They were often graded down because of their appearance, even when they were more fluent than their instruc-tors (see, Brazil 1990). Finally, in those cases where negative sentiments weren't directly voiced to the native speakers who were courageous enough to continue in the class 'for the love of the language and the pride of a culture', their presence was constantly viewed as an impediment — an obstacle to the instructor's cultur-ally sanctioned efforts to minister to the particular needs of the children of the dominant linguistic group of the nation: Anglo Saxons. Oftentimes native speak-ers were subjected to public humiliation for using forms of popular or rural Spanish with which instructors were not acquainted or which they did not want to address for fear of contamination.[2]

In short, the Chicano's 'linguistic capital' was not rewarded by the educational system, pedagogical exercises, language instructors, or Spanish departments across the Southwest, all of which favored more classic materials. Instead of building on the native students' natural resources and their capabilities, in order that they might contribute productively to a socially and culturally diverse national identity, these students were reprimanded, humiliated and ignored because of the peculiarities involved in the Spanish of Chicanos (for an account of some of these unique characteristics see Hernández-Chávez, Cohen and Beltrano, 1975). This, of course, in addition to the fact that many of those Chicanos who entered Spanish classes were already well schooled in the principles: 'French is exotic: Spanish isn't', and in the requirements of a public school system which declared: 'No Spanish on the courtyards' a requirement which, interestingly enough, was exactly the opposite for Anglo students who were encouraged to 'speak Spanish outside of the classroom' in order to improve their expression. If this were not enough, Chicano students, who were relentless in their pursuit to study their language, often encountered a eurocentric bias on the part of instructors, instructors who proclaimed that *the* Hispanic cultures and civilizations of the globe were Latin American and Spanish, and that everything else was a grotesque barbarism — the most vile of all cultural conditions: hybridism.

To be successful in a Spanish language course with these types of impediments to one's expression at the most basic and intimate of levels, it was necessary to attempt to blend in: to cleanse oneself of one's *pochismos*, *anglicisimos*, and of one's unfortunate affiliation with a culturally, socially, and politically underrepresented 'native' ethnic group. It was to speak like a Spaniard, act like a Mexican national, proclaim the glory and grandeur of Spanish civilization, or to publicly announce a cultural heritage which was not one's own. And it was to engage in what Octavio Paz (1961) so clearly defined as *el ninguneo* — that is, to engage in a mental operation consisting of pretending to oneself that one did not exist as a Mexican *American* subject. This was a purposeful intervention; for as Frantz Fanon (1952/1967) so correctly ascertained in the case of the black of the Antilles: 'The Negro of the Antilles will be proportionately whiter — that is, he will come closer to being a real human being — in direct ratio to his mastery of the French language.' (p. 18).

Spanish language programs were of course not the only culprits. The attitudes reflected therein were part and parcel of a hegemonic process, an 'expropriation of identity' which, as Fanon describes in *The Wretched of The Earth*: (Fanon, 1961/ 1968) 'cripples and deforms. . . .' This colonial expropriation 'is not satisfied merely with holding a people in its grip' . . . but 'it turns to the past of the oppressed people, and distorts, disfigures, and destroys it.' (p. 210). Given the sinister logic behind the colonizing grip, it is not surprising that it did not occur to many of our predecessors to teach the Spanish language through Chicano literature to native speakers. The very idea of the existence of a corpus of Chicano literature was foreign to scores of language teachers, who doubted that there was anything closely resembling a Chicano culture and civilization, anything closely resembling a Chicano literary corpus that could be brought into Spanish classes. How could there be when Chicanos were cast as 'brute', 'vulgar' and even pathological entities? They were considered to be the shadow of Euro-American cultures, the secret other which as Octavio Paz (1961) claimed 'could only be met in the secret or the darkness.' (p. 14). In its public forms Chicano culture was usually associated with *tacos*, *fiestas* and *piñatas*.

Given the type of ideological climate of the fifties, where assimilation and the melting pot theory prevailed, instructors of the Spanish language probably felt that they were reinforcing the national cultural identity as much as that of the Hispanic world by suppressing any traces of Chicano literature and culture in their courses. Anyway, they could always fall back on a line of thought which proposes: 'if it doesn't exist, why fix it?' After all, the erasure of Chicano cultural history from national textbooks and cultural productions had reinforced this particular line of thinking. But thanks to the social and political struggles of Chicanos in the sixties, Chicanos who vehemently challenged this Euro-American lingo-centrism, combatted institutional racism and rallied support for the implementation of educational programs, this painful scenario was to be profoundly altered. Briefly stated, these Chicano movement intellectuals succeeded in creating the climate for rewriting the canon of Spanish language teaching by incorporating students' own native cultural milieu as a basis for strengthening their language skills.

Canonical readjustment in the light of the aforementioned obstacles was — and continues to be — a complex process, for it has depended on the creation and effective interfacing of three bodies of knowledge which are directly implicated in this type of instruction: first of all, the creation of a solid body of Chicano literary criticism entrusted with formulating standards and assumptions with which to teach and evaluate Chicano literature; secondly, the development of a solid body of sociolinguistic studies of Chicano Spanish and English with which to illuminate the properties of Chicano Spanish; and thirdly, the development of critical pedagogical studies in education designed to elucidate the types of processes involved in teaching Spanish to the native speaker. The development of Chicano studies as a domain of scholarly inquiry has also contributed to alternative language programs for Chicanos which implement Chicano literature as an instructional means. In fact, much of the available scholarship concerning the use of Chicano literature for teaching Spanish to native speakers has depended on the cultural perspectives and the institutional support of Chicano studies programs, scholars and theoretical perspectives.

One of the most lasting contributions to emerge from this convergence of disciplines with the Chicano movement, was the creation of an alternative perspectives concerning the linguistic expression of Chicanos. As Carlos Monsiváis (1977) so candidly pointed out in a critical volume of essays which references the scholarly contributions of Chicanos from '*La otra cara de México*' (The other face of Mexico):

> *No se trata de aplaudir o de lamentarse sino de situar el problema históricamente. . . . Por lo demás, desde el punto de vista cultural, la mera presunción de 'hablar bien' es sospechosa porque no suele remitir a la vivacidad y a la inventiva idiomática sino a la petrificación e immovilidad de un tipo de habla cuyo genuino rigor es el 'rigor mortis.' (p. 16).*

(The point is not to applaud or complain but to contextualize the problem historically. . . . Beyond that, from a cultural perspective, the mere assumption of 'speaking well' is suspicious because it does not tend to remit vivacity or idiomatic inventiveness but a petrification or immobility of a type of speech whose real rigor is 'rigor mortis').

In the old tradition, Chicanos were reprimanded for *por su insuficiencia verbal* (verbal insufficiency) or *por su olvido homicida del español* (for their homicidal forgetting of Spanish) particularly in elementary Spanish classes. There was little cognizance of the value of the creative, vibrant and linguistically complex expression Chicano students brought with them. In the new tradition, an emerging body of Spanish language materials undertook a serious examination of the wide range of linguistic utterances of Chicanos and sought to familiarize the Chicano Latino population of the United States with the various linguistic options open to them, as well as with the feasibility of using Spanish language instruction as a basis for examining and mastering a variety of standard and popular dialects.

Chicano literature played an important role in this regard insofar as it enacted a deliberate, and often highly stylized rendition of these different forms of expression, ranging from rural to urban, from vernacular forms of speech to the highly academic. The writers of Chicano literary texts, particularly those texts in Spanish, were themselves conscious of their contributions to strengthening the Spanish language expression of Chicanos in the United States through the written word. Miguel Méndez (1976), author of the widely divulged *Peregrinos de Aztlan*, summed up the prevailing sentiment upon prognosticating to his public well in advance of critical studies documenting the success of using Chicano literature for language instruction (Méndez, 1976):

Vamos a decir que nuestra literatura consiste de varios idiomas, pero que nace de un solo corazón. También para la literatura chicana que aparece en lengua española veo un futuro muy luminioso. Ya verás, no pasarán muchos años sin que lo nuestro logre el aplauso de propios y extraños. Me refiero también a Latinoamérica y a España. En cuanto a la función de las obras chicanas escritas en español, está entre otros motivos el de revitalizar y preservar nuestras raíces más profundas. Nuestra cultura ancestral se finca primordialmente en el idioma español y nos llega a través de la genealogía que emerge y se continúa con el transcurso de incontables generaciones. Es un tesoro que ayudaremos a salvaguardar con nuestra aportación. Se me occurre que también enriqueceremos el idioma español con la aportación de muchas palabras nuevas nacidas al amparo de nuestra historia aquí en los EE.UU. (p. 6).

(Let us say that our literature consists of several languages, but it is born out of one heart. I also see a very bright future for Chicano literature that appears in Spanish. You will see, before long, that which is ours will be applauded by our own people as well as others. As for the function of Chicano works written in Spanish, it is among others to revitalize and preserve our deepest roots. Our ancestral culture is rooted primarily in the Spanish language and it is transferred to us through a geneology that emerges and continues with the passing of countless generations. It is a treasure which we will help to preserve with our contribution. It occurs to me that we will also enrich the Spanish language with many new words born as a consequence of our history here in the United States).

As we enter the nineties, instructors of the Spanish language who wish to incorporate Chicano literature into their courses for native speakers are, in fact, doing so from a position of relative privilege when compared to their Chicano/a Latino/a predecessors. These lacked any specialized texts that incorporated Chicano literature within instructional manuals designated for teaching Spanish to the native speaker and found themselves in the unenviable predicament of having to create programs from scratch — without any predecessors in the country. Moreover, these also lacked the benefit of departing from cultural perspectives such as the one voiced by Miguel Méndez. Contemporary instructors of Spanish also enjoy the benefits of drawing from an ever-growing body of Chicano literary and critical texts and the benefit of participating in programs which, by all accounts, are thriving. They may even have the occasion of eliciting the praise of mainstream scholars who are relieved at the prospect of not having to contend with highly fluent Spanish speakers in their elementary courses. Nonetheless, there are still substantial problems to be reckoned with in this type of pedagogical activity.

The most serious problem which must be reckoned with is the continued underrepresentation of this subject matter in college curricula, textbooks and pedagogical studies. After all, the sprinkling of Spanish language programs implementing Chicano literature for the study of Spanish by native speakers hardly constitutes integrating the curriculum. There are long, difficult roads to be traveled, especially when we consider that these Spanish for native speaker curricula are being implemented in institutional sites which do not incorporate Chicano literature within the Spanish major, which continue to lack graduate programs in Chicano literature, or sensitive instructors of the caliber of Miguel Méndez (1981). Yet, at this point in history, it behooves us to be optimistic at the prospects for future growth of these programs, while tempering such optimism with a realistic assessment of the problems to be contended with by instructors who aspire to incorporate Chicano literature into the language curriculum for native speakers. These problems require the purposeful intervention of the instructor at the level of policy, the development of the curricula, and the accessing of instructional materials. The following section examines these problems and offers the reader measures to counteract some of them.

Using Chicano Literature to Teach Spanish to Native Speakers: Problems, Resolutions and Purposeful Intervention

One of the few pedagogical studies to address the use of Chicano literature in university and college level courses in the Southwest is a dissertation by Elia Mar Díaz-Ortiz (1987). Díaz-Ortiz sent questionnaires to professors of Latin American literature regarding the use of Chicano literature in Spanish language courses, and she found that, indeed, Chicano literature was being used in five southwestern states for the purpose of Spanish language instruction. Furthermore, the majority of the respondents queried did agree that Chicano literature belonged in the Spanish language curriculum and that it was of benefit to the students. Although Díaz-Ortiz' study is confined to this specific region and to professors of Latin American literature, who may have a more favorable inclination toward Chicano literature than other professors, her findings seem to confirm a trend towards supporting (at least at the theoretical level) the use of Chicano literature in courses for Spanish speakers within select universities, colleges, and high schools.

However, simply attesting to the viability of using Chicano literature to teach Spanish does not suffice. To quote a familiar Mexican saying: '*Del dicho al hecho hay un gran trecho.*' ('Easier said than done.') That is, instructors entrusted with this mission must contend with a particular set of circumstances which are not common when canonical national Hispanic literatures are incorporated into Spanish language courses. It is not simply that instructors must reckon with a complex linguistic expression which is often not accepted by the official institutional academic culture or with a literary expression which is not widely diffused in popular reference works.

As Díaz-Ortiz (1987) and Sánchez (1981) indicate, in the case of Chicano literature, opinions held by professors towards the viability of teaching and studying Chicano literature may be an obstacle, even when these professors may outwardly be in favor of using Chicano literature. The instructor who proposes to use Chicano literature to teach Spanish to native speakers thus enters (whether willingly or unwillingly) into the unsettling terrain of ideology — that is, age-old social attitudes surrounding the linguistic expression, innovation, native culture, the 'literary' quality of Chicanos and Chicano literature, etc. These attitudes are deeply rooted in a majority of Spanish language professors, ranging from a naive instructor who might worry, 'Is this good enough, it's so different,' to an entire social network, including colleagues, students and administrators, all of whom must also be convinced, largely because of the prevailing stereotypes surrounding minority culture and the novelty of Chicano literature within institutional settings.

These realities came home to me personally one day as I was rushing to my Spanish for native speaker's class. One of my colleagues said to me: 'Can you believe it, a *Chicano writer* next to Borges in a Spanish language text?' He had obviously never heard Chicano students ask me 'Why do we have to study Borges?' The student would have rather studied Anaya. This anecdote points to the fact that the successful implementation of Chicano literature into the Spanish language curriculum requires much more than the enthusiasm of an individual instructor, an instructor who, in this particular case, was privileged enough to have Spanish for native Speakers taught on her campus for almost two decades. As Díaz-Ortiz (1987) points out: 'Chicano literature can be difficult to nurture in the curriculum if it is not recognized and accepted by the curricular "gatekeepers", whether these be faculty, administrators, public officials or community representatives' (p. 62). In addition, Díaz-Ortiz (1987) elaborates that the level of acceptance of Chicano literature will depend largely on the willingness of those involved in curriculum policy-making to explore ways in which Chicano literature can enhance the education of students of all racial, ethnic and cultural backgrounds. But this alone will not suffice. As my anecdotal narrative points out, wide-scale education of professors, staff and educators should be pursued if these types of prejudices surrounding noncanonical traditions such as Chicano literature are to be eradicated. In addition, this endeavor requires a solid institutional commitment to those Chicano Latino professors who would naturally be called upon to launch such undertakings because of their expertise and vested interest in promoting these programs.

Of course, not all of the problems associated with this type of incorporation of Chicano literature into the Spanish curriculum stem from pejorative opinions; as Díaz-Ortiz (1987) pointed out in her study: some instructors actually failed to incorporate more Chicano literature into their courses because they didn't believe that much of it could be found in Spanish. Thus, part of the problem is rooted in ignorance. It is safe to speculate that many of the professors who made these comments never actually studied Chicano literature in college and that their exposure to it was seriously limited. It is not uncommon for these instructors, to equate the whole of Chicano literary production with *Yo soy Joaquín* or solely with Chicano literature disseminated in the sixties or written in English or in Caló. Many of these instructors would probably be surprised to discover that Chicano literature includes the highbrow: romanticism; *costumbrista* pieces, literary biographies, sophisticated ballads, along with popular forms and classic 'movement literature'. Undoubtedly, many of the misconceptions surrounding Chicano literature within educational circles can be attributed to the lag which exists between the time it takes to produce Chicano literary scholarship, the time it takes to disseminate it and the time it takes to translate it into instructional publications for secondary and college level course work.

To add to the instructor's dilemma, few of the Spanish language texts for bilinguals actually contain Chicano literature, and until the publication of Armando Miguélez and Maria Sandoval's (1987) *Jauja*, which promises a greater, more representative grouping of literary pieces, the selection was extremely limited in those which did. *Nuestro Español: Curso para Estudiantes Bilingües* by Hugo A. Mejías and Gloria Garza-Swan (1981) can be said to be representative of these earlier texts, which tend to focus their attention on providing the student with general cultural readings such as 'La joven americana', 'Disco dancing', 'La fiesta de la quinceañera', 'La cocina mexicana en los Estados Unidos', and 'La bruja con cara de caballo.' These readings are often enlisted with the end of affirming the student's own native cultural formation (legends and folktales), strengthening vocabulary and exemplifying the linguistic phenomenon examined in the chapter. A predecessor to this text, Guadalupe Valdés-Fallis and Richard V. Teschner's (1978) *Español Escrito* contains a wide variety of exercises, but even fewer readings, and the ones which do appear are of the general cultural variety such as 'La educación bilingüe y temas relacionados', 'La lectura y la obra literaria' and 'La inmigracion ilegal.' It goes without saying that Spanish languages texts for bilinguals such as these have tended to underrepresent Chicano literature or to subordinate it to strictly linguistic functions and that a greater balance between grammatical and literary pieces is in order in future texts of this nature.

Pedagogical studies concerning the use of Chicano literature in Spanish courses have not made a substantial improvement in this area either. As Díaz-Ortiz (1987: 55) noted in her study of at least seven of the most prominently reviewed sources on teaching Chicano literature, only *one* source sometimes includes teaching Chicano literature in the *Spanish* language curriculum. Thus, the instructor who bypasses all of these lacunae and finds a Spanish for bilinguals text with Chicano literature interlaced between grammatical exercises may well be fortunate. However, this individual may also be very surprised to see that the text's representations of Chicano literature are seriously dated.

To further complicate matters, much of Chicano literature has yet to be recovered. This translates into the added problem that the instructors who elect to incorporate Chicano literature largely through their own personal initiative (given the state of affairs with combined grammar and reading books) faces the additional difficulty of selecting a representative body of texts in a tradition whose contours are changing daily. Throughout the course of my own work, *Conversations with*

Chicano Critics: Portrait of a Counter Discourse (Chabram Dernersesian, 1993), which involves a series of in-depth interviews with prominent critics of Chicano literature, I have had occasion to learn first-hand of the number of Chicano literary excavations which have been undertaken in recent years by contemporary Chicano literary critics such as Rosaura Sánchez, María Herrera Sobek, Yolanda Broyles, Luis Leal, Francisco Lomelí, Nicholas Kanellos, and Juan Rodríguez. These critics have identified scores of Chicano/a memoirs, biographies, novels, chronicles, short stories, theater and ballads unknown to most Chicano literary histories of movement years. This, of course, does not include the significant literary production which has appeared since movement years. For this reason, it is not surprising that, at this point, to speak of Chicano literature in terms of its already familiar 'canon' is to betray one's profound ignorance of the rapid growth of its ever changing literary panorama.

Further yet, within the area of Chicano literary scholarship, we are far from anything closely resembling a definitive Chicano literary history (if such a concept can still be applied in this period of canonical readjustment which has all but dissipated the idea of a linear literary history), although various seminal works exist which merit serious attention. This in itself should not be surprising to those eager instructors who seek to populate their courses with the writings of Chicanos and Chicanas since Chicano literature as a domain of literary activity was institutionalized not more that twenty years ago, and sparingly at that.

Yet, with all of these problems, there are some reference works (dictionaries, guides, partial literary histories and bibliographies) which offer basic information concerning the identification and periodization of Chicano literature. Any of these reference works would be of use to the instructor who is frequently called upon to define Chicano literature and to deliver an exposé of its attributes. The most basic include: *Literatura Chicana*, a translation of *Chicano Literature*, authored by Charles Tatum (1982) and published under the Twayne Series; *Chicano Literature A Reference Guide* (Lomelí and Martínez, 1984) (which includes bibliography and notes on Spanish-speaking writers); a special volume on Chicano Literature soon to be published as *Concise Dictionary of American Literary Biography* (1989); Tina Eger's (1982) indispensable *A Bibliography of Chicano Literary Criticism*; and *The Chicano Periodical Index* (Castillo-Speed, Chabrám and García-Ayvens, 1989) can offer useful information in this regard. Recent years have witnessed a proliferation of monographs of Chicano literature which would also be of use to those interested in pursuing further study of genres, authors or problems. A cursory survey of the most significant monographs produced within the last decade or so would list over twenty. (See Appendix, for a complete listing).

To this list, several issues of literary journals dedicated solely to the diffusion of critical essays can be included, along with a significant body of unpublished dissertations on Chicano literature, a representative sample of which can be found in Evangelina Enríquez' (1982) dissertation, 'Toward a Definition of, and Critical Approaches to Chicano(a) Literature', University of California, Riverside.

For instructors whose sole objective is to acquire a general background concerning the development of Chicano literature, the best sources continue to be such seminal literary scholarship as: 'Mexican American literature: A historical perspective' (Leal, 1979), 'Notes on the evolution of Chicano prose fiction' (Rodríguez, 1979), and, lastly, a critical piece entitled, 'Critical approches to Chicano literature' (Sommers, 1979), which includes a general introduction on Chicano literature and a lengthy exposition of the different critical approaches to the analysis of Chicano literature. *Beyond Stereotypes* and *Third Woman* journal are important because they document Chicana literature, a domain of Chicano literary production much neglected by early Chicano/a literary historians. Many of these critical texts can be read in intermediate and advanced Spanish courses for bilinguals, and they are themselves an important source of cultural history and discussion for students.

Exposing students to the changing perceptions of Chicano literature with regard to its corpus, periodic development and its basic criterion and definition can be readily achieved by contrasting the opinions of literary historians from different generations or schools of thought. A flavor of the types of animated discussions which might ensue from such a dialogue can be seen by contrasting the opinions of critics describing their own criteria. These critical dialogues taken from *Conversations with Chicano Critics* (Chabram Demersesian, 1993), reproduce some of the basic literary scholarship and divergent points of view which prevail with regard to Chicano literature in these literary histories:

Critic #1. So what I eventually proposed was this: that the principal criteria in defining Chicano literature is specificity of reference in terms of the conflict between Anglo-Americans and Chicanos. In which case Chicano literature begins in the early nineteenth century when those conflict circumstances first come into being, and find expression in various forms, both popular and formal. . . . The earliest example of Chicano literature, according to this definition, is the 1826–27 travel account by José María Sánchez, who was sent by the Mexican government into Texas (at that time, it was called 'the northern frontier') to investigate conditions on the northern border between Mexico and the United States. So Sánchez kept a diary of this trip, and in it he refers to existing conflicts between Anglos and Mexicanos; he predicts the loss of Texas in 1827 after surveying the Austin colony, and he describes the Mexicanos who were living there among the Anglos in a way that. . . . Well, he could be talking about people today, he says the same kind of thing you hear today: these Mexicanos aren't even Mexicano anymore, they don't speak Spanish, they don't know their Mexican history. They act just like Anglos. That was back in 1827! (Rodríguez, J.).

Critic #2. First of all, I had to define what I understood by a Chicano. In the article I said that anyone of Mexican descent born in the United States or who lives here permanently and is acquainted with both cultures (Anglo culture and Mexican culture), is a Chicano. Before 1848, you don't have these requirements met, so everything is Mexican. So then you say, 'Does this belong to Mexican literature or not?' Finally, you come up with the fact that it's Mexican literature, but produced in the Southwest. That leads you to the next step: When the Southwest becomes part of the United States, its literature changes too — it becomes Chicano literature because, like the land and the native population, the literary corpus is incorporated into another national state. (Leal, L.).

Critic #3. I take issue with the kind of criticism, which in my opinion, wants to see the history of Chicano literature as an unbroken evolutionary line that descends from the Spanish chronicles of the sixteenth and seventeenth centuries. This, of course, is a problem of literary history, but one which we will be dealing with for some time to come, especially now with the accelerated development of both Chicano literature and criticism.

The Spanish chroniclers are Spaniards of the sixteenth and seventeenth centuries. However, something happens with the introduction of the Anglo element. Recently, I have listened to some very interesting papers . . . that have dealt with specific nineteenth — and early twentieth — century texts written by Mexican Americans. Until this work is done, I agree with José Armas that we can't speak of a Chicano tradition that extends centuries into the past. . . . Why search for origins, when the past is already present with us. Of course, my observations pertain to a literate tradition. The persistence of a mestizo culture is another matter which will go unquestioned.

Given the circumstances, without a readily available context for Chicano literature, the logical direction to look was towards Mexico. Writers and critics pursued this course. Fine and good because we didn't have much else in terms of context for Chicano literature. But it bears repeating that Chicanos are not Mexicans even though some Mexican intellectuals are beginning to reclaim us. Now I think we've reached a wider perspective, we're asking 'What's American literature? What does it include?' (Calderón, H.).

Critic #4. In that essay of mine I take issue with the idea that Chicano literature dates all the way back to the Aztecs, what with its evocation of themes found in Aztec poetry. . . . I wanted to point out that the Chicano literature you see developing in the Southwest comes out of Spanish tradition. In fact, for numerous reasons — many of which were certainly not admirable — early Chicano literature deliberately de-emphasized any Indian aspects. If you look at an early play like *Los Comanches* it's obvious that there was a high degree of resentment between the people that saw themselves as Mexican, and the Indian population. However one chooses to view the experience of colonialism, the Spanish influence is deeply planted in the Southwest, and was formative in the development of Chicano culture.

This is why we see a strong relationship between Chicano literature and other forms of Latin American literature: they both came out of that Spanish-colonial experience, and developed along the same lines. When I read anthologies of Latin American literature that go back to the seventeenth and eighteenth centuries, I'm struck by the fact that Chicano literature, in a telescoped way, repeats much the same historical process of development. Here, as I say, the process has been shortened, but it's still essentially the same cycle. (Paredes, R.).

Discussion of the various contrasting opinions of Chicano critics with respect to Chicano literary history might be structured around the following sub-themes: a) origins of Chicano literature (chronological); b) literary influences (Spanish, Mexican, Anglo Saxon); and c) social, cultural and historical factors bearing on the definition of Chicano literature. Instructors might simply elect to present the different hypothesis surrounding the development of Chicano literature, and ask students to comment on their own perceptions of the material represented. Instructors also have the option of adding life to the session by bringing in representative texts (mentioned in these essays) from each of the periods of Chicano literature so that students would have the opportunity to experience the diverse themes and forms of expression utilized by Chicano literary writers throughout the decades.

This, of course, requires that the instructor have access to a wide range of Chicano literary texts, and access to these texts can be problematic given that much of Chicano literature continues to be published by small presses and journals rather than large-scale corporate presses. Arte Público, Third Woman, and Bilingual Press continue to be the most important organs for the diffusion of Chicano literature and criticism, although in recent years Chicano criticism has appeared with greater frequency in university presses and mainstream journals. Given the fact that many of the classic Chicano literary works are either out of print or else locked in archives in special collections of important universities, the instructor who wishes to incorporate these materials may need to photocopy materials with the consent of the involved parties.

Accessing those literary works which are available in paperback is most successful when the instructors contact Chicano vendors such as Relámpago Books, Bilingual Press and other such operations, given that general bookstores rarely carry a suitable selection of Chicano literary pieces. Similarly, instructors who seek to locate reference materials surrounding Chicano literature would do well to visit the Chicano university libraries at Berkeley, Stanford, Davis, Santa Barbara, and Los Angeles since their holdings in the area of Chicano literature far exceed those housed in most university libraries. An option which is oftentimes overlooked by instructors in their haste to develop course materials is inviting Chicano writers to high school and university campuses for lectures and symposia. Direct contact with authors creates more appreciation for the material as students are afforded the opportunity to converse directly with the source concerning literary influences, personal motivations and experimentation with forms.

Once instructors are informed as to the chronology and availability of Chicano literature, they are faced with the selection of appropriate texts, and this selection is usually undertaken by way of chronology, region, or theme. Some of the important themes that have penetrated Chicano literature are: immigration, acculturation, women's lives, aging, urbanization, the migrant experience, oppression, racism, a variety of human dilemmas and many other experiences pertaining to the Spanish-speaking population. Instructors contemplating the selection of specific texts are also usually motivated by linguistic considerations, namely: what to do in the light of a bilingual bicultural corpus of literary works? For those who adhere to the rule of thumb: only Spanish language texts in Spanish courses, a selection of Spanish language Chicano literary texts can be found in many *corridos* and legends, as well as in the writings of authors such as: Miguel Méndez, Gina Valdés, Lucha Corpi, Tomás Rivera, Rolando Hinojosa-Smith, and Alejandro Morales. Two Spanish language literary texts which include the works of Chicanas have been very successful in Spanish language courses. These are: a translation called *Esta Puente mi Espalda* (Moraga and Castillo, 1988), which provides many literary and cultural essays in Spanish concerning Chicana feminism, and *Puentes y Fronteras* (Valdés, 1982), a series of *coplas* in which the themes of love, immigration and work are brought together under the muse of a literary voice which echoes *La Llorona*.[3] While any course designed to instruct native speakers of Spanish in the language would naturally draw from a variety of Spanish language texts, students as well as the instructor would benefit immensely from using Chicano literature written in English, given that some of the most representative texts are in English or else are bilingual. Of course, these texts would be utilized for discussion, compositions and oral and written summaries in Spanish. As Rosaura Sánchez (1981) notes: 'Stories and articles not available in Spanish may be broken up into parts and translated collectively by groups of three or four students. The isolated parts may either be read aloud to the entire class, written out and shown with a projector on the wall, or typed out, mimeographed, and distributed to all class members.' (pp. 95–96). It goes without saying that students would continue to perform the majority of class functions in Spanish.

Thus far this chapter has examined some of the anomalies involved in incorporating Chicano literature into the curriculum, describing institutional constraints as well as the particular types of literary, scholarly and linguistic issues which are brought into play when Chicano literature is incorporated into the Spanish curriculum, and proposing alternate routes for dealing with traditional subject matter. In each of these cases, the purposeful intervention of the instructor has been required, whether it be convincing unsympathetic administrators of the value of Chicano literature, developing literary course materials for review in courses, and/or seeking out organs for the diffusion and promotion of Chicano literature. Such active intervention may seem excessively troublesome for those who are accustomed to pedagogical routines which regurgitate 'what's there', or who are themselves baffled at the prospect of having to go to such extremes to implement the literary trajectories of a *local* mode of cultural expression. The question which inevitably emerges is: Is it worth it? In answering this question, one might, for example, point out, as Gelfant (1981) did not so long ago, that similar trajectories would be required for American literature 'when American literature did not exist at all as an academic subject, when it was defined as substandard English Literature or as popular writing that anyone could read without instruction.' (p. 776). Chicano scholars, linguists, educators, and Spanish teachers have travelled great distances in accepting Chicano literature as an academic subject which is not defined as substandard or condemned as 'barrio crap', although this is a constant effort — obstacles and prejudices continue to exist. Other considerations oblige the author of this essay to answer: yes, it is worth it, and follow that answer with a second 'we can't do without this type of purposeful intervention.'

This response is based on sound pedagogical theory as much as it is on a concern for the not-so-distant future when the proliferation of the Spanish-speaking population of the United States will itself require well seasoned programs, developed materials, as well as experienced professors who are in the advantageous position of being well experienced for contending with the large number of students expected to join Spanish for native speakers classes. Yet none of these rationales suffice without first examining the role which Chicano literature plays in teaching Spanish to native speakers and without examining some of the concrete ways this literary expression can succeed in achieving the objective of imparting a greater knowledge of Spanish to native speakers.

Role of Chicano Literature in Teaching Spanish to Native Speakers

Using Chicano literature to instruct native speakers in the Spanish language can act as a stimulus for instilling a sense of cultural pride and awareness in those native speakers who have not had the opportunity to learn about their own cultural heritage in high school or other university classes. This heightened cultural awareness often triggers more interest and pride in the Spanish language itself, especially among students who are self-conscious of the encroachment of English on their Spanish. This awareness can stimulate the student to study harder and master the unforeseen difficulties encountered along the way. Chicano literature may also provide exposure to alternative perceptions of Chicano language, culture and social relations between groups and help the student overcome the effects of pejorative attitudes towards their own expression. Here I am referring to attitudes that have been passed down from insensitive Spanish professors who might have equated dialectal variation of Spanish with illiteracy, as occurred this past year at a local university where students alleged that they were repeatedly insulted and humiliated because of the way they spoke Spanish.[4] Using Chicano literature in bilingual settings which are sensitive to the students' background and speech, may also assist in overall retention of students of Mexican descent in high schools and colleges. As Rosaura Sánchez (1981) points out in her article, 'It may well be that the Spanish class will become the one spot on campus where Chicano students may come together to discuss questions that their standard university courses never focus on.' (p. 94).

As havens from the pressures of alienating environments, these Spanish classes can offer the student a bridge between past and present experiences, especially for students in transition from migrant and immigrant backgrounds whose contact with the educational system has been irregular or limited. Literary texts such as *De la Vida y el Folclore de la Frontera* by Miguel Méndez (1986) for example, provide the students with an overview of cultural panoramas from the border that treat problems associated with immigration and culture contact, problems that bear heavily on those students whose passage from home life to the university can be tantamount to crossing an international border. A number of the stories in this volume such as '*Los viejos mexicanos de los Estados Unidos*' can offer the student uplifting testimonies of perseverance, pride and group cohesion which are indispensable to them, particularly in university settings where their numbers are scarce and where they often encounter discrimination, or lack a sufficient number of Chicano Latino role models. Texts such as. . . . *Y no se lo Tragó la Tierra* by Tomás Rivera (1971) and *House on Mango Street* by Sandra Cisneros (1983) focus on the adolescent experience, providing the reader with a glimpse of the the trials and tribulations of this human segment as well as with some of the obstacles which Chicano/a youth encounter while growing up in the educational system and in the family. Poems such as 'The Ballad of Gregorio Cortez' (Paredes, 1982) and *coplas* such as the socially-oriented selections found in *Puentes y Fronteras* (Valdés, 1982) can provide students with examples of culture conflict and social tensions which have historically involved the Mexican community in the United States, providing them with the courage and the strength to resist encroachments on their civil rights.

Instructors who would like to furnish students with an idea of the positive links between Chicano literature and other literary traditions might well consider interlacing Chicano literary texts with Mexican and Latin American literary texts along the lines of particular thematic clusters, so that students may gain an awareness of the international dimensions of their literary history. Chicano literature may also help students gain an understanding of the dynamics of other ethnic groups and relations. As Luis Leal pointed out in an interview (Chabram Dernersesian, 1993) in which I asked him a question regarding the function of Chicano literature:

> So to answer your question, for me Chicano literature is a field that's just as important as any other. Once it's represented in an egalitarian fashion, Chicano literature, like black literature, will benefit Anglo American literature. Chicano literature will also create a greater interest in Mexico, particularly among international scholars, who will recognize the Mexican roots of Chicano literature. In this sense, Chicano literature is like a bridge: it enables us to read Anglo American literature from a Chicano/ Mexican perspective and Mexican literature from a Chicano perspective. (Leal, L.).

Instructors who wish to animate their courses should consciously seek to go beyond the printed word to incorporate films, recordings of Chicano literature, and theatrical renditions of Chicano plays given that much of Chicano literature forms belongs to this oral multi-media tradition. Films such as 'I am Joaquín', 'The Ballad of Gregorio Cortez' and 'Zoot Suit' are all available for instructional use and can be complemented with printed counterparts. A productive exercise in this regard involves comparing and contrasting, for example, the poem 'I am Joaquin' with the film; comparing 'The Ballad of Gregorio Cortez' with the *corrido*, and the poem 'El Louie' with the play 'Zoot-Suit.' For class discussion students may be asked to discuss the manners in which a given narrative changes once it is translated into film or music, and to comment on which medium they feel is most effective for delivering the message of the literary piece in question.

Incorporating this type of an exercise into Spanish classes can be a treat for those students who form part of a mass media society and whose Spanish classes have unfortunately consisted of boring drills and forms of cognition which do not tap into those forms of cognition which they experience in their daily lives at home. Action-oriented exercises which involve the students' participation in the reproduction of Chicano literary texts have also been successful in generating group discussion, augmentation of vocabulary and improvement of grammatical structures. Students might, for example, be encouraged to write a class play in Spanish surrounding a Chicano cultural experience and then given the needed support to perform it before the public. Or they might be encouraged to take a poem such as 'The Ballad of Gregorio Cortez' (Paredes, 1982) and dramatize it by reading it aloud with different voices. A popular Spanish language version of the poem reads like this:

> El el condado El Carmen
> miren lo que ha sucedido,
> murió el Cherife Mayor
> quedando Román herido.

> Otro día por la mañana
> cuando la gente llegó,
> unos a otros dicen:
> **-No saben quién lo mató.**
>
> *Se anduvieron informando*
> *como tres horas después,*
> *supieron que el malhechor*
> *era Gregorio Cortez.*
> ....
> *Venían los perros* jaunes,
> *venían sobre la huella,*
> *pero alcanzar a Cortez*
> *era seguir a una estrella.*
> ....
> *Allá por El Encinal,*
> *según por lo que aquí se dice,*
> *se agarraron a balazos*
> *y les mató otro* cherife.
>
> *Decía Gregorio Cortez*
> *con su pistola en la mano:*
> **-No corran,** rinches **cobardes**
> **con un solo mexicano.** (pp. 158–160)
> ....
> ....
> ....

For this exercise, students could alternate reading the parts of the narrator of the story and of the anonymous public. Students could also be made aware of the presence of non-standard popular forms of speech which have been legitimized in the popular imagination of Spanish-speaking populations of Texas such as *jaunes*, (hound dogs), *rinches* (rangers), and *cherife* (sheriff). As much as possible instructors should refrain from instilling a corrective function in cases such as these. A more productive route is to offer students a range of semantic possibilities so that they do not undermine popular variants, but rather incorporate them with other options. Years of teaching Chicano literature to native speakers has taught me that students are more than delighted to learn standard variants; most of them are comfortable with who they are, and they take pride in their popular variants, but they want to improve their grasp of the breadth of the Spanish language. In their compositions on Chicano literary pieces such as 'The Ballad of Gregorio Cortez' (Paredes, 1982), the students wanted *more*: more vocabulary, transitional phrases, and idiomatic expressions in Spanish.

Other types of productive exercises can be elicited when students are encouraged to collect legends, tales and sayings in Spanish from their communities or from their elders and then disseminate this material in the form of oral presentations in the classroom. These types of exercises, which incorporate community involvement, can have the same impact on the Chicano student that a visit to Mexico or Spain can have on non-native students of the Spanish language. The end result of these types of immersions into the local community is close contact with a lived culture and spoken linguistic expression.

Students can also be encouraged to write legends, *cuentos*, and/or *corridos* in classes on the basis of their own direct experience with these forms, or on the basis of research. A favorite exercise is reconstructing 'The Diablo Story', which tells the fate a young Chicana who goes to a party without her dad's consent, and consequently meets a young handsome lad who turns out to be the devil in disguise, and who subsequently drags her all over the roofs of El Paso (according to my mom, at least). This exercise can be used for a variety of purposes, including eliciting the students own Diablo Stories; introducing themes regarding parent-child relations; discussing male/female relationships; and drilling difficult structures such as irregular preterites; the contrast between preterite and the imperfect; and future and conditional verb forms. Students can also be encouraged to do conditional clauses, assuming the roles of devil, daughter or parent; '*Si yo fuera la hija, haría tal y tal.*' If composition is the objective, students may be asked to rewrite the legend, giving it a more contemporary social ending, perhaps even a feminist reading. Students may also be asked to write rebuttals and/or hypothetical case studies on the function of these types of Diablo stories in the Chicano/Latino communities of the Southwest.

The legend of *La Llorona*, on the other hand, provides the instructor with a wealth of possibilities for discussion and grammatical exercises because of its many variants and cultural forms. Students might be expected to collect *llorona* narratives from their communities, and then to pinpoint the differences which emerge in her physical appearance. (Sometimes she has the face of a horse, other times she is a beautiful Indian woman, and other times, she has no face, just a shrill). Other differences might be elicited in terms of her fate, the nature of her crime, and the rationale for her break with social norms. *La Llorona* is also a productive legend for multi-media presentations and contrasting views of familiar narratives. For example, Joan Baez's *La Llorona* (included in her *Gracias a la vida* album) can be used as a contrast to Rudy Anaya's (1984) *The Legend of La Llorona* and the students' own collected variants of *la llorona*. What emerges from this contrast is usually the bad woman/good woman syndrome: *La Llorona* as the blessed mother and symbol of universal suffering dressed in blue like the virgin de Guadalupe, and *La Llorona* as Malinche (Malintzin Tenepal), or criminal and perpetrator of matricide. These versions can also be contrasted to contemporary Chicana feminist readings of *la malinche* which view this figure sympathetically and identify the *malinchista* ideologies which have surrounded this much misunderstood figure of Chicano and Mexican cultural histories. Including contemporary Chicano literary texts on *La Llorona* always has the added effect of showing alternatives and changing values towards women within the Chicano community. In both the *Legend of La Llorona* by Anaya (1984), and *Puentes y Fronteras* (Valdés, 1982), for example, *La Llorona* is transformed, and dealt with in a more sensitive, more humane fashion. In the first she is the victim of Cortez, in the second, she is a benevolent (albeit, political) Chicano fairy godmother type who watches over her children as they cross the border. She hears their sufferings and dreams, and help them in their resistance to domination.

Aside from the rich social themes which are elicited from discussing *la llorona*, all types of basic grammatical exercises are made possible with *La Llorona*. Collected *Llorona* narratives can be used for familiarizing the student with popular and standard variants of the Spanish language. Students can pick out the non-standard dialect in a text, then offer a series of synonyms as alternatives. Students can also identify non-standard verb formations which are prevalent among the Spanish-speaking populations and drilled in texts such as *Nuestro Español* (Mejías and Garza-Swan, 1981). In exercises such as these, where students are called upon to examine bilingual texts or popular texts, dictionaries of *chicanismos* and *mexicanismos* furnish the instructor with an excellent complement to a traditional dictionary or a dictionary of synonyms.

Together these exercises attest to the wide range of possibilities for using Chicano literature to teach Spanish to native speakers and for counteracting prevailing stereotypes which assume that Chicanos lack a rich literary history. It would be misleading to suggest to the instructor who embarks on using Chicano literature as a basis for instructing native speakers that there will not be obstacles to be encountered along the way. Many of these obstacles have been brought to light here with the express purpose of soliciting the instructor's purposeful intervention. Yet instructors who embark on this course must rewrite the canon, interfacing academic and nonacademic communities, and 'voicing' the silences which have been levied by historical documents. Such instructors are then in the advantageous position of making a substantial mark on the pedagogy of language teaching, as well as on their students. Their students will benefit from a form of instruction which privileges their own cultural formation and dignifies their own linguistic expression. Thus contemporary instructors are also in the position of helping to alter the social fabric that wove the devastating portrait which inaugurates this essay and will participate in a much needed endeavor: the diffusion of Chicano literature to its intended public, and the creation of a community of readers. As Luis Leal points out (Chabram Dernersesian, 1993):

> Well . . . the function of Chicano literature is that of forming a community of Chicano writers and readers. There are great regional divisions — Texas, New Mexico, California, Chicago — that separate Chicanos, and our literature furnishes us with a means of bringing together this culturally diverse Chicano community. Over and above that, I'd say that Chicano literature has its own unique way of reconstructing the Chicano cultural experience which complements other domains of Chicano scholarship. (Leal, L.).

Beyond that, Luis Leal points out that for him, the function of Chicano criticism 'is just a way of bringing people together — letting others know the value of Chicano literature.' To the degree that instructors of Spanish language courses for native speakers incorporate Chicano literature in their courses, they too will comply with this highly commendable and much needed critical function.

Notes

1 I would like to thank Zare Dernersesian for his valuable assistance in the preparation of this manuscript.
2 According to the San Francisco Examiner (National edition), as recently as 1990, this painful scenario was experienced by native speakers at the University of

California, Davis, who 'were made to feel "foolish", embarrassed and insulted by UC-Davis teachers in Spanish because of their accents and the way they used the language.' (Brazil, 1990).

3 *Corridos*, a 'narrative form of ballad in eight-syllable verse, . . . brought to Mexico and hence to the Southwest' (Campa, 1979:240) are popular songs that commemorate the daring accomplishments and troubles of popular heroes. They tend to be repetitive in musical tones and illustrate folk culture at its best. They include macho stories of fierce popular leaders facing death with courage after taking revenge for injustices suffered.

A *copla* is a 'four-line stanza with its distinctive wit, wisdom, or satire. . . . Whether the subject was love, hate, envy, sarcasm or any other human emotion, there was always a *copla* to sum it up succinctly.' (Campa, 1979:240). Taken from the Castilian use of stanzas in a poem or song, *coplas* are a unit with self-contained meaning in a poem, story or a song. It is more frequently associated with singing and dancing than just with the written form.

La Llorona, literally the 'crying woman' is 'that nocturnal mourner who roamed at night looking for her lost children . . . her constant crying was like the wailing of a siren approaching and dying faintly in the distance.' (Campa, 1979:201). *La llorona* is a ballad of ancient origin portraying the story of a woman who killed her children and returned after death to cry about her crime forever. It is a sad story that goes with popular belief about the presence of certain spirits roaming around. (ACD and HT).

4 The *San Francisco Examiner* (Brazil, 1990) quoting Henry Trueba, who chaired the University task force, reported: 'We saw students who were so angry they were almost crying. These students had gone through hell.' (p. A-2). See also, The *Sacramento Bee* (Natt, 1990) which reported that 'their (students') ability to speak Spanish was judged unfairly because of their skin color. Even though they came from a Hispanic background, some said, they spoke mostly English. When they tried to learn their native language, some whites accused them of trying to get "an easy A", and some teachers ridiculed their colloquialism.' (p. B-4).

References

ANAYA, R. (1984) *The Legend of La Llorona*, Berkeley, CA, Tonatiuh-Quinto Sol.

BRAZIL, E. (1990, May 15) 'Spanish-speaking students accuse UC-Davis of bias: Castillian-oriented profs are insulting them, they say', *San Francisco Examiner* [National edition], p. A-2.

CAMPA, A.L. (1979) *Hispanic Culture in the Southwest*, Norman, OK, University of Oklahoma Press.

CASTILLO-SPEED, L., CHABRÁM, R. and GARCÍA-AYVENS, F. (Eds) (1989) *The Chicano Periodical Index*, 7, 2, Berkeley, CA, University of California.

CISNEROS, S. (1983) *The House on Mango Street*, Houston, TX, Arte Público.

Concise Dictionary of American Literary Biography, (1989) Detroit, MI, Gale Research.

CHABRAM DERNERSESIAN, A. (1993) *Conversations with Chicano Critics: Portrait of a Counter Discourse*, unpublished manuscript, University of California Davis, CA.

DÍAZ-ORTIZ, E.M. (1987) *The Use of Chicano Literature in University and College Spanish-language Courses in the Southwestern United States*, Austin, TX, University of Texas, University Microfilms International, 256, 8717397.

EGER, T. (1982) *A Bibliography of Chicano Literary Criticism*, Berkeley, CA, Chicano Studies Library.

ENRÍQUEZ, E. (1982) *Toward a Definition of, and Critical Approaches to Chicano(a) Literature*, unpublished doctoral dissertation, University of California, Riverside.

FANON, F. (1967) *Black Skins White Masks*, MARKMANN, C.L. (Trans.) New York, NY, Grove. (Original work published 1952).

FANON, F. (1968) *The Wretched of the Earth*, FARRINGTON, C. (Trans.) New York, NY, Grove. (Original work published 1961).

GELFANT, B.H. (1981) 'Mingling and sharing in American literature: Teaching ethnic fiction', *College English*, **43**, 8, pp. 763–72.

HERNÁNDEZ-CHÁVEZ, E., COHEN, A. and BELTRANO, A. (1975) *El Lenguaje de los Chicanas: Regional and Social Characteristics of Language Used by Mexican-Americans*, Arlington, VA, Center for Applied Linguistics.

LEAL, L. (1979) 'Mexican American literature: A historical perspective', in SOMMERS, J. and IBARRA-FRAUSTO, T. (Eds) *Modern Chicano Writers: A Collection of Critical Essays*, Englewood Cliffs, NJ, Prentice-Hall, pp. 18–30.

LOMELÍ, F. and MARTINEZ, J. (Eds) (1984) *Chicano Literature: A Reference Guide*, Westport, CT, Greenwood Press.

MEJÍAS, H.A. and GARZA-SWAN, G. (1981) *Nuestro Español: Curso Para Estudiantes Bilingües*, New York, NY, Macmillan.

MÉNDEZ, M. (1976) *Peregrinos de Aztlán*, Tucson, AZ, Editorial Peregrinos.

MÉNDEZ, M. (1981) Entrevista, *La Palabra*, **3**, 1 and 2, pp. 1–17.

MÉNDEZ, M. (1986) *De la Vida y el Folclore de la Frontera*, Tucson, AZ, Mexican American Studies and Research Center, University of Arizona.

MIGUÉLEZ, A. and SANDOVAL, M. (1987) *Jauja: Método Integral de Español para Bilingües*, Englewood Cliffs, NJ, Prentice-Hall.

MONSIVÁIS, C. (1977) 'Prólogo', *La Otra Cara de México: El Pueblo Chicano*, México, El Caballito, pp. 1–19.

MORAGA, C. and CASTILLO, A. (Eds) (1988) *Esta Puente, mi Espalda*, San Francisco, CA, ISM Press.

NATT, L. (1990, March 15) 'UCD aid to Hispanics taking Spanish is called inadequate', *The Sacramento Bee* [Final], p. B-4.

PAREDES, A. (1982) *With his Pistol in his Hand: A Border Ballad and its Hero*, Austin, TX, University of Texas.

PAZ, O. (1961) *The Labyrinth of the Solitude: Life and Thought in Mexico*, KEMP, L. (Trans.) New York, NY, Grove. (Original work published 1950).

RIVERA, T. (1971) *. . . Y no se lo Tragó la Tierra*, Berkeley, CA, Quinto Sol.

RODRÍGUEZ, J. (1979) 'Notes on the evolution of Chicano prose fiction', in SOMMERS, J. and IBARRA-FRAUSTO, T. (Eds) *Modern Chicano Writers: A Collection of Critical Essays*, Englewood Cliffs, NJ, Prentice-Hall, pp. 67–73.

SÁNCHEZ, R. (1981) 'Spanish for native speakers at the university: Suggestions', in VALDÉS, G., LOZANO, A. and GARCÍA-MOYA, R. (Eds) *Teaching Spanish to the Hispanic Bilingual*, New York, NY, Teacher's College, pp. 91–9.

SOMMERS, J. (1979) 'Critical approaches to Chicano literature', in SOMMERS, J. and IBARRA-FRAUSTO, T. (Eds) *Modern Chicano Writers: A Collection of Critical Essays*, Englewood Cliffs, NJ, Prentice-Hall, pp. 31–40.

TATUM, C. (1982) *Chicano Literature*, Twayne's United States Authors Series, 433, Boston, MA, Twayne.

VALDÉS, G. (1982) *Puentes y Fronteras*, Los Angeles, CA, Castle Litograph.

VALDÉS-FALLIS, G. and TESCHNER, R.V. (1978) *Español Escrito: Curso para Hispanohablantes Bilingües*, New York, NY, Scribners.

Appendix A

BINDER, W. (1985) *Partial Autobiographies: Interviews with Twenty Chicano Poets*, Erlangen, W. Germany, Plam & Enke.

BRUCE-NOVOA, J. (1982) *Chicano Poetry: A Response to Chaos*, Austin, TX, University of Texas.

BRUCE-NOVOA, J. (1982) *Chicano Authors*, Austin, TX, University of Texas.

BRUCE-NOVOA, J. (1983) *La Literatura Chicana a Través de sus Autores*, MASTRANGELO, S. (Trans.) México, Siglo Veintiuno Editores. (Original work published 1980).

CANDELARIA, C. (1986) *Chicano Poetry: A Critical Introduction*, Westport, CT, Greenwood Press.

DAYDI-TOLSON, S. (Ed) (1985) *Five Poets of Aztlan*, Binghamton, NY, Bilingual Press.

HERRERA-SOBEK, M. (Ed) (1985) *Beyond Stereotypes*, Binghamton, NY, Bilingual Press.

HERRERA-SOBEK, M. (1990) *The Mexican Corrido: A Feminist Analysis*, Bloomington & Indianapolis, IN, Indiana University.

HUERTA, J. (1982) *Chicano Theatre*, Ypsilanti, MI, Bilingual Press.

JIMÉNEZ, F. (Ed) (1979) *The Identification and Analysis of Chicano Literature*, Binghamton, NY, Bilingual Press.

KANELLOS, N. (1983) *Mexican American Theatre*, Houston, TX, Arte Público.

LEAL, L., DE NECOCHEA, F., LOMELLI, F. and TRUJILLO, R. (Eds) (1982) *A Decade of Chicano Literature (1970–1979): Critical Essays and Bibliography*, Santa Barbara, CA, La Causa.

LEAL, L. (1984) *Aztlan y México Perfiles Literarios e Históricos*, Binghamton, NY, Bilingual Press.

LEWIS, M. (1984) *Introduction to the Chicano Novel*, Houston, TX, Arte Público.

OLIVARES, J. (Ed) (1986) *International Studies in Honor of Tomás Rivera*, Houston, TX, Arte Público.

RODRIGUEZ DEL PINO, S. (1982) *La Novela Chicana Escrita en Español: Cinco Autores Comprometidos*, Ypsilanti, MI, Bilingual Press.

SALDIVAR, J. (Ed) (1984) *The Rolando Hinojosa Reader*. Houston, TX, Arte Público.

SALDÍVAR, R. (1990) *Chicano Narrative: The Dialectics of Difference*, Madison, WI, The University of Wisconsin.

SÁNCHEZ, M. (1985) *Contemporary Chicana Poetry: An Approach to an Emerging Literature*, Berkeley, CA, University of California.

SOMMERS, J. and IBARRA-FRAUSTO, T. (Eds) (1979) *Modern Chicano Writers: A Collection of Critical Essays*, Englewood Cliffs, NJ, Prentice-Hall.

SOMOZA, O. (1983) *Nueva Narrativa Chicana*, México, Diógenes.

TATUM, C. (1982) *Chicano Literature*, Boston, MA, Twayne.

VÁZQUEZ-CASTRO, J. (1979) *Acerca de la Literatura: Diálogo con 3 Autores Chicanos*, San Antonio, TX, M&A Editions.

VERNON, L. (Ed) (1986) *Contemporary Chicano Fiction*, Binghamton, NY, Bilingual Press.

Chapter 10

Using Elements of Cooperative Learning in the Communicative Foreign Language Classroom

Sidney Gorman

Several documents recently adopted by the California State Department of Education, including the *Foreign Language Model Curriculum Standards* (1985), the *Handbook for Planning an Effective Foreign Language Program (1985)*, and the *Foreign Language Framework* (1989), together with the *Statement on Competencies in Languages Other Than English Expected of Entering Freshmen* (1986), which has been ratified by the Academic Senates of the California Community Colleges, the California State University and the University of California, have established functional communication in the target language as the goal for California's public school foreign language programs. While foreign language teachers have always intended to enable students to use the target language, in recent years foreign language educators have learned to look at the way we reach this goal somewhat differently. We have come to recognize that knowing about language — defining grammar structures and conjugating verbs — does not equate with using language to complete a communicative task. We have recognized as well that in order to learn to use language effectively, students must be provided many and frequent opportunities to practice language in communicative settings.

The growing awareness of the importance of communication has led to radical changes in the look of today's foreign language classroom. More and more commonly today, teachers are abandoning the traditional format, with rows of students chanting responses to structure and pattern drills, and establishing instead paired and grouped activities, where students struggle to exchange messages or information in realistic contexts.

Not surprisingly then, many experienced foreign language teachers are finding themselves in much the same place as they were at the beginning of their careers; they are looking for ways to establish and foster the appropriate communicative atmosphere, and to manage a very busy and dynamic classroom. It is here that the practitioners of Cooperative Learning have much to offer foreign language teachers. This chapter will not attempt to define or describe any of the popular models of cooperative or group learning, nor to provide a blueprint for classroom management. Teachers who want a deeper understanding should refer to the bibliography for further reading and/or seek out one of the many workshops or seminars available. The goal of this chapter is to demonstrate the application of some of the tenets of the cooperative models to the communicative foreign language classroom and to look at the role that native language speakers might play in a communication-based classroom.

Greta D. Little and Sara L. Sanders (1989) found in research they conducted in beginning French and German classes that 'a sense of classroom community is a crucial prerequisite to truly communicative interaction' (p. 277). They report that 'communication does not actually take place in the classroom unless the language learners are a community' (p. 277). This would suggest that teachers must intentionally provide activities or situations where students within the class develop a common pool of knowledge about one another, and learn to see their classmates as partners and resources. This also seems to suggest that native speakers in the class can most likely assume the important roles of resource persons for their groups.

One element considered indispensable in any cooperative learning model is that of team building. By extension, the foreign language teacher should also consider class building. By this we mean that individual participants in a group activity must develop a sense of membership and ownership in the group's results. Team building strategies thus serve two essential purposes in the foreign language classroom: they help to form a sense of community and they provide language practice.

In a lower level class, where language is severely limited, an activity such as 'Four Corners' allows class members to learn about one another while they practice language likely to be taught at that level. In this activity, the teacher directs students to group themselves in the four corners of the room based on some shared quality. For example, if the class has learned the names of the days, months, seasons, and how to say the date, the teacher may hang pictures representing Spring, Summer, Fall and Winter, one in each corner of the room. Students are told to group themselves according to the season of their birthdays. Once they are divided into four groups, they are directed to line up in order of their birthdays. This generates questions and answers from group members. They are then told to make sure they know the names and birthdates of the individuals on both sides. They can then make sure that all members of the group know each other by introducing their neighbors to the rest of the group. If they have the language, they can be asked to discuss whether they like or dislike their birthdays and to tell why. The teacher can then direct questions to various groups, asking members about other people in the group, asking people from Spring to recall something that was said about someone in Winter, etc. The activity can be extended by then directing students to move to the season they would prefer to have been born in and to talk in the new groupings about why they did or didn't move. Again information can be shared by the whole class.

A variation of Four Corners designed to allow students to discover native and non-native resource persons in the class might be to ask students to estimate the number of Spanish-speaking persons they know personally. Then ask the students to go to one corner of the room if they know from 0 to 5 Spanish-speaking persons, to another corner if they know from 6–10 Spanish-speaking persons, to another if they know 11–15 and to the remaining corner if they know 16 or more. Ask the students to line up in their respective corners according to the number of Spanish speakers they know. Then ask them to find out from each other if any of the people they know are from another country, and if so, what country.

Extend the activity by directing students to move to the corner that represents the total number of Spanish speakers they would prefer to have met and to talk in their groups about why they did or did not move. Have them share their reasons with the class.

At a higher level, where the students control more language, African-style Introductions provides an ideal class building activity. In this activity, each individual is spotlighted one at a time (perhaps not all in one day). Class members are invited to tell all the good and admirable things they know about the person, thus introducing that person in a positive light. Other class members are encouraged to express their admiration and to ask questions to get further information. In the event that no one seems to know very much about a person, things such as 'He has a nice smile', or 'I like her perfume' are allowed and often generate more information than might be expected.

In a classroom where much time will be spent in small groups of two to four, many teachers choose to establish permanent or semi-permanent teams of students. These teams should be encouraged to develop a team community. Teams can agree upon a team name and a symbol to represent the team. The name and symbol should be a reflection of common interests or qualities that the group identifies. Teams can then identify themselves and explain their symbol to the whole class, providing both team and class building.

Activities 10.1–10.3 are additional exercises designed to strengthen the sense of a team community.

Activity 10.1: Los escudos (*The coat of arms*)

Purpose:	To design coat of arms for team.
Method:	Each team of 3 or 4 students works together to design an original *escudo*. Each *escudo* must have: 1. an original shape, and within that shape 2. a symbol that represents each member of the team, 3. a symbol that represents the team's home base, 4. a secret symbol that only has meaning for team members, 5. a motto that expresses the team's essence.
Time:	Teams should be allowed a few minutes each day over a 2 to 3 week period to plan their *escudo*.
Evaluation:	Each team must give an oral report to the class on the meaning of its *escudo*. Points are given based on creativity and participation.
Benefits:	Students work together to agree on appropriate symbols that represent all team members. Native speakers are valuable resources of both symbols and vocabulary. Opportunities for discussion of contrasting cultural perceptions of symbols.

Activity 10.2: ¿Quién soy? (*Who am I?*)

Purpose:	To demonstrate the ability to ask and answer questions about personal biographical information, description and identity.
Method:	Teacher prepares slips of paper with the names of famous people, personalities, characters and pins a name on each student's back. Students are not allowed to see their own slip but may see anyone else's. Their task is to find out their own identity by asking yes/no and information questions of other students in the class. They must also provide answers to other students' questions. They may not ask 'Who am I?' or any question which will tell them their own identity directly. Questioning must continue until all students have enough information to guess their own identity.
Time:	10–15 minutes.
Evaluation:	Points given based on ability to discover own identity as well as on participation and exclusive use of language.
Benefits:	Use of names like José Canseco, Plácido Domingo, Don Quijote, Moctezuma, will draw students attention to important contemporary and historical Hispanic figures.

Activity 10.3: ¿Qué hemos hecho? (*What have we done?*)

Purpose:	To demonstrate the ability to tell things students have done, experiences they have had and to inquire about others' experiences.
Method:	Students share personal experiences and activities until each member of the group has identified one thing he or she has done that no other member of the group has done and one thing everyone else has done that he or she has not done. Groups agree on the most interesting activity or experience and report it to the class.
Time:	15–20 minutes.
Evaluation:	Points given based on participation and exclusive use of language.
Benefits:	Students learn about others' accomplishments and talk about their own. They also find out what they have in common.

A second element of cooperative learning models is that activities must promote a sense of positive interdependence. Students must recognize that the group's success requires that each member participate and contribute. Such interdependence adds to the individual's sense of community since each member of the group feels that to some degree his/her participation is essential to success.

Activities for the foreign language classroom that promote this sense of positive interdependence would be those in which the task cannot be accomplished without the participation of each member of the group. Any paired activity where each partner knows only one part of the information required would meet this requirement. Good examples are found in *Look Again Pictures*, J. Winn-Bell Olson (1984). In these activities, each partner is given a picture which only he or she may look at. The two pictures are identical except for a limited number of differences. The partners describe to each other what they see until the differences have all been identified. In another, similar paired activity, students compare datebook pages until they can find a two-hour block of time when they can get together. The storytelling activity and the reading jigsaw activity described in the next section demonstrate the element of positive interdependence for groups larger than two. Activities 10.4, 10.5, and 10.6 promote a sense of positive interdependence among students working in pairs, or small groups.

Activity 10.4: Dos artistas (*Two artists*)

Purpose:	To demonstrate the ability to give directions and to use vocabulary related to the rooms of a house and furniture.
Method:	In pairs, back to back, student A describes the arrangement of her/his room (or any room in the house) as s/he draws it. Student B draws the same room based on the directions given by student A. Students switch roles.
Time:	15–20 minutes.
Evaluation:	Points given based on the accuracy of their drawings, participation and exclusive use of language.
Benefits:	Students learn about each others' homes. Non-native and native speakers find out how their homes may be quite similar or quite different.

Activity 10.5: La guía telefónica (*Telephone directory*)

Purpose:	To demonstrate the ability to tell, request, understand and write names, addresses and telephone numbers.
Method:	Copy a page from the telephone directory, if possible one with all Hispanic names. Ask each student to select a new identity with address and phone number. Have students write this information at the top of a blank sheet of paper. Each student then asks 2 or 3 other students for name, address and phone number, and writes down the information. As students give the information, they spell their new names and street names as necessary. After the exchange of information, each student verifies that the written information is correct.
Time:	10–15 minutes.
Evaluation:	Points given based on the accuracy of written information, participation and exclusive use of language.
Benefits:	Students get practice using Hispanic names and, for the length of the activity, see themselves as being Hispanic.

Activity 10.6: ¡Vamos a almorzar juntos! (*Let's do lunch*)

Purpose:	To demonstrate the ability to ask and tell about common, daily activities, and to establish day, date and time.
Method:	In pairs, students will try to find a two-hour block of time when they can 'get together'. Give student A a prepared date-book page; student B gets another version of the prepared date-book page. Both pages indicate a variety of previous commitments such as doctor's visit, football practice, dance lesson, etc. Their task is to find a two hour block of time when the two of them can meet, since they are old friends who haven't seen each other in a long time. Date-book pages are set up to have only one possible meeting time. They should consider not only the activities scheduled for the week, but also time needed to get where they are going or to prepare for what they are going to do. They may not look at each other's date-books. They must ask one another about various days, dates and times, and explain whether they can or cannot meet. And if not, why not.
Time:	10–20 minutes.
Evaluation:	Points given based on originality, creativity, participation and success in completing the task.
Benefits:	Date-book pages can be set up to compare and contrast the type of home and family responsibilities non-native and native speakers have.

A third quality recognizable in any cooperative model is that activities must incorporate both individual and group accountability. Each member of the group must be responsible for an active contribution to the result, and the group must be responsible for a complete product. For this reason, any activity should be debriefed in some way; what the group has experienced should be shared with the whole class, be it in a formal presentation by the team or in an informal discussion to which all contribute.

Activity 10.7, Tell Me A Story, is one such activity. Working in pairs, student A reads Story A and student B reads Story B. The selections should, of course, be appropriate to the level and content of the class. They may be short, humorous anecdotes or longer, more serious pieces. Chicano legends, such as *La Llorona* (The Weeper) and *diablo* (devil) stories, or the story-line of Chicano *corridos* (type of Mexican songs) work well in this activity. Students are told ahead of time that they will be responsible for telling the information to their partners, and that all will take a quiz covering all the material. After enough time to read the selection thoroughly, the pairs of students tell each other about what they have read. They should be encouraged to ask questions for clarification or detail and to summarize what they have been told. At the end of the time allowed, all students take a quiz covering all of the material. Thus, both partners must read, tell, and recall both parts of the information provided. The reading, retelling, discussion, and quiz are all in the target language, of course.

Individual accountability is readily recognizable in activities 10.7 and 10.8. Activity 10.9, called Favorite Teacher, demonstrates the concept of group accountability.

Activity 10.7: ¡Cuéntame un cuento! (*Tell me a story*)

Purpose:	To demonstrate the ability to narrate, question for confirmation or detail, and to respond to questions asking for confirmation or detail. Also, to demonstrate comprehension of oral narration.
Method:	In pairs, student A is given Story A and student B is given Story B. Sufficient time is allowed for students to read stories silently. They may not read each other's story. Copies of the stories are collected. Student A is given five minutes to tell his or her story to student B. B may ask questions to clarify or get details or confirmation. Then student B tells his or her story to student A.
	All students then take a short quiz on both stories A and B.
Time:	15–30 minutes.
Evaluation:	Scores for both quizzes are combined to make one score (grade), which each student in the pair receives. (Students should be told this ahead of time — it will make them conscientious about both telling and understanding.)
Benefits:	Excellent opportunity to use Hispanic legends and folk tales.

Activity 10.8:   ¡Rompecabezas! (*Reading jigsaw*)

Purpose:	To demonstrate the ability to read, understand, summarize and report facts.
Method:	Students form 'home' groups of 4 or 5. Within each group, students number themselves from 1–4 or 5. All #1 students in the class are asked to read Part 1 of the reading assignment and be prepared to share the information read with the members of her/his home group, #2 students read and share Part 2, #3 students read and share Part 3, etc.
	After students have read their sections of the assignment, all the #1's, etc., get together in a group and discuss the section together, agreeing on what it says and what is important to share with home groups. Then they go to their home groups and each student summarizes his or her section for the group.
	All class members then take a quiz covering the information in all the sections of the reading.
Time:	30 minutes (Varies according to content).
Evaluation:	Points given based on individual scores on quizzes, participation and exclusive use of language.
Benefits:	Excellent opportunity to use Hispanic legends and folk tales and for Hispanic students to excel.

Activity 10.9:   ¡Mi profesor favorito! (*My favorite teacher*)

Purpose:	To demonstrate the ability to describe people and to list characteristics as they listen to descriptions.
Method:	In pairs, students describe their favorite teachers. As student A speaks, student B lists on chart paper the characteristics that A mentions. Students switch roles. When they are finished, the charts are posted for comparison with others from the class.
	Looking at everyone's list, each pair then considers the qualities that the ideal teacher would have, then writes a paragraph describing the ideal teacher.
Time:	10–15 minutes.
Evaluation:	Points are given to each pair based on participation, on the accuracy of the list of characteristics and on the paragraph on the ideal teacher.
Benefits:	Non-native speakers are likely to learn new adjectives as they listen to native speakers' descriptions.

The last element common to all cooperative learning models is processing. Students need to be aware of the dynamics of group interaction and to know how to change and improve those dynamics. They gain these skills by noting and discussing the actual group process. Many communicative activities lend themselves to developing processing skills. For example, in Activity 10.10, The House Problem, a team of four students must solve a puzzle about who lives in which house by reading a list of clues and manipulating pieces of paper which represent five different owners, their houses, their pets, their favorite foods, and their favorite drinks. The language required to complete the task is appropriate to a beginning class late in the year or to an intermediate class. Different groups will approach the task in different ways, some notably more successfully than others. After the task has been completed, the class should discuss what worked, what didn't, and what kinds of behaviors and problem-solving skills are needed to make such an activity succeed.

Activity 10.10: ¡Cinco casas! (*Five houses*)

Purpose:	To demonstrate the ability to work cooperatively while reading statements, asking questions, agreeing and disagreeing, and offering alternatives to solve a puzzle.
Method:	Working in groups of four, each student in a group receives five of the following clues in the language being studied. The goal is to rearrange the puzzle items in order to satisfy clues 1–19 and answer the questions in clue #20. Students are then allowed to proceed as each group chooses, provided all group members are allowed to participate.

The problem and clues:
1. There are 5 houses, each a different color.
2. The man who lives in each house is of a different nationality.
3. Each man has a different pet.
4. Each man eats something different.
5. Each man drinks a different drink.
6. The Frenchman lives in the orange house.
7. The Spaniard has a dog.
8. The man in the green house drinks coffee.
9. The green house is immediately to the right of the white one.
10. The Russian drinks milk.
11. The man who eats salad has a cat.
12. The man in the yellow house eats ice cream.
13. The man who drinks wine is in the house in the center.
14. The American lives in the first house on the left.
15. The man who eats bananas lives next door to the elephant.
16. The man who eats ice cream lives next door to the horse.
17. The man who eats omelettes drinks orange juice.
18. The German eats hot dogs.
19. The American lives next to the blue house.
20. Who drinks water? Who has the giraffe?

The puzzle: (cut in separate squares)

WHITE	SPANISH	CAT	ORANGE JUICE	HOT DOG
GREEN	RUSSIAN	DOG	MILK	OMELETTE
YELLOW	GERMAN	HORSE	COFFEE	SALAD
BLUE	AMERICAN	GIRAFFE	WATER	ICE CREAM
ORANGE	FRENCH	ELEPHANT	WINE	BANANA

The solution:
House #1: yellow, American, elephant, water, ice cream
House #2: blue, Russian, horse, milk, banana
House #3: orange, French, cat, wine, salad
House #4: white, Spanish, dog, orange juice, omelette
House #5: green, German, giraffe, coffee, hot dog

Time:	30–45 minutes.
Evaluation:	Points given based on participation and exclusive use of language.
Benefits:	Students use critical thinking skills as they learn to agree and disagree and to offer alternatives to a problem being solved.

Many foreign language teachers are ready and anxious to use communicative activities such as those described here in their classrooms and many of those will meet with great success — increased student interest, enthusiasm, and accomplishment. But all teachers need to consciously and carefully plan strategies for managing the communicative classroom. Research by a number of scholars has indicated that application of cooperative learning strategies results in higher achievement, increased intellectual development, better attitudes towards peers, school, learning and school personnel and increased self-esteem and motivation (Kagan, 1985). In terms of foreign language specifically, the research of Little and Sanders (1989) suggests that we cannot develop real communication in the classroom without developing a sense of community among class members. The cooperative approach, then, is clearly one which can and will enhance the foreign language classroom for both native and non-native speakers of the language.

References

CALIFORNIA STATE DEPARTMENT OF EDUCATION (1985) *Foreign Language Model Curriculum Standards*, Sacramento, CA, Author.

CALIFORNIA STATE DEPARTMENT OF EDUCATION (1985) *Handbook for Planning an Effective Foreign Language Program*, Sacramento, CA, Author.

CALIFORNIA STATE DEPARTMENT OF EDUCATION (1986) *Statement on Competencies in Languages Other Than English Expected of Entering Freshmen*, Sacramento, CA, Author.

CALIFORNIA STATE DEPARTMENT OF EDUCATION (1989) *Foreign Language Framework*, Sacramento, CA, Author.

KAGAN, S. (1985) *Cooperative Learning: Resources for Teachers*, Riverside, CA, University of California.

LITTLE, G.D. and SANDERS, S.L. (1989) 'Classroom community: A prerequisite for communication', *Foreign Language Annals*, **22**, pp. 277–81.

OLSON, J. (1984) *Look Again Pictures for Language Development and Life Skills*, Hayward, CA, The Alemany Press.

Further Readings

ARONSON, E., BLANEY, N., STEPHEN, C., SIKES, J. and SNAPP, M. (1978) *The Jigsaw Classroom*, Beverly Hills, CA, Sage.

COSTA, A.L. (1983) *The Enabling Behaviors*, San Anselmo, CA, Search Models Unlimited.

JOHNSON, D.W. (1983) *Reaching Out: Interpersonal Effectiveness and Self-actualization*, Englewood Cliffs, NJ, Prentice-Hall.

JOHNSON, D.W. and JOHNSON, R. (1975) *Joining Together: Group Therapy and Group Skills*, Englewood Cliffs, NJ, Prentice-Hall.

ROY, P. (Ed) (1982) *Structuring Cooperative Learning: The 1982 Handbook*, Minneapolis, MN, Cooperative Network.

STANFORD, G. (1977) *Developing Effective Classroom Groups*, New York, NY, Hart Publishing Co.

YORKEY, R. (1985) *Talk-A-Tivities Problem Solving and Puzzles for Pairs*, Reading, MA, Addison-Wesley Publishing Company.

Chapter 11

Folk Art in the Classroom

Beatrice Carrillo Hocker

In the following essay, Beatrice Carrillo Hocker, an educator at The Mexican Museum since 1978, addresses the effectiveness of folk art as a curriculum tool and as a bridge for multicultural awareness. The Mexican Museum of San Francisco was founded in 1975 by Mexican American artist, Peter Rodriguez. Since its inauguration, the Museum's education department has conducted student art programs related to the collection and exhibitions which encompass five areas of Mexican art: pre-Hispanic, Colonial, Mexican and Mexican American fine art and folk art.

Since its inception fourteen years ago, The Mexican Museum has recognized the inherent appeal of folk art to people of all ages and has used it as an effective tool in the fulfillment of its mission, which is to promote an awareness, understanding and appreciation of the cultural and artistic heritage of the Mexican people. All school programs are directed to achieving this end and the most effective means of accomplishing this goal has been by relating 'the Mexican experience' to the everyday experiences of the students. Folk art has facilitated this crosscultural connection.

For example, the Museum presented the exhibition, 'Lo del Corazón: Heartbeat of a Culture', wherein the symbol of the heart — el corazón — in its myriad forms and aspects, served as the unifying theme. Pre-Hispanic, Colonial and Chicano art provided a visual vocabulary of the core values, beliefs, attitudes and goals which give form or are at the heart of Mexican culture. The works encompassed themes on God, life and death, good and evil, life style, justice and human compassion. The challenge for the education staff was to make the exhibition relevant to non-Hispanic students, and folk art provided the solution.

We decided to implement an in-museum workshop based on the art of the Otomí. The contemporary Otomí Indians of the State of Puebla cut out ritual paper figures which reflect their religious beliefs and practices as well as their life concerns. After viewing the exhibition, the students created facsimiles of the Otomí figures but used images and symbols that expressed their own beliefs, goals, life styles and concerns.

The following activities are part of a museum kit designed to reinforce the Otomí Indian display.

153

Activity 11.1: Making paper spirits

Title:	Paper Spirits of the Otomí Indians of the State of Puebla, Mexico.
Background:	The Indian lives in a world full of spirits. Everything in nature has a spirit and all during his or her life, the Indian must try to stay on good terms with those spirits in order to have good health and prosperity in the form of good crops. The Indian therefore performs special ceremonies to the spirits as he feels that if he fails to do so, the spirits may punish him with sickness and bad luck. The Mexican Otomí Indians, who live in the village of San Pablito in the State of Puebla, cut out paper spirits for use in their special ceremonies.
Method:	Imagine yourself under these circumstances and make your own paper spirit.

1. Decide what type of spirit you would like to create: plant, animal, human or evil spirit. As an example, you might make a corn, flower or bird spirit.
2. Use brown or white paper, no larger than 9" × 11" and no smaller than 5" × 7".
3. Fold sheet of paper in half. On one side of paper draw an outline of one-half of your figure with the center of the figure being next to the folded edge of the paper. Be sure to draw symbols that represent the nature or characteristics of your spirit.
4. With scissors, cut along drawn outline of figure with paper still folded in half. In order to cut out the eyes easily, a second fold can be made on the eye area and a small half circle or triangle can be cut on the folded edge of the paper.
5. After you and all your classmates have completed the paper spirits, exhibit them pinned to a colorful paper or cloth backing. Be sure to include an identifying label for each spirit.

Materials Needed:	5" × 7" or 8½" × 11" sheets of white and brown paper, scissors, pencils, Colored paper for mounting (optional).
Benefits:	Students learn about the rich Indian folk art heritage. Hispanic students may be able to identify certain family traditions and serve as resource persons when discussing the spirits.

This workshop not only made clear to the students the similarities and differences between Mexican culture and their own respective cultures, but it also provided them an opportunity to learn about themselves.

To offer another example, folk art is facilitating the instruction of Mexican history to students at The Mexican Museum. The Museum recently presented an exhibit of some 100 contemporary folk dance masks. The faces of mythical creatures, Christian personages, Spanish Conquistadores, *diablos*, *negritos*, and *Malinches* relate the intriguing story of pre-Hispanic belief systems, the Spanish Conquest and the merging of indigenous and European cultures. History comes alive for the students through these objects. They point their fingers at the masks and ask: 'Why are blacks pictured in Mexican masks? Did the Indians believe in the devil before the Spanish arrived? Who is Malinche and why did the maskmaker make her look so ugly? Who wears the masks and when are they worn?' Masks are valuable reservoirs of cultural information. Their imagery and use reveal historical events and antecedents, social practices, myths, legends and artistic traditions. The masks also generate a natural curiosity and interest that a history book often fails to ignite.

Activity 11.2: Making a facsimile of a Mexican bark painting

Title:	Bark Painting of the Otomí Indians of Puebla, Mexico
Background:	Before the Spaniards arrived in Mexico, paper made from bark was used by the Indian civilizations of Mexico for religious ceremonies, as offerings to gods, for decorating temples and palaces and as paper for their books.
	Today this bark paper is still being made by the Otomí Indians of the State of Puebla, Mexico. They make paper from the inner bark of two types of trees, mulberry and wild fig, which is called *amate*. The mulberry bark produces paper with a white tint and the fig tree produces paper with a brown tint. Since 1959 artists from the state of Guerrero paint brightly colored paintings on *amate* in a style similar to that of their pottery, which is decorated with flowers, scrolls and fanciful animals and birds. The *amate* bark paintings may be bought in native markets or in city shops all over Mexico.
Method:	Create your own facsimile of a Mexican bark painting.
	1. Cut a piece of the shopping bag to the size bark painting you desire.
	2. Wad the paper into a tight ball, and place in warm water.
	3. Unwrinkle and flatten the paper.
	4. Tear around the edges to give sheared appearance.
	5. Lightly cover the paper with the mixture of brown and black paint and let dry.
	6. Paint design on brown paper with fluorescent paints and let dry.
	7. Outline the design with a black marker.
Materials Needed:	Brown grocery bags, containers with warm water, brown and black paint, brushes, multi-colored paints (preferably fluorescent), black felt pens or markers.
Benefits:	Students learn how native American Indians were making and using paper before the arrival of the Spaniards in Mexico.

Other educators are now recognizing the potential of folk art to enrich school curriculum. At a conference on Perspectives of Mexican and Mexican American Folk Art sponsored by The Mexican Museum (1987), San Francisco educator Yolanda Garfias Woo illustrated with a Guatemalan toy backstrap loom and a Mexican miniature floor loom how folk art can be used to integrate the study of cultures into all areas of the curriculum. Initially the students are presented with background information, which in this instance might cover looms in general, the weaving process and the countries of origin. She suggested that in the areas of history and social sciences, the looms could be linked to a discussion on pre-Hispanic, Colonial and contemporary trends in textile production; in language arts for the introduction of new vocabulary words associated with weaving; in mathematics for practicing computations on the buying and selling of folk art objects in US dollars, Mexican *pesos* and Guatemalan *quetzales*; as well as to research and creative writing projects. Woo is a strong advocate of this teaching method, as can be seen in the proceedings from the 1987 conference, when she states that educators have the responsibility of exposing children at a young age to world cultures in order to 'teach sensitivity and cultural awareness . . . so that people will *not* seem so strange and *not* so foreign' (1989).

Another San Francisco educator, Ricardo Reyes, used a $5000 grant from the San Francisco Education Fund to purchase a folk art collection. This collection serves as the basis of a multi-cultural education program at Horace Mann Junior

High School. Students create a cyclical exhibit with a different focus each month of the year. Themes have included black history, Chinese and Mexican Days of the Dead, Ching Ming and punk rock and street art. The interpretation of each exhibit is inter-disciplinary and cross-cultural. Reyes develops a curriculum packet each month for each social studies teacher and relies heavily on the racially-diverse student body as a resource (1989).

There are many Spanish language classes that come to The Mexican Museum, since gallery tours are conducted in Spanish or bilingually upon request. It has been demonstrated over the years that the students have little or no knowledge of the cultures of those who use Spanish as their native tounge. A surprising number of students do not know that Spanish was introduced into the New World in the sixteenth century. Many do not realize that prior to this time the indigenous peoples spoke a multitude of Indian languages of which many still survive throughout North, Central and South America. The fact that Náhuatl, the language of the Aztecs, serves as the root of many Spanish words (and some English words) such as *coyote*, *aguacate*, *chocolate*, *tomate*, and *maiz* is a surprising revelation to them. It does not seem logical to provide students with the facility of speaking a foreign language but not with a cultural understanding of the peoples with whom they will be conversing and the countries they will be visiting. Language is only one aspect of culture; a world view, traditions, beliefs and myths constitute the 'wholeness' of culture. Since folk art is the visual manifestation of the cultural environment of a people, it is concerned with all of these things. A language teacher can easily use folk art objects as conveyors of cultural information and also as catalysts for curriculum related activities.

The folk art objects brought to the classroom need not be exotic or one-of-a-kind, because it is sometimes the simple common items that provide more insight into the lives of their creators and their users. For example, the *piñata* is a folk art form recognized by almost all students but few know its history and its use within its cultural context. Its name is derived from the Italian words *pignatta* and *pigna* (meaning cone-shaped) and was the object of a sixteenth century court game in that country. Consequently the *piñata* was used in Spanish Lenten ritual and later introduced into Mexico by the Spanish.

Eventually the Mexicans began to decorate the clay pot and to use it as part of the ritual festivities of the Christmas *posada*. The process and materials used reveal the French influence of papier mâché and the use of tissue paper, or *papel de china*, makes reference to the initial importation of this paper to Mexico in Spanish galleons from the Philippines during the Colonial period. Piñata forms now include Santa Claus, Halloween pumpkins and US comic book characters. The possibilities of classroom-related activities based on this information are multiple and intriguing.

Activity 11.3: Making miniature bird piñatas

Title: *Piñatas*
Background: An important and playful complement to Mexican Christmas festivities is the *piñata*. Its origin is somewhat uncertain, though it is known that *piñatas* were brought to Mexico by the Spaniards who in turn learned about them from the Italians. It is believed that Marco Polo brought this idea to Italy in the twelfth century after he saw them used in China in agricultural spring ceremonies. The Chinese placed seeds in hollow forms

of cows, bulls or water buffalos which scattered when the vessels were broken with sticks of different colors. The Italians later used the piñata as a court game.

By the middle of the sixteenth century, the Spanish had adopted the custom of breaking the *piñata* on the first Sunday of Lent, designated as *piñata* Sunday. This custom was introduced into Mexico but the *piñata* went through several changes. It became associated with Christmas and with the availability of tissue paper, the Mexicans began to decorate the plain clay vessels to create figures of animals, stars and fruits. They are filled with seasonal fruits like tangerines, as well as nuts, candy and sometimes with favors and toys. At Christmas time the favorite shape is the star, as it symbolized the star the appeared so brightly the night of Christ's birth.

The symbolism of the brilliantly decorated jug is the devil, or the spirit of evil that attracts humanity; the prizes inside are the unknown pleasures that cause this attraction; and the blindfolded person who, with a stick, must break the suspended jug, represents faith, which should be blind, and which is held responsible for destroying the spirit of evil.

Method: Instructions for making miniature bird *piñatas*:

1. Create a paper cone with heavy weight paper. Glue edge down and tape at base of cone to hold in place until dry.
2. Cut out a triangle (approximately $1\frac{1}{2}$" high) at opening of each cup with point facing toward base of cup.
3. Punch hole above each triangle.
4. String yarn through the hole of one cup and through the hole of the other cup. Tie ends of yarn into a knot.
5. Tape Styrofoam cups together matching both triangles. Use 2" masking tape.
6. Tape 3 oz. dixie cup with 1" tape to one end of Styrofoam cup.
7. Tape paper cone to 3 oz. Dixie cup.
8. Glue fringed strips of tissue paper to body of piñata *starting at tail end* of bird piñata.
9. Tape crepe paper streamers to base of cup to create a tail.
10. With pencil punch through paper at opening.

Materials Needed:

1. Styrofoam cups, 8.05 oz. (2 per piñata)
2. 3 oz. bathroom Dixie cups (1 per piñata)
3. yarn — cut into approximately 18" lengths
4. heavyweight paper cut in approximately $4\frac{1}{2}$" × $3\frac{1}{2}$" squares
5. hole punchers
6. scissors
7. tissue paper cut in $1\frac{1}{2}$" strips and fringed
8. masking tape in 2" and 1" widths
9. Elmer's glue

Benefits: Students learn history of a very popular Hispanic tradition. Native speakers can explain the various occasions when they have used a *piñata*.

Of the many ways to look at an artifact, the seven outlined by Fred Schroeder of the University of Minnesota, Duluth, can be very helpful to teachers and students.

1 *Reading with your hands:* The first way of looking at an artifact is to study how it was made;
2 *How was it used?*: The second method shifts from studying materials and manufacturing process to the practical function of the artifact within its society;

3 *What was its environment?*: The third method concerns itself with the question, 'what was the total environment within which it existed'?
4 *Development through time*: The fourth way of looking at an artifact is to put the artifact into a chronology;
5 *Cross-cultural comparisons*: The fifth way of looking at an artifact is to compare it with similar artifacts from other cultures;
6 *Noting the influences*: The sixth way examines the influences that can be discerned in the design and decoration of the artifact;
7 *Functional meanings or values*: The seventh way to look at an artifact has to do with examining deeply rooted value systems, aesthetic, mythical and iconological.

There are now many resources on folk art, especially on ethnic folk art. Most museums now have teacher check-out materials, a willing and cooperative education staff, and shops with a generous amount of folk art objects and books. Neighborhood cultural centers are another resource and students and their families may prove to be the most valuable resource in terms of their own ethnic possessions and the oral history to bring the objects to life.

The integration of the study of culture in all areas of study is not only very possible, it is now becoming imperative. The heavy influx of immigrants into US communities and schools necessitates that educators bear the responsibility of helping young people understand and respect the culture of others. It is only through the students' recognition of the similarities and differences between cultures that the stigma of being foreign or weird can begin to disappear. The common denominators that exist in the folk art of all peoples and the unique character which sets apart the folk art of each culture beautifully accommodates this particular need.

Further Readings

CORDRY, D. and CORDRY, D. (1968) *Mexican Indian Costumes*, Austin, TX, University of Texas Press.
CORDRY, D. and CORDRY, D. (1980) *Mexican Masks*, Austin, TX, University of Texas Press.
ESPEJEL, C. (1978) *Mexican Folk Ceramics*, Madrid, Spain, Editorial Blume.
HARVEY, M. (1973) *Crafts of Mexico*, New York, NY, MacMillan Publishing Company, Inc.
HARVEY, M. (1978) *Mexican Crafts and Craftspeople*, Cransbury, NJ, Associated University Presses.
PETTIT, F. and PETTIT, M. (1978) *Mexican Folk Toys*, New York, NY, Hastings House Publisher.
SANDSTROM, A.R. and SANDSTROM, P.E. (1986) *Traditional Papermaking and Paper Cut Figures of Mexico*, Oklahoma City, OK, University of Oklahoma Press.
TOOR, F. (1947) *A Treasury of Mexican Folkways*, New York, NY, Crown Publishers, Inc.

Museum Exhibit Catalogs

1978 *Art of the Huichol Indians*, The Fine Arts Museum of San Francisco, New York, NY, Harry N. Abrams Publishing, Inc.

1988 *Behind the Mask in Mexico*, Museum of International Folk Art, Santa Fe, NM, Museum of New Mexico Press.

1988 *Mexican Masks*, **62**, Los Angeles, CA, Southwest Museum.

1989 *The Mexican Museum*, Monograph, San Francisco, CA, The Mexican Museum. (pp. 102–5).

Chapter 12

Effective Computer Uses for Teaching Spanish to Bilingual Native Speakers: A Socioacademic Perspective

Christian J. Faltis and Robert A. DeVillar

Within the field of teaching Spanish to native speakers (SNS), there are two well-defined schools of thought with respect to how to most effectively and efficiently teach Spanish to bilingual speakers (Faltis, 1990). The first school of thought posits that the best way to improve the language abilities of bilingual students is by replacing certain non-standard features used among native bilingual speakers with their standard equivalents. Accordingly, classroom activities center upon extirpating deviations from the standard through extensive drill and practice. This approach to language instruction has been labeled the 'limited normative' approach (Valdés-Fallis, 1978). Materials overtly reflecting the limited normative perspective are *Español: Lo Esencial para el Bilingüe* (Quintanilla and Silman, 1978); *Español: Material para el Hispano* (León, 1978); and *Español para el Bilingüe* (Barker, 1972). As US Spanish usage spans generations, socioeconomic classes, and geographic areas, the limited normative approach may well be doing students a disservice, since it can only serve to alienate them from the very community which creates, uses, sustains and develops this dialect (Faltis, 1984).

The second school of thought maintains that language development depends greatly on the extent to which the standard variety is used as a medium of instruction rather than exclusively as the primary objective of instruction. More specifically, this approach asserts that bilingual students will develop standard Spanish if they are provided skills and practice in talking, reading, and writing about a variety of topics within a classroom context which uses standard written and spoken Spanish. This approach to SNS has been termed the 'comprehensive' approach to language instruction because it aims to extend the student's oral and written communicative competence primarily by having students learn to read and write in standard Spanish for diverse purposes and to a variety audiences (Valdés, 1981). Teaching materials reflecting the comprehensive approach are *Español Escrito: Curso para Hispanohablantes Bilingües* (Valdés-Fallis and Teschner, 1978; 2nd ed. 1984), *Cómo se Escribe: Curso de Secundaria para Estudiantes Bilingües* (Valdés, Hunnum, and Teschner, 1982), and *Mejora tu Español: Lectura y Redacción para Bilingües* (de la Portilla and Varela, 1978). The ultimate goal of the comprehensive approach is to help bilingual native Spanish speakers acquire what Valdés (1988) calls the *norma culta*, that is, educated standard Spanish.

Although the two approaches to SNS differ in many respects, they share two significant points. First, both assume that language is learned synthetically. From this perspective, language is broken down into discrete units, which are then taught separately in a lock-step fashion. Accordingly, language is presented to students first in terms of sentence and sound patterns. In the limited normative approach, this is done so that non-standard forms can be contrasted with standard uses and then these can be practiced individually. In the comprehensive approach, students start out focusing on basic skills such as spelling, accent rules, word formation rules, and other isolated writing conventions before engaging in more substantial reading and writing activities. Once the basic language forms are mastered, paragraph-level skills are introduced, modeled and practiced. In both approaches, the models for paragraph-level exercises are derived from traditional literature and other standard language resources (Faltis, 1981).

Their second commonality relates to the dominant role which teachers hold over students in the instructional process. Both approaches, by giving primacy to skill development over authentic language use, reflect what Freire (1970, pp. 58–73) refers to as the 'banking concept' of education because the teacher, as holder of knowledge, presents information as deposits. Further, the teacher presents knowledge in the form of bits and pieces about language, and students are expected to reproduce the knowledge fragments on tests and other display assignments. Thus, there is little value placed on the students' ideas, since the teacher, as holder of knowledge, determines what students need to learn. Under these circumstances, students are prevented from being true partners in the process of inquiry and from talking and working together on problems that matter to them. Consequently, we conclude that neither of these approaches provides students with the minimal necessary conditions for language and literacy development to occur.

An Alternative Approach: A Socioacademic Perspective

In this chapter, we advocate an alternative to both the limited normative and the comprehensive approaches to SNS. The alternative downplays skill development and instead advocates a much stronger role for communication, social integration, and cooperation in the classroom. Although knowledge and skill development are important to language growth, the relevance accorded these components depends greatly on the purpose they serve in assisting learners to further develop their language. In the case of bilingual Spanish speakers, we believe that knowledge about language and the development of oral and literacy skills must be secondary to using language for authentic purposes to explore topics of real interest to learners. Thus, we propose that native bilingual speakers will further develop language and literacy to the extent that the following three conditions are met:

1 Students are encouraged to talk with peers and the teacher about topics and themes that matter. (See Faltis, 1990);
2 Students of differing social backgrounds and language abilities interact socially;

   3   Students work together cooperatively to share and consider each other's ideas.

The theoretical framework upon which we base our argument is presented in DeVillar and Faltis (1991), and we invite the reader to consult this work for a full description of the framework. Briefly, the first condition speaks to the importance of talk for second language and literacy development. Students acquire oral and written language competence by actively talking, writing, listening, and reading about topics that are drawn from experiences that are meaningful to the students. Wong Fillmore (1985, p. 26) points out that active interaction allows students 'to figure out what is being said, how the language is structured, and how it is used socially and communicatively' by its speakers and writers. In the classroom, interaction requires that students are physically and socially integrated in ways that necessarily require them to talk to one another about topics that matter to them, and in this way use language for authentic purposes. Thus, the second condition seeks to integrate students from various backgrounds and language abilities to share experiences that are relevant to their lives, using whatever language abilities they have to express themselves. The third condition advocates the use of small groupwork organized around cooperative learning principles such as positive interdependence, interpersonal skill development, individual accountability, and face-to-face interaction (Johnson, Johnson, Holobec Johnson and Roy, 1984; DeVillar, 1987). DeVillar (1991) characterizes cooperative learning as

   . . . generally concerned with structuring a learning environment where
   students, whatever their particular range of performance, cultural, or
   other selected characteristics, can work together (rather than against one
   another) in order to enable every student to engage actively in the learning process, thereby improving their outcome opportunities (p. 183).

Organizing students around cooperative principles supports the first two conditions and at the same time, aims to promote a sense of camaradarie among students of diverse abilities and experiences.

Integrating the Computer in the SNS Classroom

As the decade of the 1990s begins, the field of Spanish for Native Speakers has been largely unaffected by the computer revolution, a phenomenon which has otherwise resulted in the introduction of computers for learning subject matter at virtually every level of schooling. To the best of our knowledge, no computer software packages have been developed specifically for either of the two major approaches to teaching SNS. Instead what we have found is that three traditional kinds of computer software are available to support second language instruction in general, and that the three types vary considerably in the extent to which they meet the three conditions for effective language and literacy development. In the following sections, we critique the three kinds of computer software that may well be incorporated into SNS classroom in the years to come. We discuss their strengths and limitations in terms of our three conditions of social interaction, social integration, and cooperation among students. We hope that the discussion with respect to the integration of computers also serves as an example of the kind of alternative SNS classroom environment we advocate.

Drill and practice

There are a number of Spanish software programs available for Spanish as a foreign language. As might be expected, the overwhelming majority of these programs are designed to reinforce basic vocabulary and/or provide drill and practice on selected grammatical structures that have already been presented in class (see *Hispania*, 72, 2, 1989, pp. 470–73 for a listing of Spanish language computer software reviews from 1984 to 1989). We refer to this type of computer use as drill and practice, although it is also known disparagingly as 'drill and kill'. Drill and practice computer uses reflect the banking concept of education (Freire, 1970), since the computer controls the knowledge to be learned, and the students are allowed to reproduce only what the computer accepts as knowledge. Drill and practice tasks are virtually useless for bilingual native speakers of Spanish because they offer little opportunity for students to use Spanish for two-way communicative purposes or to interact with peers about meaningful topics that matter to them. While students could talk and work together on drill and practice activities, the narrowness with respect to what is considered a correct response, seriously hinders their usefulness for language learning purposes.

Simulations

The second type of computer use for language learning involves simulations of real life events which place students in the role of collaborator with the computer in order to solve simple to complex problems. Computer simulations place much greater responsibility on the students for their learning than do drill and practice exercises. In computer simulations, students must make decisions to direct the activities and actions that occur within the simulations. Thus, simulations have the potential of invoking two-way communication, social integration, and cooperation among students working together to solve the problems presented in the program. An example of a Spanish language computer simulation program is *Juegos Comunicativos, Spanish Games for Communicative Practice* (Underwood, 1986). In this simulation, students are treated to five types of games, all of which are presented entirely in Spanish, as are the instructions for playing them. In Game A, students are presented a series of five images on the computer screen, and asked to describe several differences between the image on the left and the one on the right. As each difference is described, the student receives a star. When all of the differences have been described, the program proceeds to the next image.

Game B is titled *El Detective* (The Detective) and centers on a theft that occurred in a room full of people. The computer knows who the thief is, and the student has to discover which one of the characters is the culprit in a manner similar to traditionally popular detective boardgames. Students begin with questions about the room in which the theft occurred, and then move on to ask questions about the individuals who were in the room during the perpetration of the crime. Answers to the questions enable the students to correctly determine who the thief is and thus, to solve the crime.

In Game C, *El aeropuerto*, (The Airport) the objective is to help Mr. Sotero arrive at the airport by responding to his questions and giving him directions and instructions. Proper responses to Mr. Sotero's questions are suggested by a series of images presented on the computer screen.

Game D is called *El restaurante* (The Restaurant). In this game, students are given the opportunity to express likes and dislikes, wants and preferences. The student is placed in a restaurant and given a menu full of Spanish viands. The objective is to order a complete meal by responding to the waiter's questions and cues.

In the final Game E, *La vida diaria*, (Daily Life) students are guided first in present tense, and then in the preterite, through a narration of a daily routine that begins with rising in the morning and ends with going to bed at night. The sequence of events to be described by the students is suggested by images and an accompanying clock which indicates the time of day.

This set of simulations enables students to use language to solve cognitively demanding problems that are presented in relatively contextualized settings. Moreover, the nature of the games encourages students to talk and work together cooperatively. The benefit derived from these types of programs, however, is limited to beginning language learners, since in simulation games the computer is programmed to validate only a certain number and type of language responses. Feustle (1987, p. 709) notes that '[a]s long as students playing [these games] have only a very limited knowledge of Spanish, and as long as just the vocabulary and structures for each game are used, problems are kept to a minimum.' Thus, SNS students who have more than basic communicative language proficiency in Spanish may be frustrated with simulation games when logical and grammatically appropriate answers are not accepted by the computer as being correct.

Text editing and language mastery

The problem of language use that is restricted to the program design is reduced significantly when the computer serves as a facilitator in literacy development, that is, when students use the computer for word processing to produce and read their own text. In this third type of computer use, students may generate meaningful text through one of many available text editing software packages. Text editing offers students the opportunity to work and talk together as they develop text about topics that matter to them.

The assumptions upon which the text-editing approach rest may be contrasted with the traditional pedagogical approach to formal language and literacy learning, as well as with computer-integrated language learning activities described above. Within the text-editing approach to comprehensive language learning, language development is viewed as resulting from a process in which talking, reading and writing coincide and inform one another as students interact with their peers in meaningful language-eliciting/language-producing computer-supported activities. The notion of audience is also extended beyond the teacher and immediate classroom peers within this approach, since students can transcend geographical borders through computer conferencing. In summary, the social and communicative language learning aspects of text-editing, together with its electronic features, combine to produce a uniquely powerful alternative for language mastery attainment among bilingual native speakers of Spanish.

The uses of text-editing at the beginning language learning level, within a telecommunications context, and as a means to develop various writing styles, are described in the following section. These uses will also serve analogously to illustrate the potential developmental aspects associated with the text-editing process.

VALE: A beginning level integrated language arts program

Torres-Guzmán (1990) has described the *Voy a Leer Escribiendo* (VALE) program in detail. Essentially, VALE is a program which takes operational advantage of several key pedagogical trends, particularly computer-supported instruction, collaborative learning between peers, contextualized curriculum, and cultural diversity. Within this pedagogical framework, the computer is one of five stations that in their totality form the essence of the students' language development experiences. The computer is used essentially to introduce words and syllables through computerized voice prompts and to enable literacy-related keyboard/ screen activities. Computer use, in turn, is complemented by work journals, writing/reading activities, books and audiotaped stories and manipulatives. Language development within this program, then, is attained through exposure to and participation in skill-based activities which coincide with creatively guided reading, listening and writing experiences. These latter experiences are designed to promote and validate self-expression in conjunction with particular language and cultural values from the student's community.

The pedagogical and programmatic elements characterizing VALE appear theoretically sound, extending the student's present knowledge base in four ways:

1 through contextualized content and activities complemented by peer interaction;
2 computer interaction in the form of voice and image;
3 a variety of media-integrated activities supporting introduced elements; and
4 teacher guidance.

Through these primary language activities (primary dialect activities would perhaps be a more appropriate descriptor), moreover, the program's goal extends to enabling students to attain mastery of the language skills considered necessary for socio-personal empowerment (Torres-Guzmán, 1990). From a practical perspective, however, there is insufficient evidence to ascertain the degree to which VALE achieves its goal, and whether it is appropriate for adolescent learners who already read and write in another language. While the internal structure of the program appears sound, the external elements upon which it depends — time allotted, days scheduled, amount and quality of teacher guidance, students' understanding of the dialect and vocabulary selected, for example — represent important variables that can affect VALE's effectiveness for language and literacy development.

De Orilla a Orilla (From Shore to Shore): Student Learning and Empowerment through Technology

Cummins and Sayers (1990) provide a persuasive argument for learning within the culturally diverse classroom that is not only linguistically and intellectually dynamic, but which also promotes interdependence among students within this setting. Citing research conducted by Cuban (1984), Goodlad (1984), Sirotnik (1983) and Sizer (1984), Cummins and Sayers eschew the popular rhetoric of misguided progressive trends in education and the rhetoric espoused by conservative educators that a 'back to basics' model of education is now needed to remediate the lackluster performance of the nation's student populace. Instead, the authors demonstrate that US elementary and secondary classrooms have historically and typically favored passive learning controlled by the teacher over other types of instructional modes. Skill-attrition on a mass scale is almost certainly a necessary by-product of such an educational model, and US schools are unhappily in conformance with the dictates of its preferred instructional mode. The risk associated with continuing in this educationally passive tradition is already evident, but subject to increases in type and degree. Continuing in this passive tradition, for example, will inevitably lead to more critical levels of massive school retention, school desertion, and graduates with less-than-acceptable literacy and thinking skills, among others. Cummins and Sayers (1990) point out that education of this nature is especially ironic and meaningless in light of the global complexities in the areas of science, environment, culture and economics which currently face students in the near and long term. Within the United States, the future also appears bleak in that educational institutions are failing to prepare students in terms of intercultural awareness, understanding and conviviality, in spite of the dramatic increases in 'minority' students. The term 'minority student' in states like California is certainly a demographic misnomer, or perhaps, a euphemism for a politically-based human condition, as this category currently represents the majority of students in grades K through 6. Nevertheless, ethnolinguistic segregation and chauvinism prevail in US educational settings, making intergroup cooperation particularly difficult to accomplish.

According to Cummins and Sayers (1990), within the context of passive, monocultural, monolingual education on a national scale, the creative learning potential associated with the introduction of microcomputers is immediately and effectively neutralized as it is absorbed within the educational machinery. Students, then, continue to remain passive and segregated as computer-based curricula are doled out on the basis of socioeconomic circumstance, gender, ethnolinguistic group, race and academic standing. As a result, to the historical issues regarding educational equity, we now must add the contemporary phenomenon of selective rather than democratic computer-integrated learning, and the effects that differential access and participation exert upon the benefits derived by particular groups within society (see DeVillar and Faltis, 1987). Equity considerations also must extend to the realm of educational software, where Spanish language software packages are virtually absent.

The particular computer-supported learning alternative which Cummins and Sayers present reflects a well-grounded pedagogical framework in the democratic tradition which challenges student passivity and powerlessness as it celebrates active learning with others as a means to critical consciousness, intercultural conviviality, and individual empowerment. The principles associated with this particular framework are, of course, not dependent upon computer technology, although there are distinct (but perhaps not disproportionate) advantages to applying them through this medium. The model Cummins and Sayers present is historically based upon the Modern School Movement (MSM) originated by Celestin

Freinet in 1924 in the French Alps (Cummins and Sayers, 1990). Interestingly, the elements which comprised the MSM model during the first quarter of this century are identical to the elements espoused by educational reformers as the century draws to a close; namely, cooperative learning; educational technology; a contextualized curriculum infused with an active language arts program; meaningful intercultural linkages promoting information sharing and generation, intellectual development and cultural understanding; critical consciousness; and student empowerment. Cummins and Sayers (1990) report that the MSM model continues to thrive in thousands of classrooms in thirty-three countries, but that its methods, although practiced and published throughout Eastern and Western Europe and Latin America, remain virtually unknown and unavailable in English-speaking countries.

De Orilla a Orilla (From Shore to Shore) represents a recent exception to the almost universal lack of attention paid by the US to the Freinetian educational model, as Cummins and Sayers (1990) point out. The program is exceptional also in addressing the language and literacy competencies and development needs of Spanish-speaking language minority students. The primary objective of the project remains multifold: increased first and second language proficiency, enhanced academic performance and self-esteem, and improved interpersonal skills, all within a cooperative learning format emphasizing language arts, social studies, math and science. The project is also viewed as a means to reduce prejudice and to promote positive intergroup relations, a standard goal with cooperative learning that appears to reflect its early roots: sociopsychological studies of human behavior within interracial contact settings (see Allport, 1954). From the perspective of literacy development, meaningful and contextualized, writing, reading, listening and speaking activities geared to local and extended audiences ensure that the language is approached as a developmental process. For language minority students who are bilingual in Spanish and English (regardless of their degree of proficiency in each language), participation in projects such as *Orilla a Orilla* — that is, projects that are based on the principles of the MSM model — would certainly tend to result in positive and rewarding learning experiences not available to them presently in either the limited normative or the comprehensive approaches to SNS.

From contextualized to decontextualized writing

In this section, we describe computer-supported projects that have incorporated to various degrees principles of social learning theory, particularly those associated with the use of cooperative learning within a contextually-rich setting. In these learning settings the learning resources and ambience which tend to be more familiar to the students, for example, language, topics, behaviors, than they are strange, such as operating a computer, are used to lead the student toward new knowledge and fluency. Within an initial literacy-learning setting such as VALE, for example, the juxtaposition of words, the writing of stories employing invented spelling and accompanied by illustrations, and other early developmental writing strategies tend to appropriately emphasize and elicit experiences actually lived, vividly imagined or otherwise sensed by the student.

Computer-supported literacy settings such as *Orilla a Orilla* offer SNS students the means to engage in meaningful learning experiences through activities that result in broader, more penetrating contact with their surroundings. At the same time, moreover, these settings extend the notion of 'surroundings' to include the indirectly familiar as well as the environment which the students physically inhabit. Interscholastic exchanges (Cummins and Sayers, 1990) across cultures are means by which students participating in Freinetian-based programs strengthen and extend their experience. These exchanges also assist students in their intellectual movement from the parochial to the universal and in their ability to articulate it. At one level literacy skills in general are enhanced through interscholastic exchanges, in that speaking, reading, listening with comprehension and writing abilities are developed locally through the rigorous editing process that each student progresses through prior to sending his or her work to another site. Literacy development is further reinforced through reading and responding to works received from partner sites. At another level, the Freinetian model would appear also to develop students' ability to compose for different audiences by employing appropriately diverse composition techniques. Teachers at different sites involved in partner relationships structure learning exchanges that in their written expression reflect formal (i.e., transactional) exchanges as well as personal and creative writing exchanges (Cummins, 1988), all of which ideally, but all too rarely, form part of the students' literacy development experience. The acquisition and refinement of these different writing styles are especially important to bilingual Spanish-speaking students as their general educational experience characteristically results in fossilization, and even loss, of primary language and literacy skills, a circumstance which does not readily assist in, and may well hinder, the acquisition and development of second language literacy.

Conclusion

There are several interrelated principles with respect to literacy development of bilingual Spanish-speaking students that we can reaffirm based on the present analysis. First, language and literacy development is largely a function of guided social interaction within a personally meaningful learning setting. Second, guided interaction with one's peers in meaningful activities that extend knowledge through capitalizing upon behaviors and resources familiar to the learner are fundamental to self-expression. Third, with the above context, direct and indirect contact with diverse settings or cultures through interactive engagement by the learner with a member from another setting/culture will extend the student's sense of what he or she considers familiar and favorably will influence the development of multiple writing styles. Fourth, participation in the above contexts, which meet the three favorable conditions for language and literacy development outlined above, will strengthen and extend the primary language and literacy abilities of bilingual Spanish-speaking students.

The use of computers presents an effective, but not indispensable, means by which to communicate across distances. Their indisputable advantage is the speed at which communication is made possible, especially in providing the means for virtually instantaneous screen-to-screen and printer-to-printer dialogue between discussants.

Another potential advantage is that students who use computers and whose learning efforts are not diminished by their use, such as the inappropriate reliance on or use of drill and practice programs, not only learn the required subject matter, but also learn to operate a computer. Nevertheless, the pedagogical principles inherent in VALE and in the MSM remain intact whether or not a computer is used and, indeed, require the use of other, more traditional and accessible, Spanish language resources and activities. In the same manner, the programs also necessitate that peers and adults play a significant role in each student's learning. This leads us to our fifth principle: Since the computer's role in learning, as we presently understand it, is one of teacher-support rather than teacher-substitution, the inclusion of computer-supported learning activities to the SNS classroom enhances opportunities for active learning and increases the complexity of the learning setting. Thus, the extent to which bilingual Spanish-speaking students will flourish in their learning settings is directly (although not absolutely) proportional to the SNS teachers' ability to meaningfully operate the three major socioacademic conditions for language and literacy learning within classroom settings.

References

ALLPORT, G.W. (1954) *The Nature of Prejudice*, New York, NY, Doubleday Anchor Books.

BARKER, M.E. (1972) *Español Para el Bilingüe*, Skokie, IL, National Textbook Company.

CUBAN, L. (1984) 'School reform by remote control: SB 813 in California', *Phi Delta Kappan*, **66**, pp. 167–72.

CUMMINS, J. (1988) 'From the inner city to the global village: The microcomputer as a catalyst for collaborative learning and cultural interchange', *Language Culture and Curriculum*, **1**, 1, pp. 1–14.

CUMMINS, J. and SAYERS, D. (1990) 'Education 2001: Learning networks and educational reforms', in FALTIS, C. and DEVILLAR, R.A. (Eds) *Language Minority Students and Computers*, Binghamton, NY, The Haworth Press.

DEVILLAR, R.A. (1987) 'Variation in the language use of peer dyads within a bilingual, cooperative, computer-assisted instructional setting', unpublished doctoral dissertation, Stanford, CA, Stanford University.

DEVILLAR, R.A. (1991) 'Cooperative principles, computers, and classroom language', in MCGROARTY, M. and FALTIS, C. (Eds) *Language in School and Society: Policy and Pedagogy*, Berlin, Germany, Mouton de Grutyer, pp. 181–92.

DEVILLAR, R.A. and FALTIS, C.J. (1987) 'Computers and educational equity in American public schools', *Capstone Journal of Education*, **8**, 4, pp. 1–8.

DEVILLAR, R.A. and FALTIS, C.J. (1991) *Computers and Cultural Diversity: Restructuring Schools for Socio-academic Success*, Binghamton, NY, State University of New York Press.

DE LA PORTILLA, M. and VARELA, B. (1978) *Mejora tu Español: Lectura y Redacción para Bilingües*, New York, NY, Regents.

FALTIS, C.J. (1981) 'Teaching Spanish writing to bilingual college students', *NABE Journal*, **6**, 1, pp. 93–106.

FALTIS, C.J. (1984) 'Reading and writing in Spanish for bilingual college students: What's taught at school and what's used in the community', *The Bilingual Review/La Revista Bilingüe*, **11**, 1, pp. 21–32.

FALTIS, C.J. (1990) 'Spanish for native speakers: Freirian and Vygotskian perspectives', *Foreign Language Annals*, **23**, 2, pp. 117–26.

FEUSTLE, J.A., JR. (1987) 'Review of *Juegos Comunicativos*', *Hispania*, **70**, 3, pp. 708–10.

FREIRE, P. (1970) *Pedagogy of the Oppressed*, New York, NY, Herder and Herder.

GOODLAD, J. (1984) *A Place Called School: Prospects for the Future*, New York, NY, McGraw Hill.

JOHNSON, D., JOHNSON, R., HOLOBEC JOHNSON, E. and ROY, P. (1984) *Circles of Learning, Cooperation in the Classroom*, Alexandria, VA, Association for Supervision and Curriculum Development.

LEÓN, F. (1978) *Español: Material para el Hispano*, Manchaca, TX, Sterling Swift Publishing.

QUINTANILLA, G.C. and SILMAN, J. (1978) *Español: Lo Esencial para el Bilingüe*, Washington, DC, University Press of America.

SIROTNIK, K.A. (1983) 'What you see is what you get — consistency, persistency, and mediocrity in classrooms', *Harvard Educational Review*, **53**, 1, pp. 16–31.

SIZER, T.R. (1984) *Horace's Compromise: The Dilemma of the American High School*, Boston, MA, Houghton Mifflin.

Software Reviews in *Hispania* 1984–1989, *Hispania*, **72**, 2, 1989, pp. 470–3. (no author).

TORRES-GUZMÁN, M.E. (1990) '*Voy a Leer Escribiendo* in the context of bilingual/bicultural education', in FALTIS, C. and DEVILLAR, R.A. (Eds) *Language Minority Students and Computers*, New York, NY, The Haworth Press.

VALDÉS, G. (1988) 'The language situation of Mexican Americans', in MCKAY, S. and WONG, S.C. (Eds) *Language Diversity: Problem or Resource?*, New York, NY, Harper and Row, pp. 111–39.

VALDÉS-FALLIS, G. (1978) 'A comprehensive approach to the teaching of Spanish to bilingual Spanish-speaking students', *Modern Language Journal*, **62**, pp. 102–10.

VALDÉS, G. (1981) 'Pedagogical implications of teaching Spanish to the Spanish-speaking in the United States', in VALDÉS, G., LOZANO, A.G. and GARCÍA-MOYA, R. (Eds) *Teaching Spanish to the Hispanic Bilingual*, New York, NY, Teachers College Press, pp. 3–20.

VALDÉS-FALLIS, G. and TESCHNER, R.V. (1978) (2nd Edition, 1984) *Español Escrito: Curso para Hispanohablantes*, New York, NY, Charles Scribner's Sons.

VALDÉS, G., HUNNUM, T.P. and TESCHNER, R.V. (1982) *Cómo se Escribe: Curso de Secundaria para Estudiantes Bilingües*, New York, NY, Charles Scribner's Sons.

UNDERWOOD, J. (1986) *Juegos Comunicativos, Spanish Games for Communicative Practice*, New York, NY, Random House College Software.

WONG FILLMORE, L. (1985) 'When does teacher talk work as input?', in GASS, S.M. and MADDEN, C. (Eds) *Input in Second Language Acquisition*, Rowley, MA, Newbury House, pp. 235–53.

Chapter 13

An Introduction to Computer-Assisted Spanish Language Learning

Nidia González-Edfelt

The use of computers in the acquisition and learning of Spanish as a first as well as second language has immense potential that is slowly being realized. From the early years of the mainframe computer to today's accessible micro/personal computer, the computer is perceived by an increasing number of Spanish language teaching professionals as a tool capable of greatly enriching the teaching and learning processes. This chapter presents an overview of how the on-going development of both hardware and software is allowing the computer to break away from its early limitations as a language teaching tool.

The chapter addresses language educators who teach Spanish either to second language learners or to native Spanish speakers. The focus is on teachers who are just venturing into the world of computers and would like to know more about the major issues and developments surrounding computer use in language learning. The brief historical review at the beginning of the chapter will serve as a reminder that, from its very early years and in spite of early limitations, the computer was seen as a viable tool for second/foreign language learning. The second section examines the many contributions the computer can make in language acquisition and language learning, including the varied and sometimes opposite roles it can assume and its continuously emerging capabilities. The section discusses how the possession of 'voice, ears and sight', high quality software programs, and the power to coordinate several other media can allow the computer to assume the role of orchestrator and facilitator of a language rich environment. The final section briefly discusses some areas in computer-assisted language learning (CALL) that are in dire need of attention.

Brief Historical Overview

Early years

The beginnings of computer use in foreign/second language learning can be traced back to the birth of CAI (Computer Assisted Instruction) in the early 1960s. At that time, lessons were delivered by mainframe computers accessed by students from computer terminals. The large scale projects which characterize this first stage are best exemplified by the Russian language project at Stanford University (Van Campen, 1968) and the German language project at the State University of New York at Stony Brook (Adams, Morrison and Reddy, 1969). Some smaller programs, such as the ELSE project for French at Dartmouth College (Allen, 1971), were also developed. However, because most professionals involved in this work were computer specialists and psychologists, rather than language teachers, little attention was paid to the language teaching methodology employed. Toward the end of the 1960s and early 1970s, several projects which depended on complex and sophisticated technology were developed. Examples of these are the PLATO system at the University of Illinois, which offered programs on a wide range of subject areas including foreign languages (Ariew, 1974; Chapelle and Jamieson, 1983), and the FRAND project at the University of Alberta (McEwen, 1977).

The early 1970s saw increasing interest in the methodological and pedagogical aspects of the programs over technological ones (Holmes and Kidd, 1982). This new attitude resulted in smaller programs, such as the DECU/TUCO project for German at Ohio State University (Taylor, 1979), the MONIQUE program for French at the University of Richmond (Terry, 1977) and the CARLOS program for Spanish, French, and Danish at Westchester College (Smith, 1976). Although these projects were the beneficiaries of language teachers' direct involvement and input, most of them continued to reflect a programmed instructional approach to learning (Johnson, 1989). Moreover, the impact of the computer in the educational field continued to be minimal, as its use was limited to the few large universities that could afford the high cost. This inaccessibility was drastically changed in the early 1980s, when the advent of the microcomputer finally put the computer at the reach of most schools. The full impact of the microcomputer in education, however, has not yet been realized, as its influence continues to increase daily.

Research on computer effectiveness in second/foreign language learning

Interest in the use of the computer in schools has generated a growing body of research which attempts to evaluate its pedagogical effectiveness. Although these studies have generally found a positive impact in several academic subjects (Kulik, Kulik and Bangert-Drowns, 1985) the effect is less conclusive in second/foreign language learning, an area in which there have been few empirical studies. Although qualitative studies in this field suggest that computers affect positively student behavior, increasing their confidence and motivation (Quinn, 1990), quantitative data showing achievement effects are inconclusive (Roblyer, Castine and King, 1988).

One important reason for the lack of reliable statistical evidence in computer assisted second/foreign language learning is given by difficulties in research methodology. One difficulty, for instance, is caused by the confounding effects of evaluating the specific software program rather than the use of the computer as a medium of instruction (Hope, Taylor, and Pusack, 1984). These methodological problems arise when the studies attempt to compare the effectiveness of computer assisted practice with traditional teaching methods. Because computer assisted learning is not a teaching method *per se*, the studies are flawed. Unfortunately, most research to date has been of this type. Lately, there has been an increasing awareness of the need to utilize more appropriate research methods and questions; these include changing the research focus from the medium (i.e., the computer) to examining both the message (i.e., the content of the software program, including methodology and type of task) and the learner (Dunkel, 1987). In other words, the focus needs to be on the process, rather than the product, of computer-based language learning.

Slow acceptance of computers in the second/foreign language teaching field

In general, the use of computers in second/foreign language teaching has proceeded rather slowly. Some reasons include the high cost of hardware and software acquisition and teacher and administrator training. The slow start could also be interpreted as a function of the time-lag between the availability of microcomputers and their full use in the classroom. Although these causal factors could be applied to all fields of study in general, a different picture emerges when other subjects are considered. While in mathematics, for example, the microcomputer has been viewed as a natural fit and is readily adopted as a valuable learning tool, its acceptance by second/foreign language teaching professionals has been slower and more controversial. The most frequent explanations given in the literature have been 1) a general skepticism on the part of second/foreign language teachers toward educational technology; 2) the low quality of software programs which have been produced; and 3) the lack of capability on the part of the computer to deal with human speech. These are discussed below.

1. Skepticism on the part of second/foreign language teaching professionals

The perceived skepticism is believed by many to derive from the association of computers with the language lab and the unfulfilled expectations it engendered in the 1960s. In addition, because the language lab resulted in great part from the behaviorist theory of language learning prevailing at the time, many language teachers equate educational technology with audiolingual exercises, and consequently, believe that the computer only allows for a methodology based on behaviorist principles (Wyatt, 1983).

Researchers and practitioners such as Wyatt (1984), have pointed out that critics of CAI have confused the medium with its content and that it is possible to develop software programs which are based on differing and even opposing learning and teaching philosophies. The attempt to clarify this confusion has led to repeated assertions in the literature that computers are not grounded on any specific theoretical or psycholinguistic theory of language learning (e.g., Bickes and Scott, 1989). The computer is a mere tool, and, like other tools, such as pencils, overhead projectors, textbooks, videotape machines, and so on, its effectiveness is determined by the methodology on which it is based as well as by how effectively it is used. In addition, it has been frequently argued (see Kenning and Kenning, 1983) that the use of computers is not incompatible with the present emphasis on oral communication and practice.

2. The (low) quality of foreign language software programs

Although the computer is a neutral tool, independent of any specific language learning philosophy or methodology, the equation between computer and behaviorism has been reinforced by the fact that most software programs developed for foreign/second language teaching have taken the form of 'drill and practice'. In 1983, Sanders and Kenner argued that most of the existing second language teaching software represented the audiolingual tradition. Today, drill and practice exercises continue to represent the most common activity in software programs on the market (Burston, 1989).

In light of the current emphasis on 'communicative' and 'creative' language teaching, this use of what has been called 'technology of the 1980s with courseware of the 1960's' (Sanders and Kenner, 1983) has constituted one of the main barriers to accepting computers in the second/foreign language field and has greatly contributed to frequent disappointment on the part of language teachers trying CAI programs for the first time. Because many of these programs are based on exercises that seem to have been taken directly from a textbook, many educators see computer capabilities reduced to that of an 'electronic workbook'. Unfortunately, while the development of hardware, with its concomitant decreased costs, has proceeded at a tremendously rapid pace, the production of well-designed instructional software in appropriate quantity has lagged behind. Dunkel (1987) argues that this has been determined in great measure by reluctance on the part of publishers to risk CAI publication because of low profitability. Among the causes of low profitability, Dunkel includes a) the high cost of software development; b) the meagerness of the CAI market; c) the low volume of software programs sales (when compared to other school materials such as textbooks); and d) the short life expectancy of software programs due to the rapid pace of technological development.

The fact that form and content of most software programs for foreign/second language learning have been similar to the form and content of traditional media (e.g., books) and even of other older technology (e.g., television and film), shows that it takes time to learn how to use technological innovations to their fullest potential. Like other developments, the computer is being implemented with what has been termed (McLuhan, 1964) the 'rear-view mirror' approach. This approach refers to the historical tendency to first apply the content of older media to a new medium until the unique capabilities of the latter are discovered and exploited to their fullest. As McLuhan (1964) pointed out, the content of the first motion pictures were staged plays and that of the first television programs were old movies. Papert (1980) believes that this phenomenon explains why courseware development has followed not only the format but the content of textbooks, which in turn has caused the computer to be used as a 'page turner'.

Another contributing factor to low-quality software programs has been the lack of teacher involvement in production, due, in great part, to the time consuming nature of the task. As a consequence, a majority of programs have been developed by computer experts who lack knowledge of, and expertise in, foreign language teaching (Quinn, 1990). There are, however, signs that this state of affairs is changing. An increasing number of programs which reflect current second/foreign language learning theories and which use to a fuller extent the capabilities of the computer have appeared on the market. In addition, a number of universities are actively participating in the development of instructional materials. Two examples are The Athena Language Learning Project at MIT (Morgenstern, 1986), and Project Jefferson at the University of Southern California (Chignell and Lacy, 1988).

3. Inability on the part of the computer to deal with speech and free expression.

In light of the fact that natural language involves primarily speaking and listening skills, and that current theoretical communicative trends emphasize the spoken language, the inability of the computer to deal with human speech has been an important element preventing its full acceptance. Another factor has been the machine's limitation to operate within a predetermined, preprogrammed frame, which renders it unable to react to free written expression. Although interaction with the user is considered its most important advantage, many argue that this interaction lacks the creativity, complexity, and freedom of human speech.

It has been pointed out that the perceived disadvantages of the computer derive from the capabilities of the machine being judged against unrealistic expectations, such as the belief that it should be able to communicate intelligently and creatively. Accordingly, because the computer is not 'intelligent', it is considered deficient for language learning purposes. Bickes and Scott (1989) argue that this perspective ignores the concept that language teaching methods include a great variety of approaches and activities which aim at developing not only listening and speaking, but reading and writing as well.

What the Computer can Offer to Language Learning

One major advantage the computer offers is that whereas in any other learning tool the information goes only one way, from the medium to the student, computers provide for two-way activities by accepting, reacting to, processing and responding to student input. Although some researchers have called for a clearer definition of the term 'interactivity' (Meskill, 1987), the latter has generally referred to the computer's capability to react to student responses or requests through immediate feedback. This capability transforms students into active participants, because if they do not in turn respond, the activity on the screen stops. Interactivity becomes even more valuable because it is coupled with individualization — the computer's ability to adjust instruction to different student levels, branching into appropriate tutorials or exercises, giving extra help or more advanced activities which match students' needs and abilities (Underwood, 1984; Wyatt, 1984).

Among other advantages, the computer provides the student with: self-pacing, as in most programs the students can adapt the speed of the activity to their individual needs; a consistent, unbiased and emotionally neutral learning medium; tireless and accurate practice; a pedagogically neutral tool, not tied to any particular philosophy or methodology; and a medium which has proved attractive to students (Hope *et al.*, 1984; Pusak, 1983, Wyatt, 1984).

The changing role of the computer as an instructional tool

The argument has been made (Ahmad, Corbett, Rogers and Sussex, 1985) that the limitations of the computer seem especially important when the machine is viewed only in its role as instructor, a role which the computer plays mainly through the use of drill-and-practice and tutorial programs. A more recent attitude is to see the computer as having different roles in the learning process, the role of taskmaster being just one of them. Wyatt (1984, 1988) argues that apart from teacher, the computer serves two other important functions, that of facilitator, through such programs as word processing, and that of collaborator, through, for instance, simulation programs. While the computer as taskmaster transforms the student into a passive recipient of information and follower of machine instructions, the computer as collaborator or facilitator permits students to control and take responsibility for their own learning.

Papert (1980), the developer of LOGO, viewed the computer as a tool to explore rather than as a teacher to instruct. He believed that the optimal use of the computer is to create environments which allow for 'discovery learning'; this would only be possible, however, if the child learns to program (i.e., control) the computer rather than the other way around. His beliefs marked the beginning of a change in the theoretical emphasis from instructional to collaborative uses of the computer in language learning. It is now generally accepted that it is as collaborator that computers can offer the most benefits for language learning.

This new attitude was reflected by the shift in preference for a term to designate the use of computers in language learning. Although the most commonly used term in the United States, until a few years back, was CAI, for Computer Assisted Instruction (or CALI, for Computer Assisted Language Instruction), there was a reaction in the 1980s to the word 'instruction' in the acronym. It was pointed out (e.g., Ahmad *et al.*, 1985; Wyatt, 1984) that this term presents the computer in only one role: that of teacher or taskmaster. The term CAL for Computer Assisted Learning (and CALL for Computer Assisted Language Learning), used originally in Great Britain, was seen to focus on the learning rather than on the teaching aspect of the process. The latter, consequently, is now the preferred choice in the United States.

With this new perspective, a constant theme throughout discussion of CALL has been the 'magister-pedagogue' metaphor (Higgins and Johns, 1984). This metaphor mirrors the concept of 'banking' vs. 'generative' education, first proposed by Freire (1968/1970). In banking education, the learner is assumed to be passive and receptive, ready to absorb the information transmitted by the source of all knowledge, the teacher. In generative education, on the other hand, the student is seen as active and capable of taking responsibility for his or her own learning, and the teacher is an equal partner in this process. Similarly, in the 'magister-pedagogue' metaphor, the computer can be perceived either as a master (magister) who controls the student's learning, or as an obedient tutor-slave (pedagogue) who, under student control, provides students with an environment capable of developing qualities of initiative and responsibility for learning.

Typology of activities in software programs

Developing a typology of software programs for second/foreign language learning is difficult because programs generally include different types of activities (for instance, tutorials frequently include drill and practice, and simulations may include instructional games). Because of this, the following classification applies to activities, rather than to entire programs. The programs mentioned below have been developed for students of Spanish as a second/foreign language; however, some of them could be used profitably by native Spanish speakers. Language learning programs that have been designed for the specific needs of the latter are practically nonexistent.

1. *Tutorial* activities present new information to the student through explanations, diagrams, tables, definitions of terms, exercises and appropriate branching (Hope *et al.*, 1984). A good example of this for Spanish learning is given by *Lecciones de Español Conduit* (Phillips, 1984). The program focuses on some grammatical points which cause difficulty to Spanish as a second language learners, such as *por* vs. *para*, *ser* vs. *estar* and *pretérito* vs. *imperfecto*. There is an optional grammar review followed by exercises including fill-in sentences, multiple-choice questions, transformation fill-in sentences and English sentences to be translated into Spanish (see review of this program in Virgulti, 1985). Another example is the tutorial program *Spanish Microtutor* (c. 1989), which covers grammar points for beginning and intermediate levels. Each lesson gives the student the choice of a Pre-Test, Tutorial, Exercises, or Post-Test. The tutorial section presents clear grammatical explanations with abundant examples (see Hernández, 1989, for a review of this program). Although many tutorials present thorough and clear grammatical explanations, the weakness of these types of activities for students of Spanish as a second/foreign language is that they follow grammar-translation and audiolingual approaches and do not present instruction in a meaningful context. For native Spanish-speaking students, however, whose interest might lie in the learning of the standard variety of Spanish or specific grammatical points, these activities might provide useful information and practice.

2. *Drill and practice* activities reinforce the students' command of material and concepts which they have already covered. This format is very common in computer packages accompanying textbooks. The package for the third edition of *¿Habla Español?* (1985), for example, provides drill and practice as well as tests and quizzes; the three formats used are true/false, multiple choice and fill-in (see review of this program by Raschio, 1989). As in tutorials, the weakness of this type of approach is that the items are usually presented in isolation rather than in context, and the activity becomes a mechanistic exercise devoid of meaning.

3. *Problem solving* activities present specific problematic situations which students solve through their use of the target language. A good example is an activity in the software program *El Mundo Hispánico* (1985), which takes students on a tour of Colombia, Puerto Rico and Spain. In this particular activity, which takes place in the streets of Pamplona during the Festival of San Fermín, the student must answer questions correctly in order to outrun the bulls (See review of this program by Kiss, 1988). Another example is given by most of the activities in *Juegos Comunicativos, Spanish Games for Communicative Practice* (Underwood, 1986), a program discussed in greater detail below in the 'Answer Processing' section of this chapter. The advantage of the problem-solving approach is that it allows greater student control over their choices, and the animated graphics usually place the language in greater context than do drill-and-practice type activities. Although, unfortunately, there are no research data comparing the effectiveness of different computer activities on language learning, this approach seems to have great potential for both Spanish as a second language and native Spanish-speaking learners.

4. *Instructional games* are activities in which students have to use their knowledge of the target language to overcome impediments in their progress to an objective. In *Batalla de Palabras* (1984), for example, students race against a timer in answering multiple-choice quizzes or completing sentences in a game format (see review by Perales, 1985). Another example is *Caminando* (Chamorin and Gómez, c. 1989). In this program, the action takes place in a school, home, hotel and train station, which are located in a city represented on the screen as a map. The goal of the game is to move a 'tortoise' from one point of the city to another; to make this possible the student answers linguistic and cultural questions at different points (see review by Taylor, J.S., 1990). Like problem-solving activities, instructional games can increase the motivation of students because they are both fun and challenging.

5. *Text manipulation* activities present text which has been rearranged or altered by the computer in order to challenge the learner with a puzzle (Stevens, 1990). Among the several types of text manipulation, text reconstruction is the most popular type of program currently used in language teaching (Quincey, 1986). Text reconstruction has been defined as 'recreating the original form of a text which has been transformed in some manner' (Hubbard, 1990, p. 2). This transformation is accomplished through four basic types of activities: *deletion* (of every nth word, verb forms, prepositions, etc.); *insertion* (of extra letters, sentences, or paragraphs); *movement*, the most common of which is scrambling (at the level of the word, sentence and paragraph); and *replacement*, where, for instance, each letter is systematically replaced by another (Hubbard, 1990). A good example of deletion activities is *Spanish Hangman Vocabulary Builder* (c. 1982) in which the student receives points for completing the word before the hangman's body is revealed (see review by Cruz-Sáenz, 1984). Another example is *Cloze Encounters in Spanish* (Neff and Whitney, 1987), which permits teachers to create their own cloze exercises (see review of this program by Cohen, 1988). An example of movement activities are the syntax exercises for *Software for Churros and Chocolate* (Mohler, 1988), where students are presented with scrambled sentences in the form of lists of four to nine words (see review of this program by Weaver, 1989).

There is disagreement regarding the range of activities that can be considered text reconstruction and which of them actually result in language learning. Many practitioners and researchers (e.g., Stevens, 1990) view reconstruction tasks as valuable activities that permit learning by discovery. However, because in text reconstruction the goal is to restore the text to its original form (which means that students are penalized if they answer with correct alternative forms), its pedagogical value has been questioned. The approach seems especially problematic as a learning activity for native Spanish speakers. The fact that there is only one predetermined correct answer might penalize speakers of dialects different from the one in which the software program was written, and convey the message that certain expressions or lexical items are wrong or preferable over others. It seems fair to recognize, however, that this is a recurrent problem in any type of software program where the answers are predetermined. As a native Spanish speaker, I have more than once suffered the frustration of receiving a 'Wrong! Try again!' message on the part of the computer for having answered '*rojo*' instead of '*colorado*', or '*linda*' instead of '*bonita*'. This also brings into focus the troublesome decision on the part of software program writers to determine what constitutes standard Spanish, a decision especially complex and problematic at the lexical level.

6. *Text generation* programs give students the opportunity to create their own text. The amount of structure within which the student works ranges from creating poems or stories within a predetermined framework to the open-endedness of word-processing programs. The latter is not only the most commonly used form of text generation but has been a much studied educational computer-based activity. Research on students (native speakers of English) writing in English has suggested that word processing results in an increased positive attitude toward writing, with students writing more and with fewer mistakes than when using pen and paper (see Hawisher, 1989, for a review of this research). In addition, word processing has been found to change students' writing strategies (Daiute, 1985) and to encourage students to be more flexible and creative in their writing of stories (Grabe and Grabe, 1985). Many researchers (e.g., Jex, 1988) believe that because word processing is so suited to creating and editing text, it constitutes the best use of microcomputers for language instruction. Similarly, research on second/foreign language learners suggests that writing compositions at the computer is a valuable language learning activity; students feel that word processing motivates them to write more (Piper, 1987), and that it increases their interest and willingness to experiment with grammatical elements (Jex, 1988). These findings would seem to suggest that these types of activities are very valuable for the learning of Spanish writing skills by native Spanish speakers, an area in which research is practically nonexistent. In the case of native Spanish speakers who are literate in English and actually transferring their English writing skills to Spanish, the freedom and flexibility given by this medium would indeed seem to motivate them to learn freely and to try as many times as necessary.

In addition, in word-processing tasks the computer can be used as an electronic chalkboard, either for demonstration purposes or for working with the entire class at, for instance, creating and correcting a composition or changing the end of a story. In the Spanish language class these activities are facilitated by the fact that some word-processing programs have been translated into Spanish. An example is *WordPerfect 4.2, Spanish Version* (1986), which is a translation of the widely-used English version (see review by Irizarry, 1988).

7. *Simulation* is a general term which covers a range of activities involving decisions based on data from specific situations (Higgins and Johns, 1984). Simulations attempt to imitate a real environment in which students have the ability to intervene and make decisions which influence the direction of the activities and the results. The students communicate their responses to the computer through the keyboard, and see the consequences of their actions on the screen. Simulations have been classified according to the following types (Kenning and Kenning, 1983):

a. *Chit-Chat or conversational simulations*, in which the computer acts as one of the interlocutors in a (written) dialog with the student; the dialog gives the appearance of being open-ended and unpredictable. For instance, in a program for Spanish as a second language learners, *Spanlap* (Jehle, 1987), which is discussed in more detail below under 'Answer Processing', the student asks questions and the computer responds in a free-form dialog format.

b. *Situational simulations*, which represent real life situations, such as a visit to the doctor or a job interview. These programs have much in common with chit-chat simulations; they differ from the latter in that the conversation is limited to a specific task (e.g., getting a job). In the *Spanish Eliza* (Underwood, 1984), discussed below under 'Language Generation', (see p. 193) the students visit a psychotherapist with whom they maintain a conversation regarding their personal problems and mental health.

c. *Adventure simulations*, in which the student has to assume a role (e.g., a detective on a murder case) and make decisions based on the information presented or requested.

d. *Adventure games*, which present the student with a dangerous task. As in adventure simulations, the program starts by describing a small, artificial world; the student enters this world by typing a sentence which reflects a decision based on information previously presented. The program reacts to this input by showing through graphics and/or text the consequences of the student's decision. The most well known program of this type for Spanish as a second language learners is *Montevidisco* (Schneider and Bennion, 1983) discussed in this chapter under 'Interactive Videodisc.'

In line with the perception of the computer as facilitator and collaborator, rather than drillmaster, there has been a growing interest in text manipulation, text generation, and simulations. These programs are seen as bringing CALL in line with recent second-language learning theories. Rather than presenting the material in grammatical sequence, they place students in more naturalistic and communicative settings by providing language choices and presenting language in context rather than in isolated sentences. Moreover, they give the student a more active role by permitting a certain amount of control over what happens on the screen.

Programming languages, authoring languages and authoring programs

Computer-based foreign/second language learning lessons can be developed by three means:

1. General purpose programming languages, such as BASIC, LOGO and Pascal. These require both a great deal of training to master and time to use (i.e., to develop a lesson using them).

2. Authoring languages, such as PILOT, EnBASIC, and MICROTUTOR. These require a less difficult level of training and offer greater ease of use (than do programming languages) and greater programming freedom (than do authoring programs). However, they still require considerable training, expertise, and time.

3. Authoring programs, which are also called, 'authoring systems', 'templates' or 'shells'. These programs allow a person without prior programming knowledge or technical expertise to create language learning activities. They are based on the template principle, that is, copies of a template (which provide a structure without content) are used to develop diverse lessons by filling in the appropriate information. The programs are usually 'menu-driven', (i.e., the users are presented with a menu or a list of choices regarding the types of exercises).

In addition, clear instructions along the way lead users through the process of creating the lesson. Unfortunately, the ease and simplicity of this approach — its main advantage — also causes its main disadvantage — lack of freedom over the type of lesson that is possible to develop. The user is restricted to the structure of the template, and the resulting activities are usually of the drill and practice kind.

There are currently on the market a wide variety of authoring systems for foreign language lessons. Examples are *The Language Coach* (1988), *Cloze Encounters in Spanish* (Neff and Whitney, 1987), *Private Tutor* (Clausing, c. 1988) and *Mac-Lang* (Frommer, 1988). *Private Tutor* uses the MacIntosh's pull-down menus and can be applied to any language. *MacLang* allows teachers to develop lessons in several languages, including Spanish, and offers a range of possible activities such as branching, fill-in-the-blanks, vocabulary drills, multiple choice questions, reading comprehension, scrambled sentences, and cloze questions. In addition, it allows for the integration of interactive video.

Giving ears and mouth to the computer

As has been pointed out above, the perception of the computer as a 'silent tool', and consequently, as incapable of assisting in the development of listening and speaking skills, has constituted a significant drawback to its acceptance. Technological advances in the last decade, however, are succeeding in providing the computer with a voice. Today, the main approaches to the adding of listening and speaking capabilities to the computer include the use of peripheral audio and of digitized and synthesized speech. There have also been developments in speech processing systems which help students in their pronunciation of the target language. These approaches are discussed below.

1. Peripheral audio devices

The attachment of a random-access cassette recorder (RACR) to the computer brings together the ease of use of the cassette recorder and the advantages of the random-access audio-disc system. The microprocessor in the RACR allows synchronization of the audio messages with screen display (See Dunkel, 1987, for a more detailed description of this technology). This makes it possible for the student to read text and simultaneously listen to the spoken passages. In addition, the device permits both the recording and playing of the voice. The advantage over the computer generated synthetic speech is the 'natural' quality of the voice, because what is heard is actual human speech. Frommer (1989) points out that while in the language lab listening can become a passive activity, a computer-controlled audio environment requires the active participation of the student, because the computer progresses only in response to student feedback. In addition, random-access frees the program from the linear mode of delivery of the language lab.

The use of RACR to acquire Spanish presents clear advantages for both native Spanish speaking and Spanish as a second language learners. The device seems particularly promising for improving the listening comprehension skills of intermediate and advanced second language learners. In addition, the fact that students can record and hear their own voice makes it possible for 'passive' bilinguals as well as Spanish as a second language learners to produce language in the privacy of a computer environment, and to hear and compare their own production to that of 'model' speech. Finally, the device permits the bringing of dialectal varieties to the classroom, thus enriching the language learning environment.

2. Digitized speech

In digital audio, a person's speech is digitized (i.e., converted into numbers in binary code) and then stored. For playback, the numbers are regenerated into speech. (See Ahmad *et al.*, 1985, for an explanation of this technology). The advantages of digitized recording are many: a) Speech does not deteriorate with time; b) Sounds can be retrieved almost instantaneously at any desired point or in any sequence with extreme precision; c) Audio material can be manipulated in the same way as any other computer data: it can be stored (in memory, in floppy, hard and optical disks, and in digital tapes), and electronically transmitted via networks; d) Computer controlled audio material can be synchronized with the appropriate display on the computer screen; e) It not only allows for pre-recorded audio to be played for listening activities, but the student can record her or his own voice and play it back; f) Although the sound fidelity varies from one brand of computer to the other, in general, digital audio can produce very high-quality sound, often nearing that of taped recordings; this makes it highly adequate for second/foreign language learning purposes (Fischer, 1986; Parker and Davis, 1989).

The main disadvantage of digitized audio, apart from the fact that it can only be created with special hardware, is the large amount of memory it takes for recording, storage and output. Although the increasing availability of hard-disks, with their much greater storage capabilities, would help solve this problem, the use of a new technological innovation, CD-ROM (Compact Disk-Read Only Memory), seems to offer the best solution. The advantage of the CD-ROM is that it provides tremendous storage space and allows for instant random access. In this combination, the instructional software program containing the digitized human voice is stored on a CD-ROM disk, which is accessed by students using the program through headphones plugged into the CD-ROM drive. (see the section below entitled 'CD-ROM' for a more detailed discussion on this technology).

Another technological innovation, the low-cost sound digitizer and its accompanying authoring software, has made digitized sound very accessible for the development of courseware which incorporates pictures and speech. An example is the MacRecorder (c. 1988), a hardware-software package that is inexpensive, and easy to use, and permits users to treat sound like any other data in the Macintosh (see Chun, 1989, for a description of this package).

In recent years several CALL software programs which utilize digitized speech have appeared in the market. An example is *Acumen* (c. 1988), a drill/tutorial system for ESL aural comprehension practice. In this program the student listens to an item presented within a context and answers multiple choice questions appearing on the computer screen (see Hubbard, 1989, for a review). For Spanish as a second language, several Hypercard- and MacRecorder-based programs have been developed (see Larsen, 1990, for information regarding these programs). One example is *Spanish Pronunciation Tutor With Sound* (c. 1990), which gives the student choices from among several lessons, such as 'Stress and Accents', 'Consonants', 'Linking', etc. (For a review of this program, see Varela, 1991).

The flexibility of digitized speech, the high quality of its voice sound and the capabilities of coordinating voice with pictures and graphics add greatly to the potential of the computer as a pedagogical tool in the second/foreign language classroom. Digitized speech eliminates the earlier constraints of the computer as a setting which could only offer students silent reading and writing practice. In allowing the development of programs for aural understanding, digitized speech makes possible a comprehension approach to learning in the computer environment. This new capability seems extremely valuable for acquirers of Spanish as a second language, who need a rich natural context conducive to greater comprehensible input. It seems particularly worthwhile for students whose training has been mostly grammar-based, and are thus in dire need to increase their Spanish aural understanding.

3. Synthesized speech

While digitized audio stores digital signals which correspond to actual human speech sounds, synthesized speech is generated by the computer through the manipulation of machine produced phonemes. The most common form of synthesized speech sound today is phonemic synthesis. The Votrax chip, for example, uses phonemic approximations of the IPA (International Phonetic Alphabet) or WES (World English Spelling) (Dunkel, 1987).

The greatest advantage of synthesized speech is that memory requirements are minimal. In addition, because it allows for the generation of spontaneous utterances rather than being constrained to prerecorded material, it offers much greater flexibility than digitized speech. Its greatest disadvantage, however, renders it almost unacceptable for second/foreign language learning purposes. Synthesized speech is of low quality and difficult to understand; it has such a strong 'computer accent' that it is still a long way from resembling human speech. This problem is even more pronounced in multilingual speech synthesis devices, which have been generally based on revised English synthesizers. One method for developing Spanish synthesizers, for example, has been to approximate Spanish phonemes through a combination of English phonemes. The resulting sound quality has been very poor. Current efforts to achieve better Spanish synthesizers include the work of Tritton (1991), who is developing a library of Spanish sounds, the first step in achieving high quality Spanish synthesized speech. However, this technology is still in its formative stages and it will be a few years before it has improved to a level of speech acceptable for language learning purposes.

4. Speech processing

A variety of speech processing systems have been applied to the teaching of pronunciation and accent reduction. The last decade has seen the development of many inexpensive machines which combine the analysis of pronunciation with the production of computer graphics to provide audio and visual feedback to students working on their pronunciation and intonation. Today, there is a wide range of hardware and software speech analysis products in the market for the IBM and Macintosh personal computers (see Chun, 1989, for a detailed discussion).

The instant display of speech signals in these machines permits students to compare a native speaker's pronunciation with their own. Molholt (1988) argues that these machines can be effective even with people whose pronunciation shows signs of having fossilized. This effectiveness is believed to derive from the fact that the visual displays provide concrete, objective feedback that helps students identify and concentrate their efforts on their specific problem areas. The machines address three levels: phonemes (i.e., sounds in isolation), words and sentences. Some displays show the student's and the native model's pitch, intensity and duration of words or complete sentences.

An example of a program to teach pronunciation is *Babel* (Vila and Pearson, 1990). This system combines computer graphics, speech synthesis, and artificial intelligence to reproduce auditorily and visually the sounds of a text in any language which uses the Latin alphabet. Its objective is to help students learn the pronunciation of phonemes by reproducing words and sentences by a speech synthesizer and simultaneously displaying the correct positioning of speech organs on the computer screen. The program displays two animated graphics: a front view of a face and a phonetician's side view of the throat and jaw. When students type the words they are working on, *Babel* reproduces them acoustically and displays, through the animated graphics, the synchronized movements of the lips and cross-sectioned speech organs, so students can see how the correct pronunciation is achieved.

Some machines use spectrographic displays which show sound waves of the human voice. Spectrographic displays can be used for teaching phonemes as well as intonation, stress and rhythm. For example, to teach the aspiration of the stop /p/ in initial position in English words, a phoneme absent in Spanish, and consequently causing difficulty to Spanish speakers learning English (with the reverse difficulty experienced by English speakers learning Spanish), a spectrographic display exhibits the native speaker's pronunciation and that of the student's, thus showing in a visual and concrete manner the differences between the two (Molholt, 1988).

The Computer as the Heart of a Rich, Multisensory Environment

Other significant hardware and software developments are changing our perception of the computer from a silent, solitary machine to the orchestrator of a learning environment enriched by diverse sources of information and modalities. The following sections will discuss interactive videodisc, hypertext, hypermedia, CD-ROM, telecommunications and artificial intelligence *vis-à-vis* their application in Spanish as a second/foreign language teaching and the teaching of Spanish to native speakers of the language.

Interactive videodisc

The new interactive videodisc technology, also known as AVC (Audio Visual Computer), is making inroads in the educational field and is seen by many as exceptionally well suited to foreign/second language learning. The equipment needed for an interactive videodisc station includes a computer, a videodisc player, a video monitor, and the corresponding software program. The practically inde-structible disc is read on a laserdisc player (LDP) by a laser beam. Sound-tracks allow users to combine the video with the audio component.

The many capabilities of this new medium provide enormous potential for language learning. Each side of a CAV (constant angular velocity) video laserdisc can contain 54,000 still images or half-hour of moving pictures and/or text. Any picture or segment of moving pictures can be accessed randomly and almost instantaneously and with precision. This, added to the disc's ability to store aud-itory information, allows the display of visual situations synchronized with natu-ral speech, thus bringing to the student language in context.

The advantages of AVC over videotape for foreign language learning are obvious. Whereas video is basically a passive, linear activity, interactive videodisc offers nonlinear viewing and random access requiring active participation on the part of the student (Frommer, 1989). In addition, the capability of videodisc for complex branching permits meeting the different needs of the students. The main disadvantages of AVC at present are: a) the expense of setting up videodisc sta-tions, b) the scarcity of videodisc materials for the learning of foreign languages in the market, c) the 'rear-view approach' exhibited by most available materials, and d) the lack of a foreign language videodisc pedagogy.

Pioneering efforts in applying videodisc technology to foreign language teaching are represented by two simulations developed at Brigham Young Uni-versity (Schneider and Bennion, 1983). In one, called *Montevidisco*, the student in-teracts in Spanish with the inhabitants of a Mexican town. The course of events, as well as the places visited (a market, a bullfight, a restaurant, a hotel, a hospital, etc.), are determined by the student's own decisions. The second simulation por-trays a day in the life of a Mexican worker and, as in the previous one, student responses determine what happens at each step.

Although videodisc programs developed expressly for foreign language pedagogy have been increasing in recent years, their availability is still very lim-ited. There exist a few videodiscs for Spanish language learning use (see Rubin, Ediger, Coffin, Handle, and Whiskeyman, 1990, for a list). An example of a Spanish interactive videodisc project is *Zarabanda* (Hogan, c. 1986), based on a soap opera produced by the British Broadcasting Corporation for the teaching of Spanish. In this program, the student, after viewing segments of the videodisc, is asked questions and then given the option to answer them or to choose from among other activities (e.g., vocabulary, matching, cultural or dictation exercises, etc.) for further study and review (Stevens, 1987).

There are currently on the market a variety of authoring programs integrating reading materials with interactive video. As mentioned previously, *MacLang* is a good example of this approach. The program is menu driven and uses pull-down windows, boxes and buttons. Simply by clicking a button, students can see and hear an instantaneous replay of any segment as frequently as needed, and exercises can be presented in such a way that it is impossible for students to complete them unless they understand the aural component. This capability transforms the com-puter in an ideal tool for listening activities. In addition, conditional branching permits students to create story trees (Frommer, 1989).

Authoring programs with audio and videodisc interfaces present an answer to the scarcity of videodisc programs developed for Spanish language learning, especially for the segment of students for whom software programs of any kind are practically non-existent — native Spanish speakers who need to work on their speaking and literacy skills. With authoring programs, teachers can enter any content and use any tape (including commercially produced ones) to develop exercises and learning activities that fit students' needs.

Hypertext

Envisioned by Nelson (1974) almost twenty years ago, hypertext represents a new way of organizing and retrieving computer-based information. Hypertext can be defined as electronic texts that follow a nonsequential structure: each segment of the text is interconnected to other readily accessible texts which in turn are connected to the broader structure. In a clear description of what hypertext looks like, Feustle (1989, p. 461) points out that

> [it] does not function in terms of pages, chapters, or volumes, but rather of files and their links. One does not open hypertext and find the traditional table of contents with corresponding page numbers, as there are none. A more useful and correct beginning for a hypertext document . . . is a diagram of the major files and their links.

As an example of the way hypertext works, we can imagine the following sentence on the computer screen: '*Pasamos la tarde conversando, bailando y cantando.*' A highlighting or boxing of any of these words, or the presence of a button, indicates a link, that is the possibility of following a new path or obtaining extra information. Clicking the highlighted word '*bailando*', for instance, might bring to the screen a definition and/or an example of a sentence using the same verb in other contexts; clicking a button could bring a picture of people dancing, or additional information, such as explanations of grammatical constructions, a review of tense forms of the verb '*bailar*', a description of a particular aspect of the target culture, comprehension questions, and so on.

There are great advantages in such an environment for both Spanish as a second language and native Spanish-speaking learners. The absence of a predetermined sequential order in hypertext allows students to determine the direction of their learning, to explore freely and to decide how much time to spend on each activity. Because of this, materials that otherwise would be inappropriate for some students, for instance, fluent Spanish speakers with unique grammatical or lexical needs, are rendered appropriate by the nonlinearity and freedom that permit students to follow a learning path according to their own interests and needs.

HyperCard

HyperCard (1987) expanded on the idea of hypertext by making it possible to easily integrate, organize, link, store, search and retrieve a variety of media, including text, graphics, animation, and digitized and synthesized sound. *HyperCard* is a lesson-authoring package with a built-in programming language (called

'HyperTalk'). It incorporates the easy to use mouse-driven menus and buttons of the Macintosh, as well as paint capabilities that make it highly visual.

The underlying metaphor of *HyperCard* is a stack of cards (or screens). The 'home card' contains numerous icons or buttons representing the several stacks that come with the program. Each card presents and stores information in 'fields' and 'buttons'. Text is entered in a field, whereas a button is a 'hot spot' on the screen which, when clicked on with the mouse, allows the user to perform a task, such as navigate freely to another media or another 'card' (a different screen), get additional interconnected information, play a sound, etc. Buttons link cards with each other; they are represented by icons which take different shapes, such as arrows, check boxes, pointing fingers, and so on. The desired content of each card is first typed or painted and then linked by buttons or by using HyperTalk.

Since *HyperCard* was first introduced in the August 1987 Macworld Exposition, there have appeared in the market a great number of applications. One interesting example was its use by ABC's Peter Jennings to cover the 1988 presidential campaign. The *HyperCard* stack was especially designed to instantly retrieve information regarding the election and the candidates. One of the cards, for instance, contained digitized faces of the candidates; a click on the face of Mr. Dukakis, for example, would bring to the screen a card with up-to-minute information regarding his delegate count, his stance on different issues, or information on his staff, finances, and personal background (Davis, 1988). One HyperCard stack in Spanish being developed incorporates sound. Entitled *The Evolution of Spanish* and intended for students of Spanish linguistics, it presents an interactive approach to the study of the evolution of the sounds in the Spanish language (see Hernández, 1990, for a review of this program).

HyperCard's interactivity and visual capabilities make it an excellent tool for language learning purposes. By making it possible for students to navigate freely among interconnected information and media, it gives them a great deal of power to control information, and consequently their own learning. As with hypertext, this capability increases the pedagogical effectiveness of the computer as it transforms it into an extraordinarily flexible tool which can adapt itself to the different student needs, both to those of native Spanish speakers and of students in their beginning Spanish course. The applications of *HyperCard* in first and foreign/second language learning are discussed below.

Multimedia, interactive multimedia and hypermedia

Although the term multimedia is sometimes used to refer to the incorporation of different media (i.e., hardware such as print, slides, record, film, video, etc.) in a single computer document (Stefanac and Weiman, 1990), it has been proposed (Finkel, 1990) that the word 'interactive' only be used when the media are controlled by a computer, to distinguish the latter case from the use of several media without the mediation of a computer. Thus, a presentation using two or three media, such as an overhead projector, a slide projector and a videotape player, for example, would be termed 'multimedia'; on the other hand, the term 'interactive multimedia' would mean that all of the above media are integrated and controlled by a computer.

What differentiates multimedia from interactive multimedia, then, is the interactivity of the latter. It has been said that the difference between them is like that between watching a mystery vs. solving it (Finkel, 1990). While multimedia is linear, interactive multimedia offers random access, thus allowing students to make decisions, such as going through the text, engaging in additional practice activities, testing themselves, and so on. This is not possible with noninteractive multimedia.

With the easy integration of text and graphics with other media, made possible by software programs such as *HyperCard*, interactive multimedia has begun to be referred to as hypermedia. Hypermedia expands on hypertext and on interactive multimedia, as it represents the utilization of additional media to present information visually and aurally. The difference between hypertext and hypermedia is that, although both represent a nonlinear organization, the former is limited to text, while the latter adds to text graphics, animation, audio and video. Whereas in hypertext the user can move from one text to another, in hypermedia the user can, in addition, move from one medium to another.

Similarly, the difference between interactive multimedia and hypermedia is given by the fact that the latter connotes the presence of a wider integration of media, which could include text, graphics, video, still and moving pictures, sound, music, and voice recordings, animation, digitized photos, and so on, into a single computer-controlled learning system. As an example of a hypermedia environment, Underwood (1989) describes an experimental geography program, in which the user can 'fly' over a world map displayed on the computer screen while the video monitor shows a synchronized image of the corresponding overhead view. The user also can, through a click of the mouse at any point on the map, bring to the video screen still images of that particular region. This richness of context could be extended even more by not only bringing to the screen still and moving images of the particular area, but its sounds, including songs, music and voice. It is easy to perceive the potential of such types of programs for first and second language learning. We can imagine a program where Spanish language learners can fly to any part of the Spanish-speaking world, interact with the locals and ask questions, in Spanish, of course, about their history, culture, and so on.

Hypermedia is changing the way the computer is perceived from a stand-alone tool, to 'the heart of a multimedia learning station' (Quinn, 1990, p. 297). Because of its wide range of delivery modes, such a station offers an environment which is able to address not only the different linguistic levels of the students but their different learning modalities as well. Research has indicated that several differing information sources improve learning (Parker and Davis, 1989). In addition, the integration with video allows for the presentation of language in the larger cultural context in which the foreign language is spoken, rather than in the isolation of the written mode. The characteristics of this kind of setting are in line with the trends toward a generative or exploratory approach to foreign/second language learning, with its emphasis on a learner-centered environment.

Moreover, a hypermedia setting, in allowing the integration of sound and video, addresses concerns generated by the 'silent' computer, by making possible activities which can help students acquire speaking and listening skills. For instance, in a hypermedia station, Spanish language learners can see pictures and/or names of objects, while simultaneously hearing the words pronounced. They might click the pronunciation icon (in the form of a mouth) and hear a digitized pronunciation of the word or of a full passage while reading it on the screen, or they could check lists of words derived from dialogs, click on one of the words and hear the segment of the dialog in which it occurs.

One of the major disadvantages of a hypermedia environment is the high cost of both hardware and software. The expense of producing video materials is especially high. Because of this, developers of second language learning hypermedia programs have resorted to 'repurposing' video, that is, using an existing video as the basis of the new program. In addition, there have recently appeared on the market several hypermedia authoring systems which permit teachers with no previous training to develop hypermedia lessons which integrate text with a variety of other media. Examples of these are *Course Builder* (1987); *Course of Action* (1987); the previously discussed *HyperCard* (1987); *HyperCALL* (Blake, c. 1989), which comes with a Spanish-teaching demo, and integrates graphics, videodisc and sound; *IDI Author* (c. 1989), based on *HyperCard*, and which allows for the integration of tape recorder and laserdisc; and *The Thinker* (c. 1988), an inexpensive hypermedia word processor program developed for the Amiga. The latter program offers the capability to open up to eight document windows on the same screen at the same time. Taylor, M.B. (1990, p. 19) describes this program in the following manner:

> . . . when reading about a country, the user might call up a variety of text files on different topics, a map of the continent, a map of the country, a picture of the native dress, etc. Foreseeing a need further on in the main text to refer to the maps again, the user can stick them in a corner and dismiss the other links. When, indeed, the need arises to see where something is located, the right map is at hand.

There are also *HyperCard*-based adventure games which include graphics and text and which can also be used as an authoring system to create other adventure games.

An example of a prototype *HyperCard* program for Spanish as a second/foreign language is *The Zarabanda Notebook*, developed by Underwood (1989) and based on *Zarabanda*, the interactive videodisc project for the teaching of Spanish discussed above. In this program, the student sees a drawing of the main character's (i.e., Ramiro's) room. Each object in the room, such as the book, the table, the bed, the newspaper, etc., is a *HyperCard* button which represents a link to further information. Clicking on the map on the table, for instance, brings to the screen a map of Ramiro's village. Each labeled item on the map represents in turn a button which when clicked brings to the video screen a picture of that part of town. By clicking on other appropriate icons, the student can bring to the screen additional information, such as a brief presentation of the characters in the story or a 'story map', that is, a representation of the sequence of events. Each of the icons on the latter map represents a link to a set of videodisc player commands; clicking on one of them brings to the video screen a short preview of the particular scene.

Several universities are at present developing ambitious hypermedia projects. Examples are Project Perseus (Harward, 1988), at Harvard and Boston Universities, which integrates ancient Greek literature, history, maps, digitized images of monuments, vases, and other works of art; Project Shakespeare (Frielander, 1988), at Stanford University, which combines text, drawings, still photos, and animated digitized images; Project Athena (Morgenstern, 1986), at MIT, which permits the development of interactive video material based on combinations of text, digitized color videodisc, cable television, digital audio, and high resolution graphics. (For a review of these programs, see Feustle, 1989).

Project Athena's Language Learning Program, a component of the MIT Athena Project mentioned above, has as its goal the development of prototypes for beginning and intermediate courses in several foreign languages, including Spanish. The programs stress a communicative approach by using a simulation format and having students interact with characters of a story; the characters become real people when showed in videotaped segments. The program includes two projects for Spanish language acquisition. The first, titled 'Encuentros', is a simulation of a Hispanic setting which allows students to interact with several characters. The second, 'No Recuerdo', simulates a setting in Bogotá through the use of segments from films, documentaries, and other sources: the plot revolves around two characters, Gonzalo and Elena, with whom students interact. (For more information about these programs see Morgenstern, 1986).

Although the prototype programs described above are for students learning Spanish as a second/foreign language at the intermediate level, it is obvious that a hypermedia approach offers tremendous promise for the development of Spanish skills on the part of native Spanish-speaking learners, whose goal might be to expand their vocabulary, general knowledge of, and ease with, the language. Language programs that have the native Spanish speaker in mind would employ a much more sophisticated vocabulary, focus on standard grammatical points or other aspects of the language which second or third generation Spanish speakers in the United States tend to lose, and include activities to develop literacy skills.

CD-ROM

The problem of the necessary space to store the large amount of information in a hypermedia environment has been solved by the development of a new, inexpensive storage technology, the CD-ROM (Compact Disc-Read Only Memory). Its combination of a tremendous storage capability with instant random access offers great potential to a language learning environment. The CD-ROM is a prerecorded (i.e., it is impossible to write on it), nonerasable disc, which looks much the same as an audio compact disc (CD), from whose technology it derives. A CD-ROM holds at least 550 megabytes of digital data. This is about the capacity of 700 double-sided Mac floppies, that is, enough room for 150,000 text pages or 15,000 images or several large *HyperCard* stacks or one hour of digital sound (Meng, 1988). Or, stated in yet another way, it would take eight years of full-time work to type enough text to fill a CD-ROM (Stevens, 1987). In addition, the storage capabilities of the CD-ROM permit the use of sound and video. Because graphics, sound, and animation are encoded digitally, it is possible to mix all of them on a CD-ROM.

A few foreign/second language programs which apply CD-ROM storage technology to interactive multimedia have been developed. One example is an ESL project by Willetts (cited in Hanson-Smith, 1988). The program combines text, graphics, animation, digitized pictures and sound, and includes an authoring system. The student can choose from among a range of activities, such as doing Cloze exercises, a crossword (with visual and sound effects), a jigsaw puzzle with graphics, or seeing the text while hearing it. Students can choose either a word in isolation, or a sentence and have the digitized voice repeat it. Access to any segment of the program is instantaneous and precise.

To my knowledge, no programs applying CD-ROM storage technology to interactive multimedia have yet been developed for Spanish language learning. As Stevens (1987, p. 1) stated more than five years ago, technology has developed at such a fast pace that it has been difficult for educators and software program writers to keep up with it. It is hoped, however, that programs for Spanish language learners, including native speakers, are soon developed based on this technology, which offers so much promise for language learning.

Telecommunications

Telecommunications allows people to interact easily and in real time with persons from other cities and countries. The communication can take place directly between two or more users through their respective personal computers and modems and a telephone line. However, it commonly occurs through the use of a large central computer, accessed by the users by means of terminals or their own personal computers and modems. The medium offers an inexpensive approach once the basic hardware (a computer, a modem or a terminal, and access to a telephone line) is in place.

In making it possible for students to communicate with their counterparts in other countries, telecommunications constitutes a very promising language learning medium. Through this application of computers, learners of Spanish as a second language as well as native Spanish speakers can be provided with the opportunity to practice the language and to exchange information with native speakers in different areas of the Spanish-speaking world. Sayers and Brown (1987) point out that telecommunications seems to meet the needs of both native Spanish speakers and students learning Spanish as a second language. The former are acquiring and maintaining literacy skills and need authentic contexts for writing in their first language; the latter also need authentic contacts and a great deal of practice with native speakers, in order to develop cultural awareness and communicative competence.

One of the most well known telecommunication projects is *De Orilla a Orilla*. This program connects students from bilingual and Spanish as a second language classes in the United States with students from several other countries (Argentina, French-speaking Canada, Mexico and Puerto Rico). The project's goal is to promote bilingual literacy in both bilingual education students and students in second/foreign language classes (Sayers and Brown, 1987). The program has been found successful in increasing student language proficiency (Mulligan and Gore, 1989). At present there are several telecommunications projects throughout the United States (see Mulligan and Gore, 1989) and, as awareness of the power of this approach to language learning grows, many others are being installed.

Artificial intelligence

The goal of artificial intelligence (AI) or 'machine learning' is to replicate by machine certain aspects of human cognitive abilities. CALL-AI (i.e., the use of artificial intelligence in computer-assisted language learning) attempts to model the cognitive behavior of a language teacher (Bailin, 1988). A general belief among many language teaching professionals is that it is only through AI that a truly communicative computer environment will be achieved.

It has been pointed out that an intelligent CALL system needs not only knowledge about the target language itself, but also knowlege about the kinds of errors students are likely to make, as well as about the most appropriate pedagogical strategies for dealing with them (Vernick and Levin, 1986). The branch of AI that attempts to give the computer the capability to understand, analyze and process a human language, such as English or Spanish, is called natural language processing (NLP). Answer processing and language generation are two areas of NLP that have been the object of a great deal of research and work by scientists interested in the application of these areas to second/foreign language learning.

a) *Answer processing.*   Answer processing, or response analysis, is the branch of NLP that attempts to develop programs which are able to anticipate, process and react logically to student responses. Because the pedagogical worth of CALL programs depends not only on the quality of their content but also on the quality of the feedback provided to the student, the way in which the program analyzes student input for errors is extremely important. 'Intelligent' programs should be able to determine the appropriate type and frequency of feedback, react to correct responses and to errors, indicate specifically what is incorrect, offer continuous available help and provide tutorial and branching according to the student's individual needs.

'Intelligent' CALL programs are based on effective parsers, or grammatical analyzers, which are able to analyze human speech input and thus interpret students' responses, recognize correct and incorrect structures and respond appropriately. There are a number of computer parsers designed for foreign language study. An example for Spanish is the already mentioned program *Spanlap* (Jehle, 1987), in which students engage in a written dialog by asking questions. The program analyzes the student's input morphologically, syntactically and semantically, and responds by either generating an answer or selecting a teacher-written response.

A program's ability to parse intelligently is made possible by the fact that it operates within the limits of the micro-world displayed on the screen. An example of a 'semi-intelligent' program is the above mentioned *Juegos Comunicativos*, (Underwood, 1986) a series of language games presented in the form of problems which students solve using their linguistic skills. The program analyzes input both semantically and syntactically. While the semantic analyzer determines if the response is appropriate to the situational context, the syntactic analyzer, or parser, analyzes the structures to detect grammatical errors. If the latter are present, hints guide the student to discover and correct them.

However, in spite of the great deal of research and work on parsing conducted in the last decade, computer interpretation of, as well as feedback to, student input is still in its early stages of development. In general, programs continue to be very limited as to how much they can interpret learner input, anticipate possible errors and distinguish between significant and insignificant mistakes. A good example of this is given by *Juegos Comunicativos*. In spite of the fact that the program was designed, in the words of its author, 'to accept a wide range of student input and still provide intelligent feedback' (Underwood, 1987, p.1) and that it was based on the premise that there is more than one correct way to say things, it still has significant limitations. The answers given by the students have to be strictly limited to the vocabulary and structures specified for each game. Consequently, answers given by an educated, fluent speaker of the language not following these constraints might not be accepted by the computer; at the same time, grammatically correct constructions with no logical meaning, such as '*la mano no tiene café*' are accepted (see review by Feustle, 1987). In spite of these limitations, however, the program is a very valuable first step in the right direction.

The constraints discussed above pose an even greater challenge to the development of Spanish language learning programs for native speakers of the language. The more advanced the student language ability, the wider the range of differing but correct possible answers he or she can give. Hence, the difficulty in developing programs for native speakers increases. This difficulty is compounded when the numerous regional variations throughout the Spanish-speaking world are taken into account. A truly pedagogically sound computer program would not reject answers simply because they do not conform to one predetermined Spanish language variety. In sum, although the potential of this type of intelligent programs for native Spanish speakers is extremely exciting, there is still a lot of work to be done.

b) *Language generation.* In language generation, the goal is to make the machine produce appropriate utterances and responses, and thus communicate meaningfully with students, both native speakers and second language learners. This attempt is best exemplified by conversational-type programs, which permit the student to maintain a simulated dialog with the computer, via the written mode. The few existing programs for foreign/second language study have been modeled on the pioneering program of this type, *Eliza*, written in 1965 by Weizenbaum (1976). This program, which employs pattern-matching rather than parsing, permits the computer to assume different roles according to the script, and can be used to write other programs. In one of the most well-known versions, the computer assumes the role of a psychotherapist, with the program simulating an open-ended conversation between 'therapist' and user. For Spanish learning, there is an experimental Spanish version of *Eliza* and another called *Familia*, both developed by Underwood (1984). While Spanish *Eliza* is modeled very closely on the English version, in *Familia*, the conversation is limited to one topic (the family) and focused on one grammatical aspect of the language (the use of the verbs *ser* and *estar*). This narrower domain permits the program to identify ungrammatical responses and correct them in an indirect, expansion-type strategy, for example, Student: '*Mis padres están del Perú*'. Computer: '*¿Quieres decir que tus padres son del Perú?*' (see Underwood, 1984, for a detailed description).

Although these programs give the impression of understanding what the user is saying, they actually answer with canned responses which react to key words within a restricted domain; if the conversation deviates from this domain, the program cannot respond. The usual solution on the part of the computer is to cover up its lack of understanding by, for instance, asking the user to continue speaking or by changing the subject. Underwood (1984) points out that these programs are still at a level in which they neither discover all syntactical errors nor understand much of the student's input. There is, therefore, much work to be done in this promising area of CALL.

Conclusion

Computer use in second/foreign language learning has been increasing in recent years. There is a growing belief in the worth of CALL as well as in the perception of the computer as a powerful learning tool that can be used in different roles. There are several factors which have contributed to this increased interest. First, an emergent methodology in CALL finally seems to be freeing the computer from the constraints imposed by the rear-view approach. Software programs, which constitute the key to computer pedagogical effectiveness, are moving away from behaviorist approaches and becoming more challenging, communicative, and pedagogically sound.

Secondly, interest in computers for language learning has been favorably affected by rapid development of hardware and software. Innovations such as interactive videodisc and hypermedia have allowed the easy integration and co-ordination of diverse media, and brought controlled and random access to them. Thirdly, technological advances and commercial competition have brought greater availability and affordability of computers, thus making them more accessible to educational institutions.

However, in the process of writing an overview such as this one, it becomes painfully obvious how much remains to be done. Research, for instance, sorely needs attention. Unfortunately, very few studies have been carried out in computer environments and much less on the different areas touched upon here. It seems as if the technological and software advances are taking place at such a rapid speed that there is little time to pause to study their effects. Research needs to be conducted, for example, on the learning process which takes place with different types of software activities as well as on the relationship between these activities and the student language level. Are simulations, for instance, more appropriate for Spanish as a second language learners than for native Spanish speakers? Are activ-ities that concentrate on reading and writing more useful for the latter? These are just a few of the questions that need to be researched.

A second area in dire need is the development of computer materials for native Spanish speakers. Software programs for second/foreign language learning have been developed at a very slow pace, and their number and selection are small even for the most commonly studied languages in the United States, such as Spanish and French. Within this general poverty of software programs for language learning, the ESL field has fared the best. Language programs for the native Spanish speaker, however, are practically nonexistent. Most Spanish language professionals are now aware that the needs of native speakers of Spanish are different from those of students learning Spanish as a second/foreign language. This needs to be reflected in software development.

At present, extraordinary hardware and software development efforts are being invested in giving the computer voice and ears (such as peripheral audio devices and digitized and synthesized speech), a mind (such as artificial intelligence), a greater 'long term memory' capacity (such as CD-ROM), and the power to address the different modalities of students (such as hypermedia). These will eventually succeed in bringing the full potential of the computer to the service of language learning. It is to be hoped that the development of software programs, which constitutes the key to what actually happens in the learning process, can keep pace with hardware developments and respond to the challenge. Meanwhile, the computer continues winning converts among language educators. Although, as has been pointed out, '[t]here can be no better "communicative" learning environment than the warm and responsive presence of other human beings' (Underwood, 1984, p. 80), the computer offers many significant uses and exciting potential that the language teaching professional cannot afford to ignore.

References

Acumen [Computer program] (c. 1988), Albany, CA, Bardon Data Systems.

ADAMS, E.N., MORRISON, H.W. and REDDY, J.H. (1969) 'Conversation with a computer as a technique of language instruction', in ATKINSON, R.C. and WILSON, M.H. (Eds) *Computer-assisted Instruction: A Book of Readings*, New York, NY, Academic Press.

AHMAD, K., CORBETT, G., ROGERS, M. and SUSSEX, R. (1985) *Computers, Language Learning and Language Teaching*, Cambridge, England, Cambridge University Press.

ALLEN, J.R. (1971) 'ELSE at Dartmouth: An experiment in computer-aided instruction in French', *French Review*, **46**, pp. 902–12.

ARIEW, R. (1974) 'Teaching French on PLATO IV', *System, A Newsletter for Educational Technology and Language Learning Systems*, **2**, 1, pp. 1–7.

BAILIN, A. (1988) 'Artificial intelligence and computer-assisted language instruction: A perspective', *CALICO Journal*, **5**, 3, pp. 25–45.

Batalla de Palabras [Computer program] (1984), New York, NY, Gessler Educational Software.

BICKES, G. and SCOTT, A. (1989) 'On the computer as a medium for language teaching', *CALICO Journal*, **6**, 3, pp. 21–32.

BLAKE, R. (c. 1989) *HyperCALL* [Computer program], Rochester, NY, The University of Rochester (Department of Foreign Language, Literatures and Linguistics).

BURSTON, J. (1989) 'Towards better tutorial CALL: A matter of intelligent control', *CALICO Journal*, **6**, 4, pp. 75–89.

CHAMORIN, G. and GÓMEZ, A. (c. 1989) *Caminando* [Computer program], New York, NY, Gessler Educational Software.

CHAPELLE, C. and JAMIESON, J. (1983) 'Language lessons on the PLATO IV system', *System*, **11**, 1, pp. 13–20.

CHIGNELL, M. and LACY, R. (1988, September) 'Project Jefferson: Integrating research and instruction', *Academic Computing*, pp. 12–17, 40–45.

CHUN, D.M. (1989) 'Teaching tone and intonation with microcomputers', *CALICO Journal*, **7**, 1, pp. 21–46.

CLAUSING, S. *Private Tutor* [Computer program] (c. 1988), Santa Barbara, CA, Kinko's Academic Courseware Exchange.

COHEN, H. (1988) [Review of *Cloze Encounters in Spanish*], *Hispania*, **71**, p. 462.

Course Builder [Computer program] (1987), Knoxville, TN, TeleRobotics™ International, Inc.

Course of Action™ [Computer program] (1987), Minneapolis, MN, Authorware, Inc.

CRUZ-SÁENZ, M. (1984) [Review of *Spanish Hangman Vocabulary Builder*], *Hispania*, **67**, p. 701.

DAIUTE, C. (1985) *Writing and Computers*, Reading, MA, Addison-Wesley.

DAVIS, G. (1988, September) Macworld News, 'Stacking up candidates at ABC', *Macworld*, pp. 117–19.

DUNKEL, P.A. (1987) 'Computer-assisted instruction (CAI) and computer-assisted language learning (CALL): Past dilemmas and future prospects for audible CALL', *The Modern Language Journal*, **71**, pp. 250–60.

FEUSTLE, J. (1987) [Review of *Juegos Comunicativos*], *Hispania*, **70**, pp. 708–10.

FEUSTLE, J. (1989) 'Hypertext for the PC and PC-Compatibles', *Hispania*, **72**, pp. 456–64.

FINKEL, J. (1990) 'Word abuse', *CUE Newsletter*, **12**, 5, p. 7.

FISCHER, W. (1986) 'Comparison of sound digitizers for Macintosh', *CALICO Journal*, **4**, 1, pp. 85–9.

FREIRE, P. (1970) *Pedagogy of the Oppressed*. (RAMOS, M.B. Trans.) New York, NY, The Seabury Press. (Original work published 1968).

FRIELANDER, L. (1988, May/June) 'The Shakespeare Project: Experiments in multimedia education', *Academic Computing*, pp. 26–9, 66–8.

FROMMER, J. (1988) *MacLang* [Computer program], Santa Barbara, CA, Kinko's Academic Courseware Exchange.

FROMMER, J. (1989) 'Listening, looking, and learning with MacLang', *CALICO Journal*, **6**, 4, pp. 51–71.

GRABE, M. and GRABE, C. (1985) 'The microcomputer and the language experience approach', *The Reading Teacher*, **38**, pp. 508–11.

¿Habla Español? [Computer program] (1985) New York, NY, Holt, Rinehardt and Winston, Study Disk Software, Inc.

HANSON-SMITH, E. (1988) 'Applying CD-ROM to CALL' (summary of conference presentation by John Willetts), *CALL Digest*, **4**, 3, p. 5.

HARWARD, J. (1988, May/June) 'From museum to monitor: The visual exploration of the Ancient World', *Academic Computing*, pp. 16–9, 69–71.

HAWISHER, G. (1989) 'Research and recommendations for computers and composition', in HAWISHER, G. and SELFE, C. (Eds) *Critical Perspectives on Computers and Composition Instruction*, New York, NY, Teachers College Press, pp. 44–69.

HERNÁNDEZ, N. (1989) [Review of *Spanish Microtutor*, Version 2.0], *CALICO Journal*, **7**, pp. 91–3.

HERNÁNDEZ, N. (1990) [Review of *The Evolution of the Spanish Language*] *CALICO Journal*, **7**, 4, pp. 82–4.

HIGGINS, J. and JOHNS, T. (1984) *Computers in Language Learning*, Reading, MA, Addison-Wesley.

HOGAN, A.F. (c. 1986) *Zarabanda: Spanish Interactive Video Project for the Spanish Basic Course*, Monterey, CA, Defense Language Institute.

HOLMES, G. and KIDD, M.E. (1982) 'Second-language learning and computers', *The Canadian Modern Language Review*, **38**, pp. 503–16.

HOPE, G.R., TAYLOR, H.F. and PUSACK, J.P. (1984) *Using Computers in Teaching Foreign Languages*, New York, NY, Harcourt Brace Jovanovich.

HUBBARD, P. (1989) [Review of *Acumen*] *CALICO Journal*, **6**, 3, pp. 75–9.

HUBBARD, P. (1990) 'Exploring text reconstruction activities on computers', *CAELL Journal*, **1**, 2, pp. 2–4.

HyperCard™ [Computer program] (1987), Cupertino, CA, Apple Computer, Inc.

IDI Author [Computer program] (c. 1989), Orem, UT, CALI.

IRIZARRY, E. (1988) [Review of *WordPerfect 4.2, Spanish Version*], *Hispania*, **71**, p. 736.

JEHLE, F. (1987) 'A free-form dialog program in Spanish', *CALICO Journal*, **5**, 2, pp. 11–22.

JEX, W. (1988) 'Microcomputers and English language instruction: A few years later', *CALICO Journal*, **5**, 3, pp. 84–9.

JOHNSON, N. (1989) 'CALL: The state of the profession', *CALL Digest*, **5**, 7, pp. 1–4.

KENNING, M.J. and KENNING, M.M. (1983) *An Introduction to Computer Assisted Language Teaching*, Oxford, England, Oxford University Press.

KISS, M. (1988) [Review of *El Mundo Hispánico*], *Hispania*, **71**, p. 997.

KULIK, J., KULIK, C. and BANGERT-DROWNS, R. (1985) *Effectiveness of Computer-based Education in Elementary Schools*, Unpublished manuscript, Ann Arbor, MI, University of Michigan.

The Language Coach [Computer program] (1988), Hercules, CA, RAM Software (Language version(s): Spanish, Portuguese, French, German, Italian and Russian).

LARSEN, M.D. (1990) 'Queues and answers: Spanish CAI for the Macintosh', *Hispania*, **73**, pp. 1196–98.

MacRecorder [Computer hardware/software package] (c. 1988), Berkeley, CA, Farallon Computing, Inc.

McEWEN, N. (1977) 'Computer-assisted instruction in second language learning: An Alberta project', *The Canadian Modern Language Review*, **33**, pp. 333–43.

McLUHAN, M. (1964) *Understanding Media: The Extensions of Man*, New York, NY, Signet Books.

MENG, B. (1988, April) 'The dawn of laser storage', *MacWorld*, pp. 155–61.

MESKILL, C. (1987) 'Interactivity in CALL courseware design', *CALICO Journal*, **5**, 1, pp. 9–14.

El Mundo Hispánico [Computer program] (1985), Lexington, MA, DC Heath Educational Software.

MOHLER, S. [Computer program] (1988), *Software for Churros and Chocolate*, Martin, TN, University of Tennessee at Martin (Department of Modern Languages).

MOLHOLT, G. (1988) 'Computer-assisted instruction in pronunciation for Chinese speakers of American English', *TESOL Quarterly*, **22**, pp. 91–111.

MORGENSTERN, D. (1986) 'The Athena Language Learning Project', *Hispania*, **69**, pp. 740–45.

MULLIGAN, P. and GORE, K. (1989) 'Telecommunications and CALL', *CALL Digest*, **5**, 8, pp. 6–9.

NEFF, R. and WHITNEY, T. [Computer program] (1987), *Cloze Encounters in Spanish*, Westerville, OH, Lingo Fun.

NELSON, T. (1974) *Computer Lib/Dream Machines*, Chicago, IL, Hugo's Book Service.

ORTUZAR-YOUNG, A. (1991) [Review of *Spanish Microtutor*, Version 2.0], *Hispania*, **74**, pp. 457–68.

PAPERT, S. (1980) *Mindstorms: Children, Computers and Powerful Ideas*, New York, NY, Basic Books.

PARKER, R. and DAVIS, R. (1989) 'Digital audio, networks, and foreign language instruction', *CALICO Journal*, **7**, 2, pp. 71–82.

PERALES, A. (1985) [Review of *Batalla de Palabras*], *Hispania*, **68**, pp. 888–9.

PHILLIPS, B. (1984) *Lecciones de Español Conduit* [Computer program], Iowa City, IA, University of Iowa, Oakdale Campus.

PIPER, A. (1987) 'Helping learners to write: A role for the word-processor', *ELT Journal*, **41**, pp. 119–25.

PUSACK, J.P. (1983) 'Answer-processing and error correction in foreign language CAI', *System*, **11**, 1, p. 53.

QUINCEY, P. DE (1986) 'Stimulating activity: The role of computers in the language classroom', *CALICO Journal*, **4**, 1, pp. 55–56.

QUINN, R.A. (1990) 'Our progress in integrating modern methods and computer-controlled learning for successful language study', *Hispania*, **73**, pp. 297–311.

RASCHIO, R. (1989) [Review of software program for ¿Habla Español?], *Hispania*, **72**, p. 462.

ROBLYER, M.D., CASTINE, W.H. and KING, F.J. (1988) *Assessing the Impact of Computer-based Instruction: A Review of Recent Research*, New York, NY, The Haworth Press.

RUBIN, J., EDIGER, A., COFFIN, E., HANDLE, D. and WHISKEYMAN, A. (1990) 'Survey of interactive language discs', *CALICO Journal*, **7**, 3, pp. 31–56.

SANDERS, D. and KENNER, R. (1983) 'Whither CAI? The need for communicative courseware', *System*, **11**, 1, pp. 33–9.

SAYERS, D. and BROWN, K. (1987) 'Bilingual education, second language learning and telecommunication: A perfect fit', *CALL Digest*, **3**, 5, pp. 1–2.

SCHNEIDER, E.W. and BENNION, J.L. (1983) 'Veni, vidi, vici via videodisc: A simulator for instructional conversations', *System*, **11**, 1, pp. 41–6.

SMITH, P.O., JR (1976) 'A computer-assisted instructional review of basic Spanish', *System*, **4**, 3, pp. 182–90.

Spanish Hangman Vocabulary Builder [Computer program] (c. 1982), Troy, MI, Computations.

Spanish Microtutor [Computer program] (1989), San Diego, CA, Harcourt, Brace, Jovanovich, College Department (software).

Spanish Pronunciation Tutor With Sound [Computer program] (c. 1990), Knoxville, TN, The HyperGlot Software Company.

STEFANAC, S. and WEIMAN, L. (1990, April) 'Multimedia: Is it real?', *MacWorld*, pp. 116–23.

STEVENS, V. (1987) 'Impressions of the CALICO '87 symposium in Monterey', *CALL Digest*, **3**, 4, p. 1.

STEVENS, V. (1990) 'Text manipulation: What's wrong with it anyway?' *CÆLL Journal*, **1**, 2, pp. 5–8.

TAYLOR, H.F. (1979) 'DECU/TUCO: A tutorial approach to elementary German instruction', *Foreign Language Annals*, **12**, pp. 289–91.

TAYLOR, J.S. (1990) [Review of *Caminando*], *CALICO Journal*, **7**, 3, pp. 80–2.

TAYLOR, M.B. (1990) 'Hypermedia authoring on the Amiga', *CÆLL Journal*, **1**, 1, pp. 19–20.

TERRY, R.M. (1977) 'Students work with MONIQUE and learn French', *Foreign Language Annals*, **10**, pp. 191–7.

The Thinker [Computer program] (c. 1988) Palo Alto, CA, Poor Person Software.

TRITTON, P.J. (1991) 'Automatic translation of Spanish text to phonetics: Using letter-to-sound rules', *Hispania*, **74**, pp. 478–80.

UNDERWOOD, J. (1984) *Linguistics, Computers, and the Language Teacher: A Communicative Approach*, Rowley, MA, Newbury House.

UNDERWOOD, J. [Computer program] (1986), *Juegos Comunicativos, Spanish Games for Communicative Practice*, New York, NY, Random House College Software.

UNDERWOOD, J. (1987) *Juegos Comunicativos/Jeux Communicatifs/Kommunikative Spiele* [Instructor's guide], New York, NY, Random House.

UNDERWOOD, J. (1989) 'HyperCard and interactive video', *CALICO Journal*, **6**, 3, pp. 7–20.

VAN CAMPEN, J. (1968) *Project for the Application of Mathematical Learning Theory to Second Language Acquisition, with Particular Reference to Russian* (Final Report), Washington, DC, US Department of Health, Education, and Welfare, (ERIC Document Reproduction Service No. ED 026 934).

VARELA, B. (1991) [Review of *Spanish Pronunciation Tutor with Sound*], *Hispania*, **74**, pp. 227–8.

VERNICK, J. and LEVIN, L. (1986) *Intelligent Grammar Tutoring in ESL*, Paper presented at the Annual TESOL Convention, Anaheim, CA.

VILA, J. and PEARSON, L. (1990) 'A computerized phonetics instructor: BABEL', *CALICO Journal*, **7**, 3, pp. 3–29.

VIRGULTI, V. (1985) [Review of *Lecciones de Español Conduit*], *Hispania*, **68**, pp. 226–7.

WEAVER, R. (1989) [Review of software for *Churros and Chocolate*], *Hispania*, **72**, p. 217.

WEIZENBAUM, J. (1976) 'Computer power and human reason: From judgment to calculation', San Francisco, CA, W.H. Freeman.

WordPerfect 4.2, Spanish Version [Computer program] (1986), Orem, UT, WordPerfect Corporation.

WYATT, D.H. (1983) 'Computer-assisted language instruction: Present state and future prospects', *System*, **11**, 1, pp. 3–11.

WYATT, D.H. (1984) *Computers and ESL*, New York, NY, Harcourt Brace Jovanovich.

WYATT, D.H. (1988) 'The Logo syndrome', *CALICO Journal*, **5**, 4, pp. 76–82.

Part III

Case Studies of Curriculum and Program Innovation

Chapter 14

Spanish for Spanish Speakers: A Curriculum

Lorraine D'Ambruoso

Demographic changes in the seventies and eighties have had an unexpected and dramatic impact on foreign language education and its attendant curriculum, especially in states like California, where the minority population is now the majority population. School districts throughout the country now recognize the need to extend the foreign language curriculum to include primary language instruction along with the more commonly taught languages.

Of the minority language programs currently in stages of development or already in existence, Spanish for Spanish Speakers has the highest priority, not only in California, but in states such as Florida, New Mexico, New York and Texas as well. The sudden need for development of Spanish primary language courses is forcing educators to seek out existing programs that may serve as models for the development of new programs. These programs, although few in number, can often be quite exceptional in meeting the special needs of a student population for whom English is not the primary language. One such program is the Spanish for Spanish Speakers Program developed for the East Side Union High School District in San Jose, California by Irene Silvas, Sisulío Testa and Ruthie Ayala. This chapter will look at this program in detail. (In 1988, the ESUHSD expanded its program to include Portuguese for Portuguese Speakers and in 1991, it added Vietnamese for Vietnamese Speakers).

It is the first day of school. You are a teacher of Spanish. You walk into your Spanish 1 class only to realize that there are students in your class who do not simply speak Spanish; rather, Spanish is their primary language. Frustration quickly sets in as you try to deal with two vastly different groups of students, each with completely different needs. Try as you might to meet the needs of every student, the native speakers are quickly bored by the slow pace of the class while the non-native speakers panic at the oral fluency of the native speakers. You find yourself in an untenable situation.

With an overall Hispanic population of 32 per cent, this scenario used to be the rule rather than the exception in the East Side Union High School District. Like most districts at that time, ESUHSD Spanish language classes had always

Table 14.1: Mastery objectives for English 1 and Spanish 1-SS and Spanish 2-SS

Writing	Reading	Listening	Speaking
Paragraphs with a clear arrangement of ideas using chronological and spatial order, or order of importance.	Identify main idea, supporting details, protagonist, antagonist and supporting characters.	Provide evidence of comprehending an oral presentation.	Deliver a three to five minute speech.
Expository composition consisting of introduction, three body paragraphs and a conclusion.	Also identify point of view, trace elements of plot, setting elements of a poem, synonyms, antonyms and analogies.	Take class and discussion notes appropriate to reading level.	Demonstrate competence in various oral presentation techniques: simple description and narration in present, past and future time.
For a variety of purposes: autobiographical, cause and effect, comparative and contrastive.			
For a variety of specific audiences: self, friend, relative, professor.			
Expository composition about literature.			
Sentences using various grammatical elements.			
Revise composition to improve unity, development, order, clarity, word choice and organization.			
Revise writing to improve word choice and transitions.			

been directed towards the student who wished and needed to learn a foreign language.

The ESUHSD's educational philosophy states that one of its goals is 'to help each student realize his/her potential as much as possible through a varied and flexible curriculum which reflects a concern for individual differences'. Clearly, Spanish classes with both native and non-native speakers address the needs of only the non-native speakers, effectively ignoring the needs of the native speakers.

Faced with a Hispanic enrollment of 63.9 per cent, teachers at William C. Overfelt High School in San Jose realized that it was time to address this issue. Through the efforts of Irene Silvas, William C. Overfelt High School implemented a series of Spanish for Spanish Speakers courses. These courses are now in place at six of the district's ten comprehensive high schools.

The unique aspect of the ESUHSD's Spanish for Spanish Speakers program is that its sequence of courses parallels the sequence of courses in the English program. Spanish 1SS and Spanish 2SS parallel English 1 (Table 14.1); Spanish

3SS parallels English 2 (Table 14.2); Spanish Reading, a non-academic course which meets neither the college entrance requirement nor the ESUHSD's graduation requirement, parallels Language Arts 1, and English as a Second Language course. This means that in the Spanish SS courses, students are working on improving sentence structure and note-taking skills, on writing coherent paragraphs, compositions and research papers, and on preparing oral reports and debates (Table 14.3). The benefit of this parallel approach is that the students can transfer what they learn in their primary language classes, Spanish in this case, to what they are studying in their English classes, effectively improving their English language skills.

Table 14.2: *Mastery objectives for English 2 and Spanish 3-SS*

Writing	Reading	Listening	Speaking
A short research paper. Revise writing to improve word choice and transitions.	Identify protagonist, supporting characters, point of view, trace elements of plot, setting, theme, mood, irony, elements of a poem, synonyms, antonyms and analogies. Define and use selected vocabulary.	Accurately take class and discussion notes.	Identify, prepare and deliver a speech from one of the three major categories in public speaking: to inform, to persuade, or to entertain. Demonstrate competence in various oral presentation techniques: narrate, describe in detail, hypothesize, support opinions, persuade, tailor language.

Table 14.3: *Mastery objectives for ESL language arts I and Spanish reading*

Writing	Reading	Listening	Speaking
Paragraphs written at the lower end of the holistic scale: lack good organization or development and include frequent mistakes. Identify principal parts of verbs and parts of a simple sentence.	For oral practice pronunciation and conversation.	Demonstrate listening skills sufficient to follow class instructions.	Oral participation, oral reading, group dialogue and role playing.

Table 14.4: Spanish courses: Content, orientation and focus

Traditional Spanish Courses		SS Spanish Courses	
Sp.1	• Acquisition of basic receptive and productive skills: can order a meal, request information, ask for and follow directions, take messages, complete application forms, etc.	Sp.1-SS	• Refinement of receptive and productive skills. • Development of critical thinking skills at the convergent level: able to draw conclusions, given certain information. • Parallels Mastery Objectives for English 1 (See Table 14.1).
Sp.2	• Systematic review of key Sp.1 concepts • Continue *acquisition* of receptive and productive skills	Sp.2-SS	• Continue *refinement* of receptive and productive skills. • Systematic review of key concepts of Sp.1-SS • Continue development of critical thinking skills at the convergent level. • Parallels Mastery Objectives for English 1.
Sp.3	• Advanced course • Systematic review of all previously learned material. • Continue *acquisition* of receptive and productive skills. Goal is proficiency.	Sp.3-SS	• Advanced Course (AP) • Continue *refinement* of receptive and productive skills. • Development of critical thinking skills at the divergent level: able to hypothesize. • Parallels Mastery Objectives for English 2.
Placement:	Contingent on successful completion of previous Spanish course, except for Spanish 1 which has no pre-requisites.	Placement:	Contingent on results of 'Spanish for Spanish Speakers Placement Test' developed by the Second Language Education Department in the San Diego City Schools Education Center.

The Spanish for Spanish Speakers courses differ from the traditional Spanish courses. In a typical foreign language class, the goal is language acquisition; in the Spanish Speakers classes, the goal is refinement of already existing language skills (Table 14.4). In order to preclude discrimination, extra care is taken to avoid tracking. Hispanic students are not automatically placed in SS classes because they understand and can speak a little Spanish or because they might have Hispanic surnames. They enroll in the SS classes because they possess advanced linguistic ability. Once in the SS program, these students are grouped according to their needs into the appropriate academic or non-academic Spanish language classes.

The mastery or performance objectives for both the traditional and the SS courses encompass the goals set forth in the California Model Curriculum Standards. These standards, as developed by the California Department of Education, mandate teaching the skills of listening, speaking, reading, writing and culture as tools to communication and cross-cultural understanding. The SS courses, however, approach these goals in reverse order, emphasizing first writing and reading, and then listening and speaking. The program provides progressive skill development and upward mobility for all students. For example, students who complete Spanish 3SS are prepared to enter Advanced Placement courses for which they can earn university credit in Spanish.

The benefits of courses such as Spanish for Spanish Speakers far outweigh the inconveniences. In the ESUHSD program, Spanish teachers, regardless of the courses they teach, experience far less frustration as they address the needs of their students and they have fewer discipline problems in class. The teachers of the SS classes express satisfaction at their ability to use the Spanish language at an adult level, oftentimes enhancing their own fluency; they enjoy the opportunity to challenge their students to operate at a higher level of critical thinking and to reach a higher level of mastery of their primary language. Most of all, teachers in the SS program experience a strong sense of satisfaction knowing that they are providing a long-neglected service and, as a result, fulfilling a professional responsibility.

From the students' point of view, there is satisfaction in the realization that they are refining their knowledge of Spanish in ways that parallel and refine their English language skills. Equally important, although perhaps not as obvious to these students, is the fact that they learn to appreciate their Spanish language and heritage as an integral part of their cultural identity. This, in turn, helps the students develop positive self-esteem.

This program is not without its detriments, both to teachers and to students. For teachers in the SS program, the work load is more intense, for the teacher usually has more and different classes to prepare for each day, but no additional time for this preparation. But the heaviest burden is the result of the lack of instructional materials. Since there are few materials published specifically for native-speakers' classes, the SS teacher is obliged to continually develop new units of study. Finally, for the teacher who does not have native-speaker fluency, the students can be intimidating.

The students also find some disadvantages to the program. Students enrolling in the SS courses find that they have to study considerably more than if they were enrolled in traditional classes where there was nothing new to master. Because the course work is commensurate with the students' abilities, there is a higher level of expectation, both in the SS courses and in the students' English progress as well.

In an effort to lighten the workload for SS teachers, the ESUHSD has provided funding for summer workshops to develop a curriculum guide for the program, with thematic units of study as well as suggested teaching strategies.

The district has documented the results of the Spanish for Spanish Speakers program. The initial data was very positive; the continuing data confirms the original assumptions. SS students, when surveyed, felt that the courses, rather than segregating them by ethnicity, emphasized the intrinsic values of their culture. SS students are moving into honors English classes and are receiving the highest scores possible on the Spanish Advanced Placement Examination. Finally, we have seen concrete evidence that these courses motivate students beyond the high school curriculum; more SS students continue on each year to post-secondary education.

Chapter 15

Tapping a Natural Resource: Language Minority Students as Foreign Language Tutors

Rosalinda Quintanar-Sarellana, Thom Huebner and Anne Jensen

Introduction

Two facts about American education seem irrefutable. First, the demographics of public schools are undergoing a dramatic change. The number of Hispanics and Asians attending public schools is increasing at a faster pace than the Anglo population. In 1986, the ethnic configuration of the school-age population in California was distributed as follows: 52 per cent Anglos, 29 per cent Hispanic, 10 per cent black, 7 per cent Asian and 2 per cent classified as 'Other'. Projections for the year 2030 show the Hispanic population rising to 44 per cent, an increase in the Asian population to 16 per cent with the Anglo and black populations decreasing to 33 per cent and 6 per cent respectively (Olsen, 1988). Second, the graduates of American public education are not as competitive internationally as they once were. International comparisons repeatedly show American students performing significantly below Chinese, Japanese and Taiwanese students (Stevenson, Stigler, Lee, Lucker, Kitamura and Hsu, 1985).

In an attempt to improve the performance of graduates of American public education, the National Academy of Education has defined the following as educational priorities:

1 programs and assessment which reflect the context within which students will be expected to perform outside of the school setting;
2 programs that bolster the achievement of historically underserved, minority students; and
3 collaboration among teachers, students, and researchers in designing educational programs (James, 1991).

This chapter describes the start-up year of a three-year project funded by the California Academic Partnership Program which touches on each of these priority issues. The goal of the project is to develop a curriculum which allows

Spanish-speaking high school students to develop their language and literacy skills by employing them as tutors for Spanish foreign language students.

Rationale

Within the state of California, and increasingly nationwide, two issues loom large in the areas of foreign language curriculum development and assessment. First, traditional measures of achievement in high school foreign language courses often have little or no relationship to functional proficiency in the use of the language, and in fact, after four years of study of a foreign language, students often have little ability to communicate in it (Krashen, 1982). Second, increasingly larger numbers of students come from Spanish speaking homes, and while the Spanish language skills of these students vary widely, traditional Spanish foreign language courses are inappropriate for this population (Valdés, Lozano and Garcia-Moya, 1981).

Recent Trends in Foreign Language Instruction

Foreign language enrollment in public secondary schools is currently higher than at any time since 1915, when record keeping of these enrollment figures began (Dandonoli, 1987). This increase in enrollments is attributed to increasing numbers of postsecondary schools reinstating foreign language requirements for either entrance or graduation; to demographic changes in the United States which may have sensitized students and parents to the need for proficiency in foreign languages; and to national and state mandates relating to foreign trade, math/science/foreign language study and teacher education (Dandonoli, 1987).

At the same time, evaluation of what constitutes the fulfillment of foreign language requirements has shifted from 'seat time', or a display of declarative knowledge of linguistic structure, as measured by pencil and paper tests, to functional proficiency (e.g., Byrnes and Canale 1987; Freed 1987; Huebner and Jensen, 1992). Proficiency is developed through practice in the communicative use of a foreign language. Currently, a significant body of research in curriculum and instruction in foreign language education is focused on ways to provide this kind of meaningful practice.

Language minority education. In addressing the low level of foreign language proficiency in the United States, two of the more recent presidential reports on education (President's Commission on Foreign Language and International Studies, 1980; National Commission on Excellence in Education, 1983) have cited as untapped resources, language minority students, who by being 'brought into the mainstream of education and employment opportunities' (President's Commission of Foreign Language and International Studies, p. 14) can 'build on their existing linguistic resources so that they may contribute more to American education, diplomacy and international business' (President's Commission of Foreign Language and International Studies, p. 19; Bernhardt and Hammadou, 1987; Brown, Rosen, Hill and Olivas, 1980).

Unfortunately, it has long been observed that based on achievement test scores and dropout rates, the academic success of language minority, and especially Mexican-American students, is lower than that of their native English-speaking peers. Two factors are frequently cited as contributing to this relatively low academic performance: language proficiency and social status relationships (Olsen, 1988; Wong-Fillmore, 1986; Carranza, 1977; Carter and Segura, 1979; Celce-Murcia, 1983; Coste, 1983).

Cummins (1981) identifies two types of language proficiency: 1) 'basic interpersonal communication skills', used in everyday interactions; and 2) 'cognitive/academic language proficiency', required for academic work. While the first can be attained within a few years of exposure to a second language, the second is less universal and continues to develop throughout the school years and beyond. Furthermore, some of these cognitive/academic language skills can transfer from the first language to a second. An obvious example is literacy-related language skills, which involve students' abilities to analyze and manipulate context-reduced cognitively demanding texts. One reason language minority students often fail to develop high levels of academic language skills in English is the lack of opportunity to look at their own first language analytically (Cummins, 1981).

Another frequently cited cause of academic failure among language minority students is their perceived status relationship to the rest of the school community. Work on expectation states (Cohen, 1980; Cohen and Sharan, 1982) has found that group members use the previously established perception of each other's status to evaluate probable competence on new and unrelated tasks. High-status members are expected to be more competent on new tasks, and to contribute more; their contributions, as such, are evaluated more highly. Within this framework, language minority students are perceived to be low status, reinforcing stereotypes of inferiority (Cohen and Sharan, 1982). The literature on expectation-states theory suggests that modifications in perceived status relations through a treatment which accords expert status to low-status participants will affect interactional patterns and learning unilaterally (Cohen, 1980).

Status may also affect the acquisition of a second language for mainstream students as well. For example, in some two-way bilingual education settings involving the teaching of both Spanish and English to both majority and minority group members, Edelsky (1982 and 1991) has found that the English speakers learn little if anything of the minority group's language. The problem, she maintains, is that the members of the majority group are socially dominant even when they are outnumbered (Freire, 1970).

Low academic achievement for the low status student is frequently a by-product of unequal status relationships in classrooms. Recent research on language minority students contends that members of subordinate ethnic groups are often disempowered as a direct result of their interactions with representatives of the dominant groups (e.g., educators and majority peers) (Ogbu, 1978). Cummins (1986) points out that one reason compensatory educational programs have failed to improve academic achievement rates for language minority students is because the educational programs have not significantly altered the relationship between educators and minority students. Academic programs designed for members of subordinate groups are most successful when the relationships between students and educators are significantly altered, and the students' language and culture are integrated into the curriculum (Au, 1980; Cummins, 1986; Freire, 1970; Hernández-Chávez, 1984).

Setting

The Campbell Union High School District (CUHSD) in suburban San Jose exemplifies the issues in foreign language education mentioned above. Within the CUHSD, the study of foreign languages is a prime example of a discipline undergoing a radical change in both philosophy and approach. Since 1984, as an outgrowth of the recommendations by the American Council on the Teaching of Foreign Language (ACTFL) and the California State Department of Education Model Curriculum Standards, emphasis within the CUHSD has shifted from understanding the structure of the language being learned to becoming functionally proficient in the target language. This refocusing of instruction stresses the practical uses of language in casual, social and working conditions. To facilitate the development of this concept, a proficiency interview, modelled after the ACTFL Oral Proficiency Interview Test is now a component of all language studies beyond the first year (Huebner and Jensen, 1992).

Although the CUHSD Foreign Language Department has been successful in building a high enrollment throughout the district, it has never been successful in building the enrollment of Spanish-speaking students in Spanish courses. These students already have the valuable asset of speaking another language, but their command over academic language, and especially their Spanish reading and writing skills, vary greatly. In Spanish foreign language classes, Spanish-speaking students are bored with oral work, but often do not perform well on written tasks. As a result, Spanish-speaking students often have low self-esteem and attempt to hide the fact that they speak another language.

The academic performance of this population of students lags behind that of their language majority peers. For example, in Campbell Union High School District (CUHSD), Hispanic students comprise 20 per cent and 21 per cent of the student populations at Del Mar and Blackford High Schools respectively; but they comprise 32 per cent and 33 per cent of the dropouts from those schools. In addition, although 44 per cent of the students from these two high schools go on to college, only 6 per cent and 5 per cent of the Hispanic populations continue with higher education. It should also be pointed out that the Hispanic populations at these high schools is growing by 2–6 per cent per year.

Spanish-speaking students need a vehicle whereby they can improve the Spanish they already know. They need to see the value of their language skills at school, in the workplace, and as preparation for college. They need to see the connection between the Spanish used in their communities and the Spanish used in the classroom (Faltis, 1984).

The Program. To meet these needs and at the same time provide maximum opportunities for Spanish foreign language students to practice their communicative use of the language with native speakers, the CUHSD, in collaboration with faculty from San Jose State University, have established a Spanish for Spanish Speakers course in which students are trained and employed as peer teachers and proficiency testers in the Spanish foreign language classrooms. Other components of the curriculum include a sociolinguistic strand, computer literacy, Latino and Chicano literature, career awareness and parent involvement. The objectives of the course are listed below:

1. *Peer Tutoring.*   We like to think of peer tutoring as the heart of the program, because it is this component that involves the most radical change in relationships within the school community. By tutoring their native English-speaking peers, native Spanish speakers are made aware of the value, economic as well as cultural, afforded to proficiency in Spanish. (Because of outside funding, we are able to pay students for time spent as tutors. While not all districts would be able to do that, some form of public recognition for their skills is absolutely essential.) They are also recognized for their skills, by teachers and peers alike, as having expertise in a skill area that their native English-speaking peers are trying to develop. At the same time, the tutorial sessions benefit the Spanish foreign language students in that they have opportunities to practice using Spanish in communicative contexts with native speakers of the language, thereby developing proficiency in it. In designing this program, it was hypothesized (see Huebner, Bartolome, Avelar-LaSalle and Azevedo, 1989 for the report on a pilot study) that by reversing the expert-novice roles that exist in traditional classrooms, the perceived status relations among the two groups would also change. As this component is implemented, students from the Spanish for Spanish-speaking class go to Spanish foreign language classes to tutor their native English-speaking peers in Spanish once every week or two. This activity requires coordination between the teachers of both the Spanish for Spanish Speakers and the Spanish foreign language classes. It is also necessary for the Spanish-speaking students to prepare and practice their lessons before going to the tutorial session. They are eager to do this, since they do not want to lose face in front of their peers. But by preparing to tutor, they must also review and thoroughly understand the grammatical points, punctuation and accent rules, etc. presented in the text. This becomes a vehicle for developing and refining their own literacy skills.

Typical activities for the tutorial sessions include games, interactive stories, and interview protocols. These protocols typically focus on one grammatical functional point or situation, and are designed to guide tutors in conversing with their tutees about topics of interest to adolescents. Initially, protocols were designed by the teachers, taken from the list of communicative activities found in the textbook, or were games familiar to everyone. For example, games used early on to provide communicative activities included *Lotería* (Bingo), and *Serpientes y Escaleras* (Chutes and Ladders). Gradually, however, students made up their own protocols. For example, for beginning Spanish learners, the Spanish-speaking students found pictures in magazines which they mounted on cards and used for labeling activities (*¿Qué es esto? ¿Qué están haciendo?* etc. What is this? What are they doing?). A sample student-made protocol, focusing on the form and use of the past tense, and taking simple question-answer form, is found in Appendix 1.

2. *Oral Proficiency Testing.*   To emphasize the importance of proficiency in the foreign language classroom, students in the SSS course were trained in the administration of a modified version of the ACTFL Oral Proficiency Interview (OPI). CUHSD has developed and has had extensive experience administering this modified OPI to its students of foreign languages for several years (Huebner and Jensen, 1992).

3. *Development of Sociolinguistic Awareness in Spanish.*   In order for the tutorial component to succeed, it was not sufficient to be sure that students knew some

basic fundamentals of teaching. Because the students in the Spanish for Spanish Speakers classes typically come from a variety of ethnic, geographic and social backgrounds, it was necessary that they understand and appreciate the linguistic diversity inherent in the many dialects represented in the class. Furthermore, we wanted the Spanish-speaking students to be able to articulate the differences between their own dialects and those represented in a typical Spanish foreign language textbook, should one of the English-speaking students question them on it.

Therefore, sociolinguistic units were included in the course, in which students were provided with tape recorders and asked to collect samples of the Spanish spoken by their family, friends and other members of the community. Recordings included such things as oral histories, recipes, proverbs, home remedies, jokes, etc. These recordings were then brought to class, transcribed and analyzed for such topics as phonological, lexical and syntactic variation, code-switching, linguistic borrowing, etc. For example, after having brainstormed about regional and age dialect differences based on casual observations of each other's Spanish, students in one class made formal hypotheses about the use of specific lexical items in Spanish. They then constructed a dialect survey reflecting these hypotheses (see Appendix 2). The next step was for each student to administer the survey to three to five of their relatives or friends. They brought their results back to class and analyzed them to either verify or refute their original hypotheses. Finally they reflected on the steps they had just gone through to illustrate what is meant by the scientific method.

4. *Chicano and Latino Literature.* To increase student awareness of the literature of their local community and its relationship to other Hispanic literature, students read from a sampling of Chicano and Latino literature. These readings included legends and short stories and were selected using three principal criteria: 1) high interest level for adolescents, 2) representativeness of the cultural background of the students, 3) readability of text.

5. *Development of Computer Skills in Spanish.* Through a grant from IBM it was possible to set up computer labs in the project high schools for the exclusive use of the Spanish for Spanish Speakers and the Foreign Language classes. The data that students collected in the sociolinguistic component of the project, together with their writing assignments from literature studies, were then saved in the students' files. At the end of the year, students published a 'cultural reader', based on these assignments using a desktop publishing program (see Appendix 3, *Q-Vo*, as an example of this reader).

6. *Career opportunities for bilingual professionals.* An important priority for the program is to help language minority students gain access to the existing educational and economic opportunities available to them by virtue of their bilingual proficiency. Several guest speakers informed the students of the different career options for bilingual professionals. In addition, students visited San Jose State University and Stanford University, where they talked to minority students who explained financial aid and their experiences in higher education. During these visits, the high school students received a lot of encouragement from college teachers and students (Peck, 1987).

7. *Parent Involvement.* To sensitize and inform parents of targeted students for the SSS course about effective participation in the academic needs of their children, a parent training and involvement program was developed. A newsletter was mailed to all the parents informing them about the course and the different activities in which the students participated during the school year. A Parents' Night was held in which parents had an opportunity to talk to the teachers and some of the faculty from San Jose State University who were involved in the project.

Collaboration between CUHSD, Middle Schools and San Jose State University

To provide a coordinated articulation model, this project facilitates targeted foreign language students' progress through middle and high school toward admission to a four year college. Often high school, middle school, and college faculties work in isolation, although all have long realized the need to work more closely together. Project staff believe that as the partnership creates closer ties between teachers and administrators, students will become more successful.

Evaluation and Discussion

During the first year of this program, data were collected through student written journals and interviews with the project staff. These data were discussed through a series of meetings attended by the evaluator, the co-principal investigators and the project staff. According to these interviews and journals, the major successes and contributions of the project thus far can be identified qualitatively as follows:

1   Increased awareness of career options available to bilinguals;
2   Positive reactions and raised self-esteem among the Spanish-speaking students as a result of peer teaching;
3   Recognition of the value of Chicano/Latino art and literature;
4   Interest in the Spanish language, particularly in reading and writing, among the Spanish-speaking students;
5   Opportunities for exchanges of varied cultural experiences using the students as resources;
6   Increased awareness of dialect variation in the Spanish language;
7   Raised educational and professional goals as evidenced by students' enrollment in institutions of higher education;
8   Increased awareness on the part of the Spanish-speaking students of effective tutoring techniques;
9   Assumption of greater responsibilities for learning on the part of the Spanish-speaking students;
10 Support for the program and its teachers from colleagues, especially from the foreign language teachers;
11 Development of friendships among Spanish-speaking students and Spanish foreign language students.

Although the previously mentioned outcomes are very positive and encouraging, it is more important to emphasize the lessons learned during the first year of the project. The sociolinguistic component was taught one day a week throughout the academic year. This format did not provide the continuity that was needed to cover the content in the sociolinguistic component. After examining the process, it was decided that it would be more efficient to teach the sociolinguistic component in concentrated periods of time, i.e., one whole week three times a semester. Another important piece of information that was revealed in the process was the need to sequence data collection in a different order. For example, students were initially very reluctant to interview friends and family members about their life histories. This reluctance may have been the result of shyness about educational level and social status, or perhaps, more likely, immigration status. In any case, it was easier to get students to collect data on recipes and home remedies (less personal data) initially, and then ask for life histories after the students had developed interview skill and interviewees had developed a sense of trust.

The tutorial component was another area that required a closer look and reorganization. The success of the tutoring session depended to a great extent on the coordination between the Spanish for Spanish Speakers class and the Spanish foreign language class. Obviously, the tutorial topics were an extension of the content being covered in the Spanish foreign language class. Release time was provided so that teachers from the Spanish for Spanish Speakers class and Spanish foreign language class could plan in advance. Ideally, the schedule should allow teachers from both classes to have the same prep period in order to plan and coordinate activities.

The project has presented students with an interesting and challenging course. Students have reacted very positively to the enrichment activities included in the curriculum. In this course students are active participants, as they become interviewers in the community, tutors of foreign language students, Spanish oral proficiency testers, writers and publishers of their own work. The collaboration of Campbell Union High School District and San Jose State University also enabled students to explore career options and to establish personal contacts with college students and professors. In the future, the project will be measuring the effectiveness of the course in increasing students' awareness and appreciation of dialectal variation in Spanish-speaking communities. The project will also be monitoring the participants access to higher education.

Appendix 1
Spanish for Spanish Speakers — CUHSD
Sample Tutorial Activity

Preguntas para iniciar una conversación sobre el fin de semana.
(Questions to initiate a conversation about the weekend.)

1. ¿Adónde fuiste durante el fin de semana? (Where did you go during the weekend?)
    ¿Qué hiciste durante el fin de semana? (What did you do during the weekend?)

2. ¿Fuiste a un restaurante? (Did you go to a restaurant?)
    ¿Cómo se llama el restaurante? (What is the name of the restaurant?)
    ¿Dónde está? (Where is it?)
    ¿Qué comiste? (What did you eat?)

¿Qué bebiste? (What did you drink?)
¿Con quién fuiste? (Who did you go with?)

3. ¿Fuiste al cine? (Did you go to the movies?)
¿Qué película viste? (What movie did you watch?)
¿Con quién fuiste? (Who did you go with?)
¿Te gustó la pelicula? (Did you like the movie?)
¿Qué hiciste dispués del cine? (What did you do after the movie?)

4. ¿Tuviste tarea durante el fin de semana? (Did you have homework during the weekend?)
¿Hiciste la tarea? (Did you work on your homework?)
¿Fue dificil? (Was it difficult?)
¿Qué hiciste después de la tarea? (What did you do after finishing your homework?)

5. ¿Fuiste a la iglesia? (Did you go to church?)
¿Con quién fuiste? (Who did you go with?)
¿Viste a unos amigos? (Did you see some friends?)
¿Charlaste con tus amigos? (Did you talk to your friends?)
¿Qué hiciste después de la iglesia? (What did you do after church?)

6. ¿Fuiste de compras el sábado? (Did you go shopping on Saturday?)
¿Qué compraste? (What did you buy?)
¿Dónde lo (la) compraste? (Where did you buy it?)
¿Cuánto costó? (How much did it cost?)
¿Cómo es? (How is it?)

7. ¿Viste la televisión? (Did you watch television?)
¿Qué programa miraste? (What program did you watch?)
¿Qué te gustó? (What did you like?)
¿Qué no te gustó? (What did you dislike?)
¿Qué ocurrió en el programa? (What happened in the program?)
¿A qué hora fué? (What time was the program?)

Appendix 2
Spanish for Spanish Speakers
Dr. Thom Huebner

Estudio sobre dialectos: (Study about dialects)
Estoy haciendo un estudio sobre dialectos (variaciones gramaticales, fonéticas, y en vocabulario) en español para mi clase de español para hispanohablantes. Espero que Ud. pueda ayudarme.
(I am studying dialects (grammatical, phonetic and vocabulary variations) for my Spanish for Spanish Speakers class. I hope you can help me.)

Datos importantes sobre la persona entrevistada: (Important information about the person interviewed:)
Edad: (Age) 15–20 21–35 55–65 65+
Nació en (Place of birth):
Años de estudio: (School years) 0 1 2 3 4 5 6 7 8 9 10 11 12 13 14 15 16
Tiempo que ha vivido en San José o en el Condado de Santa Clara: (How long have you lived in Santa Clara County?)

¿En qué otras partes de este país ha vivido? (In what other parts of this country have you lived?)

¿Cuánto tiempo vivió en cada país o ciudad anotada? (How long did you live in each country or city?)

¿En qué otros países o ciudades de latinoamérica ha vivido? (In what other countries or cities of Latin America have you lived?)

¿Cuánto tiempo vivió en cada país o ciudad? (How long did you live in each country or city?)

Preguntas: (Questions)

1. ¿Cómo le llama a la mamá de su mamá? (respuesta posible: abuela, nana, mamá grande) (What do you call your mother's mother?)

2. ¿Cómo le llama al papá de su papá (abuelito, tata, papá grande) (What do you call your father's father?)

3. ¿Cómo le llama a una bebida fresca y gaseosa que no tiene licor? (agua gaseosa, refresco, soda) (What do you call a carbonated drink that has no alcohol?)

4. ¿Cómo le llama a la verdura que usamos para hacer guacamole? (aguacate, avocado, palta) (What is the name of the vegetable that is used to make guacamole?)

5. ¿Qué expresión usa Ud. cuando alguien junto a Ud. está por caerse? (aguas, cuidado) (What expression do you use when somebody near you is about to fall down?)

6. ¿Cómo le llama a lo que manejamos al trabajo o a la escuela y que tiene cuatro llantas y puertas? (auto, carro, coche, automóvil) (What do you call the vehicle you drive to school and/or work?)

7. ¿Cómo le llama al la fruta verde y picante que usamos para hacer salsa? (ají, chile, picante) (What do you call the green fruit that we use to make hot salsa?)

8. ¿Cómo le llama a lo que carga una mujer en su hombro o en su mano; y que usa para guardar dinero? (bolsa, cartera) (What do you call the object women use to carry their money?)

9. ¿Cómo le llama al objeto que usan los estudiantes para sentarse y escribir sus notas? (escritorio, pupitre, mesa banco, silla) (What do you call the object that students use in school to sit down and take notes?)

10. ¿Como le llama los a demás hijos de sus padres ademas de sus nombres? (carnal, hermano) (What other words do you use to refer to your siblings?)

11. ¿Cómo le llama al objeto que usan los muchachos para abrigarse cuando hace mucho frío? (chamarra, chaqueta) (What do you call the object youngsters wear in cold weather?)

12. ¿Cómo le llaman a los varones menores de doce años? (chavos, muchachos, chicos) (What do you call young males under 12 years of age?)

Appendix 3: Sample of high school newspaper

¿**Q-vo?**

Conversaciones con Hispanohablantes
de San José

Oaxaca

JUEGOS

Catherine *by Karia Duarte*
BLACKFORD HIGH SCHOOL

K: Esta es una entrevista de español para el hispano hablante. Su nombre no me lo necesita decir. ¿Qué juegos usted judaba cuando era peqieña?

C: Bueno, cuando era pequeña, yo jugaba mucho con mis amigos y intentaba muchos, eh, juegos asi imaginativos, jugaba muchos deportes también.

K: ¿Cuál era su actividad favorita?

C: Eh, pues a lo mejor, los deportes portque jugaba mucho al softball y también nadaba.

K: ¿Cuál era su dia típico?

C: Día típico–¿Cuando tenía cuantos años.?

K: Cuando era pequeña.

C: ¿Como diez años de edad o asl? Pues, irme a la escuela, y siempre que iba a la escuela tenfa que hacer el trabajo, y luego jugaba en la escuela durante el recreo, y después de la escuela me fui–a veces me fui a casa de un amigo o de unas amigas y, ahmmm, jugaba un poco los deportes, el basketball o lo que queriamos, y cenaba siempre con la familia, pero muchas veces mi papá no estaba porque

hacia muchos viajes. Entonces, miraba la televisión, después de haber canado, y ahmmm, no se si tenía muchos estudios cuan-do era pequeña, pero algunos, y luego me fui a la cama sobre las diez, nueve o diez.

K: ¿Cuáles son algunas de las cosas que hacía antes, y que ahora no hace?

C: ¿Qué ahora no hago?

C: Jugar con mis amigos.

K: ¿Qué hace usted en los días feriados o sea holidays?

C: Mmm, pues, últimamente, mi marido y yo trabajamos mucho en la casa porque es-tamos añadiendo una–eh, ϲ sea estamos haciendo una adición a nuestra casa. Entonces, este fin de semana, por ejemplo, el lunes tenemos vacación, y, ahmmm, nosotros es-taremos poniendo ladrillos enfrente de la casa-que es mucho trabajo, y muchas veces vamos al cine por la noche, y hay slempre mucho que hacer por la casa.

Appendix 3: (cont.)

"Anna" *by Olidia Mejorado*
BLACKFORD HIGH SCHOOL

O: Estoy haclendo un reporte para mi clase de Español y me qustaría saber de su vida de joven.

A: Bueno yo soy de un estado de Durango en un pueblo muy chiquito. La vida es muy diferente allá en México que aquí en los Estados Unidos; allá en Mexico uno se para bien temprano, como las cuatro de la mañaña y se va uno al monte con sus padres a atener los animales y a atender las milpas que tiene uno de elotes, fruta, y verduras; entonces uno se la pasa en el monte hasta las doce de la tarde. Llega uno a su casa y come se prepara para a veces estudiar. Cuando no iba a la escuela de todos modos llegaba y estudiaba. Allá en mi casa pasan uno má tiempo con su familia–porque en la vida, el paso de la vida es más simple. Aquí en los Estados Uniods, la vida es muy rapida y muy pronto. Aquí, uno va a la escuela, llega uno y se pone a ver la televisión. En Méxlco, de donde yo soy, en el pueblo no había televisión; apenas hace poco empezaron a llever televisiones de differentes pafses, o también de Méxlco compraba uno televisiones; entonces la vida era muy simple. Allá tenemos las costumbres de nostros. Son más sencillas las fiestas, y los juegos. Todos lo juegos que tenemos son inventados por uno misom–los niños. Cuando esta uno niño, allá tenemos la vida muy simple. Allá nostros ibamos a lavar al rio y también ibamos mucho a misa los Domingos. Nos juntábamos todos juntos como una familia y aunque uno quiere tener tiempo para su familia. En veces no tiene tiempo porque está uno trabajando, y allá cuando uno trabaja con toda la familila junta en el monte. Tenemos muchas constumbres sencillas. Como mi favorito tiempo fué cuando tenía 15 años, y me hicieron mis quince años. Aquí, se nombran el sweet sixteen. Nosotros allá, la quinceañera es cuando uno va enfrentarse al altar de Dios, y le da gracias por darle vida,

y por poder sequir su joventud adelante, y eso es algo muy hermoso y una constumbre fantástica en México que a mi me gustaba. Era mi fiesta de 15 años. Este era mi cumpleaños más hermoso, y más lindo de mi vida, Mi familia es muy sencilla. Tenemos todas las constumbres de México. Mi madre nunca nos dejaba ver la televisión porque dice que es mejor uno tratar las cosas sencillas, y levantar un libro leer, y platicar uno con su hermano o su hermana en vez de estar uno viendo televisión, o estar viendo afuera y andar de compras o algo como allá en mi pueblo. No hay tiendas de ver. Tratamos todos de estar juntos y eso lo hace a uno tener la familia más fuerte, y más sencilla, y las costumbres más bonitas.

O: ¿Cuánto tiene en los Estados Unidos, y le gusta o se siente aml o bien en el país se quiere regresar?

A: Bueno ahorita ya tenge 20 años aquí en el país. Mi vine cuando tienía 17 años.

O: ¿No gusta decir otra cosa?

A: No gracias.

Yucatan

References

Au, K.H. (1980) 'Participant structures in a reading lesson with Hawaiian children: Analysis of a culturally appropriate instructional event', *Anthropology and Education Quarterly*, **11**, pp. 91–115.

Bernhardt, E. and Hammadou, J. (1987) 'A decade of research in foreign language teacher education', *Modern Language Journal*, **71**, pp. 289–99.

Brown, G.H., Rosen, N.L., Hill, S.T. and Olivas, M.A. (1980) *The Condition of Education for Hispanic Americans*, Washington, DC, Government Printing Office.

Byrnes, H. and Canale, M. (Eds) (1987) *Defining and Developing Proficiency Guidelines, Implementations, and Concepts*, Lincolnwood, IL, National Textbook Company.

Carranza, M. (1977) 'Language attitudes of Mexican American adults: Some sociolinguistic implications', unpublished doctoral dissertation, South Bend, IN, University of Notre Dame.

Carter, T.P. and Segura, R.D. (1979) *Mexican Americans in School: A Decade of Change*, New York, NY, CEEB.

Celce-Murcia, M. (1983) 'Problem solving: A bridge builder between theory and practice', in Alatis, J.E., Stern, H.H. and Strevens, P. (Eds) *Applied Linguistics and the Preparation of Second Language Teachers: Toward a Rationale*, Washington, DC, Georgetown University Press, pp. 97–105.

Cohen, E.G. (1980) 'Expectation states and interracial interaction in school settings', *American Review of Sociology*, **8**, pp. 209–35.

Cohen, E. and Sharan, S. (1982) 'Modifying status relations in Israeli youth', *Journal of Cross-Cultural Psychology*, **11**, pp. 364–84.

Coste, D. (1983) 'International aspects of teacher training', Alatis, J.E., Stern, H.H. and Strevens, P. (Eds) *Applied Linguistics and the Preparation of Second Language Teachers: Toward a Rationale*, Washington, DC, Georgetown University Press, pp. 116–23.

Cummins, J. (1981) 'The role of primary language development in promoting educational success for language minority students', *Schooling and Language Minority Students: A Theoretical Framework*, Los Angeles, CA, Evaluation, Dissemination and Assessment Center.

Cummins, J. (1986) 'Empowering minority students: A framework for intervention', *Harvard Educational Review*, **56**, pp. 18–35.

Dandonoli, P. (1987) 'Report on foreign language enrollment in public secondary schools, Fall 1985', *Foreign Language Annals*, **20**, pp. 457–70.

Edelsky, C. (1982) 'Writing in a bilingual program: The relation of L1 and L2 texts', *TESOL Quarterly*, **16**, pp. 211–18.

Edelsky, C. (1991) *With Literacy and Justice for All*, London, England, Falmer Press.

Faltis, C. (1984) 'Reading and writing in Spanish for bilingual college students: What's taught at school and what's used in the community', *Bilingual Review*, **11**, pp. 21–31.

Freed, B.F. (1987) 'Preliminary impression of the effects of a proficiency-based language requirement', *Foreign Language Annals*, **20**, pp. 139–46.

Freire, P. (1970) *Education for Critical Consciousness*, New York, NY, Seabury Press.

Hernández-Chávez, E. (1984) 'The inadequacy of English immersion education as an educational approach for language minority students in the United States', *Studies on Immersion Education: A Collection for United States Educators*, Sacramento, CA, California State Department of Education, pp. 144–83.

Holmes Group (1986) *Tomorrow's Teachers: A Report of the Holmes Group*, East Lansing, MI, Author.

Huebner, T., Bartolome, L., Avelar-LaSalle, R. and Azevedo, M. (1989)

'Integrating language education, teacher training and university-school collaboration: A pilot project', *The Modern Language Journal*, **73**, pp. 23–31.

HUEBNER, T. and JENSEN, A. (1992) 'A study of foreign language proficiency testing in secondary schools', *Foreign Language Annals*, **25**, 2, pp. 105–15.

JAMES, T. (1991) *Research and the Renewal of Education: Funding Priorities for Educational Research*, Stanford, CA, National Academy for Education.

KRASHEN, S. (1982) *Principles and Practices in Second Language Acquisition*, Oxford, England, Pergamon Press.

NATIONAL COMMISSION ON EXCELLENCE IN EDUCATION (1983) *A Nation at Risk: The Imperative for Educational Reform*, Washington, DC, US Department of Education, Government Printing Office.

OGBU, J. (1978) *Minority Education and Caste*, New York, NY, Academic Press.

OLSEN, L. (1988) *Crossing the School House Border: Immigrant Students in the California Public Schools*, San Francisco, CA, California Tomorrow.

PECK, S. (1987) 'Spanish for social workers: An intermediate-level communicative course with content lectures', *The Modern Language Journal*, 71, pp. 402–9.

PRESIDENT'S COMMISSION ON FOREIGN LANGUAGE AND INTERNATIONAL STUDIES (1980) 'Strength through wisdom: A critique of US capability', *The Modern Language Journal*, **64**, pp. 9–57.

STEVENSON, H.W., STIGLER, J.W., LEE, S.Y., LUCKER, G.W., KITAMURA, S. and HSU, C.C. (1985) 'Cognitive performance and academic achievement of Japanese, Chinese, and American children', *Child Development*, **56**, pp. 718–34.

VALDÉS, G., LOZANO, A. and GARCIA-MOYA, R. (Eds) (1981) *Teaching Spanish to the Hispanic Bilingual: Issues, Aims and Methods*, New York, NY, Teachers College Press.

WONG-FILLMORE, L. (1986) 'Teaching bilingual learners', in WITTROCK, M.C. (Ed) *Handbook of Research on Teaching*, 3rd Edition New York, Macmillan, pp. 648–85.

Chapter 16

Using Expert Teacher Knowledge to Develop Curriculum for Native Spanish-Speaking Secondary Students

Fabián A. Samaniego and Barbara J. Merino

In collaboration with:

Bridget Berlin	Catherine Balestrieri Burton
Jesús G. Solís	Antonio Maldonado Losada
Evelyn Vargas Castaneda	Arlene L. Keefe
Deborah Ottman	

Español para triunfar, a four-week summer institute for secondary teachers of Spanish who teach native Spanish-speaking students, was sponsored by the University of California at Davis (UCD), the summer of 1989. The institute was designed by Dr. Barbara Merino of the Division of Education and Fabián A. Samaniego of the Department of Spanish at UCD. It was funded by a Title II grant from the California Post-Secondary Commission and was conducted in collaboration with the Butte County Office of Education, California State University at Chico, California State University at Sacramento, and the California State Department of Education.

Twenty high school teachers from northern California (see Appendix A for names and schools) participated in the eight-hour per day, four days per week, month long summer institute. Teachers were selected to participate in the institute on the basis of their language proficiency, Advanced 3 on the ACTFL/ETS oral proficiency scale (1986) and for being from a school district with a high percentage of native speakers of Spanish (NSS). Preference was given to those who already were teaching, or were scheduled to teach, a Spanish course for NSS. The institute fellows received a $600 stipend in addition to residency and meal costs. For those who needed it, tuition costs for six university credits were also provided.

Source of Expert Teachers

The twenty institute fellows that completed the *Español para triunfar* summer institute became the pool of expert teachers from which ten were selected to participate in a series of follow-up seminars focusing on the development of curriculum for native Spanish-speaking secondary students. The seminars, which were directed by Dr. Barbara Merino and Fabián Samaniego and funded by the UCD Center for Cooperative Research and Extended Services for Schools (CRESS), consisted of four, six- to eight-hour sessions which took place on Saturdays during the 1989–90 academic year.

Pre-Institute Knowledge Base

In order to fully appreciate the thoroughness of the lessons developed by this group of expert teachers, it is important to understand their background, both prior to and after the training received in the 1989 summer institute. Although only three of the twenty fellows were already teaching NSS courses, two others indicated they were expected to design a program for NSS over the summer and have it ready to implement in the fall. The twenty participants came to the institute with a strong interest in serving their NSS community of students and eager to be helped in an area where they were either struggling along with a recently developed program or were anticipating having to develop a program in the not so distant future.

All admitted in the beginning that they were not particularly happy with what they were currently doing for NSS in their classes. Most had limited knowledge of dialect variation and of theoretical and pedagogical issues related to teaching native speakers. Attitudes toward dialect variance were measured the first and last days of the institute using the Attitude Scale on Acceptability of Dialect Variants (see Appendix B). The participants' general background knowledge was measured by having them respond, both at the beginning and at the end of the institute, to a case study (see Appendix C), which asked them to describe a quality instructional program for a six-month Spanish II class comprised of native English speakers learning Spanish as a foreign language and several types of NSS.

The Four-Week Institute: Scholarly Papers

The four-week program was designed to have expert scholars and practitioners present their research and practical applications to the institute fellows in the mornings, allowing the afternoons and evenings for practical discussions and work in groups on curriculum prototypes that fellows were asked to prepare. In the afternoons, each participant also presented a lesson to their peers incorporating effective teaching from their practice with some of the principles for working with NSS that they were learning.

The scholarly presentations were, in fact, a preliminary version of many of the papers presented in this volume. All presenters were asked to submit a paper further elaborating on the topic they addressed at the institute. The papers in this volume are updates on how current research in the areas of specialization of each institute presenter relates to native speakers in their language-learning process. A brief synopsis of the presentations, all of which are available on videocassette or in this volume, are given below.

In his talk entitled *National Linguistic Heterogeneity in International Perspective*, the keynote speaker, Dr. Joshua Fishman (1989), demonstrated from a world-wide perspective the importance of maintaining the first language of a minority community. Dr. Fishman presented very convincing data illustrating how, when a minority community's language disappears, the minority community itself ceases to exist.

In Dr. Barbara Merino's presentation titled *Dialect Variants in Spanish*, the institute fellows learned that within the Spanish-speaking world there are a multitude of dialects, each as valid as the other, and all worthy of respect. Her presentation titled *Dialect Variants in the Southwest* (1989a) made it clear that there is significant variation within the Chicano dialect of the Southwest, and, once again, that teachers must fully recognize that all dialects are valid and correct within their own communities. Perhaps the most important lesson learned during the four-week institute was that as teachers of Spanish, we must avoid telling NSS that their language is incorrect, simply because they use the dialect of their community, and that they must avoid making 'so many errors'. Rather, we should praise students for the language they already command and make them aware of those instances when their dialect does not conform to a more standard variety of Spanish.

In her presentation titled *On the Question of Standard vs. Dialect: Hispanic Students*, Dr. Margarita Hidalgo (1989) presented a number of techniques she uses to help NSS students develop an awareness of how to recognize when they are using dialect and when they are expected to use more standard varieties of the language.

Dr. Lenora Timm (1989) explained, in a presentation titled *Code-Switching and Southwest Spanish Speakers*, how her research has shown that the constant shifts back-and-forth, from Spanish to English to Spanish, are an integral part of the dialect of Hispanic communities of the Southwest. She presented a very strong case for not simply labeling this code-switching as lack of vocabulary or, even worse, a sign of ignorance. Instead, Dr. Timm stated that code-switching should always be acceptable within the context of the community of speakers that use it naturally. Without it, individuals may find themselves ostracized from their own minority community. She did indicate, however, that students who code-switch should be made aware of times when it is not appropriate to code-switch.

For their presentation on *The Dialect Speaker and Oral Proficiency Assessment*, Dr. Barbara Merino and Fabián A. Samaniego (Merino and Samaniego, 1989) showed a video made of an oral proficiency interview (OPI) they had conducted with a native Spanish-speaking high school student. The interview was a vivid illustration of how a native speaker is able to perform all the linguistic functions required at the Superior level on the ACTFL/ETS scale (1983), yet would have to receive a lower rating, because she used her community's dialect when speaking. This problem has been pointed to as invalidating OPI ratings of native speakers. (Valdés, 1989).

The second week, institute fellows heard Dr. Robert Politzer of Stanford University present *A Researcher's Reflection on Bridging Dialect and Second Language Learning: Discussion of Problems and Solutions* (Politzer, 1989). This presentation helped the institute fellows understand the relation between second dialect acquisition and teaching and second language acquisition research in psycholinguistics, sociolinguistics, neurolinguistics, classroom research and bilingual education.

In Dr. Miles Myers (1989) presentation, *Classroom Research*, the institute fellows learned that through means as simple as observation and asking students to respond to a question like 'What did you learn in class this week?' in their journal entries, teachers can empower themselves as bona fide researchers in their own classrooms.

In his presentation titled *The Role of Culture in Teaching Spanish to Spanish Speakers*, Dr. Henry Trueba (1989) focused on the importance of understanding the relationship between culture, language and literacy if one is to understand home language. He emphasized the role of home culture in linguistic and cognitive development as well as in the acquisition of literacy.

Language Loss: Implications for Teaching Spanish to Spanish Speakers, was the topic addressed by Dr. Edward Hérnández-Chávez (1989). He pointed out how his research has shown that the loss of first language skills by native speakers of Spanish is a problem that leads not only to the disruption of communication patterns, but also to the breakdown of cultural and social structures and to a generation of Hispanic youth alienated from their own communities. His message to the institute fellows, concerning the importance of helping young Hispanics hold on to the language of their community, is a message that foreign language teachers across the country need to hear.

In her presentation on *The Role of Chicano Literature in Teaching Spanish to Spanish Speakers*, Dr. Angie Chabram Dernersesian (see Chapter 9) addressed the need for reform in the curriculum development, language policy and cultural politics of foreign language departments on college and university campuses across the country. She pointed out that although 'Spanish has not been the terrain of "native speakers"', there is an ever-expanding wealth of Chicano literature available that, when used with NSS, ends up triggering a high degree of interest and pride in the Spanish language itself. Her presentation, which is included in this volume, presents a very complete bibliography and names of vendors of this, unfortunately often difficult to find, socially and culturally rich literature.

The Four-Week Institute: Applied Presentations

The first applied presentations were made by Sidney Gorman (1989). Through demonstration, lecture and cooperative activity, she laid the foundation for the institute fellows' understanding of recent changes in the foreign language classroom brought about by the communicative competence and proficiency movements. Her three presentations were titled *Cooperative Learning in the Foreign Language Classroom* (1989b), *Classroom* (1989a), and *Grading Student Work in a Communication-Based Classroom* (1989c).

In a presentation on *Developing a Curriculum for NSS*, Lorraine D'Ambruoso (1989) (see Chapter 14), presented a detailed description of a three-year program for NSS currently being taught at the East Side Union High School District in San Jose, California. This program is unique in that it sets up equivalent expectations for NSS in the district's Foreign Language Departments, as they exist in the English departments for native speakers of English.

An Overview of Computer Assisted Instruction (CAI)/Computer Assisted Language Learning (CALL) for Foreign Language Speakers was given by Dr. Nidia González Edfelt (1989). Her presentation began with a brief historical overview of the use of computers in foreign language courses, then went on to address the current use of computers in foreign language teaching including speech processing, interactive videodisc, HyperCard, telecommunications, and artificial intelligence. Her presentation was followed by one titled, *Computers and Teaching Spanish to Spanish Speakers*, by Dr. Chris Faltis of the University of Nevada at Reno and Dr. Robert DeVillar (Faltis and DeVillar, 1989) of California State University at Bakersfield. In this presentation the institute fellows had an opportunity to sit at the computer and experience first hand how to help students develop their writing skills cooperatively, using computers.

Folk Art as a Curriculum Tool in the Classroom, was presented by Beatrice Carrillo Hocker (1989) of The Mexican Museum in San Francisco (see Chapter 11). She traced the art of bark painting from its pre-Colombian roots to its current ritual use in some small Indian villages in Mexico and to its highly commercialized contemporary use in the Mexican tourist trade. She also had the institute fellows create their own ceremonial masks, after briefly explaining the art of mask making in Mexico.

Additional applied presentations given by the institute principal investigators, included *Teaching for Competency* (Samaniego, 1989a), *Testing in a Competency-Based Classroom* (Samaniego, 1989b), a panel with Dr. Joseph Lyons: *Alternative Views of the Oral Proficiency Assessment*, and *Recruiting Spanish-Speaking Students* (Merino, 1989b).

Institute fellows were exposed to an inordinate amount of theoretical and practical knowledge during the four-week program. Their evaluations of the program indicated that although they wished they had more time to discuss and talk about implications of the information presented by each speaker, they felt they learned a tremendous amount and had changed their perspectives considerably regarding NSS dialects and the teaching of NSS. These assumptions are supported by the results on their post-institute case study descriptions of a quality instructional program for a Spanish II foreign language class and by their responses to Form B of the Attitude Scale at the conclusion of the institute.

Curriculum Development Seminars

Upon completion of the summer institute, the questions that remained unanswered were 'How much carryover would there be to classes for NSS, if any?' and 'What effect would the training received in the summer institute have on curriculum development in the participants' schools?' The simple response given by the institute fellows, when told of the possibility of follow-up sessions during the 1989–90 academic year, was 'Of course we're interested. You certainly can't abandon us now! We need your help to start implementing everything we've learned.'

Realizing that to create change there needs to be follow-up training, since one workshop, seminar or institute alone does not bring about change in the classroom nor in a program's curriculum, the institute designers requested funding for follow-up work with half of the summer institute fellows. Funding granted from the UCD CRESS Center made it possible to schedule four one-day meetings on weekends during the 1989–90 academic year. Seven of the ten fellows invited to participate accepted. Participants received a stipend of $100 per session to cover their travel, meal and housing expenses.

Identification of Curriculum Platform

As part of the activities of the summer institute, fellows had to work in groups to develop a curriculum platform and a sample lesson illustrating the curriculum philosophy. Thus, having already participated in a cooperative curriculum development effort, the seminar participants were told at their first meeting that they would be expected to develop a curriculum platform that would include:

a) a statement of program philosophy;
b) a theoretical framework of guiding principles for curriculum development;
c) criteria for curriculum development for module prototypes;
d) a format for lesson design;
e) a range of themes for the modules.

After some general discussions and brainstorming on philosophy and guiding principles for curriculum development with the seminar co-directors facilitating, the seven fellows decided to divide themselves into three groups and have each group work on developing a five- (or more) day module on specific themes. It was decided that two groups would focus on second- or third-year level courses for NSS, and one group would focus on first-year level Spanish courses with native and non-native speakers of the language in the same class.

Comments on the thinking and planning that took place throughout the development of a curriculum platform and the module prototypes are well warranted. All groups were concerned with developing a curriculum that truly addressed the needs of NSS in their classes and not just one that added a little more reading and writing for NSS enrolled in the regular courses. In conducting a needs assessment, it became clear that certain needs were seen as having a very high priority in the minds of all participants. For example, all felt it necessary to develop a curriculum that would help students realize that they are an important part of a vital community of the United States. Another concern expressed by all participants was that far too many NSS in the participants' schools are perceived to have low self-esteem. All felt a need to make these students aware of their own self worth and of their rich cultural heritage. It was also deemed important to provide a variety of Hispanic role models that would motivate the NSS to think about the variety of professions open to them.

Preparation of Prototypes

With these basic tenets in mind, each group proceeded to develop prototype modules. What resulted is a nineteen-day unit on self-esteem, an eighteen-day unit on understanding and applying the concept of self-portrait, a twelve-lesson unit on better understanding and appreciating the students' Mexican heritage, and two six-lesson units on writing for a specific audience. This last unit is unique, in that it serves as a bridge between the work of NSS at the second-and third-year levels and the community's elementary schools.

In going through these modules, it is important to note the extent to which they incorporate the various trends and concepts linking contemporary second language acquisition theory and the NSS. In particular, it is worth noting the

Table 16.1: Correlation of teaching modules and trends in second language teaching acquisition

	Module on self esteem	Module on self portrait	Module on Mexican heritage	Modules on writing
Communication-Based Instruction				
1. Pair work	X	X	X	X
2. Small group work	X	X	X	X
3. Cooperative activities	X	X	X	X
4. Authentic materials	X	X	X	
5. Role playing			X	
6. Process writing				X
7. Oral testing				
Dialect Variance				
1. Accepts variance	X	X	X	
2. Only accepts standard				X
3. Contrasts dialect and standard			X	X
Chicano literature and Culture				
1. Uses Chicano literature	X	X		
2. Requires ethnographic interviews			X	
3. Focus on home culture	X	X		X
4. Focus on folk art			X	
Computers				
1. Used by students				
2. Used to teach writing				

extent to which these modules incorporate what was presented in the 1987 summer institute. Table 16.1 shows this correlation. It is impressive to see the influence of the summer institute. It is clear the participants place a high value on communication-based instruction, as reflected by the fact that almost all of them incorporated pair and group work, cooperative activities and authentic materials into their lessons. Almost all of them also seem to be making a conscious effort to incorporate the basic tenets of dialect variance and a high degree of Chicano literature and home and/or folk culture. The areas that were totally excluded are those whose applicability is greatly influenced by outside factors: the questionable value of the oral proficiency interview for native speakers of Spanish and the inavailability of computers.

Modules for Intermediate and Advanced Level NSS Courses

The first two modules presented here were developed by the two groups that focused on second- or third-year level courses for NSS. Since this is the level at which the majority of high school NSS courses should be taught, we have included the complete modules, except for the day-by-day specification of materials to be used, essential vocabulary and daily assessment.

A Nineteen-day Module on Self-esteem

Prepared by:
Bridget Berlin, *Galt Joint Union High School, Galt, California*
Deborah Ottman, *Corning Union High School, Corning, California*

Unit Goal To explore different aspects that influence one's idea of self-worth: abilities, family, name, physical appearance, education, race, integrity, concern for others and diligence. Through a better understanding of these aspects, students will take action to improve their own self-esteem and that of others.

Day 1
Goal To explore how one's abilities and one's name influence self-esteem.

Procedure Your Name and You

5 min. Name association:
Put up pictures of well known individuals that students will recognize: José Canseco, Gloria Estefan, Bart Simpson, etc. In pairs, ask students to list all qualities they associate with each individual. Then have several pairs read their lists to the class.

25 min. *'El Mejor Pintor'* (The Best Artist) from *Cuentos Simpáticos* (Likeable Short Stories) by Rubin Pfeiffer (1983a)
• If available, show pictures of artists mentioned in the story and their works.
• Review new vocabulary.
• Read short story *'El Mejor Pintor'* and discuss plot and theme with the class.

10 min. Personal name association
• Have students prepare a list of things/characteristics they associate with their own names. Then have them read their lists to each other in small groups.

Homework Journal entry: Have students use the lists they prepared in class to write on topic: 'What my name means to me'.

Day 2
Goal To explore how one's physical appearance influences self-esteem and to learn that looks can be deceiving and that it is what is inside that counts.

Procedure All that Glitters is not Gold

10 min. Surprise package.
- Write on board: *No es oro todo lo que reluce* (All that glitters is not gold). Then show students a beautifully wrapped gift box filled with junk. In pairs have them brainstorm what might be in the package. Discuss with class. Then open the package and ask class to tell you how the quote relates to the package.

25 min. '*Narcizo*' (Narcissus) reading (Berlin and Ottman, 1991b)
- Review new vocabulary.
- Ask for volunteers to read '*Narcizo*' aloud as others follow along.
- Discuss the plot and theme with the class.

15 min. '*Plástico*' (Plastic), a recording by Colon and Blades (1978)
- Have students read the lyrics silently as they listen to the song.
- Have a class discussion on how some people put too much energy into developing their physical appearance rather than their inner qualities.
- Call on volunteers to share what inner qualities they believe should be developed.

Homework Journal entry: Write about a time when someone misjudged you based on your appearance, or when you misjudged someone based on their appearance.

Day 3
Goal To explore how one's level of education influences self-esteem and learn that the value of education differs, depending on the circumstances.

Procedure '*En el Mismo Barco*' (In the Same Boat) by Rubin Pfeiffer (1983b).

25 min.
- Review vocabulary.
- Have students locate Venezuela and the Orinoco river on the map.
- Have students read the story silently.
- Discuss the value of having different skills, depending on the person or setting.
- Write on board: '*Nadie puede hacerte sentir inferior sin tu consentimiento.*' (Nobody can make you feel inferior without your consent.) (Eleanor Roosevelt) Then ask class to relate the story and discussion to this quote.

25 min. Skills inventory
- Have the students do an inventory of their own talents using *Mi Carrera* (My Career) by Denise Douglas and Robert Moreno (Douglas and Moreno, 1986).

Homework   Journal entry: Prepare two lists — one of your own strengths and one of your weaknesses. Star the weaknesses you wish to improve and explain why you wish to improve those areas and not others.

Day 4

Goal   To do a Johari Window (Luft, 1969) a creative activity in which students analyze their perception of themselves and others, and see how others perceive them.

Procedure   Johari Window

10 min.   Self-analysis
- Tell students to prepare a list of things that you and many others know about you — your physical characteristics, likes and dis-likes, abilities, personality traits, and beliefs.
- Then prepare a second list of things only you and a very small number of people (your best friend, a parent, a clergyman) know about you.
- Finally, prepare a third list of things you would like to be able to say about yourself in the future — profession, marital status, accomplishments
- In groups of three or four, share as much information in your lists as you feel comfortable sharing.

25 min.   Explanation of how to prepare a Johari Window
- Show students an example of a completed Johari Window and explain how students are to create their own.
  1. Tell them to work in groups of four.
  2. Explain that each student will get a manila folder and is to write his or her name on the folder tab.
  3. Say that you will provide each group with several magazines — both Spanish and English, if possible, and a glue stick.
  4. Tell students they will need to refer to the lists they previously prepared to make the first three of four collages their Johari Window will have: one on the front cover, one on the inside of the front cover, one on the inside of the back cover and one on the back cover.
  5. On the front cover of their manila folder they will have to make a collage of what they believe is common knowledge to many people about themselves.
  6. Tell students that on the inside of the front cover, their group members will make a collage of how they see the individual. (Students are not always aware of how others perceive them). Explain that belittling is not allowed!
  7. Tell students that on the inside of the back cover, they will make a collage of what no one or only very few people know about them.
  8. Finally tell them that on the back cover, they are to make a collage of what they hope for themselves for the future.

9. Tell students that when the collages have been completed, they will be asked to fold a sheet of paper in half, like a miniature manila folder, and on the corresponding faces, write a brief explanation of what everything in each collage represents. The group members who contributed to the inside front cover are to explain what everything in that collage represents.

10. Inform students that they will have to make one to two minute presentations of their Johari Windows to the class.

11. Explain that the completed Johari Windows will be graded.

15 min.	Begin working on personal Johari Window.
Homework	Locate or draw pictures for your collages and those of others.

Day 5

Goal	The whole period will be devoted to continue working and completing the Johari Windows.
Homework	Finish Johari Window and be prepared to turn it in at the beginning of next class.

Day 6

Goal	To share and grade the Johari Windows.
Procedure	Grading

50 min.
- Emphasize that students must show respect while others are presenting.
- Allow twenty minutes for students to share their Johari Windows with two or three classmates. Encourage students to question each other concerning any illustrations they don't understand in their group members' Johari Windows.
- Divide the class in groups of four. Have each group grade three or four Johari Windows belonging to students that are not part of the group.
- Remind students that honesty and fairness are highly valued characteristics that all should strive to develop.

Homework	None.

Day 7

Goal	To explore how race or 'being different' influences self-esteem.
Procedure	Prejudice and stereotypes

5 min.
Color associations
- As the teacher says each of the following colors, the students must write down anything they associate with each color.

Colors:

red   white   brown   black
green   yellow   blue   gray
         orange   purple

- Call on students to tell what they associated with each color and ask if others made the same associations.

30 min.   *Rainbow Wars* produced by Pyramid (1985)
- Show the video.
- Discuss the plot and theme with the class.

Homework   Journal entry: Explain what prejudice is, where it comes from, how it damages self-esteem, and how you can overcome and help combat it.

Day 8

Goal   Students explore how integrity influences self-esteem.

Procedure   'El Mecánico' (The Mechanic) by Berlin and Ottman (1991a)

10 min.   Journal entry:
- Write on board: '*Prefiero fallecer con honor a ganar por decepción*' (I prefer to die with honor than to win by deception.) (Sophocles).
- In their journals, have students explain the meaning of this quotation and mention an incident to illustrate it.

15 min.   Review vocabulary

25 min.   Recording of '*El Mecánico*' (Berlin and Ottman, 1991a)
- Listen to recording, stopping tape at the end of each page for one minute, during which students write brief summaries of what they heard.
- Working in pairs, have students discuss the plot and jot down a list of the characteristics of the two characters.
- Have two volunteers write all the characteristics on butcher paper as the class tells them what to write. Tell students to copy the butcher paper lists.
- Discuss the message of the story and how the quotation, the journal entry and the story are interrelated.

Homework   Journal entry: Write a summary of the class discussion on the message of the story and how the quote, the journal entry and the story are interrelated.

Day 9

Goal   To explore how love and giving affect self-esteem.

Procedure   *The Giving Tree* (Spanish version) (Videocassette) Westport, CT, Weston Woods (1989).

40 min.
- Show the video.
- In groups of three, ask students to discuss the movie and name each stage represented, describe them, and decide how they could be represented through pantomime with sound effects.
- Ask several groups to act out different stages.
- Discuss with the class the significance of the tree, the meaning of unconditional love, for whom do we have unconditional love, who loves them that way, and how unconditional is their love.

Homework
Journal entry: Expand on class discussion on the meaning of the tree and of unconditional love. Tell who you love unconditionally and who loves you that way. Explain how unconditional your/their love is.

Days 10–13

Goal
To explore the influence of desire, diligence and perseverance on self-esteem.

Procedure
Soy lo que creo que soy (I am what I Believe I am) (Berlin and Ottman, 1990a)

10 min.
- Show only the title of the transparency and discuss its meaning.
- Show one half of face, then quickly, the other half. Ask class to react.
- Discuss the effect of positive and negative thinking with the class.

110 min.
Stand and Deliver/*Con Ganas de Triunfar* (World Video, 1988)
- View one-third of movie over each of three days, allowing enough time for students to have an in-depth class discussion on the relevance of what they viewed each day. On the last day discuss the relevance of this movie to the various aspects of self-esteem discussed in class thus far. Questions that you may want to ask include:
  1. What did Jaime Escalante do to make the students work that was different from what other teachers did?
  2. What were some of the obstacles that the students faced in doing their homework and getting to class?
  3. What was Escalante's impression the first day of school?
  4. Why did Ángel stay in the class?
  5. Justify Ana's father's decision to pull her out of school;
  6. Why did Escalante want to teach Advanced Placement Calculus?
  7. Why did the head of the math department oppose him?
  8. Why did Escalante teach high school?
  9. Compare and contrast Angel and Finger Man.
  10. Why did the testing service assume the students had cheated?
  11. Why did Escalante make the students retake the test?
  12. What motivated the students to work so hard?
  13. In what ways did the students benefit by taking the AP Calculus class and the AP Exam?

Homework   None.

Day 14
Goal   To do an analysis of the students' own self-confidence.

Procedure   Self-esteem Evaluation Survey

20 min.
- Review vocabulary for survey.
- Ask students to complete the survey individually.
- Allow students to comment on the results of the survey and discuss with the class.

15 min.   *Soy Responsable* (I am Responsible) (Berlin and Ottman, 1990b)
- Call on volunteers to read out loud from handout.
- Discuss with class for understanding.

8 min.   'The Serenity Prayer' (Niebuhr, 1980).
- Have students copy the poem from the transparency.
- Ask students to make a list of the things in their life that they can change and of the ones that they cannot change.

Homework   Journal entry: Choose one item from previously prepared list of things in students' lives that they can change and write a paragraph explaining why they want to change it and how they would go about changing it.

Day 15
Goal   To demonstrate students' understanding of the self-esteem unit by composing a letter using process writing.

Procedure   Letter

15 min.
- Give instruction for the advice letters students are to write.
  1. Explain that they will be writing an advice letter about self-esteem, incorporating what they have learned throughout this unit;
  2. Review the different components covered in the self-esteem unit on the board;
  3. Explain the grading rubric using the transparency.
- Have students select to write a letter of advice to one of the following:
  1. a friend;
  2. their parents;
  3. a child;
  4. to Ann Landers and a response from her;
  5. the editor of the school or local newspaper;
  6. to themselves.
- Have students begin by brainstorming, listing all ideas that come to their head related to the type of letter they decide to write. If necessary, do a model brainstorming session with the entire class.

- Tell students to use their brainstorming list to write their first draft. Suggest they may want to reorganize their lists into clusters of related topics and that each cluster may constitute a paragraph in their letters.
- Have students write a first draft of the letter.

Homework   Finish the first draft of letter of advice.

Day 16
Goal   To edit each other's first drafts.

Procedure   Peer Editing

50 min
- Have students work in groups of three.
- Tell each person in group to read their partner's letters and comment on the content: Is it clear? Is there enough information? too much? too little?, etc.
- Then have each group read the letters a second time, this time focusing on structure and spelling errors. (You may want to have class focus on specific types of errors, like accentuation and preterite tense errors.) Ask students to point out any errors they find.
- After letters have been returned to their owners, have them begin writing their final draft, incorporating any suggestions and making any corrections that were pointed out by their peers.

Homework   Finish writing final draft of advice letters.

Day 17
Goal   To have peers grade the advice letters and turn them in.

Procedure   Peer Grading

50 min.
- Have students work in groups of three.
- Give one copy of grading rubric and one letter to each group. (Make sure the letter does not belong to anyone in the group.)
- Have students in each group read the letter and come to an agreement on scoring.
- Repeat process with two more letters. Each group must grade as many letters as there are people in their group.

Homework   None.

Days 18–19 (*optional*)

Goal   Students produce a video of positive statements about themselves.

Materials: • Video camera and blank cassette

Procedure

100 min.
- Have students prepare a fifteen to thirty second positive statement about themselves. Tell them they may use any of the following models or to create their own: *Me llamo . . . y me siento muy orgulloso(a) porque . . .* (My name is . . . and I feel very proud because . . .) *Soy . . . y soy muy interesante porque . . .* (I am . . . and I am very interesting because . . .) *Soy muy bueno(a) con . . .* (I am very good with . . .) *Estoy muy orgulloso(a) de . . .* (I am very proud of . . .)
- Allow students to work individually or in small groups. Do not begin videotaping until all have finished writing and are able to listen as each student is taped.
- After video is completed, all view it together.

Homework   None.

An 18-day Module on Creating a Self-portrait

Prepared by:
Catherine Burton, *Tomales High School, Tomales, California*
Arlene L. Keefe, *Ukiah High School, Ukiah, California*

Unit Goal   To develop a greater self awareness of students' bilingual Chicano/Latino heritage background by fully understanding and then creating their own *autorretrato* (self-portrait).

Day 1
Goal

To introduce the reading *Cajas de Cartón* (Cardboard Boxes), a short story by Francisco Jiménez (1984), and to get students to generate a vocabulary list for the first part of the reading.

Procedure   Anticipatory set

15 min.   Brainstorming
- Point to empty cardboard boxes in front of the classroom and ask students: *¿Qué son? ¿Qué representan? ¿Para qué son?* (What are they? What do they represent? What are they for?) List ideas on the board as students make suggestions. (There are no correct answers in this brainstorming activity.)

10 min.   Predicting
- Tell students they are going to read a short story named *Cajas de Cartón*, and ask them to write two or three sentences saying what they think this story is going to be about.

30 min.   Reading and generating a personalized vocabulary list.
- Have students read first part of *Cajas de Cartón* silently.
- As they read, tell them to make a list of at least ten new vocabulary

237

words that they do not know. Then have them look up the meaning of those words and write their definitions on a sheet of paper to be kept in their folders.

Homework   Ask students to write ten original sentences using the words in their personalized vocabulary list.

Day 2

Goal   To discuss *Cajas de Cartón, primera parte* (first part) and to describe individual characters.

Procedure   *Cajas de Cartón, primera parte*

20 min.   Review part one of story
                • Have students, working in pairs, read the story aloud to each other.
                • Tell students to look for answers to the discussion questions on board as they read.

20 min.   Comprehension check
                • Re-read story with whole class, by calling on individuals to read aloud one at a time. Ask lots of comprehension check questions after each student reads.

10 min.   Mapping
                • Map answers to discussion questions on board.
                • Explain mapping process to class as you do it on the board, a transparency or on butcher paper.

Homework   Collect previous day's homework. Give students ten comprehension check questions over the first part of the story to answer in writing.

Day 3

Goal   To work with new vocabulary in *Cajas de Cartón*.

Procedure   Vocabulary

10 min.   Anticipatory set
                • Write *-ito*, *-ita* (diminutive endings in Spanish that often imply endearment) on chalk board and ask students to scan the reading and prepare a list of all words with these endings.
                • Ask several students to read their lists. Then ask class why they think these endings are used. What do they mean?

40 min.   New vocabulary
                • Distribute vocabulary list.
                • In groups of three, have students define any words on the list that they already know.

- Individually, have students look up words they do not know and write definitions.

Homework   Collect previous day's homework. Have students do a vocabulary worksheet, focused on the new vocabulary they just defined.

Day 4

Goal   To help students become proficient with new vocabulary and to help them prepare to write about themselves.

Procedure   Writing about Self.

20 min.   Vocabulary review practice test
- Dictate ten words from the new vocabulary list and ask students to write each word and its definition.
- Have students exchange papers. Show vocabulary answer-key transparency so they may correct each others' work.
- Tell students to use their practice test papers to study for the next day's test.

15 min.   Focus on family
- Read aloud the last paragraph of the story as students listen.
- Discuss the family unit with class: number of people in family, birth order, etc.
- Have students draw their own family, indicating birth order. (Keep drawings in student folders and grade at end of unit as extra-credit homework or test points).
- Take a survey (raised hands) of where class members fit in the following categories: only child, first child, middle child, baby of family, only girl, only boy, twins. Have a student write results of survey on board as it is taken.

15 min.   Focus on birth order
- Using student's drawing, student volunteer points out advantages and disadvantages of his or her birth order. Encourage class to agree or disagree.

Homework   Study for vocabulary test.

Day 5

Goal   To evaluate vocabulary acquisition and to have students think and write about themselves.

Procedure   Advantages and disadvantages of birth order.

50 min.   Vocabulary test
- Give a vocabulary test similar to the vocabulary worksheet students did as homework.
- Review what was said yesterday about birth order. Finish discussion if not completed day before.

- Divide class in groups of three or four according to birth order. Give each group some butcher paper and ask group members to alternate writing advantages and disadvantages of being in that birth order.
- Have each group report orally to class.

Homework   Essay: *Por qué me gusta (o no me gusta) ser el* _____ *hijo (la hija) de mi familia.* (Why I like (or dislike) being the _____ son (daughter) in the family.)

Day 6

Goal   To introduce the second part of *Cajas de Cartón.*

Procedure

10 min.   Brainstorming
- Tell students that they will have to write in their journals about *El trabajo más duro que he tenido que hacer.* (The most difficult work I have had to do.) Then have students share ideas about the topic.

15 min.   Journal entry
- Allow students to write on the topic *El trabajo más duro que he tenido que hacer.*

25 min.   Personalized vocabulary lists
- Hand out the second part of *Cajas de Cartón,* and ask students to read it silently.
- Then ask students to prepare a list of at least ten new vocabulary words from this reading and their definitions.

Homework   Ask students to write ten original sentences using the words in their personalized vocabulary list.

Day 7

Goal   To discuss the central theme of *Cajas de Cartón.*

Procedure   Autobiography

25 min.   Mapping
- Read aloud the *La Genesis de 'Cajas de Cartón'* (Jimenez, 1986), comments on autobiographical nature of *Cajas de Cartón.*
- Ask students if they knew story was biographical. As they give their responses, map ideas about biographical information on board. Tell students to copy mapping ideas and keep them in their folders.

15 min.   Reading aloud
- Call on students to read the story aloud, one paragraph at a time. Ask comprehension check questions.

10 min.	Definition

- Show transparency with definition of 'theme' and ask student to copy: *El tema es la idea central de una obra o de un cuento. Es el mensaje que quiere comunicar el autor.* (The theme is the central idea of a work or of a short story. It is the message that the author wants to communicate.)
- If time allows, have class identify the main theme of *Cajas de Cartón*.

Homework	Ask student to write a paragraph identifying the theme of *Cajas de Cartón*. Insist that they give examples to support their ideas.

Day 8

Goal To define new vocabulary and to discuss theme of *Cajas de Cartón*.

Procedure Theme and vocabulary

10 min.	Review of theme

- Call on individuals to share what they had written on the theme of *Cajas de Cartón* in their homework.
- As students speak, map their ideas on a transparency.

40 min.	New vocabulary

- Write a list of active vocabulary on chalk board and tell students to copy it and keep it in their folders.
- Working in groups of three, tell students to write a definition for each word. Encourage students to write their own definitions for words they already know and to use the dictionary on new words.

Homework	Hand out worksheets and ask students to complete them for the next day.

Day 9

Goal To help students become proficient with new vocabulary and to introduce ideas on self-description.

Procedure Vocabulary and definition of 'self-depiction'

15 min.	Vocabulary practice test

- Dictate ten words from new vocabulary list. Tell students to write each word and its definition.
- Have students exchange papers and correct them as you show transparency with correct answers.
- Tell students to study from their practice test for tomorrow's test.

25 min.	*Autorretrato* from the prologue of the *Novelas Ejemplares* (Exemplary Stories) by Cervantes Saavedra, (1967)

- Write three new words from *Autorretrato* on board and ask if anyone can define them. If not, ask students to make some educated guesses.
- Hand out copies of *Autorretrato* and ask students to read it silently. Ask them to find the three words and guess at their meaning from the context.
- Read *Autorretrato* aloud to the class and ask comprehension check questions as you read. Focus on new vocabulary.
- Discuss 'self-depiction' with class — What is it? How does the author express it? What does he tell us about himself?
- As students respond, write their answers on the board or transparency in three categories: *características físicas, eventos importantes, y lo que ha hecho.* (physical characteristics; important events; and what he has done)

Homework   Ask students to count off 1, 2, 3, 1, 2, 3, 1, etc. Tell all the ones to write a self-descriptive paragraph on *características físicas*, the twos on *eventos importantes en mi vida* (important events in my life) and the threes on *lo que he hecho yo* (what I have done).

Day 10

Goal   To evaluate vocabulary acquisition and to create a sample self-portrait

Procedure

20 min.   Vocabulary test
- Give a vocabulary test similar to the new vocabulary handout students did for homework.

30 min.   Group *autorretrato*
- Have students work in groups of three. Each group should have a 1, a 2 and a 3 from previous day's homework assignment.
- Then the number 1 student reads his or her paragraph while the other two students together draw a picture from what is being communicated. The process is repeated as the number 2 student and the number 3 student take turns at reading their paragraphs while the others draw. After all have taken their turns at reading and drawing, a new, complete *autorretrato* will have been created.
- Hang the finished *autorretratos* around the class.

Homework   Journal entry: Write your thoughts about what you learned in class today.

Day 11

Goal   To practice interviewing techniques
Procedure   Interviewing

10 min.   *Encuesta firmada* (A signed interview) (Burton and Keefe, 1991)
- Have students do *Encuesta firmada*, a search activity whereby they have to find someone in the class who: *tiene más de 15 años, tiene*

su licencia de conducir, lleva dos anillos, (is more than 15 years old, has a driver's license, wears two rings) etc.
- Every time they find a classmate that fits a description, they get him or her to sign in the appropriate box. The same person's name may not appear more than once in the *Encuesta firmada.*
- When each activity has a signature, verify the signatures by calling on the individuals that signed and ask if they do the activity.
- Ask the rest of the class to indicate by raising their hand, *¿Cuántos consiguieron más de 5 firmas? ¿más de 8? ¿10?* (How many have more than 5 signatures? more than 8? 10?, etc.)

40 min.   Interviews
- Tell students to pair themselves off by birth order similarities they identified on Day 4.
- Give each student a copy of the interview questions and tell them to interview each other using the same questions.
- Tell them to take notes on their partner's responses as they will need them to do the day's homework.

Homework   Write a description of the person interviewed.

Days 12–13
Goal   To expose students to self-expression by various artists including *Frida Kahlo*

Procedure   Self-expression

15 min.   Anticipatory set
- Show pictures of self portraits of several Hispanic artists: Dali, Picasso, Kahlo, Rivera, etc., and have the class discuss what each artist tells about him or herself.

60 min.   Video: *Frida Kahlo* (PBS, 1988)
- Show sixty-minute PBS video on the life of the Mexican artist Frida Kahlo over two days.
- Discuss with class during last ten minutes of first day.
- When students have seen all of video on second day, have class discuss their impressions. Ask what they liked most, least, what they learned about self-reflection, etc.

Homework   None.

Day 14
Goal   To review information learned about Frida Kahlo.

Procedure   Frida Kahlo

10 min.   Anticipatory set
- Working in pairs, ask students to come up with a one or two sentence statement answering the question *¿Quién era Frida Kahlo?*

(Who was Frida Kahlo?) Tell them to base their response on the self-portrait and the video they saw.

40 min.   *'¿Por qué se pintaba Frida Kahlo?'*
- Call on students to read aloud *'¿Por qué se pintaba Frida Kahlo?'* (Why would Frida Kahlo do paintings of herself?) (Zamora, 1989). Ask comprehension check questions after each student reads.
- Have class reconsider their answer to the question *¿Quién era Frida Kahlo?* Ask them to discuss how they would respond to the question now.
- Have a general discussion on Frida the artist: *¿Tuvo una vida fácil? ¿Es su arte representativo de su vida? ¿Fue difícil ser la esposa de otro artista famoso?* (Did she have an easy life? Is her art representative of her life? Was it difficult to be the wife of another famous artist?) etc.

Homework   Journal entry: Have students write a paragraph or two on the topic *Yo puedo /no puedo identificar con la vida de Frida Kahlo porque . . .* (I can/cannot identify with the life of Frida Kahlo because . . .)

Days 15–17
Goal   To create students' own self-portraits in books titled *¿Quién soy yo?* (Who am I?) *Mi autorretrato.*

Procedure Self-portrait

3 days   Instructions
- Each student will create his or her own *autorretrato* book.
- Each book will be illustrated with photos, cut-outs from magazines, and drawings as well as have written narrative.
- Each book will consist of no less that twenty pages which will address the following topics:
  descripción física (physical description)
  cosas que te gustan (things that you like)
  tu familia (your family)
  lo que has hecho (what you have done)
  eventos importantes (important events)
  dónde vives y dónde has vivido (where do you live and where have you lived)
  tu trabajo (your work)
  tradiciones (traditions)
  planes para el futuro (future plans)
- Each page is to have an illustration, which may consist of photos, drawings, or cut-outs from magazines, and a written explanation of the graphics. The amount of writing per page will vary depending on the illustrations.
- Students may consult with each other, but each student must do his or her own book.
- Books will be due at the end of three school days.

Homework   Collect necessary illustrations and continue to work on *autorretrato* books.

Day 18

Goal   To celebrate the completion of the *autorretratos* with an author's party.

Procedure

10 min.   Set up for party and socialize
- Set up food and drinks.
- Eat and enjoy.

40 min.   Sharing of masterworks
- Ask each student to describe to class his or her favorite page in *autorretrato* book.
- Allow some time for students to share their books with anyone they wish to. Do not insist that everyone has to share, in case some have included very personal information in their books.

Homework   None.

Modules for Novice Level NSS Courses

Following is the module prepared by the group focused on the first-year level language courses for students studying Spanish as a second language together with NSS, and the module on writing for a specific audience. The first-year unit is a seventeen-day module designed to get students to understand and appreciate their own Mexican heritage by studying a state of Mexico of their own choosing. This version is highly abbreviated, as it just outlines the goals and procedures and does not include materials needed each day, homework nor daily assessment. The writing module is an extended writing process activity where an audience with a specific need is identified in the community and students write to meet the specific needs of that audience.

A Twelve-lesson Module on Mexico

Prepared by:
Evelyn Castaneda, *St. Francis High School, Sacramento, CA*
Antonio Maldonado Losada, *Bishop Manogue High School, Sacramento, CA*

Unit Goal   To develop a true appreciation of the students' Mexican heritage by doing an in-depth study of the geography, history and culture of Mexico.

Lesson 1

Goal   To probe students' prior knowledge about Mexico and create initial interest in its geography, history and culture by showing the video *!Esplendores!/Splendors of* Mexico (1992).

Lesson 2

Goal   To learn the names and location of at least fifteen Mexican states by having students study the map of Mexico for two minutes, then writing as many states and capitals as they recall on a blank map, and finally, comparing their partially filled maps with first one, then two more classmates and sharing information with them.

Lesson 3

Goal   To gain a deeper understanding of a particular Mexican state of the student's own choosing by randomly distributing the cut-out states of Mexico, one per student, and having students write the name of their state, its capital, bordering states, and any other information they may know about the state. Students are told to work on the state they are holding in their hand, unless some have special reasons for wanting to work on another state.

Lesson 4

Goal   To learn the names, location and important features of ten more Mexican states by taping sheets of paper with the names of the seven locations bordering Mexico in their proper location on classroom walls, assuming the front of class is north, and telling students to write the name of a new state (a new cutout state of Mexico per student), its capital and bordering states, and any other information they may know about the state. If they have difficulty identifying their state, tell them to hold it up to the map on the wall and identify it by shape. Finally students are asked to create a human map of Mexico by standing next to the persons representing their neighboring states.

Lesson 5

Goal   To introduce students to information resources and to make them aware of principle historical periods in Mexican history by giving students a handout with a visual overview of major periods of Mexican history, and generating a class discussion (with teacher playing a major role) about Mexico's history. NSS students should be encouraged to add to the discussion anything they may know about Mexico's history. Finally, the teacher accompanies students to the library and helps them begin to research their assigned states for an oral presentation and written paper they will be doing.

Lesson 6

Goal   To assess the effectiveness of the research completed to this point and to develop personal strategies to find the required information by having students complete a questionaire designed to have students list all research information thus far accumulated, then working in groups, comparing the usefulness of sources used thus far.

Lesson 7

Goal To create interest in and appreciation for different forms of art found in Mexico and to learn to classify them by generating a list of different forms of art they have discovered in their research, then asking them to classify their lists using a handout designed to focus on *ártes visuales, plásticas, dramátá, música y literatura*. (Visual arts, plastic arts, theatre, music and literature)

Lesson 8

Goal To introduce students to a variety of music and dances of Mexico and to the use of masks as a Mexican art form by showing the video: *Folkloric Dances of Mexico* (1990) and a series of teacher-prepared transparencies of the dancers' costumes. Students also read *Las Máscaras de México* (Castañeda, E. and Losada, R. 1991) (*The Masks of Mexico*) and discuss the use of masks in some of the dances viewed.

Lesson 9

Goal To understand more about the use, origins and symbolism of masks in Mexican folk art and to create a personal mask by first discussing the meaning of the Latin word '*persona*', and relating it to *máscara*, then seeing samples of various Mexican masks and discussing their symbolism. Finally students are asked to design and make their own masks using a basic pattern for mask making developed by The Mexican Museum in San Francisco (see Chapter 11).

Lesson 10

Goal To have each student give an oral presentation on the Mexican state selected and to have the rest of the class analyze each oral report in writing.

Lesson 11

Goal To test students' overall knowledge of Mexico's geography, history and culture, including information presented in student reports.

Lesson 12

Goal To prepare and perform role plays on a variety of situations in Mexico, including deciding on which package tour to Mexico to buy, teaching a university Mexican culture and civilization course, being transported in a time machine to a specific time in the history of Mexico, etc.

Two Modules on Writing for a Specific Audience

Prepared by:
Arlene L. Keefe, *Ukiah High School, Ukiah, California*
Jesús G. Solís, *Vintage High School, Napa, California*

Unit Goal To write illustrated children's storybooks and/or ABC books to be given to a local elementary or bilingual school for use by children as additional reading practice.

Children's Storybooks

Lesson 1
Goal To have class look at several children's storybooks in Spanish and English to get ideas for their own writing and to analyze the writing style and format usually used.

Lesson 2
Goal To write a first draft of a simple story which follows the style and format of children's books. Students are asked to specify the illustrations that would appear on every page to help readers with comprehension.

Lesson 3
Goal To share first draft with several classmates and get feedback on appropriateness of plot and comprehensiblity and to write second draft incorporating peers' suggestions as necessary.

Lesson 4
Goal To share second draft with peers and get feedback on spelling, punctuation and grammar usage. To prepare third draft incorporating peers' suggestions if appropriate and to turn it in for grading.

Lesson 5
Goal To take graded stories and illustrate every one or two sentences on a single 4" × 5½" or 5½" × 8" page. Illustrations may be the students' own drawings, collages made from magazine cutouts, computer drawings, photos, etc.

Lesson 6
Goal To have an authors' reception where each children's storybook author reads and shows his or her masterpiece to the class before the books are given to a local elementary school.

Children's ABC Books

Lesson 1

Goal To have class look at several children's ABC books in Spanish and English to get ideas for their own writing and to analyze the writing style and format used.

Lesson 2

Goal   To find a word beginning with each letter of the Spanish alphabet and to share word lists in small groups, checking meaning and spelling, of each word.

Lesson 3

Goal   To write a sentence using each word in a way that makes its meaning clear and to share sentences in small groups to check for comprehension, spelling, punctuation and grammar.

Lesson 4

Goal   To prepare a second draft of the list of sentences, incorporating all suggestions, if appropriate and to turn it in for grading.

Lesson 5

Goal   To take graded list of sentences and write one sentence per page on $4" \times 5\frac{1}{2}"$ or $5\frac{1}{2}" \times 8"$ sheets of paper. The key word in each sentence is illustrated on the page the sentence appears.

Lesson 6

Goal   To have an authors' reception where students share their ABC books in groups of four or five before the books are given to a local elementary school.

Summary and Conclusions

A number of in-service teacher training programs have been developed across the country, based on the premise that expert teacher knowledge already exists among our teachers in the field and needs only to be tapped and nourished a little in order for it to open up and reach students in many new creative ways. The National Writing Project and the California Subject Matter Projects (SB 1882, 1988) in Literature, Writing, Science, Mathematics, Art, Social Studies, and Foreign Languages are but two examples of these highly successful programs. The *Español para Triunfar* four-week summer institute together with the *Curriculum Development Seminars* were organized with the same premise in mind and the curriculum modules which resulted and which have been described here fully attest to its success.

To develop curriculum for NSS, this program began by identifying expert foreign language teachers interested in working with NSS and, in a four-week summer institute, provided them with a program that greatly expanded their knowledge base. Throughout the institute and especially in the follow-up seminars, the expert teachers were provided ample opportunities to collaborate with each other on the prototype modules they were developing. This collaboration, together with the ample guidance and a place for planning allowed each teacher participant to share the creative process, strengthening in turn, the work of each individual.

We believe that this program suggests a model for curriculum development that provides teachers to have release time for writing, as D'Ambruoso (see Chapter 14) indicated is essential, but also adequate time and a place for planning and collaboration with other teachers and a means of strengthening and updating the teacher's knowledge of the most current developments in the subject area. Such a model already exists and is being implemented with high degrees of success in the previously mentioned projects: The National Writing Project and the California Subject Matter Projects (SB 1882, 1988). A wealth of expert foreign-language knowledge is waiting to be tapped by teachers as they develop a superior curriculum.

Appendix A

List of *Español para Triunfar* 1989 Summer Institute Fellows

Rubén Ayala	Lincoln High School Lincoln, CA
Wendy Baskette	Tokay High School Lodi, CA
Bridget Berlin[1]	Galt Joint Union High School Galt, CA
Catherine Balestrieri Burton[1]	Tomales High School Tomales, CA
Evelyn Vargas Castaneda[1]	St. Francis High School Sacramento, CA
Sharon Crane	Ukiah High School Ukiah, CA
Mike Croghan	Ukiah High School Ukiah, CA
Catherine Fox-Anderson	Las Plumas High School Oroville, CA
Cecilla García	St. Francis High School Sacramento, CA
George Griffin	Linden High School Linden, CA
Cheryl Ingham	Hiram Johnson High School Sacramento, CA
Arlene L. Keefe[1]	Ukiah High School Ukiah, CA
Antonio Maldonado Losada[1]	Bishop Manogue High School Sacramento, CA

Karen Olberg	Kelseyville High School
	Kelseyville, CA
Deborah Ottman[1]	Corning Union High School
	Corning, CA
Ramon Muñoz	Migrant Education
	Chico, CA
Barbara Lynn Rolen	Williams High School
	Williams, CA
Jesus G. Solís[1]	Vintage High School
	Napa, CA
Lupe Vásquez	Migrant Education
	Fresno, CA
Regina Virgen	Davis Adult School
	Davis, CA

Note

1 Collaborated with Samaniego and Merino writing Chapter 16.

Appendix B

The following are Forms A and B of the Attitude Scale on Acceptability of Dialect Variants. Both forms are designed to rate the degree of acceptability of twenty Spanish sentences each illustrating a particular use of Chicano dialect. The degree of acceptability of each sentence is judged from two distinct points of view: in column A from the point of view of a community of speakers of 'standard' Spanish, in column B from the point of view of the Chicano community. Those doing the rating are asked to react to each statement as if heard being used by an employee of the telephone company in column A and as if heard in informal speech in a Chicano/Latino barrio in column B. The scale used is (5) = very acceptable, (4) = acceptable, (3) = neutral, (2) = little acceptance, (1) = not acceptable.

FORM A

ESCALA DE ACTITUD HACIA LOS VARIANTES DIALECTALES:
La lista que sigue incluye varios variantes. Reaccionen a cada variante. Marcando el grado de aceptabilidad que le daría un miembro de la comunidad de hablantes del español estandard: (en la caja A) y luego lo que le daría un miembro de la comunidad de hablantes Chicanos, (en a caja B). Para la comunidad estandard imagínense de lo que se aceptaría de un empleado bilingüe de la oficina de teléfonos. Para la comunidad Chicana imagínense de lo que se aceptaría en el habla informal en un barrio Chicano/Latino. Marquen según (5) = muy aceptable; (4) = aceptable; (3) = neutro; (2) = poco aceptable; (1) = no aceptable.

	A	B
1. Te duele el estómago por *lo* que *comistes* mucho.	☐	☐
2. Necesito un *daime* para hacer una llamada.	☐	☐
3. La *chota* le pidió sus documentos.	☐	☐
4. Si no *tenía* miedo, diría la verdad.	☐	☐
5. Por ser *gabacho* habla bien el español.	☐	☐
6. Le voy a pedir *raite* a Guillermo.	☐	☐
7. Los muchachos *dijieron* que no iban a venir.	☐	☐
8. Los trabajadores *dumpearon* arena en la calle.	☐	☐
9. Mira como me mojaste *los pieses*.	☐	☐
10. A mí no me gusta comer *ajuera*.	☐	☐
11. *Vayansen* para afuera, no estén dando lata.	☐	☐
12. Yo comí mucho, y me duele el *estógamo*.	☐	☐
13. Ese año, ya no pude *siguir trabajando*.	☐	☐
14. Los niños no sabían *'onde* esconderse.	☐	☐
15. Siempre se portan *asina* cuando no está su mamá.	☐	☐
16. De mi casa, no *truje* nada.	☐	☐
17. Ahí *'tá*, encima de la mesa.	☐	☐
18. Siempre come *muncho*, por eso está tan gordo.	☐	☐
19. Desgraciadamente la lámpara está *rompida*.	☐	☐
20. El pobre, se golpeó contra la *pader*.	☐	☐

FORM B

ESCALA DE ACTITUD HACIA LOS VARIANTES DIALECTALES:

La lista que sigue incluye varios variantes. Reaccionen a cada variante. Marcando el grado de aceptabilidad que le daría un miembro de la comunidad de hablantes del español estandard: (en la caja A) y luego lo que le daría un miembro de la comunidad de hablantes Chicanos, (en a caja B). Para la comunidad estandard imagínense de lo que se aceptaría de un empleado bilingüe de la oficina de teléfonos. Para la comunidad Chicana imagínense de lo que se aceptaría en el habla informal en un barrio Chicano/Latino. Marquen según (5) = muy aceptable; (4) = aceptable; (3) = neutro; (2) = poco aceptable; (1) = no aceptable.

	A	B
1. Bueno, y tú ¿adónde *fuistes*.?	☐	☐
2. ¿Puedes ir a la *marqueta* a comprarme leche y pan?	☐	☐
3. Ese *bato* siempre anda en moto.	☐	☐
4. Si *tenía* dinero, me iría ahora mismo.	☐	☐
5. Oye Juan, dáme un *frajo*, por favor.	☐	☐
6. Lo que quiero es un *mapeador* nuevo.	☐	☐
7. Los muchachos *dijieron* que no iban a venir.	☐	☐
8. Estos *sofases* están muy caros.	☐	☐
9. La *carpeta* quedó bien limpia.	☐	☐
10. Nos *juimos* a la casa temprano.	☐	☐
11. *Duermansen* por favor que ya es tarde.	☐	☐
12. Yo comí mucho, y me duele el *estógamo*.	☐	☐
13. Yo *nesito* más dinero.	☐	☐
14. ¿Y a *onde* vas tú?	☐	☐
15. Los domingos siempre se visten *asina*.	☐	☐
16. Es la *mesma* casa de antes.	☐	☐
17. La *botea* de vino se rompió.	☐	☐
18. Por aquí no hay *nadien*.	☐	☐
19. Me voy *pa* Mexico.	☐	☐
20. Nunca ha *resolvido* como vivir con menos dinero.	☐	☐

Appendix C

CASE STUDY

You are assigned a Spanish II class which consists of five native English speakers learning Spanish as a foreign language, five non-standard speakers of Spanish who are very fluent but who use grammatical, lexical and phonological variants of non-standard Spanish and five NSS of a standard variety who have been in the US since the age of six and who are unable to write Spanish or speak it very fluently.

Discuss how you would proceed in setting up an instructional program for a six month syllabus. Broadly outline methods you would use to address the students' unique needs as well as ways of integrating them. Describe your error correction strategies, the use of standard and non-standard variants in the class and any other issues you consider important.

References

ACTFL Proficiency Guidelines (1986) Yonkers, NY, American Council on Teaching of Foreign Languages.

Autorretrato (1967) Prologue to DE CERVANTES SAAVEDRAS, M. *Novelas Ejemplares*, in DEL RIO, A. and DEL RIO, A. *Antologia General de la Literatura Espanola, Tomo 1*, Ft. Worth, TX, Holt, Rinehart & Winston, Inc., p. 410.

BERLIN, B. and OTTMAN, D. (1990a) *Soy lo que Creo que Soy*, unpublished transparency.

BERLIN, B. and OTTMAN, D. (1990b) *Soy Responsable*, unpublished handout.

BERLIN, B. and OTTMAN, D. (1991a) *El Mecánico* (Audio cassette), Davis, CA, University of California, Davis, (available from the authors).

BERLIN, B. and OTTMAN, D. (1991b) *Narcizo*, unpublished manuscript, Davis, CA, University of California, Davis.

BURTON, C. and KEEFE, A. (1991) *Encuesta Firmada*, unpublished handout.

CARRILLO HOCKER, B. (1989) *Folk Art as a Curriculum Tool in the Classroom*, (Video cassette), Davis, CA, University of California, Davis, Media Center, No. 927936–38, (120 minutes).

CASTANEDA, E. and LOSADA, R. (1991) *Las Máscaras de México*, unpublished manuscript, Davis, CA, University of California, Davis.

COLÓN, W. and BLADES, R. (1978) *Plástico* (Audiotape) *Siembra*, New York, NY, Elektra Records, No. 4XT-JM-00537.

DOUGLAS, D. and MORENO, R. (1986) 'Estudio de Habilidades', in *Mi carrera*, Santa Clara, CA, Santa Clara County Office of Education.

!Esplendores! / Splendors of Mexico (1992) (Video cassette), Princeton, NJ, Films for the Humanities and Sciences.

The Giving Tree (1989) (Video cassette of SILVERSTEIN, S. *The Giving Tree*), Spanish version, Westport, CT, Weston Woods, (10 minutes).

FALTIS, C. and DEVILLAR, R. (1989) *Computers and Teaching Spanish to Spanish Speakers*, (Video cassette), Davis, CA, University of California, Davis, Media Center, No. 927929, (60 minutes).

FISHMAN, J. (1989) *National Linguistic Heterogeneity in International Perspective*, (Video cassette), Davis, CA, University of California, Davis, Media Center, No. 927897-97, (114 minutes).

Folkloric Dances of Mexico (1990) (Video cassette), Huntsville, TX, Educational Video, (114 minutes).

Frida Kahlo (1988) (Video cassette) Knoxville, TN, World Video, 60 minutes.

GONZÁLEZ EDFELT, N. (1989) *An Overview of Computer Assisted Instruction (CAI) / Computer Assisted Language Learning (CALL) for Foreign Language Speakers*, (Video cassette), Davis, CA, University of California, Davis, Media Center, No. 927927-8, (70 minutes).

GORMAN, S. (1989a) *Classroom* (Video cassette), Davis, CA, University of California, Davis, Media Center, No. 927904-05, (90 minutes).

GORMAN, S. (1989b) *Cooperative Learning in the Foreign Language Classroom*, (Video cassette), Davis, CA, University of California, Davis, Media Center, No. 927902-03, (100 minutes).

GORMAN, S. (1989c) *Grading Student Work in a Communication-Based Classroom*, (Video cassette), Davis, CA, University of California, Davis, Media Center, No. 927906, (58 minutes).

HÉRNÁNDEZ-CHÁVEZ, E. (1989) *Language Loss: Implications for Teaching Spanish to Spanish Speakers*, (Video cassette), Davis, CA, University of California, Davis Media Center, No. 927910, (60 minutes).

HIDALGO, M. (1989) *On the Question of Standards vs. Dialect: Hispanic Students*, (Video cassette), Davis, CA, University of California, Davis, Media Center, No. 927910, (60 minutes).

JIMÉNEZ, F. (1986) 'La génesis de "Cajas de cartón" ', in MONTROSS, C.M. and LEVINE, E.L. (Eds) *Vistas de Mundo Hispánico: A Literary Reader*, New York, NY, Scribner Book Company Inc., pp. 174–5.

LUFT, J. (1969) *Of Human Interaction*, Bethesda, MD, National Press Books.

MERINO, B.J. and SAMANIEGO, F.A. (1989) *The Dialect Speaker and Oral Proficiency Assessment*, (Video cassette), Davis, CA, University of California, Davis, Media Center, No. 927900, (60 minutes).

MERINO, B.J. (1989a) *Dialect Variants in the Southwest*, (Video cassette), Davis, CA, University of California, Davis, Media Center, No. 927898, (60 minutes).

MERINO, B.J. (1989b) *Recruiting Spanish-Speaking Students*, (Video cassette), Davis, CA, University of California, Davis, Media Center, No. 927914, (60 minutes).

MYERS, M. (1989) *Classroom Research*, (Video cassette), Davis, CA, University of California, Davis, Media Center, No. 927908-09, (90 minutes).

NIEBUHR, R. (1980) 'The Serenity Prayer', in BARTLETT, J. (Ed) *Bartlett's Familiar Quotations*, (15th Edition), Boston, MA, Little Brown and Co., p. 823.

PASKEICZ, L. (1989) *Developing a Curriculum for NSS*, (Video cassette), Davis, CA, University of California, Davis, Media Center, No. 927911-12, (90 minutes).

PFEIFFER, R. (1983a) 'El mejor pintor', in *Cuentos simpáticos*, Lincolnwood, IL, National Textbook Company, pp. 27–8.

PFEIFFER, R. (1983b) 'En el mismo barco', in *Cuentos simpáticos*, Lincolnwood, IL, National Textbook Company, pp. 40–1.

POLITZER, R. (1989) *A Researcher's Reflection on Bridging Dialect and Second Language Learning: Discussion of Problems and Solutions*, (Video cassette), Davis, CA, University of California, Davis, Media Center, No. 927907, (60 minutes).

Rainbow Wars (1985) (Video cassette), Santa Monica, CA, Pyramid Films, (20 minutes).

SAMANIEGO, F. (1989a) *Teaching for Competency*, (Video cassette), Davis, CA, University of California, Davis, Media Center, NO. 927900, (60 minutes).

SAMANIEGO, F. (1989b) *Testing in a Competency-Based Classroom*, (Video cassette), Davis, CA, University of California, Davis, Media Center, No. 927913, (60 minutes).

Stand and Deliver/Con Ganas de Triunfar (1988) (Video cassette), Knoxville, TN, World Video, (103 minutes).

TIMM, L. (1989) *Code-Switching and Southwest Spanish Speakers*, (Video cassette), Davis, CA, University of California, Davis, Media Center, No. 927899, (60 minutes).

TRUEBA, H.T. (1989) *The Role of Culture in Teaching Spanish to Spanish Speakers*, (Video cassette), Davis, CA, University of California, Davis, Media Center, No. 927909, (60 minutes).

VALDÉS, G. (1989) 'Teaching Spanish to Hispanic bilinguals: A look at oral proficiency testing and the proficiency movement', *Hispania*, **72**, 2, pp. 392–401.
ZAMORA, M. (1989) 'Por qué se pintaba Frida Kahlo', in LEVY-KONESKY, N. DAGGETT, K. and CECSARINI, L. (Eds) *Fronteras*, Ft. Worth, TX, Holt, Rinehart & Winston, pp. 408–12.

Español para Triunfar Fellows II

Catherine Balestrieri Burton teaches Spanish at Tomales High School, Tomales, California and at Santa Rosa Junior College, Santa Rosa, California. She has served as a mentor teacher in her district. She received her B.A. and M.A. in Spanish from San Francisco State University.

Bridget Berlin received her undergraduate degree from CSU Sacramento in Spanish and International Relations. She also studied Spanish literature at the University of Granada for two years. She has taught courses in Spanish for native speakers at El Camino High School in Sacramento and is currently teaching at Galt High School in Galt, California.

Arlene Keefe holds a B.A. degree in Spanish from the University of Santa Clara, Santa Clara, California. She is currently teaching Spanish and Spanish for Native Speakers at Ukiah High School, Ukiah, California, where she also directs the publication of the Spanish student newspaper.

Antonio Losada is a native of Spain who has resided in Sacramento since 1985. He received his B.A. from the University of Madrid and his M.A. from California State University, Sacramento. He has worked as a high school Spanish teacher at Bishop Manogue High School and currently teaches at Christian Brothers High School in Sacramento, California when he works in heterogeneous classes including native speakers and second language speakers of Spanish.

Deborah Ottman has an undergraduate major in English and Spanish, with a minor in Math and credential authorizations in each one of these areas from California State University at Chico. She has taught all three subjects as well as Drama and Spanish for Spanish Speakers at Corning High School in Corning, California where she also served as a mentor teacher. She is currently teaching at Emerson Junior High in Davis, California, where she teaches Spanish to immersion program students.

Jesus Solis was born in Mexico and came to the United States in middle childhood. He received his B.A. in Spanish from California State University, Chico, where he also completed his M.A. in Education. He teaches Spanish at Vintage High School and at Napa College in Napa, California.

Evelyn Vargas Castaneda was born in San Salvador, El Salvador. She has an undergraduate degree in Occupational Therapy from the University of Buenos Aires in Argentina and an M.S. in Special Education from Indiana University, Bloomington. She has been teaching Spanish at St. Francis High School since 1980 in classes that mix native Spanish speakers and second language learners. She served as Director of Espanol para Triunfar.

Part IV

Summary and Conclusion

Chapter 17

The Relevance of Theory on Language and Culture with Pedagogical Practices

Henry T. Trueba

Language is one of the most powerful human resources needed to maintain a sense of self-identity and self-fulfillment. Without a full command of one's own language, ethnic identity, the sharing of fundamental common cultural values and norms, the social context of interpersonal communication that guides interactional understandings and the feeling of belonging within a group are not possible. Furthermore, without language and a strong self-identity, the ability to learn other languages and understand other cultures is impaired. Barth (1969:10–12) indicates that while the substance of the definition of ethnicity is focused on the sharing of biologically self-perpetuating common ancestry and the sharing of common cultural values are important, 'such a formulation prevents us from understanding the phenomenon of ethnic groups and their place in human society and culture' (Barth, *ibid.*).

The roots of ethnicity are simply the sense of a common origin, common beliefs, values and goals, inherent in human society from its beginnings. According to DeVos, all mammalian societies, including humans, are organized in group systems where their rank, dominance and accommodations lead to conflict: 'On the basis of ethnic group definitions of belonging, societies can develop into highly complex formal systems of social inequality not simply of individuals but of groups' (DeVos, 1990:204). The question is why in modern times ethnicity has become the focus of conflict. DeVos feels that:

> Ethnicity is a source of considerable conflict because ethnic groups do not stay put in fixed systems of stratification. Ethnic identity, when it persists in a group, pushes toward a separateness or competitive affirmation that can be used in readjusting systems of accommodative social stratification. Therefore, one must start from a theoretical position that conflict in some form is a normal condition of society. Ethnicity implies a dynamic form of maintained separateness and instability in respect to questions of dominance that can periodically lead to overt social conflict (DeVos, 1990:205).

Ethnic boundaries and social mobility are consequently viewed by anthropologists as both essential elements of social groups and subject to continuous change. In modern societies, especially in industrial Western societies that have highly developed technologies, mobility in terms of migration waves is often a function of economic, political and social forces. It stands to reason that socio-economic, linguistic, religious and cultural differences become mechanisms to determine ethnic boundaries between 'us' and 'them', that is, between members of a given group, and 'the others'. Those forces (economic and political) are also determinant of the intensity of conflict in the cycles of tolerance or intolerance of ethnic differences. Interethnic conflict can rise to a level of misunderstanding and even cruelty that defies reason and common sense.

The very basis of a democracy that protects interethnic peace and fosters respect for each other's ethnic identity is the commitment to respect each other's language and culture, especially in the instructional context. In other words, one of the instruments of control and exploitation is to deny people their language and culture rights, as well as their right to learn effectively. The basic thesis behind this book is precisely that in order to maintain peace and preserve a strong democracy, there has to be a strong commitment to the language and culture rights of ethnic groups and that it is in the best interest of democracies to encourage bilingualism and respect for cultural differences.

The second theoretical contribution of this book is the neutralization of the destructive impact of modern deconstructionism. Behind much of the work presented here is the message that in our times, when skepticism about the unity of humankind is pervasive, when people question the scientific grounds for our biological bond as members of the same human species, and when, based on epistemological grounds we question even our ability to study and understand peoples from other cultural backgrounds, language and culture are instruments by which we can understand other peoples' values and motivations, and the psychodynamics of their behavior.

Deconstructionism (as did Ethnoscience in the 1960s) comes in handy as a means to examine in great detail, through critical analysis, the assumptions (historical and political) behind research, and to question such assumptions. Rather than throwing away all the results from previous research, deconstructionists must correct, if necessary, 1) the empirical record, the evidence on which inferences are grounded, and 2) the interpretation of the gathered data. Social scientists assume that there is an ongoing process of reinterpretation of previous data gathered and analyzed; indeed, they see the research process as a never ending one, consisting of chains of understandings and interpretations which can be modified when new evidence appears.

The goals of cultural anthropologists in the mid-twentieth century were very ambitious. The indictment against genetic or biological determinism of behavior remained strong, and the recognition of the relationship between language, culture and cognition was emphatically established by the ethnographers of communication (Gumperz and Hymes, 1964, 1972; more recently used by Hornberger, 1988a, 1988b) and ethnoscientists such as Frake (1964). The ethnographic methods were clearly enriched by the use of linguistic analysis and the sharpening of procedures for ethnographic interviews (Spradley, 1979). While the following years saw an increasing tendency to recognize the linkages between culture and cognition and the redefinition of culture in terms that cognitive codes were viewed as crucial in determining behavior, according to Spindler (1978:13–15) and other scholars (DeVos and Suárez-Orozco, 1990; Suárez-Orozco, 1993), psychological reductionism began to appear as a dangerous oversimplification of the complex psychodynamics of behavior and achievement motivation. The reaction to these currents in the 1980s and 1990s has gone beyond the 'psychophobia' alluded to by Shweder (1991, as well as in Suárez-Orozco, 1993:2). Indeed, the reaction of more recent anthropologists has been one of despair and rejection of all theoretical frames, and even one of rejection or plain skepticism about scientific research resulting in the accumulation of knowledge over time. As Suárez-Orozco eloquently states:

> The very fundamental anthropological *grande idea* that we can study, understand and explain other cultures is now rejected by many in anthropology. Melford Spiro has noted that many contemporary anthropologists have rejected this vision 'as either arrogant, misguided, or futile, if not all three. Arrogant, because it is an expression of Western, hegemonic, phallocentric, patriarchal discourse; futile, because non-Western cultures and peoples are "Other," opaque in principle to Western investigators, however well-informed, fair-minded, or emphatic they might be' (Spiro, 1992:ix). It follows then, that the idea of comparison, a key tenet in cultural anthropology until very recently, is also suspect among many contemporary anthropologists. Even the 'ethnographic fieldwork approach' that triumphantly defeated the 'armchair anthropology' of yesteryear is under assault by many as futile on epistemological grounds . . . or immoral on political grounds (Suárez-Orozco, 1993:3).

The strong case made by Suárez-Orozco in discussing Renato Rosaldo's *Culture and Truth* (1989) and the work of other contemporary anthropologists, leads the readers to believe that there cannot be objective approaches to the study of political processes or behaviors associated with such processes:

> Upon close scrutiny, Rosaldo seems to reduce the problem of 'objectivity' in social analysis to the (power) 'positions' of various subjects in a given field. By framing the problem along an outside/inside axis, the analysis is sustained by (and reproduces) unfortunate cliches: that those promoting an objectivist discourse believe that only the 'outside' ethnographer (armed with self-deluding fantasies about being 'neutral', 'impartial' and 'apolitical') can be 'objective'. The other side of that worn coin is the equally vacuous notion that according to 'objectivists', the 'insider' informant can only be hopelessly subjective and biased, the proverbial fish-in-water paradigm (Suárez-Orozco, 1993:19).

The distance placed between the researcher and the persons under study (the other) assumes that it is an epistemological impossibility to understand any other person outside of one's culture. More extreme deconstructionists want to argue that the construction of 'others' exists only in the mind of the researchers. Consequently, there is no universal or shared knowledge across cultures, because cultural systems are inherently meaningless for other than the members of the cultural group. Indeed, according to this line of thought, there are no universal continuities or shared human potentials, only culturally constructed, radically discontinuous and mutually incomprehensible systems of meaning. As Melford Spiro has recently observed, 'contemporary anthropology argues that cultural diversity is of a magnitude that renders every culture incommensurable with any others' (1992:x). Hence, in today's literature we have 'others', not 'brothers' (Suárez-Orozco, 1993: 3). The politicization of research that resulted in the rejection of other people's work, regardless of the evidence behind this work, responds to the general trend to see research as a hegemonic expression of power over others. Rejecting the possibility of valid research is equivalent to a statement of liberation, an emancipation from the yoke of intellectual power holders. The fact that some research has been a reflection of power structures and has overextended its evidence should not be used to reject the possibility of conducting good research, or of adjusting the inferences of research without making unjustified claims. In fact, the many ongoing efforts in cross-cultural anthropological research that seek to explain power differential are good reasons to accept, in good faith, the possibility of conducting valid research regardless of the cultural affiliation of the researcher.

There is no easy way to walk out of the epistemological nightmares imposed by current dilemmas in the social sciences. The issue of objectivity, or the lack thereof, leads many young scholars to give up attempts to study other people, and therefore claim that it is futile to presume that what is in their heads has any correspondence to what is in the real world, much less in the heads of other people. Social scientists have been facing this issue for many decades. As Hymes pointed out (Hymes, 1964:6), 'any thoroughgoing linguistic theory is of necessity a theory that makes ethnographic assumptions', meaning that linguistic theory makes assumptions 'not only about linguistic systems but also about ethnolinguistic systems, about the partial dependence between properties of linguistic systems (however narrowly conceived) on the one hand, and characteristics of their users and circumstances of use on the other' (Hymes, 1964:6–7).

According to Hymes, linguistics had not been recognized until 1960 as 'a source of methodological rigor and inspiration', although it was important to anthropology in the United States and historically linked with ethnographic research by Boas (1916, 1928) and his students, but never 'the only or best source of formal and qualitative methods' (Hymes, 1964: 10). Hymes suggests that linguistics is not 'a theory of what linguists do, but more importantly, a theory of the nature of language' and consequently it must play a greater role in the study of cognition and cultural behavior (Hymes, 1964:11).

After recognizing that anthropologists did not fall into the trap of ignoring the significance of speech activity in human development, and its relationship to society and culture, Hymes suggests that up to 1964 anthropology played a static role 'repeating platitudes and paeans, stressing that language is important, but without the calibration that would enable one to investigate the importance, either of language in general, or, comparatively, of particular languages'. Clearly, anthropology opposed the misconception that there were 'inferior' languages functionally, and the monolithic conception of homogeneity of language and culture (that is the correspondence to one language=one culture). At this point, Hymes makes one of his most visionary statements that redirected much of subsequent ethnographic research:

> Not that the obvious facts of heterogeneity, multilingualism, individual differences in linguistic competence, and the like were denied; they simply

did not enter into any anthropological theory of the nature of language and its cultural role. Hence there are studies of cross-cultural differences in the patterning and importance of behavior having to do with sex, weaning, magic, or almost anything one might care to name, and general theories that try to account for them, in pursuit of what has been described as anthropology's task to account for the similarities and differences in human cultures; but there is none such for language. It stands as one of the most important tasks of anthropology to constitute what might be called a comparative ethnography of communication, concerned in part with the differential role of languages, and of speech behavior, in socialization, personality, interaction and social structure, cultural values, and beliefs (Hymes, 1964:12).

As a result of this generation of scholars, ethnoscience and the ethnography of communication developed and produced a substantial amount of excellent studies (Sturtevant, 1964). Ethnoscience was developed partially on the grounds that previous anthropologists were imposing their own cultural biases and cognitive frames upon those of people being studied. Their efforts and contributions went beyond the design of cleaner and more focused ethnographic inquiry into the 'emic' perspectives of the 'others', and discovered the significant role that language plays in the interpretation of observed behavior. Studies such as those by Frake (1961, 1964), Berlin and Romney (1964), Metzger and Williams (1963), Sturtevant (1964), and others, were based not only on a very strict process of reconstructed inquiry, but on the assumption that language mediated between actions observed and the interpretation of actions. Another important discovery of ethnoscience (perhaps not altogether explicit) is that the study of other cultures was essentially the study of peoples' actions whose meaning was deciphered through their use of language. Language was used as a means to infer views of the world, expected appropriate behaviors and cognitive taxonomic structures of phenomena, such as the taxonomy of disease by the Subanum of Mindanao (Frake, 1961), the numerical classifiers of the Tzeltal (Berlin and Romney, 1964), or the organization of wedding ceremonies (Metzger and Williams, 1963). The use of linguistics in specific socio-cultural settings as a means to understand other peoples' behavior and cognitive frames was an important contribution of a parallel field in anthropology called the 'ethnography of communication' or 'sociolinguistics' developed by distinguished scholars such as Gumperz and Hymes (1964, 1972). Since 1964, Hymes recognized the potential contributions of Vygotsky's *Thought and Language* (1962) to the ethnography of communication because of the connection that Vygotsky saw between language, culture and cognitive development and his recognition of the ideological context of psychological theory (Hymes, 1964:11).

Years before the writings of sociolinguists and ethnographers in the United States emphasized the use of linguistic analysis to understand behaviors across cultures, two Soviet scholars, Vygotsky and Bakhtin, had explored theoretical territories ignored elsewhere. Vygotsky had postulated a sociocultural approach to cognitive development as a mediated action. As Wertsch explains:

Three basic themes run through Vygotsky's writings: 1) a reliance on genetic, or developmental, analysis; 2) the claim that higher mental functioning in the individual derives from social life; and 3) the claim that human action, on both the social and individual planes, is mediated by tools and signs. These themes are closely intertwined in Vygotsky's work, and much of their power derives from the ways in which they pre-supposed one another (Wertsch, 1991:19).

The fundamental premise of Vygotsky's approach was that of the unity between sociocultural and cognitive phenomena. Vygotsky was strongly influenced by the work of Darwin and Engels (Wertsch, 1991:20) and consequently he saw the transition from primates to humans as a central problem in understanding human cognitive development. He was intrigued by the problem-solving actions of chimpanzees and gorillas and developed the notion of 'tool-mediated' human action which was dependent on specific interactional contexts. As Wertsch observes, for Vygotsky apes remain slaves of the concrete situation or specific interactional context, while humans have developed 'representational means' to overcome such constraints (Wertsch, 1991: *ibid.*). Vygotsky struggled to translate the inspirational writings of Marx on sociocultural history into a more effective methodological approach to study human development and higher order thinking. With his emphasis on the unique human mental functions (higher order or advanced mental, representational functions, in contrast with rudimentary ones seen in apes) he studied the process of decontextualization. He saw children's cultural development as 'superimposed' on processes of growth, maturation, physical development and inseparable from them, constituting a 'single line of sociobiological formation of the child's personality' (cited in Wertsch, 1991:22). While it was clear that for Vygotsky the development of higher order mental functions of the individual was rooted in his/her sociocultural life (an obvious influence of Marxist philosophy), what was less clear was the nature of the relationship between the individual and the social group. Vygotsky insisted that human action in general was mediated by tools and signs, especially by symbolic sign systems such as language. The rela-tionship between the semiotic level and action was firmly established by Vygotsky in his use of the term 'mediated action' which emerged as a result of his research with preschool children in contrast with older children. Wertsch states:

> Vygotsky's account of mediation is a set of assumptions about the nature of particular higher mental functions, more specifically, his view that thinking, voluntary attention, and logical memory form a system of 'interfunctional relations' . . . He devoted the entire volume [his last, *Thinking and Speech*], in fact, to the issue of how speaking and thinking come to be thoroughly intertwined in human life, a cogent example of the interfunctional relationships that characterize human consciousness (Wertsch, 1991:30).

The most basic contribution of the Vygotskian tradition, as understood by his own students and the scholars, such as James Wertsch, who have read in the original Russian most, if not all of his works, was the realization that in order to understand conscious human action we must study human existence and the processes of behavior both in their social and historical dimensions, not in the structure of the grey mass in the human brain or in the isolation of decontex-tualized psychological phenomena (Wertsch, 1991:1–45). It was in the context of these contributions that we can also appreciate Bakhtin's originality and powerful insights.

The Soviet Union of the 1920s was in a political turmoil that resulted in the imprisonment or exile of many intellectuals. The abuse of power by the Stalin regime robbed Bakhtin of his health and freedom in 1929. Bakhtin was focused on both the nature of language and on concrete utterances, rather than on words or sentences, arguing that utterances transcend the individual and reveal specific meanings anchored in concrete sociocultural contexts or situations. Wertsch states that in Bakhtin's view utterance 'is an activity that enacts differences in values . . . , for instance, the same words can mean different things depending on the particular intonation with which they are uttered in a specific context' (Wertsch, 1991:51); that is what Bakhtin called 'different voices', applied both to oral and written communication. Voices exist in the sociocultural environment, not in isolation. Voices are therefore linked to the speaker and the addressee. Language is, therefore, seen as the dynamic exchange of voices in specific interactional settings that determine meaning. Bakhtin talks about 'dialogicality' and 'dialogic overtones' which in current terms would mean linguistic communication within restricted audiences.

The significance of Bakhtin's contribution was to find order and meaning where previous linguists saw randomness and chaos. In the past, other linguists has focused on the historical reconstruction of linguistic forms, on syntax and lexicon. Bakhtin emphasized the relationship between discourse and sociocultural milieu, and consequently, the relationship between the speaker and the social group with which he communicates. Wertsch cites Bakhtin's following statement:

> The single utterance, with all its individuality and creativity, can in no way be regarded as a *completely free combination* of forms of language, as is supposed, for example, by Saussure (and by many other linguists after him), who juxtaposed the utterance (*la parole*), as a purely individual act, to the system of language as a phenomenon that is purely social and mandatory for the individuum (Bakhtin, 1986:81, as cited by Wertsch, 1991:58).

What is particularly important for our critique of deconstructionism is that there can be no linguistic meaning or even a trace of mental representation of behavioral phenomena in the isolation of a sociocultural context. The claim that individuals' views are the only 'valid' accounts of social events betrays the intrinsic nature of communicative and mental processes which are anchored in concrete interactional contexts and therefore subject to a joint interpretation of phenomena. What permits social life and communication between individuals in a social group is precisely that which allows researchers to study other cultures and establish their own interpretation as subjective and as biased as it can be; even the subjectivity and the biases are socially shared, patterned and understandable.

If we accept some of the basic tenets of Vygotsky (1962, 1978, etc.; see set of references in Wertsch, 1991:159–60), Bakhtin and generations of other sociolinguists and ethnographers, rather than throwing away whatever knowledge has been passed to our generation, it is incumbent upon us to examine the sociocultural context that determined their interpretation of behavioral phenomena, and to re-examine the data so we can argue the value of alternative interpretations more congruently, given our sociocultural context and contemporary knowledge. This is an ongoing process in all the sciences; we reinterpret history and revise the validity of previous accounts by linking explanations to contextual factors.

This volume presents a clear example of strong theoretical and pedagogical approaches to the issues of home language (or First Language) maintenance as a requirement for meaningful pedagogical approaches. More importantly, this volume capitalizes on the work of sociolinguists and anthropologists, who defended the basic equality of all languages and the value of multilingualism, those who emphasized individual differences and the need to study human behavior with respect for differences across cultures, as Hymes had suggested since the 1960s (1964:12).

In the last few years a number of books have been written that pursue similar goals of enlightening the conflicting relationships between minority groups in modern technological societies and the dilemmas faced by teachers and professors in educational institutions. Recently, for example, Trueba, Jacobs and Kirton (1990) described the situation of the Hmong, one of the most recent immigrants to the United States, in California; Trueba, Cheng and Ima (1993) described the complex diversity within the Asian American community and their differential adaptation strategies; and Trueba, Rodriguez, Zou and Cintron (1993), ethnohistorically documented the success of Mexican immigrants who, without losing their language and culture, managed to succeed in belonging in America, in achieving well in schools and playing leadership roles in their community. The present volume, however, goes further to demonstrate the importance of understanding the inseparability of language and culture in the process of learning and the role of schools in facilitating the learning of minority students. This volume and the examples alluded to above are serious attempts at using cultural and linguistic knowledge to advance pedagogy and the quality of life for immigrant and minority groups in Western societies.

References

BAKHTIN, M.M. (1986) *Speech Genres and Other Late Essays*, EMERSON, C. and HOLQUIST, M. (Eds) and McGEE, V.W. translator, Austin, TX, University of Texas Press.

BARTH, F. (1969) *Ethnic Groups and Boundaries*, Boston, MA, Little, Brown.

BERLIN, B. and ROMNEY, A.K. (1964) 'Descriptive semantics of Tzeltal numeral classifiers', *American Anthropologist*, **66**, 3, *Special Issue: Transcultural Studies in Cognition*, Part 2, pp. 79–98.

BOAS, F. (1916) *The Mind of Primitive Man*, New York, NY, Macmillan.

BOAS, F. (1928) *Anthropology and Modern Life*, New York, NY, Morton.

DEVOS, G. (1990) 'Conflict and accommodation in ethnic interaction', in DEVOS, G. and SUÁREZ-OROZCO, M.M. (Eds) *Status Inequality: The Self in Culture*, Newbury Park, CA, Sage Publications, pp. 204–45.

DEVOS, G. and SUÁREZ-OROZCO, M.M. (1990) *Status Inequality: The Self in Culture*, Newbury, CA, Sage Publications.

FRAKE, C.O. (1961) 'The diagnosis of disease among the Subanum of Mindanao', *American Anthropologist*, **63**, pp. 113–32.

FRAKE, C.O. (1964) 'Notes on queries in ethnography', *American Anthropologist*, **66**, 3, *Special Issue: Transcultural Studies*, Part 2, pp. 132–45.

GUMPERZ, J. and HYMES, D. (Eds) (1964) 'The ethnography of Communication', *American Anthropologists*, **66**, 6.

GUMPERZ, J. and HYMES, D. (1972) *Directions in Sociolinguistics: The Ethnography of Communication*, New York, NY, Holt, Rinehart & Winston.

HORNBERGER, N. (1988a) *Bilingual Education and Language Maintenance: A Southern Peruvian Quechua Case*, Dordrecht, Holland, and Providence, RI, Foris Publications.

HORNBERGER, N. (1988b) 'Iman Chay?: Quechua Children in Peru's Schools', in TRUEBA, H.T. and DELGADO-GAITAN, C. (Eds) *School and Society: Teaching Content Through Culture*, NY, Praeger, pp. 99–117.

HYMES, D. (1964) 'Directions in (ethno-) Linguistic Theory', *American Anthropologist*, **66**, 3, *Special Issue: Transcultural Studies*, Part 2, pp. 6–56.

METZGER, D. and WILLIAMS, G. (1963) 'A formal ethnographic analysis of Tenejapa Ladino weddings', *American Anthropologist*, **65**, 5 pp. 1076–101.

ROSALDO, R. (1989) *Culture and Truth*, Boston, MA, Beacon Press.

SHWEDER, R.A. (1991) *Thinking Through Cultures: Expeditions in Cultural Anthropology*, Cambridge, MA, Harvard University Press.

SPINDLER, G. (Ed) (1978) *The Making of Psychological Anthropology*, Berkeley, CA, University of California Press.

SPIRO, M. (1992) *Anthropological Other or Burmese Brother? Studies in Cultural Analysis*, New Brunswick, NJ, Transaction Publishers.

SPRADLEY, J. (1979) *The Ethnographic Interview*, New York, NY, Holt, Rinehart & Winston.

STURTEVANT, W.C. (1964) 'Studies in ethnoscience', *American Anthropologist*, **66**, 3, *Special Issue: Transcultural Studies in Cognition*, Part 2, pp. 99–131.

SUÁREZ-OROZCO, M.M. (1993) 'Three generations in the reshaping of psychological anthropology', unpublished Manuscript, Center for Advanced Study in the Behavioral Sciences, Stanford University, Stanford, CA.

TRUEBA, H.T., CHENG, L. and IMA, K. (1993) *Myth or Reality: Adaptive Strategies of Asian Americans in California*, London, England, Falmer Press.

TRUEBA, H.T., JACOBS, L. and KIRTON, E. (1990) *Cultural Conflict and Adaptation: The Case of the Hmong Children in American Society*, London, England, Falmer Press.

TRUEBA, H.T., RODRIGUEZ, C., ZOU, Y. and CINTRON, J. (1993) *Healing Multicultural America: Mexican Immigrants Rise to Power in Rural California*, London, England, Falmer Press.

VYGOTSKY, L.S. (1962) *Thought and Language*, Cambridge, MA, MIT Press.

VYGOTSKY, L.S. (1978) in COLE, M., JOHN TEINER, V., SCRIBNER, S. and SOUBERMAN, E. (Eds) *Mind in Society: The Development of Higher Psychological Processes*, Cambridge, MA, Harvard University Press.

WERTSCH, J. (1991) *Voices of the Mind: A Sociocultural Approach to Mediated Action*, Cambridge, MA, Harvard University Press.

Notes on Contributors

Beatrice Carrillo Hocker graduated with a BA in Fine Arts from California State University, Hayward. She served as Associate Curator of Education at the Mexican Museum in San Francisco, California for fourteen years. She is currently a consultant of multicultural education working mainly with the Oakland Museum, the Museum at Black Hawk and the Mexican Museum. She is a frequent presenter in multicultural education for school districts and universities.

Angie Chabram Dernersesian is a Chicana scholar born in Monterey, California. She earned her BA at the University of California, Berkeley, and her MA and PhD in the Literature Department of the University of California, San Diego. She is currently Associate Professor in the Chicana/o Studies Program at the University of California, Davis. She is a member of MALCS (Active Women in Letter and Social Change). The author of numerous articles in the areas of Chicana feminism, ethnography, and criticism, she has recently co-edited *Cultural Studies on Chicana/o Cultural Representations* (University of California Press).

Lorraine D'Ambruoso received her BA from the University of Santa Clara and is Foreign Language Coodinator for the East Side Union High School District in San Jose, California, where she has also taught French since 1966. As Coordinator, she worked to establish the Spanish for Spanish Speakers' program in a district that is 35 per cent Hispanic. Ms. D'Ambruoso is currently the President of the California Foreign Language Teachers' Association.

Robert DeVillar is Associate Professor of Bilingual/Cross Cultural Education in the Department of Advanced Educational Studies at California State University, Bakersfield, where he also coordinates the masters and credential programs in Bilingual/Cross Cultural Education. Dr. DeVillar received his PhD from Stanford University in 1987. His principal research interest is computers in language education and he has recently published two books on this topic: *Computers and Cultural Diversity* (co-authored with C. Faltis) and *Language Minority Students and Computers* (co-edited with C. Faltis).

Christian J. Faltis earned his PhD in Bilingual Cross-Cultural Education at Stanford University in 1983. He is an Associate Professor of Bilingual Education

268

at Arizona State University where he teaches graduate courses in bilingualism, second language acquisition and bilingual education. He recently published *Joinfostering: Adapting Teaching Strategies for the Multicultural Classroom* (1993) and *Languages in Schools and Society* (with M. McGroarty, 1991). His research interests include the study of exemplary bilingual teaching, teaching Spanish to native speakers, and secondary bilingual education.

Nidia González-Edfeldt received an MA in Latin American Studies from the University of California-Los Angeles and an MA in Spanish and PhD in Education from Stanford University. She has been involved in the education of language minority students for more than twenty years and has taught at all levels. During her work at the Alum Rock Union Elementary School District in San Jose, California, she developed a successful project for in-service training in bilingual education and was the director of a computer-assisted language acquisition program for English learners. She is presently Assistant Professor of Education at California State University, San Francisco, where she also coordinates the bilingual teacher credential program. Her research and publications have been in the areas of teacher education, language acquisition, and the use of computers in first and second language acquisition.

Sidney Gorman is a graduate of the University of California at Berkeley. She has taught in Fremont Unified School District in Fremont, California since 1969, where she has also served as a Mentor Teacher and as Foreign Language Curriculum Specialist. Most recently, she has been providing in-service training for foreign language teachers under the auspices of the California Foreign Language Project. She has co-authored two school textbooks of Spanish: *Díme Uno* and *Díme Dos*.

Eduardo Hernández-Chávez, a native of Nebraska, is an Associate Professor in the Department of Linguistics at the University of New Mexico. He received his undergraduate degree in Spanish and Latin from the University of Omaha, Lincoln and his PhD in Linguistics from the University of California, Berkeley. His research interests include: bilingualism, Chicano sociolinguistics and language policy. He co-edited *El lenguaje de los Chicanos: The Language of Mexican-Americans*, the first anthology of sociolinguistic studies on Spanish in the United States.

Margarita Hidalgo is Associate Professor in the Department of Spanish and Portuguese at San Diego State University. She received her undergraduate degree from the Instituto Tecnológico, Monterey, NL. Her MA is from Michigan State and her doctorate in Linguistics is from the University of New Mexico. Her areas of specialization include: Spanish dialectology, sociolinguistics, and the teaching of Spanish to native Spanish speakers.

Thom Huebner is currently Professor of Linguistics and Language Development at San Jose State University. He holds a PhD in Linguistics from the University of Hawaii. He is a former editor of *The Carrier Pidgin* and has authored and co-edited a number of books, most recently, *Cross Currents in Second Language Acquisition and Linguistic Theories* (with Charles A. Ferguson).

Anne Jensen received a BA degree in French from St. Olaf College in 1970 and a Master's in Education from Stanford University in 1971. She also earned a Master's degree in French from the University of Northern Iowa's French program in Angers, France in 1987. For the past seventeen years she has worked for the Campbell Union High School District in San Jose, California, where she teaches French and coordinates special foreign language projects. She was named California Foreign Language Teacher of the Year in 1983.

Barbara J. Merino received her BA in French and History from the University of Southern California, holds a Certificate in French Literature from the University of Aix-Marseilles, an MA in Italian from the University of California, Los Angeles and a PhD in Education and Linguistics from Stanford University. Her research interests include bilingualism, language assessment and classroom discourse in bilingual classrooms. She is a Professor in the Division of Education and a member of the Graduate Group in Linguistics at University of California, Davis, where she also serves as Head of Teacher Education. Her articles have appeared in a wide variety of journals including: *Language Learning, Foreign Language Annals, Bilingual Review, NABE Journal, Urban Education,* and the *Journal of Applied Developmental Psychology*. Recently BICOMP, a bilingual integrated science curriculum she helped to develop, received a National Exemplary Award for Academic Excellence from the United States Department of Education.

Robert L. Politzer is Professor Emeritus in Education and Linguistics at Stanford University. He holds a PhD in Romance Linguistics from Columbia University and a second doctorate in Political and Economic Theory from the New School for Social Research. He has had an abiding interest in the study of teachers involved in teaching a second language in a variety of contexts. He is the author of over one hundred and fifty published books and articles, including, *The Successful Foreign Language Teacher*. He was the first recipient of the Pimsleur Award for research in foreign language education.

Rosalinda Quintanar-Sarellana received her PhD at Stanford University and is teaching at San Jose State University. Her research interests include teacher education, bilingual education, and language and culture. She has written recently on teachers' perceptions of minority language and culture.

Fabián A. Samaniego, a native of New Mexico, received his BA in Spanish at New Mexico State, Las Cruces and his MA in Spanish Literature from the University of Iowa. He is a Lecturer in the Department of Spanish, University of California, Davis, where he has been Coordinator of the first-year Spanish program and is Supervisor of Teaching Assistants. He is the senior author of *Dímelo Tu*, a first-year college textbook of Spanish that uses a communicative approach and *Díme*, a three-level high school series.

Rosaura Sánchez is an Associate Professor in the Department of Comparative Literature at the University of California, San Diego. She is a well-known literary critic and sociolinguist. Her publications include: *Chicano Discourse: A Socio-Historic Perspective*, Rowley, MA: Newbury House. She received her doctorate in Linguistics from the University of Texas at Austin.

Lenora A. Timm is a Professor in the Department of Linguistics at the University of California, Davis. She earned her PhD in Anthropology at the University of California, Davis in 1974. Her research and teaching interests include general linguistics, sociolinguistics — with a focus on minority language issues and bilingualism — and language and gender. She is the author of numerous scholarly articles and reviews and of the first-ever bilingual anthology (Breton/English) of a major Breton poet: *A Modern Breton Political Poet: Anjela Duval*.

Henry T. Trueba earned his BA in 1959 at the Universidad Autónoma de México. He has a MA in Theology from Jesuit Woodstock College in Maryland, an MA in Anthropology from Stanford University and a doctorate in Anthropology from the University of Pittsburgh. Dr. Trueba has taught at the University of Illinois, Champaign-Urbana, and the University of California at Santa Barbara and Davis, where he also was the Associate Dean of Letters and Science. Currently, he is the Dean of the School of Education at the University of Wisconsin-Madison and a Professor in the Departments of Curriculum and Instruction, Educational Policy Studies, and Anthropology. He has received many awards for his research on language minority students from the American Educational Research Association and the National Association for Bilingual Education. He has been a member of the editorial boards for a number of journals, including: *Journal of Contemporary Education*, *Review of Educational Research*, *Educational Researcher*, and the *Journal of the National Association for Bilingual Education*. He was chief editor of the *Anthropology and Education Quarterly* from 1988 to 1991. He has written and co-authored many books, articles, and reviews. Among the most recent are: *Healing Multicultural America: Mexican Immigrants Rise to Power in Rural California* and *Myth or Reality: Adaptative Strategies of Asian Americans in California* (both Falmer Press, 1993).

Index

accomodation 50
accountability 149, 162
achievement 9, 10, 17–19, 27, 89, 152,
    172, 209–10, 261, 266
acquisition
    of language 59–62, 69, 188, 210
    of second language 10–11, 14, 16, 26,
    45–56, 66, 78, 96, 168, 181, 183,
    190–1, 194, 210, 224, 227–8
Acumen 182
Ada, A.F. 17
Adams, E.N. 172
adaptive strategies 29, 36
age 51–2, 84
Ahmad, K. 175, 176, 182
Albert, M.L. 58
alienation 27, 58, 66, 68, 136, 160,
    225
Allen, J.R. 172
Alurista 104, 105
Alvarez, R. 36
Ammon, P. and M. 15
Anaya, R. 139
answer processing 192–3
anthropology 262–3
Aparicio, F. 117, 118, 119
appropriateness of language 50, 95, 102
Armas, J. 68
Ariew, R. 172
artificial intelligence (AI) 191–2
assimilation 58, 66, 68, 76, 79, 83, 126
attitude 50, 56, 68, 86, 88, 106–7, 125,
    129, 136, 152, 179
Au, K.H. 210
audio devices, peripheral 181–2, 194
authoring programs 180–1, 185–6,
    189–90

Avelar-LaSalle, R. 212
Avila, R. 89
awareness, cultural 136–7, 153–6, 158,
    166, 168, 191, 224–5, 227–8, 245–7
Ayala, R. 203
Azevedo, M. 119, 212

Bacal, A. 28
Baez, J. 139
Bailey, C.J. 59
Baker, C. 86
Bakhtin, M.M. 263, 265
Ballad of Gregorio Cortez, The (Paredes)
    137–8
Bangert-Drowns, R. 172
Barker, M.E. 116, 160
Barkin, F. 86, 90
Barth, F. 259
Bartley, D.E. 47
Bartolome, L. 212
Batalla de Palabras 178
Beebe, L.M. 46, 49
Beebe, J. and M. 9
Beebe, L. 20
behavior 31–4, 36, 39, 83, 87, 172, 261,
    263–6
behaviorism 173–4
Belgium, language minorities in 38
Bellugi, U. 60
Beltrano, A. 125
Bennion, J.L. 180, 185
Berlin, Bridget 229–37, 263
Bernal, M. 18
Bernhardt, E. 209
Bickes, G. 173, 175
bilingualism 5–7, 12–13, 20–1, 46, 59,
    63, 79, 86–7, 95–6, 102–4, 106–7,